Musical Representations, Subjects, and Objects

Musical Meaning and Interpretation

Robert S. Hatten, editor

JAIRO MORENO

Musical Representations, Subjects, and Objects

The Construction of Musical Thought in Zarlino, Descartes, Rameau, and Weber

INDIANA UNIVERSITY PRESS

Bloomington and Indianapolis

This book is a publication of

Indiana University Press
601 North Morton Street
Bloomington, IN 47404-3797 USA

http://iupress.indiana.edu

Telephone orders   800-842-6796
Fax orders   812-855-7931
Orders by e-mail   iuporder@indiana.edu

The paper used in this publication meets the minimum requirements of American National Standard for Information Sciences—Permanence of Paper for Printed Library Materials, ANSI Z39.48-1984.

Manufactured in the United States of America

Library of Congress Cataloging-in-Publication Data

Moreno, Jairo, date
Musical representations, subjects, and objects : the construction of musical thought in Zarlino, Descartes, Rameau, and Weber / Jairo Moreno.
p. cm. — (Musical meaning and interpretation)
Includes bibliographical references and index.
ISBN 0-253-34457-3 (cloth : alk. paper)
1. Music—Philosophy and aesthetics. 2. Music—Semiotics. 3. Music theory—History. I. Title. II. Series.
ML3845.M86 2004
781′.1—dc22
2004007629

1 2 3 4 5   09 08 07 06 05 04

Contents

Acknowledgments

Writing a first book entails accumulating debts of all sorts. In a fundamental way this book speaks to encounters with ideas that have proven intellectually invigorating for quite some time now. More than I could have realized at first, it was a single seminar I took with Alan Keiler many years ago that lit the fire of my historical imagination with respect to music theory. Another seminar, with Michel Holquist, awakened my interest in the power of signs, language, and discourse to mediate history. I am not a historian by training, let alone a philosopher or critical theorist, and so my work bears indelible marks of my autodidactic enterprise but also, I hope, traces, however light, of the imagination of Keiler's and Holquist's scholarship. And while it is not customary to acknowledge those who haven't directly assisted you by reading drafts of work in progress, I think it important to recognize here colleagues in the subdiscipline of music theory—older, younger, and contemporary, personally known and not—to whom I owe in some way or another the stimulus to tread outside of my comfort area and push the limits of what constitutes thinking historically and critically the subject of music theory. I must single out Brian Hyer's work for having decisively, if always from a distance, helped me formulate the sorts of questions I find most urgent about music theory, as well as, each in distinctive ways, Ian Bent, Leslie Blasius, Scott Burnham, Thomas Christensen, Daniel Chua, David Cohen, Peter Hoyt, Kevin Korsyn, and Alex Rehding. Allen Forte, who supervised my doctoral dissertation on an unrelated topic, taught me about caring for the work of theory. Encouragement was offered by my dear friends and colleagues Louise Meintjes and Frank Lentricchia at Duke University, and by Julie Hubbert and Philip Rupprecht. Giuseppe Gerbino, at the time of writing a doctoral student at Duke, made for intensely stimulating conversations about our methodological follies and ideological proclivities. Tadd Schmaltz from the Philosophy Department at Duke made sure that my Cartesian epistemological detours found their way back to sound. Janna Saslaw offered helpful and expert commentary on Gottfried Weber, and Kevin Korsyn generously allowed me to borrow the kernel for the idea of Romantic irony in connection with Weber's analysis of Mozart. Series editor Robert Hatten helped me avoid making unsupported claims and allowed me space to make my argument throughout all its detours. Gayle Sherwood at Indiana University Press made this book possible and patiently gave counsel beyond the call of duty during all stages of writing and production. Tony Brewer and Marvin Keenan at the Press provided superb editorial assistance and made the later stages of production extremely easy.

Key to the completion of this project was Antony John, the only person to have read through all the draft versions of these chapters, and the person who alone, I believe, could have had the patience and skill to make my exasperatingly convoluted and, I suspect, quite likely heavily Spanish-conceived prose more linear. The index and musical examples too were expertly prepared by him. Foreign language translations benefited from the expert eyes of Margo Eastlund (German) and Tamsin Simil (French and Italian). John Bauschatz is responsible for Latin translations and for checking the Greek terms and concepts I discuss. A junior faculty leave from Duke University in the fall of 2000 helped get the project started.

Finally, Sui-Man Chan offered what only she can: boundless love and care. To her and to the memory of my parents this book is lovingly dedicated.

Material from Chapter 4 was previously published in "Subjectivity, Interpretation, and Irony in Gottfried Weber's Analysis of Mozart's 'Dissonance Quartet'," *Music Theory Spectrum* 25 (1), © The Society for Music Theory, Inc., and is used here by kind permission of the University of California Press.

Note on Translations

All citations of original Italian, French, and Latin texts maintain original spellings. I have given in a glossary a short list of transliterated Greek terms alongside the originals. For transliterations I have followed the guidelines suggested by the Perseus Project (http://www.perseus.tufts.edu). I am thankful to Grant Parker of the Classics Department at Duke University for suggesting this format and to John Bauschatz for drawing up the list itself.

Musical Representations, Subjects, and Objects

Introduction

It seems self-evident that Western music theories—broadly, discourses that address the organization of musical objects—identify in a listener and/or hearer the locus of whatever kind of knowledge and understanding of music that they posit. Similarly, it is reasonable to expect that, whether describing or prescribing musical objects and phenomena, music theories necessarily articulate their object of knowledge by recourse to more or less specific languages. Furthermore, these two assumptions appear to function transhistorically, despite drastic transformations, covering everything from Greek thought to recent tonal and posttonal theory and nearly everything in between, with the exception perhaps of the most hardened speculative theorizing. Consider, for instance, Pythagoras's legendary stroll through the blacksmith's shop in which the clanking sound of hammers on anvils confirmed proportional ratios as the language of consonances. Or take, for example, the rehabilitation by late-twentieth-century North American theorists of Riemannian *Tonnetze* as a means to navigate the voice-leading intricacies of much chromatic and postchromatic music. For all their radically different aims and strategies, these cognitive gestures may be said to invoke a figure who hears, listens, and understands, as well as a means to represent what that figure hears, listens, and understands.

Musical Representations, Subjects, and Objects explores the question of what and how theories know what they claim to know, particularly when the query is concerned specifically with the very possibility of the idea of the "listener" and the modes of representation of objects by music theories. (I will return later to the anthropomorphization of "theories.") The book locates distinct modalities of thinking the subject and representation as articulated across a wide chronological expanse: Gioseffo Zarlino's *Le istitutioni harmoniche* (1st ed., 1558) and *Sopplimenti musicali* (1588), René Descartes's *Compendium musicae* (1618), Jean-Philippe Rameau's *Traité de l'harmonie* (1722), and Gottfried Weber's *Versuch einer geordneten Theorie der Tonsetzkunst zum Selbstunterricht* (3rd ed., 1832). Each chapter presents a critical reading, framed as a case study on a single theorist, that illustrates significant moments in the production of knowledge by music theories and interrogates the conditions of possibility for what and how they think—in other words, the conditions that might have made their respective modalities of thought not only possible but necessary. More specifically, each chapter offers a close reading of a theoretical writing or writings with two issues in mind: (1) the cognitive allocations that condition varying constructions of hearing, listening, perceiving, and understanding music by and for various *subjects* (which correspond largely, though not exclusively, to the "ideal listeners" of theories), and (2) the epistemic wagers that these theories place in their particular *representations* of musical objects, phenomena, and experience by linguistic and metalinguistic means. The relation between subjects and representations forms part of what I call *musical thought*, conceived dialectically. Before examining the mechanisms of that dialectic, however, I would like first to outline some general epistemological underpinnings informing the methodology of my critical readings.

Disclaimers and a First Disquisition on Foucault

Although arranged as a succession of chronologically unfolding case studies, this book does not advance a narrative of the history of the ideas of "the subject" and "representation" from Zarlino to Weber in which each successive theorist claims ever-increasing cognitive gains over his predecessors. This is a book with a general theme but no central plot. Obviously there is no attempt to carry out what would be an impossibly comprehensive study accounting for the immense density of all that may be called music theory during the period of time I consider. Less obviously there is no attempt to elucidate, from what is said in a document, what each individual writer intentionally meant, whether a theorist is right or wrong, or whether or not what a theory says is in any way truthful or, for that matter, consistent. Different from intellectual biographies such as Thomas Christensen's usefully comprehensive *Rameau and Musical Thought in the Enlightenment* which situates the totality of formulations by a theorist against a generalized epistemological, social, and institutional horizon of his time, this book attempts to establish the grounds of knowledge on which, before concepts from other fields can be adapted and before particular methodologies are adopted, a theory (not a theorist) can think its objects, represent them, and designate a cognitive figure as the arbiter for the value and usefulness of those represented objects. Each case study, then, illustrates through highly localized analyses distinct organizing principles at different moments in history. From a historiographical perspective, the emphasis is therefore on discontinuity, recognizing all the while the possibility that incommensurable modalities of thought most often overlap.

The contours for the model of historical inquiry sketched above are delineated in the work of Michel Foucault from the 1960s, his so-called archaeological period.[1] In addition to the principle of discontinuity, Foucault posits four other analytic premises to examine the coherence of thought that governs a period of time, a coherence that falls within the designation "episteme": (a) an archaeological premise dictating that the same structures of knowledge govern different fields of knowledge during an episteme; (b) an epistemological premise holding that knowledge is founded in the experience of order of an episteme; (c) a semiological premise stipulating that analysis of the structure of signs and of language as a privileged system of signs is fundamental to the reconstruction of knowledge of an episteme; (d) a discursive premise whereby the set of relations articulated in speech or writing makes possible "formalized systems" at a given episteme (e.g., the physiology of sound perception would be a mid-nineteenth-century "discourse"). For each episteme Foucault systematically delineates its experience of order, its semiology, its use of language, and finally its knowledge, a process he calls "archaeology" and applies to a sweeping study of the "sciences of man" (i.e., sciences studying life, labor, and language). Foucault reserves the term *savoir* to denote a sort of transcendental knowledge that conditions any form of thought during the episteme, while using the term *connaissance* to designate the thought of a particular discipline, or as he puts it, "the relation of the subject to the object and the formal rules that govern it."[2] The former operates at an unconscious level termed "the positive unconscious," while the latter, although dependent on the former, operates at a more conscious level.

In Foucault the notion of episteme designates both a temporal span and a spatial construct. This construct is conceived as the particular structure of thought made possible during a period of time by specific conceptions of knowledge, language, order, and semiology. (He might, for instance, exaggeratedly refer to the "episteme of Western culture," implying a monolithic enclosure conditioning all knowledge.) Less globally this structure, or "grid" as he often calls it, constitutes a cognitive area within which for a number of fields objects are defined, concepts are formed, and theories are built.[3] Foucault's own account of the trajectory of knowledge (*savoir*) divides into three epistemes: Renaissance (sixteenth century), classical (beginning with the seventeenth century), and modern (from the nineteenth century on). Foucault's series of discontinuous epistemes provides an initial historical blueprint, in the form of a priori enclosures, against which I place "musical thought." I adopt the first two of Foucault's epistemes; and when I refer to "moments" in the trajectory of musical thought, I too am invoking the dual senses of episteme as a temporal demarcation and as a spatial enclosure. But as a temporal designation, I alter Foucault's configuration. Only with Zarlino do I follow his designation "Renaissance." Beginning with Descartes, however, I make a distinction between representation, signs, and semiology, on the one hand, and subject construction, on the other. For the former, I maintain Foucault's idea of "classical representation" and "classical sign." For the latter, I adopt the label "early modern," referring to the "early modern" subject who negotiates with "classical signs," for example. I further allocate to the subject in my discussion of Rameau and Weber two distinct places within the "modern" space. Of these two, only Rameau will be said to keep the designation of "classical sign," while no specific name will be given to the sign at work in Weber.

Admittedly untidy, these changes are motivated by a desire to account for how in music theory the subject, which my readings isolate from the more generalized episteme governing a period, constitutes a more fluid construction in "musical thought" than Foucault's model might indicate. More to the point, these changes go hand in hand with two underlying theses of this book. First, I posit that, given certain protocols for representation that permit particular statements about cognition and that sanction their validity, the efforts of music theorists to explain and understand the aural expand the boundaries of those protocols. As a domain of human activity and experience, the aural, I maintain, raises the representational stakes of Foucault's epistemes. And in those moments when this happens, a repositioning of the subject inevitably takes place. The second thesis is that, departing from a time when no discrete allocation is given to a cognitive figure of hearing or listening, that figure emerges out of the logical and categorical distinction between object and subject made most sharply by Descartes. Descartes's "early modern" subject gives way to the "modern listener," the ideal cognitive agency in the process of comprehending the dynamics of harmonic successions articulated in Rameau. Supplanting the "modern listener" is the "listening subject," a self-reflexive figure for whom interpretation of music is both a trace of its consciousness and the mark of its incapacity to fully grasp that consciousness. I find that figure in Weber. Later I will address the teleological implications of the designation "early modern" and offer more detailed criteria for giving different allocations to Rameau and Weber.

The previous paragraphs anticipate themes to which I return in the course of the book, mostly in terms of my adaptation of some of Foucault's tenets. Lest the reader think that this project is restricted to a Foucauldian historiography, I will offer further epistemological underpinnings and methodological elaborations to my readings. First, a return to the relationship I delineate between subjects and representations.

Subjects and Representations: A First Dialectic

At the level of knowledge (*connaissance*) the relation between subjects and representations is one of mutual determination. In dialectical terms neither the subjects nor representations are self-identical entities, nor are each independently constituted *by* the other; instead they are actively and inextricably constitutive *of* one another.[4] Each term participates in a differential system in which neither is fully self-substantive and in which, more importantly, each determines the grounds of being (i.e., the ontology) for the other. We may consider the dialectic first by assuming that the subject constitutes an autonomous, self-contained, unitary entity. In this case we may think it intuitively adequate that the contents of an experience of musical sound by the subject will be given and comprehended in the terms dictated by representations of its own design. In the dialectical model, however, this intuition will be turned on its head so that the terms of representation are what the subject believes, imagines, or thinks itself to be in relation to music. This dialectic asks us to conceive of the relation between subjects and representations in which neither term stands in a causal relation to the other.

Admittedly giving in to Hegelian temptations (though with considerable modifications), I conceive of the relationship between subjects and representations dialectically for several reasons. Two salient features of the dialectic deployed here are: (1) The interrelationship between subject and representations does not necessarily end when representations come to form part of what the subject believes or thinks itself to be, that is, at an ontological level. (2) I identify in the claims to knowledge by music theories a historically ceaseless reflection on their thought-forms along the axis of subject-representation, that is, at an epistemological level. This ceaseless reflection functions thus: (1) The subject sets its representations in motion only to have them return, at the next level of the dialectic, as part of the subject's cognition and as the condition of possibility for self-consciousness and self-reflection. (2) At this next level the dialectic starts anew, when the subject must negotiate its self-consciousness against its initial representations. (3) Representations are themselves most often inscribed in the various musical praxes that theories seek to understand (this means that the representation does not simply result from the subject's detached cognitive contemplation of musical sound, and neither does the dialectic oscillation; I will present cases in which the reflection on representation generates, as it were, new representations and hence new forms of subject construction). In the end, instead of a straight Hegelian program of alternating theses and antitheses followed by syntheses at higher planes of knowledge, or acts of sublation whereby an element or state of thought is negated and upheld, or a systematic "negation of the negation," my readings will favor, in a nod to Adorno, the disassembly of the interrelation of subjects and representations. This disassembly will facilitate the diagnosis of the diachronic historical movement of the interrelation but also their synchronic reversals, productive contradictions, and degrees of synthesis within particular epistemes.

In my critiques of self-identical, self-substantive, and self-transparent subjects and representations the reader may no doubt recognize thematic contours commonly associated with poststructuralist thought. However, by framing the interrelationship between subjects and representations within a "dialectic," I have opted out of calling it a "binary opposition." Calling it thus would imply a critical deconstruction highlighting contradictions in and omissions by music theories (that in my view mark the positive production of objects of knowledge), or unmasking hidden cognitive hierarchies that give rise to categories such as the musical object. What matters here is that while I advocate the non-identity of each term in the dialectic to itself, I recognize that each term does not necessarily hierarchically impose itself on the other but that each constitutes a critical cognitive intervention on the other. In a nutshell, if representation by music theory might make musical objects, experience, and phenomena in any way apprehensible and intelligible to the subject, it is largely because representation is itself part and parcel of the epistemo-ontological constitution of the subject *in* and *through* the articulation of those representations. Contemplating the implications of this dialectic for the claims to knowledge of music theory will be a central task of my readings.

Representation

I should note right away (and not without a modicum of anxiety) that this book does not restrict itself to explaining various languages and meta-languages through which theorists have expressed their conceptions of music, or to a partial historical cataloging of ways in which signs have produced the musical objects they designate. Despite the emphasis on language and meta-language as the privileged material forms of representation, I do not adopt a Heideggerian hard line according to which "Man acts as though he were the shaper and master of language, while in fact language remains the master of man."[5] For if the writings I discuss deal with music, a domain generally considered, as a "cultural trope," to be extralinguistic, the theoretical writings themselves reside on the side of linguistic praxis where music constitutes its "disciplinary object."[6] Here linguistic praxis is to be provisionally understood as a recorded trace of what has been stated, prototypically in written texts (not in spoken or enacted form), through the agency of the entire apparatus of signs that statements deploy (words, sentences, propositions, charts, graphs, musical examples, narrative prose, numerical symbols, tables, etc.).[7] But linguistic praxis must also be understood broadly to encompass the dynamic field of actions, interactions, communicability, and cognition that statements entail. This dynamic field constitutes the statements' textuality. Borrowing here from Derrida's widely known theory, textuality exists not only as a condition of possibility for the communicability of statements, but in the present context it exists also as a constitutive dimension of music theories as they engage other disciplines and other forms of cognition (understanding, all along, that the very idea of closed disciplines is severely undermined by textuality). For example, an issue that will surface throughout my readings is that of how music theorists negotiate what is fundamentally an epistemology of the aural against the background of a predominantly visual epistemology in Western thought (wondering all along whether or not an "aural epistemology"—different in my account from the "knowledge of the aural"—has ever emerged from under the shadow of a visual epistemology). Any and all epistemological maneuvers performed by music theories in their efforts to give cognitive form to musical objects, phenomena, and experiences are here considered textually. And so it is that however tightly woven into the fabric of language theoretical representations of musical objects, phenomena, and experience may be, I will consider these representations not to be exhausted by the regulative force of language.

How then is representation conceived here? Representation encompasses the historically contingent organizing principles and semiotic protocols governing the production of music-theoretical discourse that allow music theories to construct their objects and make them cognitively, experientially, and perceptually available to a subject. Representation constitutes the link between the expressible and the audible, although as we will see, what "the audible" may be is itself constructed in representation. Functioning like an operating system, representation enables the connection and construction of objects, phenomena, and experiences *to* and *within* a language or metalanguage. I depart from this Foucauldian dictum, however, for my view of representation recognizes also that the praxis of music theory is fueled by human agency. Representation will therefore also be said to regulate the discursive network of cognitive, communicative, and cultural protocols that a music theory adopts or advances in trying to situate a musical object, phenomenon, or experience in a system of relations. Discursive conceptualizations of music are manners of representation embedded in the phenomenology of listening in a way that inextricably connects "music" (i.e., its sonic materiality) to what we say and think music is. I speak of representations in the plural in recognition of the fluctuating degree of transparency ascribed to representation throughout history to make objects cognitively present.[8]

Subjects

Similarly, "Subjects," in the title of this book, indicates the plurality of positions historically assigned to what is a complex of notions. My analysis of subject constructions by music theory does not presuppose their historical stability, but neither does it reduce their plurality throughout history to a radical nominalism along a series of historically dispersed names with no corresponding realities or ontological grounding of any kind. It must be made clear here that I use the term "subject" pragmatically, as shorthand for shifting conceptions of the locus of cognition on whose grounds ideas of hearing, listening, perceiving, and understanding music are constructed in music theories. Subject, in short, designates a cognitive configuration whose focus of knowledge is hearing, listening, perceiving, and understanding music.

To the musician this all may sound unnecessarily complicated, given that I could easily identify the subject with the common term "listener," even more so since I have alluded earlier that "subject" corresponds to the notion of "ideal listener" elaborated by a particular music theory. But "listener," a widely circulated term in Anglo-American theoretical and analytical discourse, is unnecessarily limiting for my case studies. For one, "listener" presumes an individual's agency in the activity of listening to music, especially, in the most common usage of the term, an attentive listener of musical compositions. Among the four theorists I discuss, only one—Weber—addresses an actual musical composition as an object of experience, while another—Zarlino—includes the listener (called a "Soggetto ben disposto") as an ancillary element of his theory of music.

Listening, furthermore, encompasses manifold activities, not all of which fit neatly into the common notion of "the listener." As Roland Barthes notes, listening may be equivalent to hearing and recognizing "indices" (in Peirce's sense)—for instance, identifying in footsteps an approaching person—or it may entail deciphering according to learned codes signs intercepted in hearing, or it may point to the source of sound on the basis of which the listener develops an "intersubjective space."[9] Corresponding to the last two types in Barthes's typology, listening to music is primarily a psychological activity of "selection and decision" that entails an empirical presence. This empirical presence—embedded in the listener—may or may not be part of a theory's definition of the locus of aurality or a theory's notion of an intentional act of audition. As my readings will indicate, sometimes this locus of aurality is defined in relation to sound more or less abstractly conceived (e.g., intervals, chords), not necessarily in relation to sound in the context of particular musical situations (i.e., compositions or passages from compositions). In other times, listening goes beyond what Barthes calls a "supervisory activity" to become a creative endeavor. Indeed, it is a central argument of this book that the movement from activity to creativity in listening unfolds historically around the dialectic of subjects and representations.

"Subjects," then, includes the general sense of listeners and music theories' "ideal listeners." But the term encompasses a much broader sense as historically unfolding cognitive configurations that condition what and how listeners listen, what and how hearers hear, what and how perceivers perceive, and how the subjects of an aural experience negotiate that experience. Historically these conditions have defined constant relocations in the relationship of subjects to objects, even and particularly when objects were identified in the experience of the subject itself or, indeed, when the subject becomes its own object.[10] It is a basic tenet of this book that music theory since the early seventeenth century had been profoundly, if not decisively, marked by the subject-object division as a fundamental determination of the structure of musical relationships.

A general overview of the "subject" finds in Aristotelian thought an early expression: *hypokeimenon,* from the verb *hypokeimai* ("to underlie, as the foundation in which something else inheres"), designates a changeless ontological substratum that underlies all things and the matter that underlies the form, opposite of *eidos* (idea) and *entelecheia* (actualization). The term also designates the logical subject to which attributes are described.[11] This dual ascription suggests important connection between Being and language that will feature in my readings. With Aristotle's definition in mind, Martianus Capella, for example, views the *subjectum* as a "primary substance which, itself, belongs to nothing else inseparably."[12] Thus understood, the condition of the subject—subjectivity—was not associated with what today we might call subjects of experience or the individual subject.[13] Interiority, that is, was not encased within the confines of the human subject, continually paying heed to outside presences within the self. The turn toward the subject of experience takes place during the seventeenth century, at which time an epistemological assignation of the concept "subject" emerges alongside a phenomenology of interiority. Since that time the subject has designated a number of fundamental and varied functions in the space of Western European thought generally understood to be "modern." The formation of modern thought coincides with the establishment of the subject as the ground of knowledge and, in a crucial consideration for music theory and music in general, as the self-reflective locus of interiority. But there is more. Reflecting on the inward turn dramatically embodied in Montaigne's *Essais,* Jean Starobinski remarks that the self is distributed as "an agent, an implement, and a point of application."[14] This distribution of the self is given unitary form in the most concentrated expression of subjectivity: Descartes's *ego cogito.*

Systematically argued and programmatically deployed in a coherent philosophy, Descartes's *ego* constitutes a historically decisive articulation of the subject, if for no other reason than Western philosophy will spend the next centuries dealing with its consequences (to which I return in the Epilogue).[15] Without anticipating my discussion in Chapter 2 at this point, suffice it to say that Descartes makes of the subject not only a first principle of epistemology and the original, transcendent, and unitary nexus of thinking and Being (in the expression "cogito ergo sum"), but also places all other things (be it thoughts, experiences, perceptions, phenomena) in relation to and outside this Being defined by thought. As a result, things constitute objects against and over which the subject now stands. Descartes: "where knowledge of things is concerned, only two factors need to be considered: ourselves, the knowing subjects, and the things that are objects of knowledge."[16] This particular cognitive order informs a wide network of uses of the "subject" associated with modern thought (n.b.: not Foucault's modern episteme), or as sociologist of science Bruno Latour puts it, "the magnificent figures that the moderns have been able to predict and observe: the free agent, the citizen builder of Leviathan, the distressing visage of the human person, the other of a relationship, consciousness, the *cogito*, the hermeneut, the thee and thou of dialogue, presence to oneself, and intersubjectivity."[17]

In Latour's list the reader may recognize vague contours of the sometimes beleaguered figure of the music listener, a figure shaped most decisively in nineteenth-century thought and characterized in this study by its attentiveness and interiority, and by the fact that for it musical experience is inescapably immediate (the degree of immediacy, or "presence to itself," will be subject to much attention in my readings). I use the expression "beleaguered figure" pointedly, with an ear in the direction of recent critiques of the centrality and self-coherence of the subject in various humanistic disciplines, including musicology. Here, for example, is another list, by one of the subject's most tenacious critics from the discipline, Lawrence Kramer: "the normative characteristics of the modern subject include identity, boundedness, autonomy, interiority, depth, and centrality."[18] "The true human subject," Kramer continues, "is fragmentary, incoherent, overdetermined, forever under construction in the process of signification."[19] It may be reasonable to regard this "true human subject" as standing opposite the "false" subject (or listener) of music theory with its aspirations of immanence, objectivity, and transcendence. But once music theories' claims to knowledge are historicized, their subject(s) too come to be seen always "en procès," to use Julia Kristeva's famous quip (implicit in Kramer's expression "under construction").

Kristeva's intuition, that subjects are always simultaneously undergoing a process of construction and are under trial, is particularly apropos in light of the historical analyses I carry out. My readings of Zarlino, Descartes, Rameau, and Weber are premised on changes in the conception of the subject as they interact with reconfigurations of their claims to knowledge. Anchoring the readings are two major philosophical articulations of Western subjectivity: Descartes's, early in the seventeenth century, and Kant's, near the end of the eighteenth century (I term these "early modern" and "modern," respectively). Each version of the subject will be seen to emerge out of taking to task notions of who we are and how we know what we know. In an oft-told story, Descartes's epistemology is said to pour the world's contents into the mental container of the self-positing thinking-I, where they are reduced to ideational content; Kant, the story continues, pours them back out in the process of outlining the structures of our consciousness and delimiting the nature and range of our cognition. This is, of course, a gross generalization of a far more complex and less linear story, one that features many other important characters, some of which will be featured in my readings (among many others, Bacon before Descartes, and Berkeley, Condillac, Hobbes, Hume, Leibniz, Locke, and Rousseau after; Herder, Jacobi, and Wolff before Kant, and Novalis, Fichte, and the Schlegel brothers after him). Descartes and Kant, as well as the philosophical tradition to which they belong, construct the subject as a contested locus of knowledge, and this knowledge as a contested field of cognition, perception, and sensation.

Historically, then, the subject has resulted from an incessant testing of its boundaries, its place in the world, and its limitations and possibilities—in short, from its being on trial. But such due process plays only an unacknowledged, even unconscious, function in music theories, often akin to what Michael Polanyi calls "tacit knowledge" or Thomas Kuhn calls "unmarked knowledge." Partly this is because it has not been their self-appointed disciplinary function to define the subject as it has been for philosophy since Descartes; and partly because music theories have historically assumed the existence of the subject as a self-positing entity who hears or listens according to the prescriptions given in the theories themselves. Thus, my efforts to elucidate the question of the subject in music theory appeal to philosophy because more than any other field of inquiry it offers the most coherent, consistent, and focused statements on the matter, and not because philosophy invents the concept of subject. Philosophy alone cannot account for the distribution of the subject along various axes of "agency, implementation, and point of application." Indeed, not only can it not contain the dispersion of the subject throughout a multiplicity of meanings, but it too is fully contingent upon a number of other areas of human inquiry and social practice. Alongside philosophical articulations by Descartes and Kant, I will invoke some of these meanings borrowed from contemporary understandings of subjectivity, often, in fact, in critical counterpoint to the statements of philosophy: the "I" as locus of phenomenological experience and perceptions or as bearer of psychological processes and states, the grammatical bearer of predicates, the discursive position of enunciations, the cognitive position from whose perspective objects are apprehended and known, and the performer of actions.[20] Returning to the *hypokeimenon*, I should note, then, that throughout my readings "subject" is reduced to neither ontological ground nor epistemological idea. It will nonetheless encompass some of the "reality" that Kramer advocates for in the "true human subject," without, however, reducing the subject to a mere effect of the social or the political, and emphasizing the fact that all epistemology constitutes human praxis and that all praxis entails an epistemological attitude.

Musical Thought and a Second Dialectic

Taking a cue from the binary Cartesian model of "knowing subjects" and "objects of knowledge," the question must be asked as to what sort of musical *objects* are thereby produced. Premised on the subject-representation dialectic, there appears an additional and codependent dialectic between the object of representation and the subject for whom the object of representation constitutes music's materiality (e.g., intervals, chords, registers, harmonic succession, metrical organization, etc.). Keeping to the dynamics of dialectical thought, the negotiation of musical objects by subjects will also be considered relationally. The "objects" of music theory therefore ontologically precede neither subjects nor representations. In a double inversion of the subject-representation dialectic, I will argue that it is in the course of articulating its object that the subject itself comes into being as such, that is, as a cognitive position conditioned by the musical object. Subjects, representations, and objects equally participate in a triangular system of mutually determining elements.[21] Any and all movement (cognitive, semiotic, representational) along this system constitutes what I call *musical thought*.

To some it may seem excessively reductive to equate "musical thought" with the efforts of music theory. I should note that I consider music theory to articulate one among several modes of negotiating music. Instead of dismissing theory's approach as mere cognitive objectification or as a misguided and myopic formalism, structuralism, or positivism, I want to take theory's efforts quite seriously and ask of it why should it make the commitments it makes in the face of a formidably daunting self-appointed task: conceptualizing aesthetically organized sound. One particular aspect of this approach seems to me to contribute a fundamental staging area for our encounter with music, namely, how music theory affords thought *in* music. How, that is, alongside and in combination with cultural, sensuous, social, spiritual, and other ways in which music forms part of our experiential reality, music theory endeavors to map the possibility of *thinking sound*. However, "thinking sound" is not thinking "music itself," to use that much maligned and, to many, now nearly disowned concept. As my readings will detail, so much that does not correspond to the ontological reality of sound goes into thinking sound that it is a moot point to insist that advocating the efforts of music theory to establish relationships (tonal, metrical, rhythmic, timbral, registral, etc.) is to insist on sound as a point of origination in all understanding of music, or to accuse theory of indulging in an autonomous epistemology, or to privilege "structural listening" over other forms of listening. In fact, by saying "relationships," I avoid alternatives such as "organizing principles" or "formal abstractions," all in an effort to echo my insistence on highlighting the mutual implication between not only the elements of musical thought, but the very textuality of musical thought itself.

Relationships are vital, I remind my first-year theory students. But they are also complicated, I continue, trying to convey the urgency to come to terms with the fact that the moment two musical objects come into contact, neither one leaves that encounter unscathed. Even more vital, I tell them, is when we realize that we are one of the parties involved, as is the case, for instance, when, a few weeks into the semester, we set about accounting for the relationship between two humble major triads lying a perfect fifth apart. Without belaboring the point that would be obvious to the expert, my students and I soon have to negotiate various conceptual notions that have gone into accounting for that particular relationship (e.g., the concept of chord itself, the notion of root, scale-chord matrices, key-relation arrays, and so on, to say nothing of the natural, psychological, musico-practical, and even theological foundations on which some of these concepts are built). What is more, such accounting is defined by a particular idea of what knowing music is (here the emphasis on voice leading and dissonance treatment), an idea that is therefore not only aesthetically, culturally, historically, institutionally, and socially contingent, but also part of a productive and to my mind inevitable interaction of my sensory encounter with music.[22] In an important way (and to step back from the classroom), it is out of sheer admiration and sympathy for what I consider a quixotic quest by music theories to establish relationships, which I find equally courageous, imaginative, at times disingenuous, and most often stubborn, that I set out to analyze their doings. Yet this romanticizing spirit is balanced by my own critical desire to call attention to commitments they make that often exceed their self-conscious task of trying to understand music. Each analysis in the book is therefore conducted with an ear on the moments of noncoincidence between what a theory says and what it does, on what is being done in what a theory says and in how it says it.

Scope

My readings aim to return a modicum of historicity to the movement along the circular semioses of "musical thought," to approach the claims to knowledge of music theory with a critical ear attuned to its unceasing, albeit not necessarily conscious, dialogue with the fundamental question of what is music, and to explore the structures of values and interests that inform responses to that question. If my project sounds impossibly general and unattainably comprehensive, I ought to note that this book has very definite limits in the body of writings it analyzes and, within these writings, in the range of questions I ask.

Chapter 1, on Zarlino, outlines a modality of musical thought whose elements are wholly dependent on a universal epistemology. Although he articulates the idea of a "well-disposed subject" characterized by its predisposition to passively perceive music, there is in his thought no subject in the modern sense—that is, Zarlino makes no separate cognitive allocation to the subject as an active agent in the proper perception and correct comprehension of music. Instead, Zarlino tenaciously subscribes to an Aristotelian doctrine of the indivisibility of form and matter, the unity of which constitutes the *subjectum* (in

Capella's sense) equally of the world and of music. This doctrine subtends all knowledge and being in a way that makes it unnecessary, from a modern perspective, to identify a separate human subject of musical thought. Human presence is fully embedded in the uninterrupted continuum of all things. Knowledge emerges as analogical connections among things in this continuum are discovered, identified, recognized, and then ordered. No signification (it is difficult to refer to "representation" here) occurs outside of an all-encompassing web of analogies. Following this well-known model of Renaissance knowledge of Foucault (and best known in musicological circles from Gary Tomlinson's *Music and Renaissance Magic*), I analyze musical thought within an epistemology of resemblance. Building from Foucault's model, I identify an epistemological saturation brought about, in Zarlino, by the simultaneous engagement with Aristotelian natural philosophy, history, Pythagorean numerology, scripture, and the *signatura rerum* creed of Neoplatonic and Hermetic provenance, on the one hand, and aspirations to rational (i.e., an "ordered account") underpinnings for *musica scientia*, on the other. For Zarlino, the unity of number ultimately provides the foundation for the intelligibility of music, while the demonstrations of mathematics guarantee the means by which to articulate knowledge of music with exactitude. Much tension stretches across these versions of knowledge: the plethoric character of universal analogies and the circumscription of *musica scientia*. A different tension—between sound as number and sound as music—is the focus of the chapter's second section. I examine the impact of the introduction of subjective criteria for the classification of intervals on the overarching epistemology of correspondences, as well as the persistence of analogical thinking in the discussion of counterpoint proper. A final section engages historical questions within the context of Zarlino's "modernity," particularly the remapping of the cognitive relation with antiquity that Zarlino sketches in the *Sopplimenti musicali* (in response to the challenges of Vincenzo Galilei and conceived in terms different from those of the *Istitutioni*).

Within the trajectory of *Musical Representations, Subjects, and Objects,* Chapter 1 introduces a modality of thought defined by epistemic constraints and possibilities radically different from those of the next three chapters. Most salient is the subsidiary position occupied by the subject in Zarlino's theory. Almost as an aside, Zarlino mentions the exitence of a "well-disposed subject" (*Soggetto ben disposto*) which he does not elaborate. A concession to sense, Zarlino's *soggetto* subject intrudes in the number-oriented space of *musica scientia* and implicitly demands an ideal space where number might accommodate sense. This raises the obvious question: why do I include Zarlino in a book focusing on the subject? As an opening gambit, Chapter 1 emphasizes the epistemic discontinuity in the conception and place of the subject in musical thought that occurs with Descartes at the turn to the seventeenth century, the focus of Chapter 2. This discontinuity in the construction of the subject is accentuated by the fact that Zarlino is the theorist whom Descartes most often cites and knows best. In the *Compendium musicae*, Descartes in essence summarizes his predecessor's influential views on consonance classification, contrapuntal rules, and modal innovations. My reading of Descartes juxtaposes this level of continuity to the discontinuity in musical thought that results from the emergence of the subject as a separate locus of cognition.

"The object of music," Descartes writes, "is sound." This motto provides the impetus for examining the criteria for the construction of sound as an object, and most importantly for inquiry about the figure to whom sound constitutes an object. For Descartes these criteria fall under the jurisdiction of the perceiver and are determined by analysis of sound in terms of measurement (calculation of identities and differences among intervals or temporal units in a composition against a common unit) and order (serially arranging the results of measurement according to degrees of complexity). The results of such analysis constitute the mark for certain, demonstrable, and intersubjective knowledge, in short, for the kind of knowledge considered to be "objective" to this day. The analytic of order and measurement in turn reconfigures the structure of the sign. Whereas the Renaissance sign functions according to a ternary arrangement in which signified and signifier are bound through a preexistence resemblance, the classical sign simply folds the signifier (analysis) into the signified (the thing analyzed). In the link between analysis and signs, the sign retreats from the world into the mind. It too gains independence from and cognitive superiority over whatever perceptions, sensations, and simple or complex ideas it designates. In my reading, the sign enters in a dialectical relation to analysis: it is constituted by analysis at the same time that it is the instrument of analysis. Combined, analysis, representation, and signs form a set of rational (i.e., reasoned) relations whose axiomatic character create the logical (i.e., accountable) context that actually defines all objects to which it is applied. Discussion of the classical sign in Descartes sets up a theme that recurs in Rameau: namely, how, in Hayden White's words, "the fundamental 'Unbehagen der Kultur' is not . . . language itself; it is the task of representation, which ascribes to language a degree of transparency that it could never achieve."[23]

The "early modern" subject, as I call Descartes's construction of the perceiver, denotes an entity whose defining characteristic is to hold a particular perspective of and over that which it perceives. This perspective is gained precisely in the cognitive allocation and ordering powers given to analysis, representation, and signs. From a Foucauldian viewpoint, the epistemology of order provides the conditions of possibility for a discursive practice that includes "subject," "object", and "intuition" among its central governing concepts, all of which appear in the *Compendium* and are given thematic form in the *Rules for the Direction of Mind* (which I consider in some detail). None of this would have been possible, however, without the coalescence of another attribute under the idea of "subject": Descartes's "I" will be studied as an object of discourse and as a privileged point of enunciation of that discourse.

Given the cognitive coordinates drawn in the *Compendium*, "musical thought" there will be said to mark the early modern, defined as the passage from the epistemology of resemblance seen in Zarlino to the epistemology of representation found in Descartes. The function of knowledge is therefore to bring the world into order instead of replicating in a plethora of multiply intersecting signs the (dis)order of the Renaissance world. But like Zarlino's "modernity," Descartes's modernity will be shown to inhabit an interstitial space between diverging modalities of knowledge. Thus, Descartes's advocacy of *mathesis universalis* as a general science of universal order, no matter how systematic its deployment, reveals a commitment to the old ideal of the interconnectedness of the world.

In identifying musical thought in the Cartesian moment as "early modern," I transpose to a later date what is customarily applied by historians of European culture and society to the period marked by events such as the beginnings of print culture, international colonization, and the Reformation. My choice reflects the use of epistemological claims to demarcate changes in "musical thought."[24] I will leave it to others to judge the adequacy of this transposition, for it may suggest that as a field of human action music theory lags considerably behind other areas. Instead, I want to register a historiographical concern: the term "early modern" does carry problematic teleological implications that I would wish to avoid, and there exists the alternative of using the widely accepted musico-historical designation of Baroque. My use of "early modern" in no way assumes an eventual maturation of thought into a midmodern stage. In fact, in Chapter 3 I emphasize how Rameau, whose theory of harmony is commonly designated as the entrance of music theory to modernity, partakes of cognitive values similar to Descartes's but deployed under different musical constraints.

Chapter 3 addresses Rameau's early theory of harmony. In conceptualizing the connectedness among successive chords, Rameau proposes a notion— *sous-entendre*—that strikes us today as being counterintuitive. "By the word *sous-entendre*," Rameau explains in the "Table of Terms" of the *Traité*, "it must be understood that the sounds to which it is applied can be heard in chords where they are not actually present."[25] For example, a seventh may be analytically assigned by means of figures (e.g., "7") over the bass root of chord where none is acoustically given. Apparently disregarding the empirical reality of music, Rameau's theoretical gesture (called "implied dissonances" here) provokes intriguing questions about representation and about the position of the listener in the notion of harmonic connection, indeed, in the notion of harmony. Implied dissonances demand further clarification of the relationship between theoretical axioms and the activities of listening and performing. That is, if the acoustical datum in a composition and/or in its performance is in a way deemed insufficient for our adequate comprehension of it, then the very ontology of sound within the theoretical category "harmony" (i.e., the conditions that determine its being) is open to question, and the epistemological stakes placed on listening rise.

An overview of the critical reception to the notion of implied dissonances reveals a great deal of suspicion, if not flat-out dismissal of what some consider as yet another of Rameau's eccentric theoretical pronouncements. Rameau himself is quite imprecise as to how the notion may form part of a phenomenology of harmony (e.g., "the fundamental bass is always implied," or "the seventh can be implied here"). Critical suspicion is perhaps understandable considering that implied dissonances may belong to an elusive order of being that I call the "musical imaginary." An adequate understanding of this musical imaginary depends upon an explanation of the function of the subject or human agent behind the implied notes, the activity I term "implication." We will need to explain how and why the human faculty of the *imagination*—the mental capacity to conceive something not explicitly perceived—should intervene so forcefully in theoretical explanations of music at this point in history.

This chapter proposes a twofold transformation in musical thought: First, there is a gradual opening of the self-reflective Cartesian consciousness toward a participatory subject who simultaneously engages its experience and manipulates reality. Second, opposite but dependent from the self-enclosed interpretation of the world from the Archimedean point of the binary classical sign, the Rameauian sign introduces a vector of temporality that transforms the structure to a ternary arrangement with the subject as the middle term. Rameau's imprecision about the nature of the subject's mediation evinces a disallowance of cognitive disruptions of both analysis and the sign at an epistemic level, which he nonetheless attempts to circumvent. I conclude that Rameau's move warrants a loosening of Foucault's analysis of the classical sign. In the domain of perception the classical sign becomes more fluid. In the end the subject will be said to enter the domain of the semiotic, to become itself part and parcel of signs. Put another way, if the classical sign formerly constituted in itself and without mediation of any kind the logic of order, the sign designating implied dissonances constitutes a grammar of order. This grammar refers to a natural and immanent order (after all, the title of Rameau's seminal writing is *Traité de l'harmonie reduite à ses principes naturels*) at the same time that it presents in itself a theory of that order. The tension here between "nature" and theory will be argued to result from a move in Rameau toward an incipient temporalization of musical thought.

Chapter 3 goes beyond study of sign structure and the active agency of the subject in the articulation of harmonic meaning. More than Chapters 1 and 2, it registers the impact of compositional and performance practice on the construction of "musical thought." Rameau's method, I claim, cannot be seen simply as deductive or inductive. The notion of implication indicates that traces of musical practice (i.e., his observation that the most "active" successions contain dissonances) form part of the first principles on which he grounds his deductive apparatus (i.e., that therefore all successions ought to contain dissonances). I propose an alternative model of method in which practice and theory enter in a triangular relationship in the middle of which stands the subject. Related to Feyerabend's notion of *counterinduction*, this alternative strategy consists in making of a particular feature of musical practice a general principle that explains other aspects of practice.[26]

In an important methodological move within the book, Chapter 3 pursues parallels between Rameau's efforts and contemporary fields where the imaginary also was deployed to stage theoretical formulations on the face of an un-cooperative empirical field, namely, French theories of education (Rousseau) and government (Montesquieu).[27] This partial archaeology will likewise be de-ployed in the final chapter.

The concern with the temporal, already seen in Rameau as a kind of incipient cognitive gesture, becomes, in Gottfried Weber, an all-consuming affair ad-dressed in the form of analytical narrative. Chapter 4 discusses Weber's analysis of Mozart's String Quartet in C Major, K. 465. The analysis largely consists of an exhaustive, note-by-note account of the stunningly chromatic opening four measures from the first movement's famous Adagio introduction. Reflecting a major shift in musical thought that attends to temporal demands, Weber's analysis dramatically encapsulates the simultaneously constructive and disrup-tive role of temporality in the formation of subjectivity during the encounter between an individual listener and the individual work. This encounter is deci-sively shaped by interpretive self-doubt and suspicion, as the figure at the center of Weber's analysis—"das Gehör"—ponders one and each harmonic interpreta-tion after the other but seldom reaches satisfactory answers.

Central to Weber's analysis is the concept of *Mehrdeutigkeit:* "Mehrdeutigkeit is what we call the possibility of explaining a thing in more than one way, or the quality of a thing, whereby it can be considered sometimes as this, some-times as that."[28] In this definition I identify a semiotic posture that I character-ize as "ironic," after Kevin Korsyn. Ambiguously situated between the ontology of musical objects ("the quality of a thing") and epistemology ("the possibility of explaining a thing"), the concept reflects an epistemic shift away from an order of things dictated from without. *Mehrdeutigkeit* makes claims for the way in which the subject, independent of first principles such as Descartes's *mathesis universalis* or Rameau's appeal to the authority of nature, gains jurisdiction over its encounter with and its interpretation of music.

The fundamental conditions for both understanding and organizing knowl-edge are conceived in Weber from the perspective of the consciousness that attains it. This consciousness—"das Gehör"—encapsulates a new subject, an "interpretive subject," and its jurisdiction over knowledge constitutes a new modality of musical thought. This jurisdiction, however, is delimited by the dia-lectic between the grids where all possible interpretations for all harmonies are given a priori (in exhaustive tables outlining chords and scale-degree correspon-dences and signified by Roman numerals) and the activity of interpretation. Whereas the former reflects the taxonomical spirit exemplified by the great eighteenth-century sciences of nature and founded on the classical epistemology of order and enumeration, the latter illustrates the subject's mediation of the static spatial domain of the tables and the temporal domain of musical context. My reading of Weber examines how the listener weaves interpretations out of and within an incessant temporal flux that in effect sabotages the former ca-pacity given to the sign to arrest things under analysis of order and measure-ment. As an exercise in interpretation under new epistemological coordinates, Weber's analysis achieves no perfect match between musical form (i.e., the materiality of harmony) and the conceptual content of *Mehrdeutigkeit*, which cannot rein in the sensuous manifold of experience.

My reading of Weber's analysis does not consider the shift toward the activity of interpretation to mark a culminating stage in the emergence of the modern subject's consciousness of its perceptions. This subject is no doubt fully conscious of its interpretive efforts, arduously writing itself in the act of listening. But caught in the anxiety of its interpretations, and, indeed, of its self-consciousness, Weber's subject is at once aware of the evanescent nature of time and constituted by it. Representation lies at once inside (in the consciousness of temporality) and outside (in the grid of possible interpretations), and the same applies to the subject. Attempting to situate this particular predicament of subjectivity, my reading casts a long glance at philosophical versions of the subject by Kant (the transcendental subject of the *Critique of Pure Reason*) and Fichte (the self-positing "I" from the *Wissenschaftslehre*), neither of which proves sufficient to explain Weber's analytical practice. In the end it is in the poetics of the early Romantics (Novalis and Friedrich von Schlegel) where I find a cognitive attitude that is, like Weber's, suspended between the possibility of representation of experience by language and the impossibility of ever reaching closure in and through any form of representation. Oscillating between these two positions, Weber's subject is said then to share in the spirit of the Romantic ironist, for whom language offers only flickering moments of cognition, even and particularly when those moments are addressed to the self.

In keeping with the ironic reading of Weber's subject, my interpretation of his analytical metalanguage—the enduring Roman numeral—highlights the tension between the rigorous order it designates and the arbitrariness of its status as sign. On the one hand, in distinction to previous metalanguages used by music theories, the Roman numeral advertises, as it were, its not being "music" (contrary to what Rameau's notation suggested) and its disassociation from performance practice (as was the case of *Generalbass* notation, used analytically by C. P. E. Bach, for instance, and by Rameau himself). On the other hand, the transparent representational relation between signified and signifier of the classical sign is now rendered more opaque, as the analytical signified hosts a number of possible signifiers. Further intensifying the insertion of the subject's cognitive agency between signified and signifier in Rameau, Weber's use of the Roman numeral positions the listening subject as the final arbiter of the signifier-signified relationship. Whereas the classical sign "existed," transparently presenting things under the cognitive logic that Foucault calls "representation," the sign through which "das Gehör" listens merely "subsists" as an index of the activity of the interpreter.

Before finishing up this introduction, I want to discuss the rationale for concluding my readings with Weber, for it may appear as if I interrupt my account *en medias res*. The first thing to say is that my choice of Weber as a stopping point is partly arbitrary and partly informed by my decision to write a partial account of subjects and representations in music theory. But there are other criteria. My reading of Weber concentrates on the emergence, at the turn to the nineteenth century, of temporality as a new domain within which knowledge of music takes place. Within this new domain there is a turn toward the existential, as listening experience and interiority become empirical addressees of musical thought. At the same time the existential marks a particularly forceful emergence of the subject into language and, vice versa, of language into the constitution of the subject. The final chapter investigates these matters through a close reading of Weber's analysis of Mozart's "Dissonance" Quartet. That analysis exemplifies how linguistic acts come to be used to define and trace the movements of the subject—which Weber calls "das Gehör." Temporality and musical experience, I argue, constitute fundamental forces shaping the grid of representation in which Weber operates. Representation can hardly be said to uphold the standards of objective accuracy and certainty available before, for instance, in the prescriptive semiotics of Rameau's *Basse fondamentale* or in C. P. E. Bach's *Generalbass* descriptions. Weber's analysis speaks, of course, to the rise of the individual musical work as an available object of cognitive attention near the beginning of the nineteenth century. In this sense classic analyses by Hoffmann (Beethoven) or Momigny (Haydn and Mozart), among many other analyses of individual works, could have served equally well to address musical experience, interiority, and temporality. Similarly, a theorist like Fétis, for whose work "historical consciousness" constitutes a primary condition of possibility, could illustrate radical shifts in the protocols of thought more in line with Foucault's scheme but would not provide the kind of systematic metalinguistic use that Weber does. More than any other nineteenth-century theorist before Riemann, Weber advocated a particular analytic metalanguage (Roman numerals, via Vogler), which in my account enables a productive comparison of the cognitive discontinuity between Weber and Rameau. That feature of Weber's work, combined with the undeniable place that his metalanguage still maintains in Anglo-American pedagogy, made his work most suitable for my critique.

The above does not yet explain why I would end with Weber. That explanation rests on three considerations: (1) musical thought in Weber hovers between two forms of rationalism, (2) these forms of rationalism become separated in the work of later theorists, and (3) there is growing scholarship on some of these later theorists.

1. Two forms of rationality coexist in Weber: a modern self-questioning subjectivity manifest in the way "das Gehör" interprets what it hears, knows itself to do so, but doubts whether its experience can be represented; and a "classical" epistemology of order illustrated in Weber's exhaustive tables of chord classification, which preserves the spirit of the great taxonomies from eighteenth-century natural sciences. The former rationality speaks to a metaphysics of interiority and self-criticism that places Weber's thought in line both with the poetics of the early Romantics and with the categorical structuring of experience in Kant. By contrast, the latter rationality manifests a sort of empirical materialism in which musical objects (e.g., chords, Weber's favored object) exist independent from context and are regarded as "things."

The coexistence of two forms of rationality comes to an impasse when Weber's subject finds itself unable to synthesize the temporal experience of music. Here one may compare his analysis of Mozart with the pragmatics of A. B. Marx's *Kompositionslehre,* where within the metaphysical underpinnings of Hegelian idealism and teleology the listener progresses through a composition gaining ever-increasing awareness and knowledge. Time, in Marx, is overcome.

2. Weber, like Marx, resorts to linguistic narrative as a medium and instrument of empirical experience. Whatever form representation and subjectivity may adopt, neither needs to be submitted to arbitration outside the analyst's assertion. Other music-theoretical efforts, however, partake of the same conditions of possibility that placed the *Naturwissenschaften* and their positive values at the center of study of human Being. With the rise of these modern sciences, their values (empirical and formalist positivism) come to dictate a separation of objective and subjective kinds of knowledge. Here science, history, and hermeneutics, which formerly could coexist in thought, are separated, or else nonscientific fields come to be upheld against the cognitive presuppositions of science. From the specific perspective of music theory, the separation is one between science-based cognition and hermeneutics, which can be seen in the most influential ideas from the second half of the nineteenth century. Take, for instance, *Tonpsychologie* (Helmholtz's systematic study of the sensation of sound) and *Musikpsychologie* (e.g., Stumpf's application of acoustics and psychology to musical cognition), or think of the polemics against hermeneutics (e.g., in Hanslick). Consider also how these discourses played constitutive roles in decisive developments such as Riemann's *Funktionslehre* or, more markedly, his "Ideen zu einer 'Lehre von den Tonvorstellungen'" (1914), where virtual spatial representations of harmonic relations operate under a psychological imperative quite simply not available to Weber.[29]

Two general points can be made here. First, Kant's critical philosophy inaugurates what Foucault calls the "analytic of finitude," a fancy name for Kant's circumscription of the domain of human knowledge of the world, his restriction of the reach of representation, and his isolation of the subject from the world. These are, for Foucault, decisive features of the modern episteme, under which the limits of knowledge become the grounds for knowledge. Second, the "analytic of finitude" carries its inversion, namely, the infinitude of knowledge in a world where the subject—as a form of transcendental consciousness—assumes a central place in the determination of what can be known and thought. This I take to mark the return of the belief in the objective values of science; I should say "return" with a vengeance: as is often remarked, in Cartesian thought (and the classical episteme for that matter) science does not subsume Being, whereas in the nineteenth-century *Naturwissenschaften* it does.

3. The third consideration is the most pragmatic. Several fundamental figures in nineteenth- and early-twentieth-century music theory have been the subject, recently, of concentrated studies, some of them similar to my own case studies in critical attitude and historical concern. I have in mind Scott Burnham's work on A. B. Marx and Riemann; Robert Snarrenberg and Kevin Korsyn

on Schenker; Leslie Blasius also on Schenker (in the most sustained archaeological effort in music theory to date); recent and ongoing work on Riemann by Brian Hyer, Kevin Mooney, and Alexander Rehding; and Lee Rothfarb on Kurth. At the same time I believe that my readings will complement existing work on Rameau and Weber,[30] that they will provide much-needed reexamination of Zarlino, and that they will inspire a renewed engagement with Descartes's modest compendium.

Further Disclaimers and a Second Disquisition on Foucault

Musical Representations, Subjects, and Objects offers a decidedly critical response to questions of value and interest to music theory that I feel need to be addressed historically. But if it offers a history, it is an extremely partial one and is, furthermore, a history that does not maintain what the pontiffs of unified, teleological histories call a "sustained argument." I conclude this introduction by addressing this issue first and then critically situating the relation of my case studies to the notion of episteme.

It will be obvious to the reader that in choosing statements articulated no less than fifty years apart from one another I have a built-in historical discontinuity. But chronological separation alone does not constitute discontinuity, which may be seen by considering notions traditionally deployed in historical explanations precisely to transcend temporal discontinuity: development, evolution, influence, and tradition.[31] Development and evolution are temporal inversions of one another, as each holds that either an idea or concept develops from a determinable point of origin or else it evolves toward a point of culmination. In either case the stages through which development and evolution take place are susceptible to the historian's analysis.[32] Influence transposes the logic of linear continuity to the level of individuals or groups of individuals while maintaining in the binary influencer/influenced the temporal dimension of development and evolution. Perhaps more than the other notions of continuity, tradition values permanence in the face of change, which it sees as occurring gradually.

Development, evolution, influence, and tradition all perform their explanatory function under the auspices of the logic of causality, aspiring by the force of that logic to give coherence to an otherwise dispersed field. These notions, moreover, make possible the establishment of discrete disciplines separating what properly belongs to the language of a discursive field (e.g., music theory) from what does not. My deployment of textuality serves to counterbalance my own tendency—due to a combination of training, intellectual proclivities, and institutional affiliations—to think disciplinary within music theory. Textuality, I believe, opens up traditional boundaries, bringing together diverse areas of discourse to bear on music theories, indicating in the process how embedded music theories are in a more general discourse of knowledge. But textuality does not erase the fact that when people read other people's work, conceptual sediments are bound to be deposited in their own work. My wager here will be to admit those sediments as part of the evidence of continuity at the level of individual authors, or of the existence of a tradition that emerges when, for instance, Weber deals with "harmony" as the result of having the notion "harmony" handed down from Rameau. There, against the apparent conceptual continuity of "harmony," stands a series of decisive discontinuities at the level of representation and subject position. I recognize, nonetheless, that in the case of Zarlino and Descartes, where influence is most pronounced, a different set of questions would emerge if one were to consider how what is "new" in Descartes affects what he merely repeats from Zarlino. By the same token, a question such as why Descartes's radical rethinking of the perceiver would not reshape what he thought of the practice of counterpoint is left unattended.

The second consideration attends to the relation of my focused case studies to the writer's work and to the episteme, more generally. In each case study I do not set out to investigate a given author's œuvre, understood either as a collection of texts "that can be designated by the sign of a proper name" or, more conceptually, as the unmediated expression of the totality of the thought and experience of an author. I trust the reader to understand that no matter how focused the ideas I analyze are, I am not reducing any theorist's thought to an essential kernel or to a conceptual contribution we may now consider fundamental. There is much more to Descartes than the articulation of a subject-object divide, more to Rameau than the *Basse fondamentale,* more to Weber than the Roman numeral. Nor am I interested in considering either the early, mature, or late statements by a theorist as a kind of definitive word: I examine Zarlino's authorial bookends, Descartes's early work, Rameau's inaugural theory (with forays into his *Nouveau système* [1726] and *Génération harmonique* [1737]), and Weber's last edition of his *Versuch.* These inconsistencies, such as they are, cannot be divorced from the epistemological underpinnings to this project. Choices of what to discuss and how much of a writing to analyze constitute forms of critique of the notion of historical evidence. My choices, which I expect some may see as "skimpy evidence" or "token samples" for large claims about how entire periods of time and entire bodies of thought are all constituted by similar cognitive values, cannot be taken to constitute evidence. Evidence implies a need for proof (usually visual) that itself demands and adopts a simple model of representation: x is evidence for y means x proves y. This logic all too easily suppresses interpretive gestures such as I make here. Perhaps the reader may object that I present as evidence only one writer, and that my case would be best made if I were to use more writers as proof, as my example might suggest. To my mind, numbers would not make a difference but would produce a different project, perhaps one of greater depth but also of greater chronological circumscription. The critique of evidence would remain in effect. For example, what sort of proof can be brought to bear on the possibility that thinkers as different as Euler, Mattheson, and Rameau constitute expressions of similar protocols for thought? As Leslie Blasius notes, the cartographies of the music-theoretical field are as numerous as are its possible historiographies.[33] With that in mind, could one not carry out profitable analyses of a more localized terrain, by studying the protocols for representation in Delair, Masson, and Saint-Lambert, whose theorizing can be said to stand on the "practical" side of musical thought? In the end I hope that readers might feel compelled to return to the vast terrain of thought of each of the authors I have chosen and reread them in the splendor of their cognitive and historical complexity.

It remains then to account for the relationship of the "theorist" to the grid of thought of the Foucauldian episteme. Foucault makes a useful analytical distinction between "author," the empirical individual, historically bound, psychological and cognitive consciousness who produced a text, and the "author function," which is something like the weight interpreters give to the author. The problem with these resides, in Foucault's estimation, not in the undeniable fact that individual authors exist who advance singularly powerful ideas or formulate influential concepts; rather, the problem occurs in forms of historical explanation that attaches to the "author function" ideologemes such as "founding subject" or unmediated "expressive function." As Foucault sees it, deploying these ideologemes unnecessarily limits historiographical inquiry to questions of intention, influence, the text, and discipline, disallowing questions about what conceptual structures may allow an author to know what he or she does. For Foucault these latter questions adopt a negative form: the mode of thought of empirical beings is not given in what it permits consciousness to say, but in what it prohibits. Naturally it is the historian's task to outline the area of knowledge where silence prevails. Foucault speaks of the "positive unconscious of knowledge," "a level that eludes the consciousness of the scientist and yet is part of the scientific discourse."[34] In psychoanalytical fashion the archaeologist lets history speak in order to establish what lies at the unconscious level.

The notion of a "positive unconscious" is not without merit, insofar as it helps explain cognitive coincidences across disparate sciences and expanded periods of time. But it is also circular insofar as it is not possible to speak of an unconscious of knowledge without accepting its inversion, the consciousness of knowledge. My case studies seek to negotiate the dialectical relation between the unconscious at the level of the episteme and the consciousness that attends to the particular discourse practice of musical thought of a theorist. What any one of these figures writes is taken as a point of entry to question how that utterance is organized, how it can move from the local level of its text to the more general level at which it makes objects and subjects of knowledge appear. This general level forms part of what Foucault calls statements, making a distinction between statements, on the one hand, and propositions, sentences, speech acts, or any other unit of discourse commonly understood, on the other. Statements do not represent; they allow representation to take place. Here a point I made early in this introduction—that theories think—becomes clear. This was not to mean that theorists do not think; rather, it meant that their individual, self-conscious thinking as authors does not adjudicate the level of statements, but only the level of propositions, sentences, and texts themselves.

Restoring some of the historical agency to theorists, *pace* Foucault, is no doubt part of my readings. This agency, however, is not sought in order to look for clues in past modalities of musical thought that might guide our analytical practices today. I say this self-consciously aware that this is a book about music that presents few musical examples, but even more aware of the fact that this is a book about musical sound. To borrow an expression by W. J. T. Mitchell, this is a book about hearing and listening that might have been written as if by a mute author for a deaf reader, a reader for whom the theorist's constructions of musical thought would provide one (ideal) way to imagine what music might be (like).

1   Zarlino: Instituting Knowledge in the Time of Correspondences

To begin, a simple question of order. By way of preface to an interval taxonomy in Part 3 of his *Istitutioni harmoniche,* Gioseffo Zarlino writes, "Before discussing counterpoint it is necessary to know the elements of which it is composed. For one cannot order or compose anything, or understand (*conoscere*) the nature of the composite unless [one] knows first the things (*cose*) that must be ordered (*ordinare*) or combined, their nature (*la natura*), and their cause (*la loro ragione*)."[1] With explicit reference to causes and natures, the language here speaks directly to epistemological values of Aristotelian natural philosophy.[2] Such values lend methodological support to a fundamental distinction Zarlino observes between *musica prattica* and *musica speculativa,* of Platonic and Pythagorean provenance. Outlining a hierarchy that places "cause" and "nature" before musical composition, Zarlino's intellectually hybrid pronouncement echoes an order of knowledge—*musica speculativa*—different from and ultimately superior to the particulars of composition and performance of *musica prattica.* The point here, however, is not so much that the passage above reinforces the hierarchy inherent in these categories and exemplified by the well-known distinction Zarlino makes between, on the one hand, *musico,* and, on the other, *cantore.*[3] Rather, the point is that conjoined in their cause-and-effect relationship, *musica speculativa* and *musica prattica* are indivisible, as are, ideally, *musico* and *cantore.* Thus, when in Part 3 Zarlino introduces the intervals in the context of their suitability for composition, he cannot forgo the foundations provided by the "causes" and "natures" first presented in Part 1 of his monumental theoretical opus.

All this may seem to belabor the obvious: Parts 1 and 2 do provide the "foundations" for Parts 3 and 4, and so Zarlino would not forgo those foundations. However, it is not without significance that Zarlino should insist on issues he had repeatedly made earlier. His prolix style notwithstanding, the insistence here reflects methodological demands arising from Zarlino's ambition to establish an indivisible musical truth. Indeed, his deft layering of various authorities in the passage above reflects consistent efforts throughout the *Istitutioni* to develop a hybrid methodology strong enough to support the congeries of aesthetic, compositional, historical, musical, poetic, rhetorical, and scientific pronouncements which constitute the "institutes" of Zarlino's title. Pythagorean, Platonic, and Neoplatonic cosmology with its numerological and mathematical underpinnings is infused with Aristotelian natural philosophy in Part 1;[4] in

Part 2 a sweeping account of ancient music (i.e., the Greek tonal system) is anchored to Pythagorean values deployed in the development of a theory of consonance that Zarlino sees as being distinctly modern; Part 3 moves into concerns of *musica prattica* proper, providing Zarlino's deservedly acclaimed and influential rules of contrapuntal practice, its elements and organization (with Willaert as a model, in the Ciceronian tradition); the materials of composition (the modes) are the subject of Part 4. In all, Zarlino's thought in the *Istitutioni* is characterized by an ambitious, all-encompassing conception of knowledge. At stake is the delicate balance he must maintain between the various cognitive pressures applied by the axiomatic dictates of Platonic and Pythagorean doctrine about the immanence and interconnectedness of all things, the explanatory method and ontological schemes of Aristotelian natural philosophy, and his recognition of indisputably changing aspects in the tonal system and style of modern music.[5] His success depends then on the flexibility of his method to withstand these pressures and attend to the dual demands of the rationality of *musica scientia* (i.e., a domain the foundations and intelligibility of which can be systematically and undoubtedly demonstrated) and the accuracy of his historical exegesis and adaptation and/or transformation of ancient knowledge in the context of his day.

Understood as a rational procedure for discovering, understanding, and providing apodictic demonstrations of the relations among things, method is indeed of primary importance to Zarlino. To give one example, as it appears in the quotation above, "order" (*ordino*) designates the rational and systematic disposition of musical things in general, or as is the case there, of the intervals of counterpoint.[6] But in a more fundamental way, "order" designates the predetermined condition in which things are given in the universe. It is the task of the *musico* to comprehend methodically these things across all domains of knowledge, and that of the *cantore* to learn how to deploy them in an orderly manner in composition or performance proper. Or, returning to Aristotelian language, the sort of empirical knowledge of individual cases of musical composition or of the matter of intervals (*demonstratio quia*—the discovery of causes through their effects) must be grounded on the structuring demonstration *propter quid* of the effect by its cause or form, for only in this way could true rational knowledge be ensured.

The objective of this chapter is to present an outline of Zarlino's thought that will serve as a key point of reference to my discussion of Descartes in Chapter 2. In the present chapter I provide examples of various ways in which Zarlino endeavors to articulate a method for a universal knowledge of music, in particular, to which the post-Cartesian notion of a self-examining consciousness is wholly irrelevant. I consider selected strands of his thought as articulated in the bookends of his music-theoretical career: the *Istitutioni harmoniche* (1558) and the *Sopplimenti musicali* (1588).[7] Two issues are of particular interest: first, the epistemological protocol guiding the conception of order found throughout the *Istitutioni*, and second, the interrelation of this protocol to the more particular sources that Zarlino deploys, appeals to, or invokes that would have made his thought possible and necessary, and that would have sanctioned it before his audience.[8]

In the first section of the chapter I describe, by appeal to passages from Parts 1 and 3 of the *Istitutioni,* what I call the epistemological saturation of Zarlino's thought. By epistemological saturation I mean two things: First, the idea that knowledge of "things," such as the intervals in the passage from Part 3 above, was informed by maximal and simultaneous associations and correspondences with other "things."[9] Second, the methodology that responds to that idea by bringing together all available sources to bear on the subject of music, be it history, Scripture, Aristotelian natural philosophy, or Pythagorean mathematics and numerology. According to the first point, more than a linear series of progressive steps toward acquisition of knowledge, Zarlino mobilizes the associative and analogical thinking connected to the *signatura rerum* creed of Neoplatonic and Hermetic provenance. According to this creed, the seen and unseen world was etched with hidden inscriptions that made it legible, and thus intelligible, to the human intellect. The second point regards Zarlino's use of heterogeneous sources to build the foundation of the "harmonic institutes." Forming part of this general epistemological background, and yet in some sense moving against its grain, appears another key element of Zarlino's thought: the rational (i.e., as "ordered account") underpinnings of his *musica scientia.* For Zarlino, number ultimately provides the foundation for the intelligibility of music, while the demonstrations of mathematics guarantee the means by which to articulate knowledge of music with absolute definition. His cognitive faith in mathematics, however, must not be taken to reflect primarily a belief in method, for it refers most importantly to the idea that music, "[like] all things created by God, was ordered by Him with the number."[10] Combined, these nested values—God, unity, number, music, mathematics—form part of and provide a conceptual framework for Zarlino's *musica scientia.* Fundamental to my analysis of epistemological saturation through this first section of the chapter will therefore be the recognition of a tension between the claims to knowledge of the epistemology based on associations and correspondences among things, on the one hand, and those of *musica scientia,* on the other.

In the chapter's second section I focus on a different tension: that between sound as number and sound as music. There I examine the impact of the introduction of subjective criteria for the classification of intervals to the overarching epistemology of correspondences. Also, I consider the persistence of associative thinking in the discussion of counterpoint proper. A final section introduces questions of method within the context of Zarlino's "modernity." Two issues are considered there: first, the influence on Zarlino's method of his teacher Adrian Willaert; second, the remapping of the cognitive relation with antiquity that Zarlino establishes in the *Sopplimenti musicali* (in response to the challenges of Vincenzo Galilei), which he conceives in terms different from those of the *Istitutioni.*[11]

1.1. The Commitments of Knowledge

Chapter 1 of the *Istitutioni* opens in grand style, with what can justly be described as a dizzying account of the origins of music. "Hearing," writes Zarlino, "will be recognized as far more necessary and better [than sight and smell] . . . in matters pertaining to the intellect," a statement he follows with the stories of Jubal finding Cain's people (*stirpe*), before the Deluge, by the sound of hammers, Mercury's rediscovery of music afterwards, and Pythagoras's discovery of the rationality (*ragione*) of the musical proportions.[12] Concluding his account, he discusses the status of music within the mathematical sciences (in the passage cited earlier), but not without connecting it to a Neoplatonic cosmology: "And such is the certainty of the said [mathematical] sciences that by means of numbers we can calculate with certainty the revolutions of the heavens, the various aspects of the planets, the lunar activities and its eclipse, and that of the sun, and infinite other wonderful secrets, without there being among them a discordant point. From this we know that music is both noble and most certain, being part of the mathematical sciences."[13]

In its exuberant erudition Zarlino's recounting appears to embrace a de rigueur protocol of learned writing, a received narrative formula that sought to connect a given writing to the authority of the ancients—keeping in mind that myth, written and oral record, and commentary on them could equally bear truth. Historical record upholds this impression. For instance, despite avowed efforts not to repeat what others have said in praise of music, Pietro Aaron goes on about the subject in a chapter longer than any other.[14] Together there we find references to Homer, a host of Greek mythological figures, a recounting of the story of Orpheus, and so on. Even when pausing to reflect about whether there is real need for such accounts, Aaron cannot contain the force of received knowledge: "Timagenes affirms that of all literary studies, music is the oldest." This is followed by other tales from Ovid about the affective power of music as well as by citations of classical loci from the *Timaeus* outlining the musical composition of the human soul, the macro- and microcosmos relation, and the musical interrelation between body and soul. Among other examples Aaron includes the restorative powers of music, music's necessary place in grammar and architecture, and, according to Hierophilus, music's effectiveness in "tempering ballistae, catapults, scorpions, and hydraulic machines."[15]

True to this tradition, Zarlino too expounds at great length on the praises of music; next to the chapter on *musica mondana* (Chapter 6), Chapter 2, on the praises, is the most extensive in all of Part 1 of the *Istitutioni*. Like Aaron, Zarlino fails in his attempt at brevity. However, in contrast to Aaron, who from the outset invokes ancient authority, Zarlino begins with a statement of fact. Absolutely nothing can be found with which music does not have the greatest convenience (*grandissima convenienza*), he proclaims.[16] Connecting music to all else, this preamble holds programmatic value, which prompts the question of what, beyond paying heed to narrative tradition, may lie behind Zarlino's retelling. As Gary Tomlinson, following anthropologist Marshall Sahlins, remarks, "[t]he precise *situation* of each *re-enactment* determines the character and significance of its events, and the particular character of these events determines the *transformational* power they bring to the structures they *re-present*."[17] It seems clear that in bringing the structures of knowledge of the preponderant Boethian and Neoplatonic traditions together with exacting claims about the certainty of mathematics and the immense depository of historical record, Zarlino's re-presentation (or reenactment) of these various intellectual traditions has as one immediate transformative effect the suffusion of each of them with the other. By simple virtue of this assigned adjacency all these structures become somehow interconnected.

But the particular situation in which Zarlino carries out his reenactment no doubt entails more than a simple juxtaposition of various kinds of knowledge. This situation is such, in fact, that it calls upon a conception of order in which knowledge(s)—in reality, one thing among all other things—itself has the greatest convenience (*convenienza*). *Convenienza* is a notion with powerful cognitive associations of agreement, accord, conformity, fitness, harmony, propriety, symmetry, and suitability. In its Latin form *convenientia* is found particularly in Cicero, who reluctantly writes in *De Divinatione:* "I shall grant this very thing, if you like, although I shall have made a great sacrifice of my case, if I shall have granted that there is any *convenientia* of nature with [internal] organs."[18] Along with a host of expressions including, among others, aemulatio, analogia, concordance, concurrence, conjunction, consonantia, harmonia, proportio, similitude, and sympathy, *convenienza* forms part of what Foucault, in a positive interpretation of the notion, calls "the semantic web of resemblance in the sixteenth century." This semantic web designates a foundational tenet of Neoplatonic and Hermetic thought available to the Italian cinquecento intellectual: namely, the condition for existence that predetermines that all things are interconnected by correspondence.[19] From a methodological perspective, the obvious question is how, in a world in which affinities connect music to all else, can anything be known about it that is not already known as part of this plethoric network of interrelationships? Put differently, if conceptual constraints may be said to keep things out of mind, and so conceptual expansions are necessary to bring things in, what would Zarlino's intellectual task be if the conceptual framework available to him already encompassed all things? For our mid-cinquecento Venetian *musico* there would have been nothing outside this framework, and so in a sense there would be no framework at all, no distinct vantage point from which to discriminate among things. Clearly, then, a fundamental task for the intellectual project of Zarlino's "harmonic institutes" would had been to outline the chains of affinities or correspondences linking things, including the place in those chains for the music he deemed exemplary.

Correspondences, Foucault argues, were established by means of visible and invisible preexisting signs inherent in things. The procedure of establishing correspondences entails a process of discovery of these signs and their interpretation. Following Foucault's analysis of such a process, I consider Zarlino's intellectual endeavor as having a twofold commitment to a semiology—the distinction of signs in their location, their constitution, and their links—and a hermeneutics —the interpretation of signs and the assignation of their meaning.[20] In the particular case of Zarlino, however, the semiological task of locating signs had already been carried out. Evidence of this is offered, for instance, in a passage from Part 1, Chapter 6, in which he cites sacred Scripture, Cicero, Plato, and a report about the inhabitants of the banks of the river Nile in connection to signs dispersed through heaven and earth that indicate Man's incapacity for perceiving disproportionate sound phenomena. Another example is a reference, in Chapter 12, to Augustine's *De Doctrina Christiana,* a locus classicus of scriptural exegesis with pronounced Hermetic influences. For Zarlino, on the other hand, the assembly and interpretation of this vast system of interconnected signs remained a fundamental necessity for his dual project of elaborating a *musica scientia* and demonstrating the validity of modern music. That he could be merely reassembling signs already interpreted is obvious, but such a reading would miss the importance of Zarlino's retelling as an interpretive act itself.

Consider his retelling, in Chapter 6, of *musica mondana.* Halfway through that chapter Zarlino defines *musica mondana* as "that harmony which is not only recognized to be among those things seen and known in the sky but also in the binding (*legamento*) of the elements, having been created by the grand architect God (as He also created all other things) in number, weight, and measure."[21] By "things seen and known in the sky," Zarlino refers to the well-known doctrines of the music of the spheres and of universal harmony. Characteristically he precedes the definition above with an exhaustive enumeration of all the possible ways in which *musica mondana* is known: by the "revolutions," "distance," "parts," "aspect," "position," and "nature" of the individual planets. He remarks, for instance, that distances between the celestial spheres are not known by sense but by reason. "Reason," in his account, has a historical basis in previously established knowledge. Thus, Zarlino relates that according to Pythagoras the distance between the Earth and the Moon is at the interval of one tone, from the Moon to Mercury a major semitone, from Mercury to Venus a minor semitone, from Venus to the Sun one tone plus a minor semitone, from the Sun to the Earth diapente, between the Moon and the Sun a diatessaron, and so on.[22] Regarding the "parts," he follows Ptolemy (*Harmonicorum Libri Tres,* Chapter 9), saying that the twelve signs of the zodiac correspond to the musical consonances. By contrast, regarding longitude, he states without citing a source that one discovers the diatonic, chromatic, and enharmonic genera, while in latitude one discovers the modes. Likewise, in the faces of the Moon are contained the tetrachordal conjunctions. According to their position, the spheres determine the virtues of people at birth and can, for instance, affect the elements themselves: if disproportionally positioned, Mars and Saturn can generate a universal pestilence in the world. This final reminder of the negative powers of astrological *convenientia* gives way, in Zarlino's retelling, to a systematic exposition of the numerical binds between the four elements (earth, air, water, and fire) and their corresponding qualities (dryness, coldness, humidity, and warmth). "Number is discovered" in each of these, which enables a most extraordinary conjunction among them by means of medial elements:

> As two square numbers come together in a medial proportional number, so similarly two of these elements are conjoined. Just as in the manner that the quaternario and the novenario square numbers come together in the senario (which surpasses the quaternario as it is surpassed by the novenario), likewise fire and water, which are two contrary qualities, are conjoined in one medial element; because fire being by its nature warm and dry, and water cold and humid, in the warm and humid air [they] are in perfect, great proportionate balance. . . . Thus they are united in such a wonderful order that there is no longer any disparity between them.[23]

As shown in Example 1.1, Zarlino illustrates this series of conjunctions along a quasi-circular path enclosed within a square frame. Earth, in a foundational position at the "bottom" of the circle, holds a sesquialtera proportion to water, the next element in the path counterclockwise. The same proportion holds for water to air, and air to fire. Connecting fire and earth is the proportion triple superpartiens, which closes off the circle. Each proportion denotes a *convenientia* between adjacent elements, which is expressed in terms of a shared or mediating quality. Earth and water stand in a 2:3 proportion, equivalent to how they convene in coldness, for instance, which is the same as saying that coldness represents the *convenientia* existing between earth and water.

The scheme of transformations in Zarlino's illustration manifests two principles: (1) all things (elements and their qualities, in this case) lie along an uninterrupted continuum; (2) in order for this continuum not to extend infinitely, it must circle back on itself. The first principle posits the existence of various kinds of correspondences distributed along a grid that conceptualizes "distance" between elements along the continuum. (This in itself denotes the primacy of "space" as the cognitive enclosure for knowledge.) The second principle reveals a peculiarity in the structure of the system: it is predetermined to repeat itself. Each of these principles must be examined in order to determine the norms according to which the knowledge of the correspondences among all things is established.

From Foucault we may borrow a taxonomy of correspondences, which he reduces to four: convenience (*convenientia*), emulation (*aemulatio*), analogy (*analogia*), and sympathy (*sympatia*).[24] First, there are correspondences among things sharing spatial proximity. This is "convenience."[25] By it, adjacent (but not necessarily similar) things share a property which nature has predisposed as the site of their immanent correspondence. "Coldness," "2:3," and "diapente": the signifying reach of each of these terms is not delimited by each of them being a *sign for* either a quality, a numerical account of parts of something, or a musical interval, in that order. Their signifying reach makes of these terms simultaneously *signs for* and *signs of* correspondences. With the expression "sign for" I shall

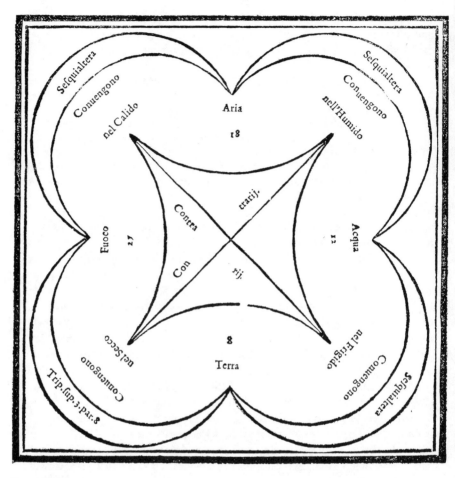

Example 1.1
Convenientiae between the four elements and the four qualities. Gioseffo Zarlino, *Istitutioni harmoniche* (1558: I, 14).

refer to a general equivalent to "word," making a distinction between that expression and the expression "sign of," which will express the idea of a correspondence between a thing and another.[26] That is, in addition to denoting a quality, parts of something, and an interval, within the *semiological* framework of correspondences, "coldness," "2:3," and "diapente" are *signs of* their proximity to one. By this account, "2:3" is a sign of "coldness," for example. Further, "2:3" is itself a sign of a convenience believed to reside in superparticular numbers (i.e., contiguous numbers in a series).[27] Lest we think that this semiological framework encloses airy abstractions exclusively, Zarlino gives a concrete and crucial application of convenience in the ordering principle that intervals are more or less perfect according to their proximity to unity. In Part 3, Chapter 3, he explains that the diapason has almost the same nature as unity, being near (*vicino*) to it.[28]

A second type of correspondence is "emulation," which, further along the graded distances between correspondences, exists among nonadjacent things: water and fire in the figure above, for example. When Zarlino, in his illustration, positions air as a mediating element between water and fire, air emerges as a sign of a hidden correspondence between nonadjacent, in fact, opposite, elements. Emulation introduces a peculiar agency to the system: it implies a striving of one element in the correspondence toward another. This agency necessarily creates a hierarchy between the elements it associates. What does it mean for the harmony of things, then, that water should emulate fire, or fire emulate water? It is here that Aristotelian natural philosophy, as a kind of ontological lubricant, helps to harmonize discordant elements and attenuates the sense of assiduous striving that characterizes emulation. As discrete and contrary elements, fire and water are conceived with consideration of the Aristotelian distinction between essence and primary substance, on the one hand, and attribute and quality, on the other. Being attributes of a thing, changes in quality do not impinge on the essence of things—here, each of the elements—which remain unaltered.[29] In this way the fact that discordant elements hold a correspondence at all matters more than the particular direction the emulation may take (i.e., from a thing to another toward which it strives). As a result, air can be interpreted *qua* air, or it can be interpreted *qua* mediant signature of the correspondence between water and fire, which is the same as saying that "18" is a sign of the proportion between 12 and 27 (i.e., as 6 is a sign of proportion between 4 and 9) and that it points (as signature) to the inherent propinquity between these two numbers. Like convenience, emulation too is brought to bear on practice, in a classic contrapuntal formulation. The stipulation that the major sixth should proceed to the octave is predicated on the fact that "each thing seeks its own perfection," in which the less perfect thing strives toward the more perfect. More specifically, Zarlino points out that the major sixth goes to the perfect octave and not the perfect fifth, which is literally "nearest to it" (more convenient), because between the major sixth and "the larger" of the perfect intervals there exists a "kinship or consensus" (*simbolo (dirò cosi) consenso*).[30] In this instance emulation trumps convenience, which Zarlino explains by remarking that "given a fact and a certain condition, I do not see how two diverse and almost opposite conclusions can be drawn from them." His explanation gives an indication of the methodological distinction between *semiology* (i.e., the fact that these interval pairs simultaneously hold diverse types of correspondences, according to either proximity or absolute size) and *hermeneutics* (i.e., the fact that these correspondences are subject to interpretation).

Following emulation, the system opens itself up to a third type of correspondence, that between relations or parts of things: "analogy."[31] Simply put, an analogical correspondence that holds between two elements also holds for another pair. Analogy does not, however, constitute a systematic means for comparing measurements; it is, rather, an expression of the irrefutable proportionality that inheres in all things and speaks to their basic numerical ontology.[32] In turn, proportionality is not a matter of mathematical measurement, although mathematics serves to demonstrate the degree of proportionality as such.

The fourth and final correspondence is "sympathy." It directs things to things through spatial movement. Here belong, for instance, qualitative changes and attraction: what is heavy is attracted to earth, what is light to air. "Fire," Foucault gives as an example, "because it is warm and light rises up into the air, towards which its flames untiringly strive; but in doing so it loses its dryness (which made it akin to the earth) and so acquires humidity (which links it to water and air); it disappears therefore into light vapor, into blue smoke, into clouds: it has become air."[33]

By itself the system of correspondences would have a significant structural flaw. As I noted before, the system is totalizing, allowing nothing to escape its reach, which means that trapped in this "Epistemology of the Like" things could potentially lose their individuality. More damaging for Zarlino's theory of consonance and dissonance, for example, would be that all things would have a correspondence in one way or another: thus dissonance would hold semiological privileges equal to those of consonance. Balancing the system, then, is a parallel network of opposites, which Foucault terms antipathies. Thanks to this virtual web of negatives, things are able to maintain a modicum of individuality. We ought to note, incidentally, that since by the tenets of Aristotelian natural philosophy upheld by Zarlino essential properties are permanent and individual, antipathies are not necessary. In Zarlino's figure (Example 1.1), antipathies are expressed in terms of opposing *qualities* (e.g., dry is the contrary of humid). Nonetheless, as a whole, the elements, like the proportions to which they are analogous and the qualities that link them, are ultimately bound in a haven of correspondence where they coexist, uninterruptedly linked along a circular path.[34] Nothing, by account of correspondences, stands isolated, everything always already points toward something else. Thus, semiologically speaking, signs for things and signs of things are predestined to fold onto one another, and lie in wait for the hermeneuticist to interpret them, to speak on their behalf.

The second principle at work in Zarlino's recount of the *musica mondana*, that of the circular structure of correspondences, raises two fundamental issues concerning signification. First, a question: how are these correspondences made into signs, how are they made to speak on behalf of the things they relate? Second, the possibility of any meaningful signification requires that the semiological motion circularly linking correspondences be arrested, and for this to happen there has to be an overriding hierarchy superimposed onto the correspondences, a metacorrespondence of sorts.

The first question goes to the heart of the sign's structure in the system of correspondences: a *sign for* something *designates* that something by virtue of a conjuncture between signified and signifier that is given by a preexisting correspondence itself.[35] The sign therefore means insofar as it *indicates* (or is a *sign of*) a correspondence between the thing signified and another thing. Correspondences are, in other words, the third term in the structure of all signs. And, in

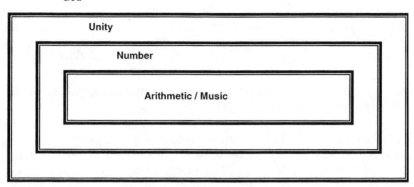

God

Unity

Number

Arithmetic / Music

Example 1.2
Hierarchy among correspondences.

a semiotic (not semiological) sense, correspondences reside outside the things they conjoin. This is an important consideration, for it points to the fact that things cannot be fully known in and of themselves, which in turn is a consequence of the inseparability of knowledge from the ontological condition of all beings. To know something is to comment on its place(s) as correspondence.[36] Let us consider an example. "Diapente" is a sign of the correspondence in the proportion 3:2. The interval's sound, its qualities as a stable and full (*piena*) concordance, and the "distance" between sounds of two large tones, one small whole tone and one large semitone apart, all form part of what is semiotically designated by "diapente," being indeed expressions of that correspondence; but these semiotic designations (i.e., signifieds) do not perform a semiological function in the constitution of the sign "diapente." That semiological function, which is the grounds for any possible interpretation, is given by the same proportion's presence in linking Sun and Earth, to give but one example. Without this predetermination—itself a semiotic echo of sorts—the sign "diapente" would hold little meaning.

Like an unending spiral ascending from the *convenientia* expressed by the adjacency between the numbers 2 and 3, through the analogy in the proportion 3:2, and all the way up to the sympathy attracting the Earth to the Sun, the system relentlessly sends all things into the uncertain wanderings of a semiotic "drift," in Umberto Eco's telling expression.[37] Against the potential aimlessness of this roving semiotics, there exists a superimposed set of what I will call absolute values, which like a parallel system of metacorrespondences arrests things in their drift through the infinite space of knowledge and simultaneously validates their signification within that space. (This is the second of the fundamental issues concerning signification in the system of correspondences.) The signifying validity of any and all correspondences is guaranteed by a nested set of hierarchies, indicated by the simple diagram shown in Example 1.2.

"[Il] grande Architettore Iddio," Zarlino reports, designed everything with a concordance of number, weight, and measurement, creating an overarching structure, the unity and limits of which He guarantees and constitutes (the unframed area represents the infinite, a cognitive space beyond the reach of representation and human knowledge). This Divine Designer stands over all things as a transcendent Being, outside of all determination. At the first level is unity, that which, emanating from the Neoplatonic One, makes possible the interconnection of all things.[38] Number appears next.[39] In Part 1, Chapter 12 ("How necessary is number in things, and what is number, and if unity is number"),[40] number is said to be furnished by God to all things, including, most significantly, human reason and discourse (ragione & discorso). The instrumentality of number as index of certainty makes it a sine qua non condition of all that is said, that is, of all that discourse accounts for. Ranging from sacred Scripture to Augustinian doctrine and Pythagorean axioms, Zarlino's account of number ultimately offers Euclid's succinct definition: "number is a manifold composed of utmost unity."[41] Unity, Zarlino says after Boethius, is not number, however, but a condition of its possibility; more specifically, unity is the principle (principio) of number. Like a point, unity is indivisible, the beginning (origine), mother (genitrice), and measurement of all things, and yet it cannot be (onto) itself, lacking a middle and an end.[42] At the next level in the illustration, as though emissaries from the quadrivium, are arithmetic and music, which Zarlino explicitly outlines in Chapter 20, entitled "The reason why music is said to be subaltern to arithmetic, and intermediate among mathematics and natural [sciences]."[43] Zarlino explains that music takes number and quantity as such from arithmetic, and measurable quantity (i.e., sonorous bodies) from geometry. These sciences depend upon principles known by natural light and cognitive sensation (lume naturale and cognitione sensitiva), such as the fact that the whole is larger than a part or that a line is length without width. Subaltern sciences, by contrast, "take" from the main ones primary elements, as perspective takes line from geometry, to which accidental elements are added. These added elements are unique to each of the subaltern sciences, such as visuality to perspective, for which visual line then becomes the exclusive subject. Likewise music has number as a common subject with arithmetic, to which it adjoins sound, making of sonorous numbers its proper subject. Zarlino writes that music possesses number (he does not say that music takes number from arithmetic) and that arithmetic is used for purposes of demonstration, which ensures true knowledge (vera cognitione) of its science. That music is only partially indebted to arithmetic is explained by the fact of their sharing the arithmetical principle of relationship, or proportion, which is used to indicate the passions (passioni) of the sonorous numbers. He further remarks that the conclusions obtained from the demonstrations of arithmetic are applied to sound or voice, which themselves are considered to belong to the natural science. From the natural sciences, sound derives "each modulation, consonance, harmony, and melody."[44] Music, Zarlino concludes, is therefore subaltern to mathematics and natural sciences, in support of which he refers to Avicenna (*Suffic. Liber,* I, Chapter 8) before offering the following, decidedly Aristotelian, disquisition:

> And as with natural things nothing is perfect so as long as it remains *in potentia* but is perfect if reduced *in actu,* thus music cannot be perfect unless it is heard by means of natural or artificial instruments. This cannot be done with rhythm (*numero*) or voices alone but the one accompanying the other, particularly since rhythm is inseparable from consonance. By this it will be obvious that music cannot be said to be simply mathematical or simply natural, but rather part natural and part mathematical and consequently mid-way among them. But since the musician obtains the reason (*il musico ha la ragione*), in the area of consonance, from the natural science of music, which [reason] consists of sounds and voices, and the reason of music's form (that is, of its proportions) is drawn from the science of mathematics . . . we can reasonably say that music is a mathematical rather than a natural science: because form is more noble than matter.[45]

The ontotheological doctrines that begin with Divine Unity give way in this passage to ontological questions that emerge once music is identified specifically in connection to science. Such ontological questions, associated here with the Aristotelian doctrine of hylomorphism (i.e., the doctrine according to which things are constituted of form and matter), are in turn subject to the logic of reason (*ragione*): "form," which gives intelligibility to things, or more precisely, "that attribute by virtue of which anything is what it is, is comprehended by reason." Matter, on the other hand, falls fully within the domain of sense.[46]

In Zarlino's passage the seamless transition from Pythagorean and Neoplatonic structures to tenets of Aristotelian natural philosophy parallels a move from *scientia*—the generalized knowledge of Creation—to *musica scientia.*[47] This musical science, that is, emerges as questions of method become necessary to explain and, more importantly, rationally demonstrate music's place in the ontological continuum of all things "that are," as he puts it in the following quote:

> Thus those who came later showed the errors made by those of the past concerning our science of music (*scienza della Musica*) and, adding to it their own authority, made it so clear and certain that they numbered it amongst the mathematical sciences. For this [musical] science, together with the others [mathematical sciences], advances the other sciences in certainty and is a fundamental truth. This fact can be recognized from its name: since mathematics is from the Greek word μάθημα (*mathêma*), which in Latin means discipline, and in [our] Italian means science or wisdom, which—as Boethius says—is none other than a means of understanding or, to put it more clearly, the capacity of things that are [to demonstrate] Truth— things which, by their nature cannot be changed.[48]

As part of the many commitments of knowledge, *musica scientia* reflects Zarlino's urgent concern with the individuality of truth: its uniqueness and absolute indivisibility.[49] This concern is dictated by the given order of things and their internal constitution, and it also informs the method by which he accounts for them. As we proceed in the next section to discussion of the structure of the *numero sonoro* and Zarlino's famous advocacy of the *numero Senario* as the matrix for musical order, we find that his institute could have been established on no other foundation than that constituted by the holistic amalgam of correspondences and number, to which the all-encompassing Aristotelian division of form and matter serves as explanatory matrix. We will consider, however, the degree to which the many commitments of knowledge force Zarlino into making strategic cognitive compromises as he approaches the particulars of *musica prattica*.

1.2. Sounding Number and Musical Sound

The importance of Zarlino's musical elaboration of the *numero Senario* is widely acknowledged and amply documented, needing no extended rehearsal.[50] It suffices to note that based on the foundational tenet of the *numero sonoro*, Zarlino audaciously rationalizes the expansion in the range of consonances sanctioned by Pythagorean doctrine, disseminated by Boethius, and upheld by music theorists up to Gaffurio.[51] This expansion is generally understood, from a musico-practical perspective, as a necessity in accounting for the irrefutable preponderance of thirds and sixths, firmly established intervals in counterpoint and recognized prior to Zarlino by Gaffurio himself (who considered them irrational, nonetheless), as well as by Lodovico Fogliano (*Musica theorica*, 1529), Bartolomé Ramos de Pareja (*Musica practica*, 1482), and Ramos's student Giovanni Spataro (*Errori di Franchino Gafurio da Lodi*, 1521).

Zarlino's rationalization is underwritten by Pythagorean numerological doctrine; departing from number and from the notions that numerical relationships speak most intelligibly in the language of proportions and that musical intervals hold a numerical rapport, the senario is advanced to a cognitive position along the coordinates delineated by that doctrine. Thus, in Part 1 of the *Istitutioni* the senario is first situated within an exhaustive taxonomy of species of numbers (e.g., simple, compound, pair, odd, prime, cubic), among which it is securely ensconced within the genus of "perfect numbers." Perfect numbers are constituted by their parts; since 6 is constituted by 1, 2, and 3, these parts can be added or multiplied, resulting in the senario.[52]

Two issues merit consideration here. First, the senario is given as part of a general taxonomy of numbers determined according to a particular conception of order. Second, as an expansion of tenets upheld by tradition, the senario cannot be sustained by appeals to musical practice alone. The question of taxonomy is pertinent. Strictly speaking, Zarlino works from a general, albeit virtual, table where all known relationships that inhere to number reside and from which he carves out a series of relationships that apply to the senario. But unlike his summaries of other types of relationships held by the senario, which take the form of tables or figures (e.g., the senario's "properties" in Chapter 15), his opening gesture here simply strings together similarity relationships as evidence of the senario's special place in the order of things. This, of course, attests to the "Epistemology of the Like" that guides the correspondences in his account of *musica mondana*. It is to this overarching epistemology that he turns in his efforts to buffer the impact of his expansion of the Pythagorean canon (the second of the issues I note above). Indeed, Zarlino goes to considerable lengths to infuse his arithmetico-mathematical discourse with the plethoric discourse of correspondences. Thus, in Chapter 13, after he has introduced the senario from a numerological perspective, Zarlino promptly slips into theological testimonial:

> Since, in His activities, God had never needed time, the great prophet Moses, in describing the great and wonderful fabric of the world, chose the number senario. So, like the one who was a complete master of every science, knowing harmony through the Holy Spirit—harmony which was contained within such a number; and which from visible things we know the invisible things of God—[that is] His omnipotence and His divinity—Moses turned to explaining and demonstrating the perfection of God's works by means of this number—the harmony contained within them, the custodian of its own being, without which nothing could last; but over all, either it would cancel itself out; or, if things truly returned to their original essence . . . the confusion of ancient chaos would once more be seen.[53]

However briefly, this account reaffirms the hierarchical structure of knowledge outlined in Example 1.2. But also introduced here is a fundamental cognitive (or, more properly, semiological) distinction: that between visible and invisible signs. In that which is apparently visible, we can know the invisibility of God, he states, which no doubt fuels the tour de force of correspondences that Zarlino elaborates in the next chapter (14), titled "That in the senario are comprised many things in nature and art."[54] The oft-quoted list he gives is comprehensive and worth recounting. Out of twelve signs of the zodiac, six are seen on the hemisphere at a given time; six the planets holding forth in that zodiac; six the circles in the sky; six substantial qualities in the elements; six the uffici naturali, without which nothing can be (size, color, figure, interval, state, and movement); six the species of movement; six the differences of position; six lines in the triangular pyramid; six faces to the cube; six the equilateral triangles contained in the circle (which demonstrates its perfection); six the times that a circumference needs to be traversed in order to be measured (from which the name sesto is given to the measuring instrument); six the degrees of man (essence, life, movement, sense, memory, and intellect); six the stages of man; and six the stages of the world (Zarlino corrects Lactantius Firmianus, who mistakenly misinterprets that sign to mean that the world would last six thousand years); six the transcendentals (entity, oneself, true, good, something, and thing); six the logical modes of propositions (true, false, possible, impossible, necessary, and contingent). Not only that, poets end their most perfect verses on the sixth foot, and, as Plato relates, Orpheus declared that the hymns must celebrate no generation beyond the sixth, since he thought that it would not be possible to sing about any other things than those in creation. "It is no wonder then," Zarlino tellingly writes, "that some have called the senario sign of the world (*Segnacolo del mondo*),"[55] for just as there is nothing superfluous in this world, the senario has such temperament that it can be neither extended nor contracted; this makes it not only perfect but also an emulation of virtue itself.[56] But then, as a kind of transition from this disquisition on the preponderance of the senario in nature, Zarlino returns to numerological properties: the senario is said to be analogous or proportional, given the manner in which it reunites its components, and it is circular, given that it is a multiple of these components. Nature, he concludes, has enclosed many things in the senario, and so it must be the case that things found in music too must be saturated with this sign. Indeed, six are the species of voice (Unisone, Equisone, Consone, Emmele, Dissone, and Ecmele); six those which are called consonances (Diapason, Diapente, Diatessaron, Ditono, Semiditono, and Unisono); six the species of harmony (Doria, Frigia, Lidia, Mistalidia, Eolia, Ionica). "It would be too long to recount one by one all those things that end in the senario," Zarlino remarks, opting to discuss its properties in a separate chapter.

Zarlino's exhaustive detailing of the omnipresence of the senario in Chapter 14 obeys a complex but strategic order of telling. Beginning with things "superior," Zarlino first introduces correspondences in a Nature that, although superlunar, is nonetheless evident and undeniably accountable; literally: the signs of the zodiac, the planets, and the way in which these mark the rhythm of time here on earth. Moving to matters articulated in the philosophical tradition (i.e., Platonic and Aristotelian accounts of position, elements, qualities, etc.), Zarlino then brings his outline to the level of "man"—an anthropological level, we might say—when describing, for instance, the way in which the senario maps the stages of our own existence. Ethical matters follow, which further implicate "man" in the senario, before Zarlino unexpectedly turns to art, that is, to the presence of the senario in poetry and song, the artifices of "man." (Throughout the chapter Zarlino intermittently issues brief apologies for not really wanting to go on too long on any matter.) His transition to discussion of the senario in music is particularly shrewd: by zeroing in on internal properties of the senario (i.e., its being analogous and circular) he establishes unassailable proof of its privileged "formal" status (i.e., its relation to *forma*). In making this move Zarlino penetrates the innermost core of knowledge and method: mathematics, the science of intelligibility. That from here he quickly turns to music—where he dwells all too briefly—suggests that all the correspondences accumulated throughout the chapter coalesce in support of music, not only ontologically, but epistemologically as well.

Throughout Part 1 Zarlino is intent on grounding knowledge on formal terms, which is a logical (i.e., orderly) procedure insofar as he observes the Aristotelian division of form and matter. As proportional relations the consonances are given, in a formal sense, in the senario, and it is these relations which render each consonance intelligible. Intelligibility is doubly associated with the necessary order that attends to things in the world and to our consequent cognitive access to them. The structural priority given to form guarantees, in a way, that its counterpart, matter, be brought into the fold of cognition. Thus, in the famous case of the minor sixth (minor hexachord), Zarlino makes an extraordinary appeal to the actual/potential scheme of Aristotelian ontology, bringing to bear on intelligibility notions that fundamentally pertain to matter (*materia*). The minor sixth is given in the proportion 8:6:5 and so is not found within the senario *in actu*. It is found nonetheless, claims Zarlino, "*in potentia*."[57] Its *forma* is given potentially in its individual parts (the perfect fourth [*diatessaron*] and the minor third [*semiditono*]), which, being contained in the senario, guarantee then the intelligibility of this "compound" interval. Here, as elsewhere, Zarlino does not fret about the inconsistency of his argument.[58] In fact, upon closer examination one has to wonder if to his mind there is an inconsistency at all. If, as I have noted, the Aristotelian hylomorphic doctrine dictates the structure of things, then there is logical and sufficient reason for Zarlino to observe the actual/potential scheme. For a committed Aristotelian, it is simply a matter of sliding further along the ontological continuum: at the level of form, even that which already is may yet be transformed. Discrepant as the methodological criteria Zarlino invokes may be, such inconsistency simply cannot overrule the ontological consistency that founds the overall scheme. By this account "being" trumps method. In the end this example illustrates his sensitivity toward the various conceptual pressures operating within his hybrid epistemology, as well as his ability to maneuver within the strictures of method to create room for the vicissitudes of *musica prattica*.

Such ability is put to a greater test when Zarlino moves, in Part 3, to a discussion of counterpoint, addressing more directly questions of matter, that is, of musical sound. At the outset of this chapter I discussed how in his introduction to the intervals in Chapter 3 he brings to bear at once the whole of his cognitive apparatus. As he proceeds further in that chapter, the primary criterion for interval classification is essentially "convenient": intervals are classified according to their proximity to unity:

> [A]s the number 2 has almost the same nature as the unity, so does the diapason have almost the same nature as the unison, whether because it is near (*vicino*) to it, as can be seen in the terms of their ratios, or because the terms of their proportions are not composed of numbers other than unity. Thus the effect resembles the nature of the cause. If harmonic numbers are the cause of harmonic sounds, and these sounds imitate the nature of the numbers, it is logical that the two sounds of the diapason should appear as one sound only.[59]

In addition to the Aristotelian language of causes found at the outset, the writing here invokes the semiology of correspondences to further cement the numerical foundation of intervals. That is to say, like numbers, sounds too are related by their *convenientia* along a spatially conceived hinge (Zarlino writes of numbers as being "neighbors") so that 2 and 1 hinge around their contiguity in a series. And since all things obey a hierarchical arrangement along the chain of correspondences, sounds too strive toward (i.e., emulate) their cause. In this case, for the emulation to occur it does not suffice that cause and effect bind things together; beyond that, the cause must be ascribed an agency (i.e., the will to imitate), essential to maintaining the hierarchy of form over matter. Thus, when Zarlino concludes that "it is logical that the two sounds of the diapason should appear as one," the expression "logical" (*ragionevole*) designates the multiple rational accountability of correspondences, causal relationships, and formal intelligibility.

As Zarlino turns to discussion of intervals lying farther from their cause (i.e., thirds and sixths), different ordering criteria enter the picture. "Consonances," he says, "are the more pleasing as they depart from simplicity, which does not delight our senses much, and when they are accompanied by other consonances, because our senses prefer composite to simple things."[60] Zarlino pursues now a comparison between the senses of hearing (*l'Udito*) and seeing (*il Vedere*), both of which prefer composite things. There is no direct evidence that Zarlino may be alluding, in his comparison, to the understanding of sense perception available to him, such as Aristotle's in *De Anima* (which he cites elsewhere in the *Istitutioni*). Different from most of his earlier comments, that is, Zarlino cites no cognitive authority in support of this view, which suggests that his comparison of the two senses is a simple analogy. But the significance of the analogy lies, I believe, in the very fact that the judgment of the senses is invoked at all. For although sense perception constitutes the acknowledged aesthetic arbiter in other domains (e.g., visual perspective), the notion of sense perception and the concomitant figure of the perceiver are hardly featured up to this point of the *Istitutioni*.[61] There is no conception of a "listener" as a discrete cognitive locus separate from objects of perception, and therefore no methodological need for Zarlino to justify this perceiver on epistemological terms. Introducing sense and perceiver at this stage, however, neither alters the basic modus operandi of the treatise nor indicates some sort of conceptual instability on the part of Zarlino. In keeping with the plethoric cognitive disposition of the treatise, the presence of a new authority (i.e., "the listener"), no matter how attenuated it may be (as is the present case), joins all other authorities without preconditions or even so much as a comment. Thus, expressions such as "sweet" or "languid" sounds, ascribed to the finals in modes 1–4, 9, and 10 (in Glarean's numbering), are conjoined with statements to the fact that in these finals "the consonances [are] arranged contrary to the nature of the sonorous number" (i.e., the fifth is arithmetically divided, as opposed to the harmonically divided fifth in the other modes). And while Zarlino preludes this by establishing an aesthetic correlation between sense and consonances arranged according to the location of the sonorous numbers in their natural positions, because sense appreciates proportionate things, the musical status of the "disproportionate" is, in the case of the minor finals, in no way diminished. There are, in fact, two distinct notions at play here that share, in the principle of proportionality, a conceptual hinge. First, we find the methodical, orderly measurement of the relation between parts of things, which is the primary use of "proportion" throughout the *Istitutioni*. Second, we find: (1) the doctrine of *propriety*: the perfect correlation between one sense and one kind of object, such as sound to hearing (Zarlino calls this a "particular sensible" [*propio sensibile*], after Aristotle),[62] and (2) the demand for a proportionality between sense and "common sense-objects" (i.e., objects affecting several senses such as movement, shape, and size). Of the latter, Zarlino states that "the more proportional such objects are to their proper sense, the more satisfying and smooth they are," adding, in a comment borrowed from Aristotle's *De Anima* and later to be loudly echoed by Descartes, that "the eye is hurt by looking at the sun, because the sun is not proportioned to it."[63] It should come as no surprise that the word *convenienza*, which I have suggested makes a programmatic appearance early in Part 1, means also "propriety,"[64] situating the aesthetic relation to sound squarely within the web of correspondences.

As musical phenomena, intervals are given to sense by virtue of their privileged status in the order of things, an ontological ground that quite simply does not require the *musico* to focus on questions of sense perception, physico-acoustic structure, or empirical observation. For an orthodox Aristotelian, it would seem odd, at the very least, not to attend to the latter, but not to Zarlino, for whom the Philosopher constituted one authority among many. Musical intervals form part of a total mode of being, known through various cognitive registers but ultimately attendant to the embedding structure of knowledge of correspondences. And within that structure Zarlino more than demonstrates how flexible his methodology can be, as his brief foray into matters of perception indicates. Such an attitude plays a greater strategic role in the *Istitutioni* the more that Zarlino encroaches into the domain of musical practice.

1.3. Redefining the Aims of Theory: The *Sopplimenti*

In Part 3 the principal aim of the *musico* is stated in clear and precise Horatian terms: "to amuse and benefit" (*delectare et prodesse*).[65] This is achieved in practice, Zarlino explains, by adhering to the well-known series of prescriptive maxims given in Chapter 26: the musician must have a subject (*Soggetto*); compositions must contain mainly consonances and incidentally dissonances; voices must proceed through the intervals dictated by the sonorous numbers; there must be variety in the movement of parts and harmony; composition must be ordered around a determinate mode; the music must complement the text.[66] Underlying the aesthetic demand for variety, a "pleasure principle" (as we may term the part of the Horatian maxim that he emphasizes at this stage) weighs heavily in his disquisition. Ancient composers disallowed successions of two perfect consonances, Zarlino observes, because they knew all too well (*molto ben sapevano*) that harmony requires things that are diverse, discordant, and contrary to each other rather than alike in every way.[67] His appeal here to the faceless voice of ancient authority does not appear, however, to ground sufficiently this widely accepted contrapuntal stricture, for in an effort to anchor more firmly compositional rule he then brings "Nature" herself to bear on the issue. The ancients, Zarlino notes, observed this particular rule confirming how true and good are the workings of wondrous nature, which does not produce identical individuals in a species but always somehow varied.[68] From this he concludes that "every composer ought to imitate the beautiful order of nature, and he will be considered excellent in proportion to the resemblance of his procedure to those of nature. . . . So we must not write consecutive unisons, octaves, or fifths, for the natural cause of consonance—the harmonic number—does not contain in its progression or natural order two consecutive similar proportions."[69] Conveniently (and I mean this literally in the sense of Zarlino's use of the word) interconnected in Chapter 29 are history, nature, and a rational account of mathematics. Together, these various strands of knowledge help subtend the imperative principle of imitation, as well as to promote through "emulation" the predetermined correspondence of art and nature. For in the end it is Zarlino's injunction to the modern-day composer to emulate nature—and with it all that nature stands alongside in the unbroken continuum of all things (history, *scientia*, etc.)—which fuels the engagement of the *Istitutioni* with *musica prattica*.

Zarlino's injunction to modern composers suggests an avenue for a critical understanding of the *Istitutioni*, namely, that the question of methodology in Zarlino is mutually implicated in his notion of a mid-cinquecento Venetian "modernity." As is amply known, in Zarlino's program that modernity is embodied in the musical aesthetic of Willaert, and by the civil, ethical, moral, and spiritual values that it represents. We may conceive of Willaert as playing a dual role in Zarlino's program. In the first place, as Martha Feldman has pointed out, Willaert constitutes the figure of the Ciceronian model, an identifiable and culturally revered foundational locus for the "harmonic institutes."[70] In the second place, within the unfolding of history (understood here in a basic sense as the passage of time), Willaert is a redemptive figure, who, Zarlino thought, would restore to music "the honor and dignity it formerly had" in the time of the ancients.[71] Indeed, Willaert's music might demonstrate modern music's universality. Reaching back to music's origins, to historical and mythological record, and to the nature of all things intelligible constitutes, to my mind, a most ambitious attempt by Zarlino to situate the "now" of Willaert's figure (and his own Venetian present) within the "ever," seamlessly infusing the present with the past and, one might well imagine, projecting its survival into the future as well. This desire for universality suggests that, along with the traditional interpretation of the *Istitutioni* as an encyclopedic synthesis of "a vast literature on music, philosophy, theology, mathematics and classical history and literature,"[72] the manner in which Zarlino accomplishes such "synthesis" might also be profitably understood as *bricolage*. Like Lévi-Strauss's *bricoleur*, Zarlino deftly cobbles together heterogeneous sources that hold prior meanings, rearranges them in novel combinations which give the unified notions of modern music's naturalness and universality a mythical character.[73] Indeed, this practice of discourse construction—which in Lévi-Strauss's formulation is characteristic of processes of mythical thought—would resonate with an actual mythology built around Venetian self-identity and Willaert's representation of it.[74]

Thus viewed, the aims of the "harmonic institutes" become ideological, investing, under criteria of objectivity and rationality, a particular musical practice with mythical values of immanence and universality. Ideology in this case is decidedly active, for Zarlino's *bricolage* both advances an operative strategy and injects a particular structural design into musical practice. By operative strategy I mean that the *Istitutioni* represents a field of action, calling into order the music making of Venice from the author's privileged position as pupil of Willaert and, at the time of the first publication of the *Istitutioni* in 1558, his potential successor at San Marco.[75] Musical action is meant also in a practical sense to benefit its listeners, in accordance with Horace's maxim. And to convey the benefit of virtue, music must itself be virtuous, as must be the beneficiary. This beneficiary is Zarlino's ideal listener, whom he identifies as a "well-disposed Subject" (*Soggetto ben disposto*), one capable of appropriately receiving a particular emotion.[76] The import of this active commitment is one we might call sociopolitical and relates to the nexus between knowledge and order, of which musical discourse and music making in Venice formed part.[77] To have any legitimacy, Zarlino's ideas about (Venetian) music had to convey the authority and *gravitas* associated with a unitary and convenient Nature and had to carry the imprimatur of reason. This is why music and the structure of its sounding matter needed to be suffused with the rationality of nature, which is what I call "injecting a particular structural design into musical practice" above. It is in the service of this structural design, then, that the Aristotelian model of form and matter constitutes a disciplinary sine qua non of the *Istitutioni*. For without that direct and unquestionable cognitive structure the inseparability of intelligibility (*forma, ragione*) and sense (i.e., sounding matter) could not have been articulated. It is not the case that "Zarlino took a step backwards by reinstating the dominance of *ratio* over *sensus*."[78] Apart from its uncritical deployment of a notion of cognitive progress, this remark fails to consider the rich dialectic between *forma* and *materia* within which Zarlino's thought shuttles back and forth, and thanks to which sound is made part of a larger ideological complex.

The ideological in Zarlino folds back onto an idea I have previously alluded to, namely, his efforts to preserve the sanctity of a unique and indivisible truth. For such efforts, I believe, make of the *Istitutioni* a costly enterprise, one whose construction and upkeep demands unrelenting epistemological anchoring, as my discussion of the many commitments of Zarlino's methodology indicates. How much tension these demands must have caused can be gleaned from the tumultuous developments that followed reception of the *Istitutioni*. For instance, work by Vincenzo Galilei (a disciple) questioned his teacher's understanding and representation of Greek theory, debunked the notion that the ratios determining musical consonance had to be confined to the senario, and demonstrated anomalies in the Ptolemaic tuning Zarlino advocated.[79] Also, Giovanni Battista Benedetti's acoustical experiments on sound production were carried out in physical terms and looked away from numerology as a source of rational explanations.[80] Taken together, these criticisms would indeed have exposed fault lines in the foundations of Zarlino's thought. His advocacy of a tuning system that corresponded to the perfect sonorous numbers of the senario, for example, was grounded in his unwavering faith in the Pythagorean ontology of sounding number. But also, because no element—be it sacred Scripture, mathematical demonstration, or the story of Pythagoras's discovery of the proportions—was deemed ancillary to the edifice of knowledge, any questions raised about his historical interpretation would have implicated the *Istitutioni*'s entire intellectual apparatus, to say nothing of the ethical and social agendas it embraced.

Aware of the potentially devastating consequences of his critics' gains (Galilei's in particular), Zarlino attempted to defuse their impact by allowing for a distinction between history and method in his *Sopplimenti musicali*, published in 1588, two years before his death.[81] Zarlino preambles this distinction by restating a long-held difference between art and science. "The truth," he says, echoing his position in the *Istitutioni*, "is that the forms of consonance and other intervals used in our time in vocal and natural composition (*cantilene*) are neither things of art nor invention of Man; rather, they are firstly produced out of Nature herself, and are positioned and registered among many things, specially in the parts of the first perfect number."[82] To pursue these natural correspondences between music and nature is science's task, while art has as its function to organize music from among the intervals found in nature, specifically in the species called "natural" or "syntonic diatonic." At first this division does little to defend Zarlino from his detractors, simply echoing the epistemological hierarchy observed throughout the *Istitutioni*. But then he draws a new distinction, between two kinds of art. When writing and thinking of practical matters, he reminds readers, his aim has always been to "teach the manner of composing that is upheld nowadays and to show the diversity of modes, not according to the customs of the ancients . . . but according to the use of the moderns."[83] The question of modernity could hardly be made in more certain terms than these: "It was never, nor is it now my intention to write about the use of practice in the manner of the ancients, whether the Greek or Latin . . . but only about the method of those who have found our manner (*questa nostra maniera*) of making many parts sing together with diverse modulations and airs, specially in the way and manner of Adrian Willaert . . . my teacher in practical matters."[84] And while for Zarlino modern polyphony achieves a triumph of sorts over ancient music, he now has to confront the real possibility of a divided history, or what would be the same for him, the devastating consequences of a divided truth.[85]

Zarlino's solution is deceptively simple: to reorganize the field of musical knowledge. This is achieved by defining anew cognitive criteria on the basis of "kind" of knowledge and "means" of acquisition. "Perfect knowledge of music is acquired from two parts, one of which we will call historic and the other methodic," he now proposes.[86] "Historic" knowledge counsels that musicians and composers follow appropriate authors on matters related to art and science and explain and declare what the ancients have written (on this, Zarlino cites Quintilian, *Institutio Oratoria*, Chapter 4). Further, Zarlino explains, historic knowledge has a dual cognitive endeavor: while "history" consists in the narration of all things memorable made in antiquity and the record of all the centuries, "exegesis" consists in the expository commentary on that record. Demanding "reason and proper method" (*ragione & buono methodo*), "methodic" knowledge subsumes all aspects of music, from composition to rational comprehension of its forms, art, and science. In essence, Zarlino's "methodic" knowledge pours into a single cognitive container the contents of the various epistemologies brought together in the *Istitutioni*.

Transparent though Zarlino's reorganization may appear to us, to his thinking its veil must have managed to protect sufficiently the notion of a unitary truth. Truth continues to reside in the indivisible ontology of sounding number. Truth also remains beholden to a holistic epistemology that bridges form and matter, nature and artifice. Erudition, formerly part of the continuum of knowledge, has been compartmentalized and has been transformed into evidence of truth, if and when appropriate. The present, Zarlino's division suggests, not only holds the past under watchful eye, it also lends it a voice through exegesis and commentary. And he does provide extended explanations of ancient knowledge, assigning individual chapters in the *Sopplimenti* to Archytas, Ptolemy, Aristotle, Theophrastus, Panaetius, Plutarch, and Porphyry. But in the end Zarlino reads the ancients in order to demonstrate the immanence of the present's values, and ultimately to affirm its superiority over the past. Further, Zarlino's conception of "method" in the *Sopplimenti* preserves the ontotheological commitments of the *Istitutioni*. Method corresponds to "knowledge" (*cognitione*), but in a sense different from and ultimately secondary to "wisdom" (*sapienza*). Together with prudence, Zarlino had written in the *Istitutioni*, wisdom was divinely furnished to man so that he could find knowledge in number.[87] Were Zarlino to yield to the pressure of his critics, he would have to admit that it is possible to know things outside of the framework of correspondences, which would indeed sever the relation of sound to number and extricate it from the continuum of things. But that, he would have said, would be neither prudent nor wise.

Zarlino's crisis is the symptom of a modernity caught in a paradoxical simultaneity of eternal immanence and change. Something had to give, for no matter how much the Pythagorean ethos and its transcendental verities may have governed the harmoniousness of music, Man, and the Divine, not to have attended to an increasing tension between immanence and change would have been unethical. And so it was that history became the first piece of the foundation of the "institutes" to be removed, the first among things to be cast away from the haven of correspondences, indeed objectified in its cognitive manipulation.[88] Zarlino's compromise, such as it is, gives a hint of a turn toward manipulative knowledge that already and inexorably had been initiated.

It has become a common critical trope to interpret the crucial moment in which disputes between Zarlino and others took place as the passage into a new stage in the development of thought. Gesturing toward investigative experimentation, mathematical proof, and questioning of received authorities, the period is said to herald the dawn of modern science. Galilei, for one, demonstrates that, besides string length, diverse criteria such as string tension or the dimension of pipes can be shown to produce consonant intervals in proportions other than those given by the Pythagorean tradition. Number, he concludes, is mute, being only a means of description, a unit of measurement.[89] It is undeniable that observation became a central criterion for the demonstration of phenomena, a criterion that would facilitate, as many are wont to say, the scientific revolution. A unitary mathematics bearing an all-encompassing internal logic would be shown to establish differences in our perception of material reality. There would emerge a crucial interpenetration of phenomenon and observation. Phenomena would no longer be subject to mere recognition. They would no longer lie in wait for our semiological and hermeneutic intervention. Phenomena had to be explained by recourse to empirical observation. This kind of observation would in turn lead to systematic experimentation—Bacon would call this *experientia literata*.[90] Systematic experimentation would provide the cognitive ground for all phenomena. There would have to be a general reconfiguration of experience, and knowledge would be made manipulative with logical rule as its instrument. The "musical thought" of Zarlino's critics bears witness, as it were, to all this, as it does to the emergence of a renewed poetics of music by the humanists and a reconfiguration of the quadrivial structures by institutions of learning. In fact, their "musical thought" could be said to have both participated in a general reorientation in the nature of knowledge as well as produced an internal reorientation such as we witness in Zarlino's *Sopplimenti*.

But to interpret these events in this way would mean getting ahead of history. I have drawn a general sketch of the motivations, commitments, and expectations of Zarlino's thought according to a cognitive semiology that responds to demands placed on all knowledge, not just by theories of sound, let alone music theory. His biases, such as they are, resonate with the epistemological commitments of a time before signs are fully extricated from their correspondences with all things. Reactionary as his thought may appear in its irrelevance to the history of problems solved by his critics, it is fully consonant with those overarching correspondences. And these cannot be rendered obsolete before knowledge in its entirety is overhauled. Galilei may have provided the basis for a reconceptualization of the ontology of sound, but there is no indication that he might have advanced a new theory of signs. In his work we witness the beginnings of a move away from the idea that number is a sign inherent in sound. Knowledge of sound *qua* thing may be thus said to reside in a cognitive area outside of itself (sound). But this knowledge is not conceived as being internal to human cognition. For one, his analysis of proportions does not arrogate the traditional authority of number. Neither does he advance mathematics as a set of axiomatic relations capable of forming a logical context that would now define the objects of our experience. It could not have done so. We must keep in mind that there are no curtain calls to cue that passage from one episode in the history of thought to the next. Thus, the numerology that Claude Palisca believes was dealt a fatal blow by the champions of experimentation (Benedetti,

Galilei, and Giovanni Fracastoro) is no more decisive a "historical" event than Cardano's early advocacy of human perception and questioning of ancient authority, which by the same logic would have instigated the revision of Scholastic knowledge.[91] An interpretation such as Palisca's, which favors future "developments," needs to be counterbalanced by consideration of writers who appear to think in past terms, so to speak. For example, Athanasius Kircher, writing in the supposed postnumerological era free of all mysticism, could still find enough intellectual ammunition in the seventeenth century to articulate a cogent universalist conception of music, refusing to separate the science of sound production and perception (the acoustics of the "new era") from music's place in the cosmos. As Frances Yates reminds us, there were "reactionary Hermetists" in the seventeenth century, Kircher being one of the most notable.[92] The notion of reactionary thinkers invites the formulation of another historical character, the "proactionary" thinker. There would belong the early experimenters, the debunkers of numerology, the scientists who would forever arrest the musical motion of the spheres. But I do not believe that we can identify Zarlino wholesale with any of these categories, unless we are willing to reduce the complexity of his thought and time. As I argue in the next chapter, the reconfiguration of musical thought after Zarlino takes place once the perceiver is extricated from all observation and becomes in fact the observer of his own observation.

2 The Representation of Order: Perception and the Early Modern Subject in Descartes's *Compendium musicae*

> When we consider things in the order that corresponds to our knowledge of them, our view of them must be different from what it would be if we were speaking of them in accordance with how they exist in reality. ([A]liter spectandas esse res singulas in ordine ad cognitionem nostram, quàm si de ijsdem loquamur prout revera existunt.)
>
> René Descartes, *Rules for the Direction of Mind* (Rule 12)

> [N]othing can be more easily and more evidently perceived by me than my mind. ([N]ihil facilus aut evidentius mea mente posse a me percipi.)
>
> René Descartes, *Meditations on First Philosophy,* Second Meditation

In the epistemology of correspondences underlying Zarlino's thought, Pythagorean, Neoplatonic, and Aristotelian strands commingle to produce a plethoric—and seemingly undisciplined—theory of music. The edifice of the *Istitutioni,* we have seen, was built atop an expansive and ultimately costly epistemological foundation. This foundation carried the enormous weight of "institutes" that included, on the one hand, the microcosm formed by mid-sixteenth-century contrapuntal practice, Venetian musico-social order, and Zarlino's (and Willaert's) place in it, and on the other, the macrocosm subtending the order of all things. As mirrors of one another, these worlds were saturated with multiple intersecting signs, signs that only the hermeneuticist could interpret and the semiologician could locate and organize. In my analysis, Zarlino was seen as an expert semiologician and hermeneuticist who deftly interpreted and accounted for music's privileged role as manifestation of order—however chaotic—and, indeed, explained it as the regulating medium that expressed that order. In this sense his musical thought brilliantly folds a *musica scientia* onto a congeries of semiological and hermeneutic practices.

The epistemology of correspondences was already under examination during Zarlino's lifetime—to wit, the distinction between "history" and "method" in his *Sopplimenti* (1588)—and would continue unabated through the first half of the seventeenth century. For example, we witness in Bacon's arguments for a new science a desire to overhaul the conception of knowledge, and we see the emergence of notions of progress designed to increase our ability to predict and control (science is understood here as systematic knowledge). Bacon argues on behalf of objectivity as a primary tenet of knowledge and introduces the question of method to achieve this goal. His failure to recognize mathematics as the language of the new science already being practiced by Galileo Galilei and others is characteristic of the intense self-questioning that takes place during the latter part of the sixteenth century, a period when the old and the new cohabit in systems of knowledge. Together, the advent of a new science and the challenges to past authorities and their methods of inquiry make possible a conception of representation that moves away from a correspondence-based epistemology. As part of this reconceptualization, the human mind—and with it the individual subject as the locus of all representations—emerges with unprecedented capacities for discernment. These capacities are self-regulated. They ground a kind of knowledge founded in an individual subject defined precisely by full awareness of these capacities. At the same time this knowledge is objective and universal. Combined, these features—intellectual self-regulation, objective knowledge, and transcendental subjectivity—can be said to instigate a number of attitudes associated with modernity: the idea of a substantive reason and an instrumental rationality.

The present chapter takes as its point of departure this appraisal of the history of modern thought. My aim is to bring into focus how a new conceptualization of the cognitive perception of sound and the representation of such perception marked fundamental steps in the articulation of the features outlined above. This articulation takes place early in the unfolding of the epistemologically defined modernity—hence the expression "early modern"—and is revealed in René Descartes's *Compendium musicae*.[1]

The *Compendium* is a private, seemingly unassuming work in which the young thinker gives his account of what would have been considered basic knowledge of music by an "honnête homme" at the beginning of the seventeenth century. In its modest dimensions (a total of fifty-eight pages in its first edition), the *Compendium musicae* (1618) is dwarfed by monumental works from the sixteenth and seventeenth centuries, most notably Zarlino's *Istitutioni*, Marin Mersenne's *Traité de l'harmonie universelle* (1627), Johannes Kepler's *Harmonices mundi libri* (1619), and Athanasius Kircher's magnum opus *Musurgia universalis* (1650).[2] Published posthumously in 1650, the *Compendium* constitutes at best a footnote in the historiography of music theory, noted more often for being the first extant complete work of its incomparable author than for its original contributions to the discipline.[3] The relative merits and stature of the treatise are further compromised by that fact that Descartes avoided systematic inquiry into sound and music in later works, and perhaps even by his candid admission of not being able to recognize intervals. With the advantage of hindsight, the Descartes of the *Meditations* could be said to have thought better than to try to incorporate the arts, in general, and sense perception, in particular, into his influential metaphysics.[4] Surprisingly, there is no specific mention of affections brought about by music in the valedictory *Les passions de l'âme* (1649).

Modern discussion of the *Compendium* has considered the work from either a philosophical and scientific perspective or a musicological one; only rarely are these perspectives combined. First, some philosophically inclined commentators consider scientific and methodological aspects of the treatise as either a mathematization or mechanization of sense perception; other commentators discuss the treatise's positions on philosophical issues vis-à-vis the development of Descartes's other intellectual interests. Some pursue the matter topically, around one single issue. Second, musicological perspectives too have emphasized methodological aspects of the treatise, focusing on Descartes's avowed interest in the mathematical and physical properties of music, his desire to confirm Zarlino's interval classification by invoking mathematics (a position usually characterized as part of his mathematization of the principle of proportionality), or his commitment to the canonist tradition of generating intervals from the monochord.[5] Other musicologists pursue the treatise's contribution to compositional matters.[6] A third group (comprised of philosophically minded musicologists) has noted the aesthetic and psycho-perceptual innovations inherent in Descartes's method. A fourth group emphasizes Descartes's separation of object and perceiver in acts of perception.[7]

My analysis assumes the perspective of cognitive perception: how the sense of hearing connects to and is comprehended by the intellect.[8] From a broader historical perspective, I view Descartes as reconfiguring the relationship between subject and object in acts of aural perception. I view this reconfiguration as a reflection of an epistemological attitude that is determined by the introduction of a new, subject-centered aesthetics sanctioned, most significantly, by a new conception of representation.[9] This new conception of representation will be seen to have an impact well beyond music theory. At stake is the place of a particular kind of knowledge in the representation both of the subject and of the cognitive perception and understanding of sound. Also at stake is the question of whether in the pursuit of questions about sound perception Descartes may have contributed to the philosophical process by which "man" would be extricated from the web of correspondences of Renaissance epistemology. On the one hand, much of Descartes's argument reflects earlier concerns about the necessary proportionality between the hearer and the material elements of music. On the other, his argument is based on a different epistemological foundation, one built on the analysis of both order and measurement of sound. Out of this, sound emerges as a distinct object of cognition. The hearer emerges as a self-grounded locus of that cognition.

My discussion centers around three passages from the *Compendium:* the introduction, the eight Preliminary notes, and the discussion of the perception of time in music.[10] I proceed in three sections. First, I address the aesthetic and methodological premises of the treatise, as manifested in Descartes's account of cognitive perception in the introduction and in the Preliminary notes. Second, I investigate the issue of representation, analyzing two examples in which Descartes appeals to the imagination. These examples—Descartes's appeals to the imagination in the perception of time in music, and his use of images to represent proportions—are seen as emblematic of a changing epistemological attitude formulated most explicitly in the *Rules for the Direction of Mind*.[11] Third, I theorize this attitude by considering representation as a transparent mark of the subject's thought itself. The analysis of representation is indebted to Foucault's theory of the classical sign, on the basis of which I articulate the formation of the early modern subject as a cognitive construction.[12]

2.1. The Emergence of a Subject-Object Relation in Perception: Descartes's Account of Cognitive Perception

The *Compendium* bears traces of the scientific enterprise of Isaac Beeckman, the Dutch mathematician for whom Descartes wrote the treatise and to whom it is dedicated. Beeckman approached sound from the field of acoustics. His agenda may be summed up in three essential points: (1) sound is considered in its physical form, not as a speculative matter; (2) music theory provides a mathematical explanation of the physical phenomenon of sound; (3) music is not considered as an artistic practice, but rather as a practical application of physico-mathematical principles.[13] During the 1610s Beeckman developed a corpuscular theory of sound, defining its transmission as a series of pulsations of "globules"; at around the same time he proved the inversional proportionality between string length and frequency. Beeckman's ideas about sound transmission are important insofar as they make more urgent the formulation of questions about sensory perception with a particular emphasis on the notion of a "hearer." In a way, by bringing aesthesis to bear in the knowledge of sound as heard, Beeckman's innovation harks back, however obliquely, to the Aristoxenian tradition that upholds the centrality of sense perception, a tradition long overshadowed by the Pythagorean proclivities of Renaissance Neoplatonists.[14]

Beeckman's influence offers a possible but not fully sufficient explanation for Descartes's particular approach to music. A complementary explanation has to do with the place that music held within a modified classification of the mathematical subjects in the *quadrivium*. Stephen Gaukroger notes how at the Jesuit college of La Flèche where Descartes studied (1607–14) a further subdivision placed music among the sensible objects that could be studied mathematically (others included astrology, perspective, geodesy, calculation, and mechanics), as opposed to those which could be known only in abstraction, separately from their matter (geometry and arithmetic).[15] Indeed, Descartes is particularly concerned with the issue of sensation. And it is in pursuing this interest that he would present a critical account of how sound as a physical, empirical phenomenon intersects with perception and cognition.

Essential to the critical account of perception and sensation in the *Compendium* is the role given to signs, in general, in the process of accounting for the human experience of the world. By way of introduction to Descartes's ideas on the matter, I will briefly consider two examples from his other writings. The following comment—from the first chapter of *Le monde,* a posthumously published treatise on light written between 1629 and 1633—is emblematic of Descartes's interest in the representation of sensation:

> Words . . . bear no resemblance to the things they signify, and yet they make us think of those things. . . . [I]f words, which signify nothing except by human convention, suffice to make us think of things to which they bear no resemblance, then why could nature not also have established some sign which could make us have the sensation of light, even if the sign contained nothing in itself which is similar to this sensation?[16]

The question is rhetorical. Descartes answers it in the negative: there is no correspondence within the sign of the object of perception to the perceiver. A preliminary outcome is that in matters of sensation there exists no semiotic continuity between "us" and the objects of sensation.[17]

In bringing sensation together with a general theory of signs, Descartes's remark constitutes a significant statement about the nature of cognitive perception. In fact, by discussing sensation as a kind of sign, Descartes succinctly outlines a central premise of his analysis of cognitive perception and of cognition in general. He proposes that the structure of sensation be divided into a thing that is sensed, a mechanism by which we sense it, and the sign by which that sensation is represented.

Two interrelated principles underlie Descartes's analysis of perception: singularity and difference. That is, object and perceiver each occupy singular positions in the order of perception and are differentiated precisely by what those singular positions can or cannot contribute to this arrangement. This is how Descartes is able to claim that whatever the mechanism by which sensations are transmitted from their origin or cause, the perceiver is in the position to represent this sensation independently from either the mechanism or the cause itself. And so, like signs, sensation observes no other protocols than those dictated by the subject.

No doubt a profound, difficult, and contentious topic, the issue of cognitive perception is strategically placed at the outset of *Le monde,* where it plays a foundational role. For it is only after Descartes has outlined cognitive perception's nature (i.e., that the world may be different from our perceptual image of it) and limitations (i.e., that our perceptual images may not constitute a reliable guide to understand how the world is and how it functions) that he can present his ambitious ideas about the world.[18] A similar strategy will be found in the *Compendium,* strongly suggesting the overall centrality of a cognitive aesthetics in Descartes's early work.

I introduce the opening remark in *Le monde* not only because it succinctly outlines Descartes's view of perception in his early thought but also because of his direct comments about the function of linguistic signs as particular media for representation. Keenly aware of the conventionality of signs, he echoes here a similar notion to that underlying the quotation from the *Rules* that opened this chapter. In the case of the *Rules* he offers an illustration from visual perception. The perception of color, he argues, can be represented in the imagination by imaginary patterns made out of lines. Furthermore, such representations are necessary for something to be grasped clearly and distinctly, for in this way they account for differences among various objects of perception.[19] Difference is understood here as an index of discrimination among things, an index that moves to the central epistemological place previously occupied by resemblance. And from here it is but a short step to the establishment of a second index of discrimination, namely measurement, that will systematically establish the differences between things. Together, difference and measurement emerge as the two central principles behind the sign (i.e., the linear imaginary patterns) with which Descartes represents his conception of cognitive perception.

These questions about perception and its representation in the *Rules* and *Le monde* strongly echo a concern made explicit by Descartes at the very opening of the *Compendium*, where he tersely states, "of this [music] the object is sound" (*huius objectum est sonus*). Uncompromisingly programmatic, the statement not only proclaims the centrality of the external, physical, and empirical manifestation of sound to his inquiry about music, but also, albeit indirectly, makes of perception the fundamental issue about knowledge of music.[20] Further, we might say that through Descartes's efforts to determine the relationship between the properties of sound (*affectiones*) and the various effects (*affectus*) that these properties may produce,[21] the *Compendium* is at heart a treatise on aesthetics (understood mainly as a theory of sense perception but one that is dependent on a theory of beauty). The *Compendium*, however, has a broader agenda: (1) the mathematical and physical explanation of sound; (2) the nature of sensory perception and the explanation of the pleasure afforded to the sense of hearing; (3) an account of the rules of counterpoint and a theory of modes. Notably, no attempt is made to build a theory of musical composition.[22] Neither is an attempt made to situate thought about music and/or sound in the context of a speculative cosmology in the manner of seventeenth-century Neoplatonists like Mersenne or Kircher, or to establish musical "institutes," akin to Zarlino's *Istitutioni*, on the innovative foundations of late-sixteenth- and early-seventeenth-century science.[23]

The foundational role of an aesthetic theory in Descartes's thought is evident from the first sentence following the proclamation of sound as music's object: "Its [music's] end is to delight and arouse various affections in us." This is a traditional view of the relationship between art and the affections, here echoing Horace's *delectare et prodesse*.[24] According to Descartes, music has two properties of sound through which to perform this function: the differences relating to time and to the intensity (*intensio*) of pitch from high to low. Left out is the issue of sound quality (timbre), which Descartes believes to be the proper domain of the physicist. Descartes then proceeds to elaborate on the relationship between sound and perception, defined as a relationship between sound-as-object and perceiver-as-subject. What, Descartes seems to be asking, must

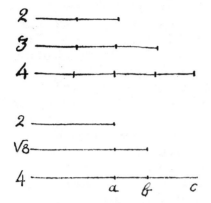

Example 2.1a
Proportion easily distinguished
visually. René Descartes,
Compendium musicae (1618
[1987]: 57).

Example 2.1b
Proportion difficultly distinguished. René Descartes,
Compendium musicae (1618
[1987]: 57).

sound be like for it to be amenable to perception and for it to produce a pleasurable effect on the senses? Answers appear in the form of eight Preliminaries
(*Praenotanda*) that introduce the *Compendium,* quoted here in toto:

1. All senses are capable of [experiencing] some degree of pleasure.

2. For this pleasure a proportion of some kind between the object and the sense
itself is required. It follows from this, for example, that the racket of guns or thunder is not apt for music, because it would evidently hurt the ears, like the excessive
glare of the sun, [that when] directly opposite, hurts the eyes.

3. The object must be such that it falls on the sense with neither excessive
difficulty nor great confusion. It follows from this, for example, that a very complex figure, even if it is regular, as is the *mater* on the astrolabe, does not please the
sight as much as another that is made up of more equal lines, like the ordinary *rete*
of the same instrument.[25] The reason for this is that the sense is more plentifully
satisfied by the latter object than by the former, where it encounters various elements that it cannot perceive distinctly enough.

4. That object in which the difference of its parts is smaller is more easily perceived by the sense.

5. We say that the parts of a whole object differ less among themselves between
which parts the proportion is greater.

6. This proportion must be arithmetic, not geometric. The reason for this is that
in it there are not so many things to notice, as the differences are equal throughout
and therefore the sense does not strain so greatly to perceive distinctly all the elements that it contains. For example, the proportion of these lines [Example 2.1a] is
more easily distinguished by the eyes (*facilius oculis distinguitur*) than the proportion of those [Example 2.1b] because in the former it suffices to consider the unity
as the difference of each line. But in the latter, it is necessary to consider the parts
ab and bc, which, being incommensurable cannot, as I judge, be known (*cognosci*)
simultaneously by the sense in any manner, except in relation to the arithmetic
proportion so that it recognizes, for example, two parts in ab where there would
be three in bc. It is clear that here the sense is constantly deceived.

7. Among the objects of the sense, the most agreeable to the soul is neither that

which is most easily perceived by the sense nor that which is perceived with most difficulty. But this object is most pleasing to the soul which does not completely fill up the sense as easily as natural desire (*naturale desiderium*)—by means of which the senses are borne onto objects—does, and which also does not do so with as much difficulty [as natural desire does], so as to tire the sense out.

8. Finally, it is necessary to note that in all things, variety is most pleasing.[26]

At this point, in the first chapter proper, Descartes proceeds to examine the "first attribute of sound," namely, "number or time."

These Preliminaries constitute neither mere guidelines to the reader for the proper understanding of the *Compendium* nor gratuitous generalizations that we may assume would have been familiar to Beeckman. On the contrary, intended as a private gift to Beeckman, the writing may not have required the aesthetic maxims in the Preliminaries were it not for the fact that Descartes felt the need to clarify the foundations of his inquiry for him. But more than anything else, the Preliminaries indicate a profound preoccupation with method. Indeed, Descartes moves carefully and systematically, beginning with the "demands of sense pleasure and ending with the structure of the object of pleasure."[27] For purposes of analysis, I subdivide the Preliminaries into three groups: 1, 2–6, and 7–8.

Tellingly, the first Preliminary stands alone. It axiomatically asserts an aesthetic maxim as the foundation of a theory of sense perception and ultimately of a theory of music. Here, as André Pirro has noted, Descartes appeals to the well-established ideas of Plato and Aristotle (later circulated by Quintillian and Augustine) to the effect that beauty and pleasure are inconceivable without order or without the regular disposition of forms.[28] Descartes's appeal to authority, however, conceals a calculated rhetorical ploy, for the privileged placement of this maxim cannot be fortuitous: it effectively raises for the reader the question of what the general conditions for experiencing pleasure may be.

Indeed, starting with the second Preliminary note, Descartes begins to specify the regulatory processes by which pleasure is experienced. First and foremost, pleasure results from a specific object-subject relation regulated, in the case of perception, by the principle of proportionality. The doctrine that considers sensation in terms of proportion is found in Aristotle: "Now if the voice is a kind of consonance, and voice and hearing are in a way one (and the same thing is in a way not one), and if consonance is a proportion (*logos*), then hearing must also be a kind of proportion. And it is for this reason too that either excess, whether high or low pitch, destroys hearing; and in the same way . . . in colours the too bright or too dark destroys sight . . . since the sense is a kind of proportion."[29] Second, Descartes presents the matter as a quantitative one, not being concerned with the suitable qualities of sound per se. Third, he establishes a position from which to elaborate on the constraints that proportionality places on the object of perception. Descartes circumscribes the range of suitable objects. In a restricted sense the burden of proportionality falls on objects. By the same token, insofar as the perceiver determines what a suitable object is, Descartes appears to be granting strategic priority to the perceiver.[30] The notion that matters of perception are evaluated from the perspective of the hearer is fundamental to Descartes's method. "It is significant," writes Heinrich Besseler, "that for the first time in the history of writings on music Descartes proceeds not from the music itself but rather from the hearer."[31] Fourth, from an epistemological perspective, Descartes's analogy between the visual (e.g., looking at the sun) and the aural (e.g., hearing thunder) is problematic, for it implies that the aural cannot be addressed outside the framework of another, presumably more reliable, sense. And while it might initially appear that there exists a community of senses (i.e., sight and hearing) attending to similar or shared demands for proportionality, it will soon become apparent that the perceptual and cognitive requirements for each sense are significantly different.

In the Preliminary notes that follow (3–6), Descartes elaborates in increasing detail the processes by which proportionality operates in perception. The third Preliminary introduces another general, albeit qualitative, principle that the object of perception must observe: simplicity. From the point of view of the subject, the senses are in no way wanting; it is rather the simple or complex structure of a particular object that may render it more or less suitable for satisfactory perception. Satisfactory perception takes place when the subject is able to discriminate the object not merely as a whole but as a complex of its parts. Simplicity masks an appeal to another, more fundamental, matter: perceptual immediacy—that is, perception—is most effective when its object can be grasped at once, and so for the subject the issue is one of sensory economics as well. Descartes seems to be interested less in the reconstruction of the object of perception and more in its perceptually unmediated cognition—where "mediation" would refer to the degree of straining needed to discriminate the parts of an object. (We will see that this distinction is crucial for his concept of intuition in the *Rules* and, more significantly, for the development of a model and a method of knowledge, and its attendant theory of representation.) To illustrate, Descartes resorts once again to a visual analogy. Despite being suitably designed as an instrument, the astrolabe is only indirectly perceptible, and so by contrast the simpler structure of the angle protractor (*rete*) constitutes a model of direct perception.

Like the third Preliminary, the fourth also addresses what I am calling an economy of perception, now expressed in positive terms: for an object to be more easily perceivable, its structure must be such that its parts differ from one another by the least possible quantity. This point is crucial, because it outlines a distinction between what is required for the object's internal organization and what is at the disposal of the sense for an effective perception of that object. Notably, here a quantifiable element is reintroduced which, in contrast to Descartes's second note, is more narrowly defined as the relationship between sense and object in terms of a comparative calculation of the parts of an object by a subject. This simultaneous bringing together and clear delineation of object and subject constitutes a point of conceptual regrouping within the narrative unfolding of the Preliminary notes. As Descartes further circumscribes the quantitative criteria for perception, he sets himself to define fully the structure of the object and, reciprocally, of sense perception in measurable terms.

In the fifth note Descartes renders the principle of simplicity as one of greater or lesser proportion among parts of an object.[32] (Proportion reappears here for the first time since the second Preliminary.) All emphasis is now on the object, with Descartes transferring the links between sense and object entirely to the internal organization of the object. We witness here a further move toward a quantification of sensation, or more precisely, the gradual emergence of analysis of the object of sensation in quantitative terms. This is not to say, as Bertrand Augst does, that "[Descartes] was applying a purely quantitative system of measuring . . . to a domain theretofore qualitative."[33] Neither do we have to concur fully with Timothy Reiss's idea that

> [I]f music did affect its hearers in some explainable way, and if, at the same time, the relations called notes, tuning, pitch, rhythm and so on could be expressed in mathematical terms, should this not mean that the affecting itself was not just rational but quantifiable? The emotional effect of the work of art, that is to say, should be able to be understood in some kind of mathematical terms: both because music itself followed mathematical rule and because human affections/ passions belonged in a material world itself increasingly thought to be subject to such rule.[34]

To my mind the difference of opinion here hinges upon defining what "quantification" might mean. For the purposes of my discussion of the Preliminaries, quantification designates the perceptual activity of measuring. This is a methodological point that I will continue to develop throughout this chapter; for now, suffice it to say that perhaps the most important conceptual contribution of the Preliminaries resides in Descartes's translation of the generalities of the principle of simplicity and the demands of perceptual pleasure into specific terms of measurement.

The sixth note specifies in detail the proportion defining the internal structure of the ideal object of perception. Descartes identifies the arithmetic proportion (i.e., a series that increases by a constant unit, as in 2, 5, 8, 11) as a paradigm for pleasurable perception, which he says is not possible in a geometric proportion. Frédéric de Buzon notes that in choosing the arithmetic proportion, Descartes implicitly leaves out the harmonic proportion, which would also account for the consonances.[35] This, I believe, represents a further effort to place the principle of simplicity at the heart of perception, and to restate the notion of immediacy (i.e., to cognize without undue processing beyond perceptual-analytic measurement that which appears before the senses). In these ways Descartes sums up with a simple mathematical explanation in the sixth Preliminary all the precepts stated in the preceding notes. (His appeal to a visual analogy will be discussed in the following section of this chapter.)

Finally, the last two Preliminary notes return to general principles, this time directed to the aesthetic demands of the soul. In the seventh note he invokes the principle of averages, according to which the sense's need for simplicity must be in balance with the more complex demands of the soul. Notably, his invocation of "natural desire" (*naturale desiderium*) may be read either as ascribing a natural origin to all that he has said about the measurement and ordering of sense pleasure, or as a contradiction or exception by which the soul cannot be explained in mathematical terms. The brief eighth note appeals to the well-established aesthetic desideratum of variety, with which Descartes couples the principle of averages. And with that note, Descartes ends with a bow to musical practice, in which mathematical perfection and all the abstractions that subtend it often yield to the demands of traditionally established aesthetic generalities.

From this initial examination of the Preliminaries we may temporarily conclude that neither a number-based account of the ontology of sound nor a metaphysical approach to cognition is any longer satisfactory for Descartes. For even though he operates within a music-theoretical model that deals with sound as number (as did Zarlino), Descartes maintains that the numerical structure of sound must first be validated by a perceiver, that is, by a subject in relation to whom the musical object must now stand. In itself this constitutes a revolutionary reorientation of the psychology of sense perception inaugurated by Aristotle in *De Anima*.[36] To grasp the implications of this reorientation, we must first consider Aristotle's ideas on the matter more closely.

Generally Aristotle regards sense perception as resulting from the affection of a sense organ or a sense faculty by an object of some kind. We have seen already that he considered perception to have a structure in which sense (with which Aristotle designates both the sense organ and its associated faculty) would be proportional to whatever object affected it. Hearing, for instance, would be said to be proportional to a sound heard. In this structure, however, sense held a secondary place. As he famously declared, "each sense . . . *is of* the sensible thing that is subject to it."[37] Two points here beg elucidation: first, the appeal to a qualitative criterion (i.e., "the sensible thing") that is common to both sense and sensible thing (which I will designate "object of perception"). Second, given this common link, what can be said to be the nature of the relationship in sense perception between perceiver and object (i.e., what does "is of" mean in the link between sense and sensible thing)?

First, Aristotle's theory of sense perception is not concerned with whether or not the sense may possess an accurate representation of the object of perception. Rather, it is concerned with the possibility of sense perception itself and with the causal mechanisms that underlie it. This he explains as the sense becoming in some way one with that object. In Aristotle's account the sense has the capacity to receive the substantial form (which he calls sensible species, e.g., redness, tree-hood, warmth) of whatever object it perceives without receiving its matter (i.e., without becoming "red," a "tree," or "fire").[38] This condition of perception we may term "aesthetic coincidence." Given that an object of perception and sense share a relation to matter and form, this coincidence might then be associated with a hylomorphic understanding of sense perception. Hylomorphism refers specifically to the doctrine holding that corporeal beings are comprised of matter and form. In the present discussion, however, I use the term to describe a correspondence between sense and sense object at the level of substantial matter. Significantly, this correspondence minimizes an absolute conceptual separation between sense and object of perception. However, the correspondence between sense and object of perception is made problematic by the transformative process of potentiality-to-actuality at play in Aristotelian sense perception. In fact, before perceiving, the sense, Aristotle believes, is hardly anything at all: that is, while a sensible species originates from the sense object, where it resides as actuality, the sense has the potential to receive that species from that object. If this process from potentiality to actuality is what Aristotle expresses when he says that "sense . . . *is of* the sensible thing that is subject to it," then the relationship between sense and object of perception could also read "sense *becomes* the sensible thing that is subject to it."

Now, to this observation we must add that, in spite of being nothing before perceiving an object, the sense is not merely a passive receptacle for qualities, a dormant capacity. This is evident, for example, in Aristotle's use of a single term—*pathos*—to mean both the experience of sense perception and the quality of the object experienced. The active character of the sense is further affirmed in this statement from *De Anima:* "just as both acting and being affected are in that which is affected and not in that which acts, so both the activity of the object of perception and that of that which can perceive are in that which can perceive."[39] It is clear that, because of the theoretical richness of Aristotle's theory of sense perception, sense and object of perception seem to exist in a conceptual interaction. As a result of this interaction, sense perception qualities, affections, and even the process from potentiality to actuality are at some level shared by the sense and the object of perception. To be sure, the object of perception holds a priority which in the end turns out to be little more than chronological, for once sense and object of perception meet, the process becomes reciprocal.

Perhaps the best way to disentangle the Aristotelian account of perception might be to rephrase the second query above. Thus, instead of asking what the nature of the relation between sense and object of perception might be, we ought to ask what the nature of the relation of the perceiver to its own sense perception might be. Difficult though it may be for us post-Cartesians to grasp, the notion that the contents of sense perception might be open to inspection either by some special overseeing sense or by the intellect is not tenable for Aristotle, for the simple reason that he believes that the sense perceives itself. For instance, he explains that the sense of sight fulfills a dual role, seeing the color that is the object of sight and seeing the perception of sight.[40] In other words, the sense both receives the object of perception (without receiving its form) and sees itself receiving that object. This conception carries a fundamental consequence for the history of perception: there is no concept of introspection in Aristotle's psychology of perception; or to put it bluntly, no mental inspection of the contents of sense perception at that stage.[41] After all, Aristotle's account in *De Anima* is not epistemological; it concerns neither whether perception brings about knowledge nor whether its contents can serve as the basis for knowledge. In the end his is an account of "how it is that we perceive that we are perceiving," as Hugh Lawson-Tancred puts it.[42] This means that there are no events of an inner mental life divorced from things in the external world, and so there is no possibility that sensations or perceptions as such may register as mental images of any kind *during* the act of perception. Thus, in response to the second query—in its original form: "what can be said to be the nature of the relationship in sense perception between perceiver and object (i.e., what does "is of" mean in the link between sense and sensible thing?")—we may conclude that the implicit structural priority of the object of perception over the sense is conveyed by the "limitations" of the latter.

The absence of anything resembling mental images in Aristotle suggests also that judgments of perceptions remain within the jurisdiction of the senses, not of the "mind." Such judgments are not really subject to criteria of rightness or wrongness. This, then, stands in stark contrast to the position Descartes articulates in the Preliminaries, in which all efforts are directed toward establishing criteria to evaluate sensorial and perceptual experience according to fixed, objective standards dictated by proportionality. To facilitate this, several structural reconfigurations take place. First, Descartes reorders the Aristotelian structure by beginning unambiguously from sense (e.g., with his axiomatic aesthetic principle in the first Preliminary) and from there gradually specifying the properties and specific structure of the object of perception. Second, he sets new criteria by which perception is organized and, significantly, judged from the perspective of sense. Third, these criteria are founded logically on the precise measurement and organization of proportions in the object of perception in relation to the sense.

Once these basic axioms are firmly established we witness the emergence of a logical separation of sense from the object of perception ("logical," from *logos*, means here [ordered] "account"). It is thus that the Descartes of the *Compendium* installs the perceiving subject and its logical analytic apparatus of measuring and ordering as the locus of perception. The consequences of this are various, and all are fundamental to the understanding of early modern aesthetics and epistemology. This marks, I would submit, a key moment in the history of musical thought. First, sensation becomes active by means of the participation of cognitive operations of the subject. Sensation, in other words, becomes a matter of cognition, becomes, more properly, what we call perception. Second, the perceiver is not only defined according to specific cognitive capacities, but is also extricated from the continuum where it had stood alongside objects of perception, which amounts to the distinction between perceiving subject and perceived object.[43] Third, the perceiving subject begins to be conceived in terms of its capacity for analyzing its perception. Fourth, in so conceiving the perceiver, Descartes begins also to define the subject epistemologically, in terms of its capacity for grounding knowledge. It is not the case, however, that Descartes approaches aesthetics epistemologically, by asking whether perception can serve as the grounds of knowledge; it is, rather, that he brings to bear on perception the criteria used to determine what the grounds for knowledge are.

It remains to be seen, then, how, in submitting perception to the tribunal of intellectual evaluation, Descartes might handle the question of presenting the evidence of sensation to the mind. For we sense an imminent structural tension in the idea of making objective something (sensation), which Descartes claims in the Preliminaries should be immediate. For Descartes, the challenge emerges through the means by which he might represent the activity of perception; how, that is, to bring together immediacy, the mental, and aesthetics, and more importantly, how it is that the mind can be staged so as to perceive itself.

2.2. Sound Scenarios: Representation and the Imagination

The turn we witness in the *Compendium* from an Aristotelian theory of sense perception to Descartes's own may be characterized as one from "impression" to "representation." In Aristotle the substantial form of the object of perception is impressed in the sense. By contrast, in Descartes's subject-centered account, perception is mediated by a unique logic ensconced in the perceiver. Fueled by the activities of measuring and ordering, this logic has no function other than to present the object of perception to the sense. Since the object of perception is presented to the intellect but is in no way impressed upon the perceiver, this process constitutes a *representation*. And, as we will find, while for Descartes the matter is one of accuracy and cognitive clarity, his account ultimately depends on a definite—and in the history of thought, definitive— separation of the perceiver from the object of perception. In this manner representation accounts for the object of perception insofar as it brings that object fully within the fold of the subject's *cogito*. This is why I will now make a distinction between the *hearer*—which is acknowledged by several writers and increasingly also by scientists prior to Descartes, *pace* Besseler—and the *subject*. The latter identifies a sentient being who submits its perceptions to cognitive evaluation. This form of evaluation is underwritten by a particular notion of mathematical analysis regulated entirely by the subject.

Indeed, we have preliminarily seen how, in discussing the nature of signs in *Le monde* and the *Rules,* Descartes throughout the 1620s had claimed for the subject the capacity to know and designate things by virtue of its capacities for analytic discrimination, including the discrimination of its own sensorial experience. But we have also seen how, in the Preliminaries, he invoked the need for immediacy as a fundamental criterion for the interaction between the perceiving subject and the object of perception. (Incidentally, for this reason, it would be erroneous to think of Cartesian representation as a "presenting-over" or secondary presentation.) Needed still was an account of the agency and cognitive mechanics by which the subject could satisfy its own demands for immediacy. Put more directly, how could it be ascertained that something which is mental might represent that which is not? Cognitive discrimination and experiential immediacy would need to be shown to be two sides of the same coin.

In the chapter entitled "Of observing number or time in sounds" (*De numero vel tempore in sonis observando*), the first chapter following the Preliminaries, Descartes introduces an analytical approach that suggests such a theory of representation.[44] There he asks how it is that we are able to comprehend a temporal series as a whole, and by what means we do so. In keeping with the aesthetics of suitable proportionality (e.g., as stated in the fourth Preliminary note), his account is predicated on absolute regularity:[45]

> Furthermore, this division [into duple and triple meters] is indicated by the beat (*percussione, vel battuta*), as it is called, to aid our imagination (*imaginationem*), so that we can more easily perceive (*percipere*) all the parts of a song (*cantilenae*) and enjoy the proportion which must prevail therein. Moreover, such a proportion is employed most frequently among the components of a song so that it aids our understanding (*apprehensionem*) in such a way that while hearing the end of one time unit, we still remember what occurred at the beginning and during the remainder of the song. This happens when the entire song consists of 8 or 16 or 32 or 64 units, etc., i.e., all divisions result from a double [1:2] proportion. For then, when we hear the first two units, we conceive them as one; then, [when] we hear a third unit, we still add it to the first two, so that the proportion is triple [1:3]; afterwards, on hearing the fourth unit, we connect it with the third, so that we apprehend them as one; then we again connect the first two with the last two, so that we grasp those four as a unit; and so our imagination (*imaginatio*) proceeds to the end, when finally our imagination understands the whole melody as the sum of many equal parts.[46]

Few, if any, passages antedating the *Compendium* match the vividness of language and detailed narration of musical experience given here. The language recounts a live experience, vividly expressed both by the use of the present tense and by the invocation of explicit subjects (witness the use of the first-person plural near the end of the passage) who simultaneously perceive, evaluate how and what they perceive, and transform what they perceive into a sort of end product of cognition.[47]

Dennis Sepper summarizes the subject's cognitive activity in this passage thus: "perception, apprehension, memory, and conception all enter into the mental process."[48] He explains the apprehension of individual sensory perceptions as a series of recursive acts that depend upon a complementary relation between imagination and remembrance. Sepper, however, does not observe that the operative role assigned to the imagination by Descartes is reminiscent of Aristotle's account, according to which the imagination mediates between individual sensory perceptions and a holistic conception and apprehension of them by the intellect. In *De Anima*, Aristotle includes the imagination and memory in the category of the internal senses, which, in contrast to the common senses (i.e., sight, hearing, smell, etc.), do not require the object of perception to be present. For Aristotle, the imagination is essential to the process by which sensory impressions of the common senses—part of the "passive," or "receptive" intellect—may be retained and re-presented (i.e., presented over). This re-presentation allows stored sensory impressions (which Aristotle called "phantasms") to enter into contact with the "active," or "productive," intellect, a contact that renders sense impressions intelligible. In a fundamental scheme for his theory of knowledge, Aristotle would argue that, first, sensations give rise to memories; second, memories give rise to experience (which, incidentally, only guarantees the knowledge [*gnôsis*] of individual cases); and, third, that through experience a generalized kind of knowledge (*epistêmê*) emerges. In the end, the importance Aristotle ascribes to the imagination may be summed up in his oft-quoted statement that "to the thinking soul images serve as sense-perceptions . . . hence the soul never thinks without phantasms."[49]

Aristotle's ideas about the interaction between sense impressions and the imagination suggest that the immediacy of sense impressions may have been a hindrance to their adequate intellectual comprehension. That is to say, sense impressions cannot be adequately accounted for in situ; after all, the senses are said to be occupied receiving the impressions of the objects of perception. Aristotle's scheme gives secondary status to the temporality of the initial impression. Conversely, Descartes's account of time in music considers the temporality of the actual experience to be fundamental for the work of the imagination; temporality is actually where the imagination operates (my spatial allusion—"where"—will become clear below). Further accentuating this difference is the fact that this temporality is subsumed within the instant of cognitive plenitude in which the totality of experience of time in music is comprehended as a unitary whole.

Aristotle attributes to the imagination a processual character, as does Descartes when he establishes the imagination as a cognitive conduit bringing together sense experience and the intellect. Similarly Descartes's account suggests that in dealing with musical time the senses can offer only a fragmentary account of experience, and so he assigns to the imagination the responsibility of synthesizing the metric proportions in music.

Significantly the synthesis that takes place in the imagination does not negate the fact that the "whole melody," in Descartes's expression, remains a sonorous and sensorial experience, however much it may be mediated by a mental activity and expressed in the language of numerical proportions. Descartes's account also suggests that he might have been interested in addressing the evanescence intrinsic to our experience of music, albeit indirectly, and thus he summons the imagination to apprehend it in a single act of perceptual cognition. An intentional agent, the imagination elevates the immediacy of sensorial experience to a higher cognitive plane. This points to the emergence of a temporal register in which the linearity of perception is integratively incorporated and eventually transformed into a single instant of cognitive plenitude. This integration is that which renders the whole experience immediate, satisfying Descartes's demands in the Preliminaries.

Descartes's maneuver entails the intentional representation of sensorial experience by the subject's imagination. Representation *by* (not merely *in*) the imagination does not constitute a less real and secondary enactment of something more authentically experienced without mediation. This understanding of perception carries an interesting extrapolation, namely, that an unmediated sensorial experience might be intrinsically deficient. It would follow then that all perceptions must become virtual apperceptions.

With this last observation we begin to answer a question asked earlier: what enables the subject to ascertain that something which is mental (e.g., the integrated experience) represents that which does not start out as such (e.g., time in music)? One may begin to address the issue by asking further whether the experience of time in music, or elsewhere for that matter, can be other than mental, time being a notoriously intractable problem for Western thought since at least Aristotle. (For one, Descartes makes no attempt to give figural form—as a geometric pattern, or an image—to what the imagination "hears.") It may be the case, then, that he regards the aural (as opposed to the visual) as an ideal subject for the kind of intentional representation the *Compendium* examines. Be that as it may, it remains to be seen how the mental/nonmental binary will be negotiated by Cartesian representation.

The proposed—and as yet unresolved—issue of mental representation begs the question of whether Descartes's representation of time in music simply describes the principles by which the imagination is able to combine individual perceptions, or whether representation instead renders these principles identical to the structure of the musical object (i.e., in this case its being divided into temporal units). We know that according to the aesthetic premises in the Preliminaries, the structure of the object must be proportional to the senses in order to satisfy them. Fair enough, one might think; however, it would be an altogether different matter to claim that the imagination operates autonomously from both the objects and the experiences it apprehends. For if one maintains that the imagination does not function autonomously, then it must reflect an objective reality (i.e., a nonmental phenomenon). And, if one affirms the opposite, then the protocols for the actions of the subjective imagination must be distinguished from the formal qualities of either the musical experience or the musical object.

Descartes would, I believe, consider this perceived dialectic between subject and object to be a moot point. He makes clear in the *Rules* that our claims to discriminate things should not refer to "some ontological genus (such as the categories in which philosophers divide things)"; rather, he says, "things can be serially arranged in various groups . . . insofar as some things can be known on the basis of others."[50] This he calls "the main secret of my method," namely, the establishment of criteria for ordering things from simple to complex. This enumerative method constitutes formal proof that knowledge of things thus arranged is certain, fulfilling one of the epistemic standards defined earlier in Rule 2 as "clear and evident cognition." There too, and in keeping with the subordinate status of ontological criteria, Descartes affirms that "in seeking the right path of truth we ought to concern ourselves only with objects which admit of as much certainty as the demonstrations of arithmetic and geometry" (Rule 2, 13/AT, X, 366). At stake is not the nature of the object (e.g., whether or not time in music might fit within the Aristotelian categories of substance, quality, quantity, relation, and so on), but rather the manner in which that object can be truthfully known. The distinction between subject and object as well as the structural priority of the subject in this distinction is, consequently, founded on an epistemological basis. We may say, then, that the *Compendium* and the *Rules* share a conception of the subject that is determined by the epistemological requisite of truth defined as certainty.

Just how important the manner of knowledge proposed in the account of time perception in the *Compendium* may have been for the development of a theory of knowledge and representation can be sensed in the following passage from the *Rules*, where Descartes illustrates the method of ordering:

> If, for example, by way of separate operations, I have come to know first what the relation between the magnitudes A and B is, and then between B and C, and between C and D, and finally between D and E, that does not entail my seeing what the relation is between A and E; and I cannot grasp what the relation is just from those I already know, unless I recall all of them. So I shall run through them several times in a continuous movement of the imagination, simultaneously intuiting one relation and passing on to the next, until I have learnt to pass from the first to the last so swiftly that memory is left with practically no role to play, and I seem to intuit the whole *thing* at once. In this way our memory is relieved, the sluggishness of our intelligence redressed, and its capacity in some way enlarged.[51]

The parallels between this account and that of time perception in the *Compendium* are unmistakable. Four such parallels stand out: (1) the role assigned to the imagination; (2) the presence of some sort of self-analytic activity; (3) the eventual synthesis of the elements of this activity into a single cognition; (4) the emergence of a definite object ("thing") as the result of that synthesis. First, the imagination constitutes the means by which the mind submits data to the tribunals of cognitive analysis, thereby achieving a unity of comprehension that guarantees clear and evident knowledge. Second, in the *Compendium,* Descartes narrates an act of perception taking place within the narrator. Likewise, in the *Rules* he describes the goal of the activity of ordering as grasping a set of relations in a single moment of cognitive plenitude: *intuition.* That he states the matter as an empirical, self-observable activity—that is, as something that can be practiced—suggests that, like the cognition of sense perception, intuition starts out as an extended temporal phenomenon.[52] Third, temporality is gradually reduced as the subject learns how to achieve the cognitive synthesis thanks to which deductive reasoning and the limits of purely serial perception and its overwhelming demands on memory (e.g., the "sluggishness" of memory) are overcome.[53] In both cases the ideal is to transform any kind of extended experience into a charged instant of absolute cognition. Imagination, which technically owes nothing to temporality, seems uniquely suited to realize this kind of transcendental and unmediated perception. Fourth, it is reasonable to think that Descartes did not start out by positing that a series of discrete magnitudes was actually a "thing." That total object results from the analytical reconstruction of the activity of measuring.[54]

Striking though the similarities between the two passages are, so too are three fundamental differences. First, although the subject from the passage in the *Compendium* achieves synthesis, that synthesis is in the full service of comprehending a sense experience. In the *Rules,* by contrast, Descartes turns the operation inward, almost completely abandoning all dependence on sensorial input. (We will shortly examine the reference to "seeing.") Thus, the Aristotelian primary sources of sensible impressions, which remain in place in the apprehension of musical time in the *Compendium,* for instance, are radically transformed by means of cognitive processes. Second, intuition, in the *Rules,* draws attention to the radical assertion of the subject's consciousness of its mental contents as undisputed locus for the cognitive discrimination of things in the world. The subject emerges as a distinct entity due in equal measure to the powers given to intuition *and* to the way in which intuition demarcates objects as entities that either exist outside of the subject or else commingle with it and are then internalized as part of the process of cognition. Whatever ontological continuity may have existed between subject and object (e.g., between sense and sound) in the *Compendium*—and there was hardly any—breaks down in the *Rules.* Third, whereas in the *Compendium* the imagination reconstructed the experience of sound and time in a kind of representational *scenario,* here intuition, though taking place in the imagination, removes objects from the temporal domain of sense experience and makes them instead into a curiously extensionless *scene* visible only to the mind. What had constituted an "integration" of experience and cognition in the *Compendium* becomes in the *Rules* a "reduction" of experience to cognition.

The complex and problematic connection between seeing and intuition demands further scrutiny.[55] To begin, Descartes assertively reinscribes the meaning of the verb "intuit" (Lat. *intueri,* "to look, gaze at") by making it into a noun (*intuitus*).[56] "[I]ntuition is the indubitable conception of a clear and attentive mind which is born (*nascitur*) solely from the light of reason" (Rule 3, 14/AT, X, 388). We recall that the trope of reason as light and of knowledge as vision had formed part of Western epistemology ever since Plato's well-known simile of the cave. That Descartes should continue to use this trope here reflects a firm commitment to an ocular theory of knowledge.[57] And while much has been said of this trope, it warrants repeating the obvious: for a theory of knowledge that so wishes to internalize things that are known, it seems paradoxical to elevate a sense perception (i.e., vision) to the highest cognitive plane. Naturally the understanding of vision here is mental, having little to do with sensation. But as Dalia Judovitz observes, "Descartes represents intuition perceptually," which means that if intuition bears any resemblance to sensation, it must be the kind of enlightened sensation that has been processed by the intellect. In sum, whether purely mental or not, the fact remains that intuition emerges from a theory of knowledge that is *figural* through and through.[58] By "figural" I mean that Descartes's theory of knowledge deploys visual representations (figures or images), algebraic equations (figures of yet a different sort), and the figuration of language itself as a set of mediating instruments in the cognition of things.[59] Descartes associates images with the faculty of the imagination. He conceives of images not as reproductions but as reconstructions of things in terms of the analytical criteria of measurement and order, very much like intuition. As such, intuition depends on the imagination, for the imagination remains that unique faculty enabling us to "see" things as images or figures without these things having to be there. For Descartes, what matters is not so much the fact that intuition takes place in the imagination, but that the imagination is a domain of the mental world of the subject.

Intuition is referred to by Descartes variously as a mental phenomenon (*mentis intuitus;* Rule 11, 38/AT, X, 408), an action (*intellectus actio;* Rule 3, 14/AT, X, 368), and a procedure (*operatio intellectus;* Rule 7, 26/AT, X, 389).[60] We arrive thus at a key point in the construction of the subject in early Descartes: in abrogating both temporality and experience in the act of intuition, subjectivity increasingly becomes defined as the capacity for active and conscious introspection. And with this, representation itself is established as a "distinct mental operation," as he puts it in the passage from Rule 7. An appropriate answer to our earlier query about how the mental can represent the nonmental is that representation is the result of the subject's analysis (i.e., measurement and order), both of objects and of its own experience of them.

To recapitulate, Descartes begins with an ontological claim about objects of perception and knowledge (the principle of proportionality) and an epistemological goal (the notion that comprehension of proportions should be cognitively immediate). Next, he elaborates a method that could objectively demonstrate precise relationships among things by means of their serial enumeration and comparison. Finally, he eliminates the inferential steps in the process of enumeration and comparison. Involving a number of faculties and capacities (the intellect, the imagination, and memory), these steps are involved into a single intellectual act by which knowledge becomes evident and, as I have stated, figural.

Descartes's belief in a figural theory of knowledge is manifest in his use of images other than the mental representations of intuition. The *Compendium* presents several examples. For instance, in the sixth Preliminary, Descartes makes use of visual images to illustrate his point that proportions may be "more easily distinguished by the eyes" when the parts of an object of sense perception hold an arithmetic proportion. His illustration, we may remember (cf. Example 2.1), consists of three evenly divided, arithmetically incrementing lines against which he juxtaposes a figure made up of three lines that, though incrementing, are unevenly divided. In the first set of lines the sense (*sensus*) perceives the nature of the differences between the divisions perfectly at once, Descartes states, but not in the second set. In similar fashion he maintains that the graphic image of a bisected string—itself a reconfiguration of the venerable monochord

—offers a view into the nature of sound, that is, its status as a measurable and ordered proportion.[61]

Images, in Descartes's analogy, contribute to our apprehension of sound what the imagination had done for rhythm. In this case the images reconstruct an auditory experience by means of a visual analogy with the goal of clarifying an otherwise diffuse sensorial perception. Moreover, the analogue here recalls Plato's use of images in the study of geometry and calculation: "They [students of geometry and calculation] make use of and argue about visible figures, though they are not really thinking about them but about the originals which they resemble. . . . [T]he actual figures they draw or model . . . they treat as images only, the real objects of their investigation being invisible except to the eye of reason."[62] But unlike Plato, who made a clear separation between images and the Ideal they help to represent, Descartes puts the sensory experience of the *Compendium* and the *Rules* on a par with that Ideal, radically shifting the relationship between sense and intellect.[63] Proportions might thereby be very much audible to the ear of reason.

Yet one could reasonably argue that, similar to Plato's, Descartes's deployment of images of sound constitutes no more than a heuristic ploy, a simple analogy designed to render visible the otherwise incorporeal experience of sound.[64] Accordingly the move would be lateral, from a less reliable sense (hearing) to a more reliable one (sight). And to a great extent such is no doubt the case, for as we have seen, as a central feature of Descartes's method, intuition remains firmly anchored by the doctrine of clear and distinct ideas that owes its epistemological primacy to an ocular conception of knowledge. Nonetheless, Descartes's use of images in the *Compendium* reflects a larger concern with the place of the imagination in representation and with the role the imagination plays in the pursuit of knowledge. This is evident in his interest in images in the *Rules*.

Visual images have a direct connection to the way Descartes conceptualizes extension and magnitude in the later Rules (i.e., 12–18).[65] In particular, there images are said to be necessary for the distinct perception of proportions. Indeed, the same concern for accounting for the measurement and order of proportions that underlie pleasurable sounds in the *Compendium* is taken up in systematic fashion in these later Rules. I believe there are two reasons why this is the case. First, as I have argued, fundamental to the aesthetic project of the *Compendium* is the clear separation of requirements for the object of perception from those of the perceiver or subject. Likewise, in the later Rules Descartes begins to detail the objects that pertain to each of the cognitive faculties of the subject (i.e., intellect, imagination, memory, and sense perception). Second, while the use of visual images in early Descartes is not exclusive to the *Compendium*,[66] the use of visual images in advocating for the immediate perception of determinable quantities in the object of perception is argued there in terms of cognitive clarity similar to that of the later Rules. The main difference is that in the *Rules* this demand is made explicit and is, furthermore, elaborated from an epistemological perspective.

Rule 12 is pivotal, for here Descartes redirects his methodological efforts from the outline of order and enumeration in the first twelve Rules toward an explanation of the nature of cognition: "Finally we must make use of all aids which intellect, imagination, sense perception, and memory afford, in order, firstly, to intuit simple propositions distinctly; secondly, to combine correctly the matters under investigation with what we already know, so they too may be known; and thirdly, to find out what things should be compared with each other so that we make the most thorough use of all our human powers" (Rule 12, 39/AT, X, 410). Following Stephen Gaukroger, we may say that the question is one of "perceptual cognition" and that for Descartes the matter centers around the question of "how we arrive at knowledge by means of sense perception."[67] In order to evaluate perceptual cognition—and thus to render sense perception cognitive—Descartes first establishes two factors attending to knowledge of things: "ourselves, the knowing subjects (*nos scilicet qui cognoscimus*), and the things which are the objects of knowledge (*res ipsae nobis cognoscendae*)" (Rule 12, 39/AT, X, 411).

Much attention was paid to the distinction between knower and known in the Preliminaries to the *Compendium*. Here, in the *Rules*, he further accentuates that distinction. However, Descartes's account in Rule 12 regards sense perception as passive, or as he puts it in Aristotelian terms, "the way in which wax takes on an impression from a seal" (Rule 12, 40/AT, X, 412). At first this binarism between an external input and an internal but passive receptacle does not differ from Aristotle's hylomorphic account in *De Anima*. But then, in an extraordinary move, Descartes maps all sense perceptions into a common object of perception: shape. "Nothing," he writes, "is more readily perceivable by the senses than shape, for it can be touched as well as seen" (Rule 12, 40/AT, X, 413). His gambit consists in reversing the order of the special sensibles (i.e., those sensibles that pertain to a specific sense) and the common sensibles (i.e., those that result from a combination of two or more senses). That is, by focusing on what is "common" about shape, Descartes is able to propose that even the differences in the perception of various colors, for instance, be understood as the differences between various visual figures (*figurae*), here independently from their proportions.[68]

Clearly then, in upholding the cognitive value of abstraction, Descartes is not, like Plato, seeking simply to extract some ideal aspect of the thing abstracted and to entrust that aspect (which, we recall, is "visible only to the eye of reason") to the reliability of visual images. Instead, Descartes is elevating the figural to a higher cognitive plane which owes its priority in the method of the *Rules* to the role that visual evidence has and which we saw at work in the construction of the notion of intuition. Further, insofar as figures permit a quantifiable account of things perceived, they become necessary for a measurable and ordered account of sense perceptions.

Descartes's account of images revolves around a small set of key concepts and ideas: the assumption of the corporeality of perceptions, the figural form of that corporeality, and the intellectual confirmation via analysis of that figural form. First, it is the common sense which gives corporeality to "ideas which come, pure and without body, from the external senses" (Rule 12, 41/AT, X, 414). But the common sense does not act alone, for that corporeality takes place in and by virtue of the imagination (*imaginatio*).[69] Again, then, we find Descartes trying to mediate between sense and the intellect by means of the imagination. For in his outline of the four faculties, the imagination lies next to the intellect (*intellectus*), and alongside sense perception (*sensus*) and memory (*memoria*) (Rule 12, 42/AT, X, 416): "[If] the intellect proposes to examine something which can be referred to the body, the idea of that thing must be formed as distinctly as possible in the imagination. In order to do this properly, the thing itself which this idea is to represent should be displayed to the external senses" (Rule 12, 43/AT, X, 416-17). The chain of steps takes us from an external sense impression (e.g., hearing a sound), to forming an image of that impression in the imagination, and from there to the external and necessary manifestation of that impression as a figure.

Having outlined this process, Descartes concludes his discussion of the cognitive domain that pertains to the knower, prescribing that these external representations be abbreviated and compact, as a safeguard against lapses of memory. These are themes that we have encountered in the *Compendium*, when Descartes talks about perceptual immediacy and the need for what I have called a "sensory economics." In short, the images of sense perception discussed in Rule 12 bring to the intellect the same clarity as did intuition in Rule 7, and as did the imagination in the discussion of time in music in Chapter 3 of the *Compendium*; namely, the reduction of sense perception to instantaneous acts of mental vision. And like the perception of time, for example, the advocacy of figures in the later Rules necessitates that intellect draw from sensory experience, but demands that what the intellect produces be not itself sensorial. This means that images, though external, must not be understood as sensorial. As a conceptual framework, this distinction not only denotes the cognitive superiority of the intellect over sensory perceptions, but also points to the emergence of the subject as someone whose *full reconstruction* of sensory perception is sanctioned by the methods of measurement and order. Epistemology, it follows, trumps ontology.

This momentous reconfiguration of the relationship between an order of knowing and an order of being is suggested by the remark from Rule 12 quoted at the beginning of this chapter: "When we consider things in the order that corresponds to our knowledge of them, our view of them must be different from what it would be if we were speaking of them in accordance with how they exist in reality" (Rule 12, 44/AT, X, 418). In truth, here Descartes is simply describing the fact that knowledge of objects entails the analytic separation of elements such as shape and extension that coexist in the object. Still, the claims on behalf of analysis help sketch a fundamental distinction between ourselves and the world which, like the subject/object distinction in the Preliminaries, defines the knower as a cognitive construction, the privilege of which is to hold a particular and generalizable perspective *of* and *over* that which it perceives.

In Rule 14 Descartes continues to discuss in greater detail the activity of instantiating sense perceptions by means of visual images. In particular, this Rule discusses the reconstruction of all things that are subject to our cognition in terms of extension and shape: "The problem [i.e., any problem pertaining to the cognition of objects in the world, including perceptions] should be reexpressed (*transferenda*) in terms of the real extension of bodies and should be pictured in the imagination entirely by means of bare figures (*nudas figuras*). Thus it will be perceived much more distinctly by our intellect" (Rule 14, 56/AT, X, 438). Descartes proposes that when no common nature exists between two things or between the "thing sought" and the "initial data," a common nature might be nonetheless present "but only by way of other relations or proportions which imply it" (Rule 14, 57–58/AT, X, 440). The goal is then to establish a common ground, which he calls "equality" (*aequalitas*), by reducing all things to magnitude.

At this point Descartes reintroduces the imagination, saying that "if we are to imagine something, and are to make use, not of pure intellect, but of the intellect aided by images depicted in the imagination (*in phantasia depictis*), then nothing can be ascribed to magnitudes in general which cannot also be ascribed to any species of magnitude" (Rule 14, 58/AT, X, 441). The species of magnitude most suited for imaginary depiction is, not surprisingly, shape (*figura*). The reason for this is that imagination itself as well as the ideas that it may contain are conceived "as being nothing but a real body with a real extension and shape." And so, while comparisons may be established between higher and lower sounds (Descartes's own example), no exact determination of that difference can be affirmed "unless we have recourse to a certain analogy with the extension of a body that has shape" (ibid.). The task of expressing proportions in the form of equalities is carried out in terms of extension and figures, all else being secondary for the intellect.

Among the key elements of the expression of proportions, magnitude is fundamental, for it alone is general to things; for instance, neither length, breadth, nor depth are common to a line, a point, or a surface. And while extension and shape are inseparable from the things we seek to compare, magnitude has the priority of being that which both *measures* and consequently helps *order* the extensions and shapes of those things.

Cleverly circular, Descartes organizes his argument so as to place method at the center of knowledge: to know is to compare and to compare is to measure, but to compare we need to establish a common standard of measurement (i.e., an index of equivalence). However, Descartes adamantly distances himself from those who think that numerical abstractions in themselves can be separated from the things they abstract. "Those who attribute wonderful and mysterious properties to numbers," he says, "do just that" (Rule 14, 61/AT, X, 447). Those "calculators" and "logicians," he says, do not know the method that guides their calculations. For Descartes, number is intrinsic to the thing being compared, be it a string length, its sound and proportion, or a surface. But number is not intrinsic to things in the sense that they possess or are made up of number. Rather, keeping in mind his comparison in Rule 12 between "things in the order that corresponds to our knowledge of them" and "how they exist in reality," number as well as magnitude and figure are all part of the analytic representation of things. By analytic representation, I do not mean merely the depiction in or transference to the imagination that Descartes proposes. Over and beyond that, analytic representation comes to signify here the totality of elements which the knower may summon in his or her claim to know things, including images, the capacity of the imagination to forge them, and the capacity of the intellect to reconstruct all perceptions on the basis of those images. Further, Descartes's insistence on instantiating things in the imagination has to do with the fact that, for instance, when one speaks of magnitude and of the numbers which account for it, the intellect may be able to conceive of these in the abstract but will have no use for them. The intellect, he says, appears to have no direct relation to the things it helps us know and understand. It is for this reason that the imagination, as a bodied, extended, and shaped faculty, must supplement the intellect by providing it with a scenario where perceptions may be set up for cognitive inspection. Gaukroger proposes a startling conclusion: "the imagination, drawing on both the intellect and the information gleaned from the sense organs, is effectively our mind as far as perceptual cognition is concerned."[70] Indeed, the degree to which Descartes emphasized the epistemological validity of giving external form to perceptions and to the notion of mental gaze indicates an equivalence between imagining and knowing.

The reductive spirit behind Descartes's use of images is made clear when he outlines the three characteristics that ought to be considered when "elucidating differences in proportion": dimension, unity, and figure. Dimension, he says, is "a mode or aspect in respect of which some subject is considered to be measurable" (Rule 14, 62/AT, X, 447). He notes, for example, that divisions in equal parts constitute the dimension in terms of which we count things, adding a crucial point: whether real or the product of an intellectual assignation, dimensions add nothing to the things that may posses them but matter only insofar as they provide the basis for measurement. Near the end of Rule 14, Descartes reaffirms that order and measure encompass all relations obtaining between things subject to analysis, and that images represent these relations. In other words, he continues to rehearse here the distinction between the knower and the known. Throughout the remainder of the *Rules*, in fact, Descartes will reiterate that distinction, which suggests that the priority given to the method of knowledge adumbrated in the Preliminaries to the *Compendium* continues to inform his work nearly a decade later.

Having explored the theoretical implications of Descartes's use of images for both the instantiation of sense perception and the representation of the intellectual cognition of perception, we can conclude by further examining Gaukroger's conclusion that in Descartes's early work the imagination is coextensive with the mind: insofar as the mental is defined by a unique kind of extension and associated with a special kind of temporality, the imagination provides those unique spaces and moments of full cognition where and during which the subject comes to know with certainty. This spatial location and this temporal domain are an integral part of classical representation. Indeed, it is the mark of the Cartesian early modern subject that it should be defined by mental introspection and self-consciousness. It is also its mark that the mental should remain bound by some sort of contact with the embodied. (Incidentally, this means that the mind-body dualism for which Descartes is routinely chastised in the *Meditations,* for example, is not yet present in the early method.) This is important to our understanding of the *Compendium* insofar as sound provides Descartes with a singular representational challenge. On the one hand, we may say that by virtue of its "invisibility" (because sound lies at the limits of perceptual intelligibility within an epistemology bent on visual tropes), Descartes opts to inscribe its perception in the materiality of images. On the other, we may say that the representation of the experience of time in music by the imagination speaks to the immateriality of intuition. There is no contradiction between these two positions, however, for Descartes's method radically expresses his conviction of the representability of all things.[71] This conviction is fueled by analysis, which, as we saw in connection with the deployment of images, reduces all perceptions and things, and in so doing is able to reconstruct them. Intuition and images are privileged signifiers because representation becomes inseparable from the analysis of perception.

Another fundamental conclusion to our discussion is that representation depends upon the conceptual separation of the perceiving subject from the objects of perception. Extricating itself from the world, as we have seen, provides the subject with the perspective from which to contemplate all things, itself included. And like the apparent contradiction between corporeality and imagination, the contradiction between the internalization of all things and the objectification of them is attenuated if we consider that mental images or pictorial figures, for instance, are visible (and in a way "external") but not sensory in the way that visual perceptions are. They are projections of the mental analysis of perception onto the scenarios of the imagination. As manifest in images, the specular nature of representation cannot, however, be fully understood without detailed analysis of the subject's agency in the process of representation.

2.3. Representation as the Analysis of Order and Measurement: The Early Modern Subject

Contemplating the nature of historical change in the intellectual (and cultural) life of Western Europe through the sixteenth century, Timothy Reiss argues that an increasing interest in mathematics was intimately bound with broader questions of "method." "Method" is understood, generally, as an orderly disposition of thought such that it would, on its own and through no recourse to syllogisms or any other authorities located in either tradition or divine rationality, account for the practice of human reason as human. Significantly, he adds that as an intellectual project, mathematical study was no less bound "with musical practice and theory" than with fields one commonly associates with the so-called scientific revolution of the seventeenth century. Music theory, in particular, is associated with the emergence of a "rational aesthetics," broadly speaking, the belief that the effects of art on a spectator or a listener could be systematically analyzable and accounted for without recourse to the traditional rhetoric/dialectic model of argumentation.[72]

My examination of Descartes thus far reaffirms Reiss's view. To be sure, the bond between music and mathematics had a long and illustrious history, having been securely ensconced within the quadrivium alongside arithmetic, astronomy, and geometry but also having maintained a relation with the disciplines of the trivium. Further, we know also that Descartes's ideas for a "rational aesthetics" would have been influenced by his Jesuit education. Particularly, ideas about the mode of inquiry into music would have been informed by Clavius's reformist quadrivium, which placed music among the disciplines studying sensible things mathematically.[73] Indeed, as I remarked at the beginning of this chapter, Descartes's inquiry in the *Compendium* would have been driven by an attempt to reaffirm the priority of sensible affects in music, to outline how the object of music produces these affects, and to determine the cognitive domain of the perceiver of these affects.

None of these aesthetic concerns were new in Descartes's writings, and neither was the methodology he engaged to pursue them. After all, late-sixteenth-century scientists like Beeckman, Benedetti, and Galilei had in one way or another methodically considered sound, its transmission, and its effects. Moreover, earlier in the sixteenth century, authors such as Fogliano and Cardano had written about the relation between the nature of sound defined proportionally and its affective qualities.[74] I find Descartes at his most original in *how* he assumed a methodological position. I do not mean experimental or systematic method, but rather "methodological" in the sense of his systematic repositioning of the perceiver in relation to the perceived. At this level the conditions for knowledge itself (and for "method" in a more traditional sense) are reconfigured. This is his most substantive contribution to a "rational aesthetics." I have already intimated that this contribution should be thought of in terms of a theory of representation—that is, that it should be conceived in terms of the believed capacity of the analysis of measurement and order to transparently outline the relationship between perceiver and perceived. In connection to this theory of representation, I have used the terms *knower* and *known* as well as *subject* and *object* to reflect an epistemological shift that is founded on the turn toward self-consciousness and perceptual introspection. In a general sense, this turn, within the context of Descartes's epistemology, may be termed *subjectivity*.[75]

We have here the establishment of a rational order underlying the systematic outline of procedures by which to obtain knowledge that is considered to be "certain," as we saw, for example, explicitly in the *Rules*, but also implicitly in the Preliminaries to the *Compendium*. The rational order manifest in these writings *prescribes* the conditions and procedures for analysis of perceptions. At the intersection of this prescriptive rational order and analysis lies *representation*. This bringing together of representation, subjectivity, and knowledge is, however, entangled in a dialectic that is as rich as it is tautological (even frustratingly so): on the one hand, measurement and order constitute the criteria for the existence of a rational order, and on the other, the establishment of a rational order owes its very existence and epistemological validity to the belief that measurement and order provide clear and distinct evidence of knowledge.

The circularity connecting analysis and representation in the early work of Descartes provides a fundamental principle for the development of new ideas of ourselves as cognizant beings. Reciprocally, "being" is defined cognitively, by the activity of thinking: that is, that the belief in an irrefutable ability to explain the world and, most significantly, ourselves is inseparable from this circularity. Put concisely, we regulate the representation of the world and our own representation thanks to the establishment of self-consciousness as the mark of the mental. Take, for instance, the epistemological values underlying Descartes's deployment of the imagination and of images when defining the cognitive parameters of aural perception:

1. Any image of a string length transparently represents not just a perceived sound but also the totality of the perceptual relationships that inhere to other strings and other sounds: the image constitutes an instrument for theoretical generalization based on the establishment of "simples."
2. This instrument is set up in the manner of a scenario, a controllable environment where commonalities can be staged and observed.
3. The subject dictates the criteria for determining what is more or less acceptable in this scenario.
4. Perception is founded upon the intentional reconstruction of sense data, which is carried out in the act of representation by the agency of the subject's imagination (e.g., intuition).
5. Whether assuming the form of extended matter or the spaceless and instantaneous form of intuition, the intentional reconstruction of sense data suggests that representation is no longer held up to standards of verisimilitude and, consequently, means that the figures (the signs of representation) gain independence from the things they denote.
6. Verisimilitude—a guiding standard in the episteme of resemblances that framed Renaissance knowledge—is superseded by the analysis of measurement and order.
7. As an axiomatic form of representation, the analysis of measurement and order is anchored to a theory of subjectivity (i.e., the mental consciousness informing the scenarios of representation), and this subjectivity will find ideal expression in the concept of intuition.

In the sum total of these values we witness the relationship binding analysis, representation, and subjectivity together under the rubric of knowledge, particularly "rational aesthetics." And yet there remain two elements underlying

Cartesian thought, which lend no small amount of credibility to these values. These two elements are *mathesis universalis* and the theory of the classical sign.[76]

For Descartes, mathesis universalis designates the logical conditions underlying mathematical disciplines: the deductive serial arrangement of things that does not depend on categories of being (i.e., ontological categories) and the instrumentality of measurement and order in arriving at such serial arrangement (the term derives from the Greek *mathêsis*—literally "learning," in a process-like sense).[77] He recognizes in these logical conditions a general science informing the order of things in the world:

> [T]he exclusive concern of mathematics is with questions of order and measure and it is irrelevant whether the measure in question involves numbers, shapes, stars, sounds, or any other object whatever. This made me realize that there must be a general science which explains all the points that can be raised concerning order and measure irrespective of the subject-matter, and that this science should be termed mathesis-universalis. (Rule 4B, 9/AT, X, 378)[78]

As an explanatory model, mathesis universalis cannot be extricated from questions of method addressed earlier. For mathesis universalis is founded on a small number of systematically arranged determinants: "quantity is the common nature—'the abstract mathematical quantity.' The fundamental property is to be equal or unequal; on the basis of this property quantities are related among themselves in simple relations ('*rationes*,' and according to some also '*proportiones*') and relations of relations or proportions ('*proportiones*,' '*proportionalitates*')."[79] Thus, while the establishment of relations of identity and difference among things by their measurement and order lends "method" a system, mathesis universalis provides the prescriptive logical criteria that ground it. And so, to say that Descartes—and the seventeenth century in general—engaged in the quantification of music would only partially represent the conceptual order fueling his intellectual project.[80] Equally inadequate would be any other reductive characterizations such as mechanization or, worse still, mathematization. In Foucault's well-known formulation, what unites these more specific practices during the seventeenth century is their debt to a fundamental conception of knowledge based on a general science of order (science being defined here as systematic knowledge).[81]

In the *Rules* such a general science of order has for Descartes the character of a project, that is, the intentional projection of a set of prescriptions of what knowledge is and how it must be attained. At stake in this project is a privileged epistemological value: certainty. According to Descartes, previous modes of thought could not guarantee certainty, blinded as they were to discrimination by the web of resemblances they sought among all things or else distracted by the vagaries of syllogisms and dialectics. Such a critique is not original to Descartes. We find critiques of the impediments to knowledge brought about by the deceptions and faulty arguments of resemblance in Bacon's *idola mentis* (idols of the mind) and *idola fori* (idols of the market) (*Novum Organum*, 1620), and much earlier, as Reiss argues, in debates in France around the middle of the sixteenth century about language and knowledge and the role that dialectics and logic played in each.[82] The main point, however, is that these intellectual developments did not seek to eliminate resemblance, stopping just short of that mark by simply diagnosing its problematic role in the acquisition of knowledge. (Bacon, we may remember, did not identify mathematics as the ideal language of the new science.) In contrast, from the outset of the *Rules*, Descartes—who in reality was the beneficiary of previous critiques—seeks to extricate knowledge from any connection with the epistemology of resemblances. "Whenever people notice some similarity between two things, they are in the habit of ascribing to the one what they find true of the other, even when the two are not in that respect similar" (Rule 1, 9/AT, X, 359). Resemblance among things can be held neither as a reliable foundation nor as a primary criterion for attaining knowledge of them, he says.[83] Further, he criticizes the dependence resemblance has on sense data, arguing that such "givens" should be first subject to analysis in order to establish their comparability. Abandoning resemblance entails embracing discrimination, which in turn entails determining exact comparisons among things. In making such moves, Descartes aims to establish certainty and indubitability as standards by which to measure the efficacy of all cognitive efforts. We may do well then to note that certainty is not guaranteed by the various mathematical calculations or geometric figures that one might bring to bear on the question of perception; these are *instruments* of order. Order itself, so to speak, resides in mathesis universalis, which is both the instrument of rationality and the logical process leading to order. As such, mathesis universalis anchors knowledge to certainty.

As the basic conceptual element in Descartes's aesthetic project, order informs both those things in the world subject to quantification and those which are not. The former correspond to the knowledge of simple natures, the latter to the knowledge of complex natures. These complex natures, Foucault explains, are "representations in general, as they are given to experience."[84] For instance, perceptions, which in the form of impressions constitute complex representations, undergo a preliminary ordering before they may serve as the basis for further knowledge. This preliminary ordering is established by transforming complex representations into simple natures (e.g., reducing objects of experience to terms such as figure, extension, or motion so that "they cannot be divided by the mind into others which are more distinctly known"; Rule 12, 44/AT, X, 418). We have seen this transformation at play in Descartes's arguments in the *Rules* on behalf of the use of images, and more informally in the *Compendium*.

The use of images obviously instantiates an analogy between seeing and knowing. This would seem at first to install resemblance anew into the operations of knowledge as well as implicitly to validate the identification of resemblances that may exist among diverse impressions. And by necessity, such recognition entails the use of the imagination, which is why we find the imagination playing a prominent role. According to Foucault, "[I]f representation did not possess the obscure power of making a past impression present once more [by means of the imagination], then no impression would even appear as either similar or dissimilar from a previous one."[85] Surely, when Descartes in the second preliminary to the *Compendium* compares the glare of the sun to the noise of guns, he is recounting two separate, discontinuous experiences. The analogy, trivial though it may first appear, foregrounds resemblance as a basic, though vague, form of experiential knowledge, one which Foucault terms "confused impressions." But with the introduction of visual images in the sixth Preliminary, Descartes engages in the analysis of the measurable elements of sense perception, out of which he extrapolates an increasingly specific relation between seeing and hearing. A curious extrapolation results: resemblance may have been moved from the center to the periphery of knowledge, but in the analysis of the perception of sound it remains very much the hub around which cognitive perception revolves. However, when Descartes articulates the notion of intuition in his analysis of perception of time in music, he has collapsed any resemblance between hearing and seeing into a sign of cognitive certainty, transforming the linear relations inherent in resemblance into a coherent and self-validating spatial virtuality. As we have seen, this transformation is carried out under the auspices of the imagination, whose job it remains to restore order to the continuous perceptions of divided units of time. Foucault terms this the "analytic of imagination," the "positive power to transform the linear time of representation into a simultaneous space containing virtual elements."[86] This space and its virtual elements are, in Descartes, intuition, nothing more.[87]

And nothing less. Intuition encapsulates classical representation in one of its most extreme forms: as the sign of thought. It is, in other words, the form and content of consciousness. It remains, then, to examine more closely how the sign is constituted as the emblematic and material expression of classical representation as well as its practical arm. The first question concerns the nature of the classical sign.

First and foremost, in Descartes's analysis of perception, the sign is coeval with knowledge itself. No longer is the sign thought to antecede our cognitive intervention in the world, as a hidden mark waiting to be discovered and interpreted. Thus, when Descartes, in Rule 12, asserts the logical priority and conceptual primacy of our knowledge of things over their status as "Beings," he is simply defining the sign as the practice of human reason. The status of the sign is entirely dependent on its function as a transparent expression of the analysis of measurement and order. The same is, of course, true for the use of images in the *Compendium*. From the perspective of the history of thought, the locus of the sign is no longer the world. It is, rather, the self-regulated mind.

Second, as an expression of the mental, the sign is intrinsically connected to the distinction between knower and known, between subject and object. The sign, in other words, becomes an index of our separation from the world. But at the same time, it is an index of our inextricable connection to a world now folded in its entirety into the *ego cogito*. This conceptual reciprocity extends to the relation within the classical sign between signifier and signified. We may think of this relation thus: (1) the sign is simultaneously the result of analysis *and* the instrument of analysis; (2) the subject treats its own thought as an object but does not recognize this self-division in the articulation of a theory of representation.

The first point is exemplified, for instance, by the moment in the *Compendium* when "finally our imagination understands the whole melody as the sum of many equal parts." What Descartes calls "understanding" constitutes a sign in that it provides a framework for identifying the simplest elements into which the perception being analyzed can be divided (this is the instrumental function of the sign in analysis); reciprocally, the sign constitutes the medium through which to combine and thus to transform those perceptions into "understanding" (here the sign is the result of analysis). If, for example, impressions and perceptions are said to be regulated by the system of relations ordering signs, are the analyses of those impressions and perceptions not signs themselves? The answer is, of course, yes.

This all means that the sign constitutes a direct representation of analysis. From this a binary structure emerges in which the only necessary link binding signifier and signified is the sign's status as analysis: that is, the sign fully signifies its object and "has no content, no function, and no determination other than what it represents." But as Foucault elaborates, a sign is not merely transparently expressive of its object *qua* mental representation. In addition, the representation contained in the sign (e.g., of the analysis of perception of time) "must be represented within [the sign]."[88] The classical sign is itself representative of its own representing function, or in other words the sign represents representation itself.[89] This complex folding of the sign within representation is termed "duplicated representation" by Foucault. As a totality of signifying relations, the sign (e.g., intuition) stands then for all the values attached to the analysis of order and measurement, the comparison of complexes once reduced to simples, and the ordering and discrimination of confused impressions as serial arrangements grasped in the immediacy of mental analysis. In short, the conditions for the possibility of the sign are given in the analytic terms of mathesis and the transparency of self-consciousness, and so are closed off to any examination.

A second question about the classical sign concerns its semiotic structure: what is the relation between the sign and what it signifies? In the powerful theory of the classical sign, however, there is an implicit blindness to an operative division, in cognitive acts, of the knower into subject and object. The knower is a subject insofar as it is a locus of representation; but as this representation is itself articulated, the knower becomes object, as, for instance, in the articulation of intuition. This division is overlooked, or is, rather, active on the level of epistemic unconsciousness, because consciousness as such is considered to be always already representational. To witness, Descartes's eventual statement to the effect that "nothing can be more easily and more evidently perceived by me than my mind" (cited at the beginning of this chapter), or his later definition of "thought" (*pensée*): "I use this term to include everything that is within us in such a way that we are immediately aware of it," and elsewhere as "everything that is made within us in such manner that we immediately perceive it ourselves."[90] To understand this aspect of consciousness, we must return to questions of method and, most particularly, of cognitive certainty. When Descartes pronounces certainty to be the goal of knowledge and the analysis of measurement and order to constitute the means by which to reach this goal, he is giving an account of how representation operates. Significantly, he is neither offering an explanation of where representation originates nor thinking of representation as the effect of some conceptually prior cause. In a way representation has no point of origin other than the self-cognizing subject defined as an *intuitus originarius* and a self-sufficient (*autarches*) being. Equally, the question of whether consciousness has the capacity to form representations or not is a moot one. Thus, the certainty of self-knowledge is never in doubt.

The self-enclosed Cartesian understanding of the representative character of consciousness comes into clearer focus by contrast to a much later but equally influential version of consciousness: Kant's. Briefly: Kant questions the representational character of thought in general, and of the "I" in particular. As we will examine in greater detail in Chapter 4, for Kant a representation of sense impressions by thought, for example, requires the mental synthesis of them. For Kant, the possibility of such synthesis does not follow from the nature of consciousness. Rather, consciousness must be appropriately structured by the forms of sensibility and the categories of understanding before it can adequately represent its objects. No longer can the transparent representation of the subject to itself be considered satisfactory. This means, among other things, that Kantian subjectivity deprives the subject of its unchallenged epistemological priority, reducing the subject to a regulatory idea of the unity of its representations and making of it one representation among many.

Throughout this chapter my working assumption has been that subjectivity, in musical thought, is associated with the conceptual separation of the perceiver (hearer) from what is perceived (sound or time in music). Yet I recognize that the subject does not exhaust its object, for the two are dialectically linked, in that features of the object determine the range of the subject's perception. I have offered a complementary account of subjectivity to that which identifies the emergence of musical subjectivity (or subjectivity in music) with the increasing inwardness of listening practices in the Renaissance musical world, or the representation of the self which is increasingly said to accompany the rise of monody and opera.[91] I have located inwardness squarely within representation, seen from the perspective of the epistemology of perception. For Descartes, and for the classical episteme at large, the cognitive autonomy of the subject is the mark of representation, while, at the same time, representation is that which provides the conditions for the possibility of a new kind of "man"—the early modern subject, in the present account. This subject, we have seen, is characterized by the ability to designate itself, imply itself, and exhibit itself in such a way that it is simultaneously authorized and authenticated by these claims.[92]

Empowering and problematic in equal measure, language plays a vital role in this articulation. As Dalia Judovitz remarks, "the subject is posited as an entity implicit in the order of representation. . . . The strategic position of the subject within representation is defined through its powers of declaration and assertion." And surely we do not need to heed Benveniste's well-known critique of the "I" as a privileged linguistic and discursive formation to concur with Husserl's statement: "[T]hat Descartes persists in pure objectivism in spite of its subjective grounding was possible only through the fact that the *mens*, which first stood by the ground of knowledge, grounding the objective sciences (or universally speaking, philosophy), appeared at the same time to be grounded along with everything else as a legitimate subject matter within the sciences, i.e., in psychology."[93]

Husserl's invocation of psychology is right on the mark. Indeed, with the *Compendium* we have examined a shift from the inaugural Aristotelian theory of impressions toward Cartesian representation that is psychological through and through (where "psychological" designates the systematic analysis of what goes on in the mind when a perceiver encounters the world). In Descartes the shift is realized most radically by bringing psychology into the fold of the scientific. Like any other domain of knowledge, the domain of the mental world is inscribed in the order of *mathêsis* and is scientific insofar as we understand *scientia* with Descartes to mean systematic knowledge based on indubitable foundations.

In the end, then, I have argued for an understanding of subjectivity and representation in Descartes's early work on music and the *Rules*, in which the very idea of what knowledge is shifts. There Descartes articulates the foundational codes for this shift. There is a well-defined object (i.e., sound), a specific subject position (i.e., the role of the perceiver in determining the aesthetic qualities of the object of perception), a concept (i.e., the idea of a rational aesthetics and perceptual cognition), and a strategy (i.e., the method by which the subject deploys the newly articulated concepts). Further, he introduces new terms (e.g., his reinscriptions of mathesis universalis and intuition) that, accompanied by their conceptual implications, amount to nothing less than sets of epistemological values to regulate the practice of knowledge. The practice of representation, as we may call Descartes's exercise in the *Compendium*, opens up the possibility for thinking of ourselves as objects of self-knowledge. This practice involves the instrumental use of the imagination as a privileged space for cognitive action. More philosophically, this practice includes a repositioning of the ontology of objects of perception in relation to our claims to know them, as well as a re-evaluation of our capacities for making such claims.

To be sure, any analysis of the claims to knowledge expressed in the *Compendium* must take into account the presence of a cognitive ambivalence in his early thought. For instance, allusions to "sympathies" which appear in the comments preceding the Preliminaries of the *Compendium*, as well as statements to the fact that "animals can dance to rhythm if they are taught and trained," or that the voice of a friend is more pleasant than that of an enemy, all give evidence to the intermingling of contrasting and even contradictory ideas of knowledge acquisition.[94] It follows that not all properties of sound are reduced to the analysis of measurement and order; some remain either unexplained or else are explained by recourse to the epistemology of resemblance. But perhaps no idea bears as indelibly the marks of previous attitudes about the possibilities of knowledge than mathesis universalis itself. Even when adamantly criticizing the esoteric grounds of Raymond Lull's "art of finding truth," Gaukroger has convincingly argued that Descartes's own belief in a universal science as the key to all knowledge is unthinkable outside of the ambitions of the universalist tradition to which Lull belongs.[95] Further, we should not read too much into the *Compendium* trying to find there a cognitively defined subject who would enclose the whole of reality and who would then draw a definitive body of knowledge. That one day Descartes was to transform the very existence of the subject into an analytic and self-evident proposition should not distract us from the epistemological contingencies of his early aesthetics. The conditions and causes of knowledge he outlines in the *Compendium* should not be fused into a "rationality" that, in a widely circulated story, will rule untrammeled later in the seventeenth century. And yet we cannot deny the ingenuity of the questions he asked of perception, the intellectual force of his appeal to the imagination, and the singular economy of his method. On their own these features of early Cartesian musical thought do not make Descartes into the primary source of the epistemology of the early modern. My exemplar—the *Compendium*—could hardly be a decisively determinant historical force for a new music theory, let alone a new philosophy, but it reveals many of the epistemological pressures encroaching upon aesthetics near the beginning of the seventeenth century. In the final analysis the matter is not primarily one of originality, but of what ideas had been deployed earlier, and with what aims. Or, as I mentioned in the introduction, analysis of claims to knowledge must simultaneously attend to the overlaps and distinctions between "author" (the individual, rational agent behind a set of ideas), "author function" (a discursive construct by which a readership transhistorically endows some discourse but not another with regulatory power over particular ideas and concepts), "text" (the specific repository of a set of ideas and concepts), and "discursive practices" (the ideas and concepts that create "the possibilities and the rules for the formation of other texts" and that inform particular ways of encountering the world).[96] On this account I can say that, understood as the complex of author-author function-text-discursive practice, Descartes's musical thought articulates the epistemological domain in which the hearer now encounters and negotiates the sound of music. The cognitive sovereignty of Descartes's hearer will be found, in my analysis of Rameau in Chapter 3, to be both expanded and under stress. Although armed with greater knowledge and understanding of nature, Rameau's subject will nonetheless further invest itself in the elusive powers of the imagination.

3 The Complicity of the Imagination: Representation, Subject, and System in Rameau

We may judge music only through our hearing, and reason has no authority unless it is in agreement with the ear; yet nothing should be more convincing to us than their union in our judgements. (L'on ne peut juger de la Musique que par rapport de l'ouïe; & la raison n'y a d'autorité, qu'autant qu'elle s'accorde avec l'oreille; mais aussi rien ne doit plus nous convaincre que leur union dans nos jugemens.)

Jean-Philippe Rameau, *Traité de l'Harmonie*
(Book 2, Chapter 18, Art. 1, "On the Establishing of Rules")

Example 3.1 shows the beginning of the second episode (m. 49) of "Les tricotets," a rondeau from the second book of the *Nouvelles suites de pièces de clavecin* (1736) by Jean-Philippe Rameau (1683–1764). In its harmonic character this episode sharply contrasts the main theme and the first episode, in both of which harmonies fall within antecedent-consequent patterns, and phrases follow clearly delineated groups of two and four measures. Here, following repetition of a two-measure group of tonic-to-dominant chords (mm. 49–52) in the local key of E minor, a powerful surge of harmonic activity in the ensuing chordal chain (m. 53) propels the passage forward, freeing the music from the regularity of the prevalent hypermeter.

Beneath the score my fundamental bass analysis indicates the root succession by fifths underlying this passage; each individual chord, the analysis claims, carries a seventh. However counterintuitive it may first appear, the addition of sevenths to each triad beginning at m. 53 expresses the lack of any stable cadential point until mm. 59–60. A more literal analysis of the passage showing two-measure groups of six-three to five-three chords would designate each triad to be a tonic, according to Rameau's theory. This would be more counterintuitive than the initial intuition that these triads are in some fundamental sense unstable. That instability is precisely what an analysis following Rameau would represent with the sevenths.

Two features of this analysis immediately stand out. First, each element operates in a distinct registral order; the fundamental bass resides, so to speak, beneath the acoustical space of the actual chords, while the dissonances occupy a higher registral space, either on the top of or within the musical texture.

Example 3.1
Fundamental bass analysis with added dissonances. Jean-Philippe Rameau, "Les tricotets," from *Nouvelles suites de pièces de clavecin, 2ᵉ livre* (1736), mm. 47–63.

(Rameau distinguishes between the *son fondamental*—a single sound lying below and controlling a chord or any sonorous body—and *sons supérieurs*—sounds that make up a harmony and are determined by the *son fondamental*.) Second, to the extent that they may be said to exist, the two elements belong to a phenomenological order distinct from the acoustical one given by the music; in this crucial sense the fundamental bass and the dissonant sevenths are implied.[1] These sevenths analytically express two axioms of Rameau's early theory of harmony: "[I]f the fundamental bass is removed . . . the harmony will remain good, for even when the fundamental bass is removed, it is always implied"; and "all conclusions of a strain in which a tonic note is preceded by its dominant are called perfect cadences. This tonic note should always occur on the first beat of a measure, if the conclusion is to be felt; its dominant, which precedes it in this

86 *Musical Representations, Subjects, and Objects*

case, should always bear a seventh chord or at least a perfect chord, for the seventh can be implied here."[2] We might conclude, then, that in spite of their familiar representation as musical notation (i.e, the fundamental bass as bass line and the dissonances as figures), neither of these analytical elements forms part of the music as it "exists in reality," to invoke Rule 12 from Descartes's *Rules;* rather, in keeping with the claims to representation of the classical episteme, they follow an order "that corresponds to our knowledge of them." And thus to the eye or ear neither fundamental bass nor dissonances exist as the sound of the rondeau; they are instead echoes of the murmuring voices of analysis, cognitive interventions motivated by theoretical claims to knowledge.

Of the two analytic elements (and for reasons that will become clearer as the chapter progresses), implied dissonances are more provocative and enigmatic, and I shall focus on them in this chapter. Their curiously inaudible character raises a host of questions. First of all, what do they represent? Are implied tones to be somehow phenomenologically experienced or imputed by the imagination of the listener during the act of hearing? Or, rather, are they to be conceptually understood but not phenomenologically experienced? To these cognitive questions we might add "practical" ones, that is, issues of composition or performance: What is the place of musical practice in this analytical formulation? In the case of implied dissonances, should keyboard players, for example, feel free to add tones that are not notated but that might be uncontroversially assumed following improvisation practices and/or general stylistic traits according to which similar sequential passages, in the case of Rameau's rondeau, contain explicit dissonances? Answers to these questions might help us both define the ontological status of a fundamental bass analysis in which implied dissonances operate and determine the order of reality in which these dissonances may exist. More significantly, Rameau's account of implied dissonances demands further clarification of the relationship between theoretical axioms and the activities of listening and performing.[3] That is, if the acoustical datum in a composition and/or in its performance is, in a way, deemed insufficient for our adequate comprehension of it, then the very ontological status of the passage in the example (i.e., the conditions that determine its being) too would be open to question, and the epistemological stakes placed on listening would rise.

Suspicions about the legitimacy of implied tones are quite understandable given their elusive nature. These suspicions are further affirmed when we consider that implied tones may belong to an equally elusive order of being, a domain we shall provisionally term the musical *imaginary.* In my interpretation this domain will designate those elements of the analysis that are not explicit in the acoustical datum of a musical composition. An adequate understanding of this musical imaginary depends upon an explanation of the function of the subject or human agent behind the implied notes, the activity I term *implication.*[4] We will need to explain how and why the human faculty of the *imagination* —the mental capacity to conceive something not explicitly perceived—should intervene so forcefully in theoretical explanations of music at this point in history. What, in other words, is the epistemology of the imagination, and how does invoking it affect the explanatory power of Rameau's inaugural theory of harmony?

In the *Traité* the intervention of the imagination—a faculty which the intellectual tradition has up until Rameau's time held under suspicion—is of significance for the history of musical thought, as it positions theoretical reflection on music within the context of an emergent theory of the subject in place since the advent of Descartes's revolutionary epistemology.[5] In confronting the consequences of this development nearly a century after Descartes, I will propose that Rameau's notion of *sous-entendre* marks the entry of music theory into the modern era—one defined by the emergence of the human subject as an autonomous agent of cognition of musical objects and by the music-theoretical construction of the subject as listener.[6] I will, however, outline three specific ways in which Rameau's appeal to the imagination stands in dialectical tension with the epistemological claims of classical representation. First, in the elliptical manner in which he represents the process of implication. Rameau surreptitiously effaces an active subject in the cognitive transaction between music and listener, resorting to passive grammatical constructions (e.g., "the fundamental bass . . . is always implied" or "the seventh can be implied here").[7] Second, in the relationship between the presence of the subject and Rameau's nature-based claims for a theory of music. To my mind there is no place where the subject's interiority more clearly encounters the purportedly all-encompassing presence of a natural—and presumably external—foundation for music theory than in the imagination (the full title of Rameau's ground-breaking treatise is, after all, *Traité de l'harmonie reduite à ses principes naturels*). The imagination, I will argue, arises both as an epistemological precondition for and validation of the foundation that nature itself, in Rameau's view, had granted harmony. It is a key issue for the history of theory that precisely at the crucial moment in which there arises a "science" of harmony founded on, of all things, nature, there also arises the need for the intervention of the subject's most elusive faculty. Third, in the relationship that what I call implication may have to musical practice. Here I will address the systematic aspects of Rameau's theory, focusing on the use he makes of existing compositional features such as the cadence and sequential progressions. Rameau's explanatory system, I claim, cannot be seen simply as deductive or inductive, for the presence of implied dissonances indicates that traces of musical practice appear as part of the first principles upon which the deductive apparatus is grounded. I will propose the existence of an alternative strategy in which practice and theory are part of a triangular relationship in the middle of which stands the subject. Akin, but not identical, to Feyerabend's notion of *counterinduction,* this alternative strategy consists in making of a particular feature of musical practice a general principle that explains other aspects of practice.[8] The prefix "counter" suggests that this general principle may contradict practice, as happens in Example 3.1, where the sevenths do not appear in the music but are part of the subject's analytical intervention.

Lurking behind my analysis of the notion of implication (and, I argue, of all that it implies for the history of theory) is the particular theory of representation that subtends Rameau's analytical expression of implied notes and the fundamental bass. After all, both the ontological foundation of nature and the epistemological contribution of the subject's reason and imagination find expression through signs. I shall take as a point of departure the claims made by Foucault and previously examined in Chapter 2: representation during the classical episteme operates according to an unmediated, transparent relation between signifier and signified. My analysis of Rameau's appeal to the imagination suggests that, unlike the domains analyzed by Foucault (language, natural sciences, and economics), music, and particularly harmony, makes necessary the presence of a third, intervening term in the otherwise binary model of classical representation: this, I will argue, alters the protocols of representation that Foucault believed to inform the order of classical knowledge. Finally, I will consider the semiotic protocols guiding Rameau's appropriation of musical notation for analytical means (i.e., the musical symbols of the fundamental bass and the figures of the implied dissonances).[9]

It may seem farfetched to base a discussion of music theory's relation to the emerging epistemology of the modern era on Rameau's notion of implied dissonances. Why should one choose to consider what, on evidence, appears to be a minor and eccentric part of Rameau's enterprise as a way to access the vast and complex question of human cognition in the early eighteenth century? The answer lies precisely in the fact that, more than any of the better-known (and understood) aspects of Rameau's thought, this element of his theory helps bring human agency from the margins to the center of musical interpretation.[10] To make my case, then, it will be necessary to delve deeply into the epistemology of the imagination, the history of its inception, and the difficult questions it has posed for our claims to knowledge. The reader will find that Rameau often recedes into the background for long stretches in my argument. I plead for the reader's patience, for in the end Rameau emerges in all his humanity as a courageous, if often self-contradictory, thinker, who to the best of his abilities tackled the challenges of musical cognition posed by harmony, and in the final analysis brought into music theory important issues pertaining to consciousness and the place of the human subject in the experience of music.

3.1. Moving Music: Rameau's Theory of Harmonic Succession

The *Traité* offers a classic example of Rameau's singular capacity for synthesis. In it he brings theoretical and musico-practical traditions together with the principle of mathesis universalis, the conception of knowledge elaborated by Descartes as a set of logical conditions subtending mathematics in their certitude. Thus one finds in the *Traité* ideas drawn from various conceptual traditions: the structuring centrality of the triad since the time of Aaron and Zarlino, the empirical knowledge of concatenating simultaneities according to the tradition of figured-bass accompaniment, incipient formulations of chordal inversion, and the contrapuntal understanding of intervallic progression. These conceptual traditions appear together with acoustic and physico-acoustic accounts of the sonorous phenomena of music (inherited from the experimental tradition of seventeenth-century acoustical science), the ancient Pythagorean tradition of considering musical phenomena in terms of numerical proportions, and the canonist practice of dividing the vibrating string (monochord) to obtain empirically those proportions.[11] The mathematical rapport between experienced and observed musical sound and music making is never doubted. According to one commentator, the physico-acoustic and mathematical frame within which these various ideas are positioned ultimately converge in the *Basse fondamentale:* A sort of "capital element," in Marie-Elizabeth Duchez's formulation, it lends Rameau's entire theoretical apparatus a unifying natural foundation.[12] But this unifying foundation must be seen to emerge simultaneously: (1) as a given (*datum*) in that it is contained in music as a natural phenomenon (i.e, the *son fondamental*) or, as Rameau puts it, "un fait d'expérience," and (2) as a construct (*factum*) in that it must be theoretically elaborated as a principle and must, furthermore, be represented (i.e., the *son fondamental* must be made present as part of the musical experience by means of the notion of *Basse fondamentale*).

Within his theoretical synthesis Rameau's systematic presentation of principles in the *Traité* gives undisputed structural priority to the *son fondamental* as the natural foundation of harmony, presented in Book 1. Books 2 and 3 reflect an ever-increasing influence of musical practice, culminating in Book 4 with a full-fledged account of accompaniment based on precepts set up in the first two books. As articulated in the order of (re)presentation, Rameau's method as a whole follows a paradoxically self-enclosed "sequence": mathesis universalis provides a set of rational relations whose axiomatic character creates the logical context that in circular fashion defines the very objects (i.e., harmonies) that this logical context seeks to explain and give meaning to. In other words, within the appearance of a logical, deductive progression from principle to generalized musical practice, Rameau's method disguises the fact that the *son fondamental* and its valorization as natural foundation are simultaneously prescriptive and descriptive. Fact and construct merge into "representative concepts at once operational and structural" that will explain and predetermine, parting from the very materiality of sound in the *son fondamental*, the permissible (i.e., natural) successions of adjacent tones of the fundamental bass (i.e., fifths and thirds), the mechanics of chordal inversion, and the generation of harmonic objects.[13]

Harmonic "objects," however, often prefigure the logical context that is supposed to explain them, complicating Rameau's systematic construction of the theoretical edifice. A telling case is that of the perfect cadence, which Rameau appropriates from compositional practice and then advances as a prototype of harmonic succession. In Book 2, Chapter 5, he takes a voice-leading description (i.e., as progressions of individual intervals) of a closing clausula from contrapuntal theory and reinscribes it as a perfect cadence (*cadence parfaite*) in terms of the fundamental bass model from Book 1.[14] According to Rameau, an *ideal* harmonic succession occurs when the following conditions obtain: (1) the fundamental bass moves by descending fifth, (2) the first in a succession of two chords contains a dissonant seventh, and (3) the dissonant seventh chord (perfect major chord plus minor third) is followed by a perfect chord (*accord parfait*). The minor seventh, which is not part of the *son fondamental* but which Rameau stubbornly elevates to the category of fundamental dissonance in Book 1,[15] becomes here a sine qua non for harmonic mobility; in its need for resolution Rameau readily identifies the primary moving force in all chordal concatenations. From now on, in order to be harmonically coherent, to form part of a harmonic chain, chords are said to connect only when impelled by the presence of dissonance. In terms of chordal categories the scheme is simple: the dominant seventh chord becomes the fundamental dissonant chord, the mark of instability against the perfect chord, the mark of stasis.[16]

Beneath the systematic veneer of Rameau's explanation of the perfect cadence lies a less systematic principle inherited from the Aristotelian paradigm of motion: the model of imperfection-to-perfection, which makes of the cadence a reinscription of the model of intervallic progression.[17] Groundbreaking, however, is Rameau's transferal of this interval-based notion to a harmonic terrain: the dissonant seventh does not stand as an independent interval; rather, its very being is confirmed by the totality of the sonority, the dissonant harmony sanctioned by the fundamental bass. Thanks to the fundamental bass, the two basic chordal categories (perfect triad and seventh chord) transcend their condition as intervallic aggregates (the sonorous simultaneities of Aaron, Zarlino, and the figured-bass tradition) and become holistic entities. More than a simultaneity of intervals, Rameau conceives of a chord as a sonority with a particular harmonic *meaning,* a meaning that is released, so to speak, when this chord connects to another chord by the lawful motion of the fundamental bass.

Harmonic meaning, then, resides in the integration of the vertical structure given by the fundamental bass into a chordal concatenation in combination with the temporal unfolding of the perfect cadence's voice-leading model. Rameau puts the matter in pragmatic terms: "[W]hen we give a progression to the part representing this undivided string [the fundamental bass], we can only make it proceed by those consonant intervals obtained from the first divisions of this string, and thus each sound will always harmonize with the sound preceding it."[18] As Thomas Christensen notes, the central claim of Rameau's conception of the passage of one chord to another is that "music is a coherent and intelligible succession of directed harmonies over real time that can be both defined and modeled with the fundamental bass."[19]

Christensen's observation suggests that for Rameau, to be intelligible (that is, to be subject to cognitive understanding), any and all successions must display at some level the conditions of the perfect cadence, with all the propulsion given by the particular interval progressions it features. It is not until Book 3 in the *Traité* that Rameau draws the broadest conclusion from this conceptualization, proposing that an ideal harmonic succession consists fundamentally of a series of interlocking evaded perfect cadences: "The succession (*suite*) of harmony is nothing other than a chain (*enchaînement*) of tonic notes and dominants, and we should understand the derivations of these notes well, so as to make sure that a chord always governs the chord that follows it."[20] The paradigm of harmonic progressivity, then, would be a succession of "dominants" moving by descending fifths to a final tonic.[21] The correspondence between this succession and a commonly used compositional idiom of mid-seventeenth to early-eighteenth-century French music—the succession of seventh chords moving by descending fifths through all diatonic scale degrees—can hardly be coincidental. Rameau, it would appear, continues to ascribe greater and more explicit significance to aspects of musical practice as he progressively elaborates his theoretical system.

At first, Rameau's idea seems to be merely an ancillary comment about the nature of harmonic progressivity. Upon further consideration, however, three fundamental and co-dependent notions of his theory emerge: harmonic connectedness, harmonic motion, and tonal hierarchy among chords. Of these, Rameau returns to the notions of connectedness and motion later in the *Traité* when discussing how to play the succession shown at the bottom in Example 3.2: "There exists such a great interconnection (*grand liaison*) within this succession of chords, which is the core of the most natural harmony." He then adds that this succession is "often picked up through practicing it rather than through learning it [intellectually]," a comment that bears on the relation of experience (i.e., figured-bass practice) and knowledge.[22] Knowledge, his remark about figured-bass practice suggests, resides in the systematic and principled account of the nature of harmonic connectedness, that is, in the explanation of what the mechanics of such harmonic motion are.[23] Furthermore, Rameau asserts here that harmonic continuity, coherence, and mobility depend upon the interconnection that might be said to exist among chords, a notion he terms *liaison en harmonie*.[24]

Integral to Rameau's model of harmonic progressivity, the notion of *liaison en harmonie* expresses both the voice-leading connection resulting from proper preparation of dissonances and the sense-making function of such dissonances in a *modulation* (i.e., how dissonances establish a hierarchy among chords that clarify and make of a tonal center a distinct goal in a musical passage).[25] To explain the concept, he draws an analogy between the intelligibility of a chord succession and that of words in a phrase; to his mind the connection among words (*liaison*) renders intelligible the sense of a phrase in the same way that the connection among chords expresses a well-constructed *Modulation*. Thus, if connectedness in general is essential for the harmonic coherence of a chordal succession, then dissonance in particular arises as an indispensable agent in its realization.

Rameau elaborates the role of dissonance in the *liaison en harmonie* by focusing on the mechanics of dissonance preparation and resolution founded in the perfect cadence model. He explains simply that a tone (*Son*) that forms a dissonance in a chord must appear in the chord that precedes it and that it must progress in a predetermined manner. The transformation of a tone from con-

Example 3.2
Progression of seventh chords and of their derivatives by inversion. Jean-Philippe Rameau, *Traité de l'harmonie* (Gossett, 408/*Traité*, 394).

sonance to dissonance as part of a *liaison,* he states, makes one desire its eventual resolution. This is most succinctly described in *Nouveau système:* "[N]ow, there is no better way to appreciate a *liaison en harmonie* than [to hear] a single tone which is used for two successive chords, and which at the same time makes one desire the tone, not to say the chord, that should immediately follow."[26]

In this context the trope of desire echoes commonplace allusions in contrapuntal theory to the effect that dissonance makes the arrival of consonance all the more pleasing. Indeed, the passage above would constitute merely a transposition to the harmonic realm of this commonplace were it not for the fact that Rameau's concept of implied dissonances calls upon the imagination to supply the connections among harmonies when none are explicitly present. Thus, the notion of *liaison* entails an abstract conception of subjective experience, a psychological intervention by the listener, if you will, indicating that the fundamental bass constitutes an incomplete representation of the melodic duties of the harmonic phenomenon. Thus, as a mechanism in Rameau's explanatory system, the notion of implied dissonances is presented as a foundational concept stipulating that chords must be connected by a predetermined voice leading that guarantees the harmonic coherence and tonal sense of a succession. That is, like the fundamental bass progressions it helps to clarify, *liaison en harmonie* both defines the motion of musical objects *and* conceptualizes what this motion might be for the listening subject. As a general principle underlying the logical, progressive, and meaningful concatenation of harmonies, *liaison en harmonie* offers an interesting point of departure for further investigation of the imaginary.

3.2. The Elusive Mechanics of Implication

Throughout the *Traité,* Rameau frequently invokes what I call implication, peppering explanations with verbs such as *entendre, imaginer, sous-entendre,* and *supposer.* As we have seen, even when removed, Rameau states, the *Basse fondamentale* "is always implied," guaranteeing that the harmonies "remain good." [27] The case that concerns us here, implied dissonance, plays a central role in clarifying the function of a chord in a *Modulation,* and at the same time constitutes the presumed agent for harmonic motion and interconnection: "All conclusions of a strain in which a tonic note is preceded by its dominant are called perfect cadences. This tonic note should always occur on the first beat of a measure, if the conclusion is to be felt; its dominant, which precedes it in this case, should always bear a seventh chord or at least a perfect chord, for the seventh can be implied here." [28] Rameau gives the impression that implication of the fundamental bass is a self-explanatory, transparent matter. By contrast, his discussion of implied dissonances is somewhat elliptical, which suggests that he might have sensed that they were less "precise," or even problematic. In any event, the agency of implication is left undefined, a compromising situation for the foundational tenets of the fundamental bass and the concept of harmonic progressivity, central contributions of Rameau's theoretical argument.

Rameau appears to have been aware of the potential misunderstanding of implication, providing an extended definition of *sous-entendre* in the "Table of Terms" preceding the *Traité:*

In music the terms "imply" (*sous-entendre*) and "suppose" (*supposer*) are considered almost synonymous; nevertheless their meanings are quite distinct. By the word "imply" (*sous-entendre*) it must be understood that the sounds to which it is applied can be heard in chords where they are not actually present. And equally, with regard to the fundamental sound, it is necessary to imagine (*il faut s'imaginer*) that it must be *heard below* the other sounds when one says that it is implied.[29]

Reception of Rameau's definition of implication is symptomatic of the ambiguity in the notion, with critics differing widely as to what he may have meant. After all, the expressions "can be heard" and "it is necessary to imagine that it must be heard" do little to clarify what the notion entails and at what stage in the act of listening it is supposed to take place. I shall consider three important discussions of implication by Thomas Christensen, Joel Lester, and Carl Dahlhaus.

Thomas Christensen explains Rameau's notion of harmonic motion in the *Traité* in a speculative way, by relating the idea to a seventeenth-century mechanical model. Motion—its causes, laws, and nature—becomes the focus of Rameau's theoretical efforts in Book 2, as he recognizes that music's temporal unfolding can be properly understood only when harmonic progressivity has been explained. Thus, in determining the cause of harmonic progressivity Rameau establishes a correlation between equilibrium and displacement, on the one hand, and consonance and dissonance, on the other (Book 2, Chapter 7). The dissonant seventh is the primal force and displacing agent in Rameau's tonal universe, a universe in which Cartesian mechanics underwrite the very idea of motion.[30] Using a kind of entropic idea of matter and motion, Rameau then describes the dissonant seventh as motion operating upon the matter of the chords. All that is missing in this analogy, then, is the musical equivalent of impact, and for this Rameau need not look too far. Music theory had already described in a memorable metaphor the rhythmic environment for the dissonant seventh as collision, or a syncopation.[31] A dynamic model of harmonic progressivity follows by which every nontonic harmony carries a seventh. One such seventh is the causative agent which, like colliding objects in the physical world, generates motion until a consonant *tonique* harmony brings music to a stop: "The ideal tonal motion in Rameau's *Traité*, then, would be a sequence of 'dominants' descending by a circle of fifths to the final tonic," Christensen writes, adding that "within a given mode, every non-tonic scale degree is ultimately analyzed by Rameau as a seventh chord, even if the seventh must be imputed by the performer or listener." He goes on to note that the notion of imputed dissonances constitutes a controversial element of Rameau's theory, given the Frenchman's proclivity for applying the idea to each and every progression.[32]

Christensen's explanation is appealing in that it provides both a conceptual framework and an intellectual genealogy of motion in Rameau's early theory. It leaves room, however, for further inquiry. For instance, to what extent does the imagination participate in the complex relation that exists between an event's empirically proven existence and its theoretical formulation? After all, why would Rameau, in articulating an analogy with, of all things, the physical world, seem so confident in conjuring the metaphysics of the imagination? To put it differently, why does Rameau seem so confident when he is metaphysically at his most daring?

In contrast to Christensen's speculative reading, Joel Lester interprets the notion of implied dissonances as a reflection of performance practice norms: "[Denis] Delair recommends that 'when perfect chords descend by fifth, the player should add a seventh after the first chord.'" Rameau, Lester further explains, develops Delair's "general suggestion" into "a general principle of harmonic progression," as he does when noting that if two successive chords bear a perfect chord, "the mind, desiring nothing more after such a chord, would be uncertain upon which of these two sounds to rest."[33] Lester finds Rameau's explanation of harmonic motion inadequate on three accounts. First, Rameau establishes a one-to-one relation between consonance and tonal stability. Any consonant chord is thus a potential tonic; if we know that a chord is not a conclusive tonic, "it is because we hear a dissonance . . . whether actual or implied."[34] Second, Rameau's model assumes hearing to be a short-range, point-to-point activity. Third, for some successions, the cadential model of harmonic progression does not work. (Lester gives the series of parallel sixth chords as a counterexample.)

Lester's observations, which highlight the incipiency of Rameau's system of "tonality," are all correct, but they too do not tell the whole story. In response to Lester's first and second points one might begin by asking, how does Rameau conceive the notion of tonal center in his early harmonic theory? Any answer would be tied in to the possibility that Rameau may have had a tonal compass with which to locate the direction of harmonic successions and the place of any given harmony within these successions. But such a compass was not available to him. On final analysis Rameau's notion of harmonic succession may be characterized as being tonally closed only in comparison to the succession by fifths through all degrees of the diatonic scale, the only case in which the final *tonique* is unambiguously defined as tonal center. Two closely related points can be made here. First, Rameau does conceive the overall succession as being expressive of the comprehensive harmonic structure of a key.[35] There is, in other words, no attempt to establish a correlation between scale degrees and fundamentals of harmonic scale steps, as no induction from cyclic progression to harmonic array built on the successive scale degrees is carried out. Progressions are thus measured in terms of harmony-to-harmony successions, tending to be, with the exception of the fifths cycle, open-ended. Scott Burnham has raised the issue, noting that Rameau's ideal in the *Traité* reflects a temporal conception of harmonic progression, one that adequately reflects Baroque music harmonic tendencies toward "a rhetoric of *Fortspinnung,* sequence, and elided cadences."[36] Second, the eventual arrival on *the* tonic is not prefigured by the harmonic succession at any given point. That is why all chords are potential tonics, provided that the preceding harmony is a *dominante-tonique.* As a center, a tonic is a secondary element of a succession, the primary tonal impetus residing within the logical progression of *dominantes* and the corresponding elements of fundamental-bass motion by descending fifth and dissonance resolution. In raising the second point, Lester, I believe, demands of Rameau's early theory that it provide a long-range approach to hearing that will not be available until *Génération harmonique* (1737), in which Rameau, under the influence of Newton's theory of gravity, shifts the focus from point-to-point concatenation of harmonies to a conception of tonic as a center of tonal attraction.[37]

Using Dahlhaus's concept of "floating tonic," according to which any chord not containing dissonance may become a tonic (though not necessarily a key center), Lester analyzes Rameau's trinity of chord quality, type of progression, and sense of key: "the quality of a chord suggests where that chord may move, while its actual movement in turn determines what its quality should be (*dominante, dominante-tonique, sous-dominante,* or *tonique*). The chord qualities and the progression determine the temporary tonic." But he adds that a simplistic dichotomy between "consonant tonics that are goals and dissonant chords that are mobile" is all that Rameau's notion of harmonic progression rests upon, remarking, furthermore, that "Rameau, the practical theorist and composer, knew that actual music can go on for long periods without any dissonances being present and still sound like it is not continuously coming to a halt."[38]

By invoking "the practical theorist and composer" Lester sets up an irreconcilable dichotomy between the speculative and practical in Rameau's work in which the practical musician "knows best," as it were. "Was Rameau speaking as a speculative theorist in adding these dissonances and chromatics, simply trying to explain the directionality of harmony? In other words, was he arguing that when we hear a triad that sounds mobile, its mobility is the result of dissonances that we add mentally because we know that the chord is not restful? Or did he mean that these dissonances should be played? Various evidence points to the latter."[39] Indeed, there exists compelling evidence to support Lester's claim that dissonances were "clearly meant to be performed" in Rameau's controversial revisions in *Nouveau système* of the figured bass in Corelli's Opus 5. There Rameau adds dissonances where there may be none in the score, and although clumsy and often unidiomatic, these added dissonances suggest an actual realization in practice. Yet there are passages in Rameau's own compositions from the 1720s and 1730s, such as that in Example 3.1, in which no dissonances appear during a prototypical succession of chords by descending fifth, in apparent contradiction of his own stipulations. Should actual dissonances be an unavoidable component of one such passage, Rameau, I believe, would have used them (sevenths could have been easily incorporated within the passage beginning in m. 53). That he did not suggests that the notion of implication served mainly a theoretical function, not a practical one. We may even speculate that Rameau may have been trying to prove his point not by using dissonances, but instead by assuming that we understand the transitiveness (and hence mobility and instability) of the passage in the absence of explicit *liaisons*. After all, progressions of this kind, more often than not, feature sevenths. The notation in the Corelli case, then, may also represent an ideal setting of that passage.

Lester's performance practice–oriented interpretation of implied dissonances

Example 3.3
Two editions (1730 and 1736) of G. P. Telemann, *Zwölf Pariser Quartette, 3. Sonata Prima.* Later edition contains added dissonances.

is not without precedent. A telling case appears in Example 3.3, which shows two editions (1730 and 1736) of the continuo from one of Telemann's Parisian Quartets. The 1736 Paris edition incorporates dissonances (in squares in the example), seemingly in response to Rameau's theoretical pronouncement.[40] I would argue, then, that Lester's critique and the editorial decisions manifest in the 1736 edition are based on making too close a correspondence between the imaginary as an *entity* with potential actuality and the imagination as an *operation* of understanding. These two ideas, though related, must be kept separate. An implied dissonance may have a corresponding version in actual compositional practice, so that it is easy to understand Rameau's claims (and his notation) as calls for realizing them. But, insofar as we can assess, the implied dissonance belongs to the realm of the imaginary and so operates as part of a theoretical explanation.

On final analysis Lester asserts that "Rameau's unconvincing insistence that all non-tonic harmonies have either actual or implied dissonances is all that is needed to demolish his argument."[41] Lester may be right in that Rameau's insistence reveals a certain anxiety in the Frenchman's attempts to overgeneralize the need for dissonance in all successions. As an example, one could cite the series of parallel dissonance-less six-three chords with which Lester both exemplifies Rameau's inconsistency in applying the notion of implied dissonances and contradicts the claim that dissonance is indispensable for the progressivity of all harmonic successions. Certainly this idiom appears frequently in the literature, and Rameau must accept idiomatic practice even if it reveals a fracture in his explanatory system. Rameau, however, is not alone in his uneasy acceptance of this particular succession.[42] We know now that, more than any other chordal succession, the series of sixth chords will resist harmonic interpretation throughout the history of tonal theory. In spite of the fact that it includes all chords available in a diatonic scale, there is no connection between its content and the root-position version of the chords, and so it is cast out as a nonharmonic phenomenon. A possible explanation, well known to advocates of linear harmony, considers this succession as being paradigmatically contrapuntal, that is, identifies it as a purely intervallic succession. The point, then, is that Rameau's failure to explain this succession does not "demolish" his otherwise insightful intuition that in the absence of a system of chordal scale degrees, the sense of either a temporary or a permanent tonic necessitates that we *conceptually* understand chords preceding the end of a strand as being *potentially* dissonant, even when they may not literally be so. Rameau's insistence cannot be separated, I believe, from the context of the conceptual necessities of his system. In fact, it is because he, the practical musician, may have had the general intuition that only certain chords in a strand are points of repose that he posits the ingenious notion of implied dissonances, however counterintuitive this may appear to us.

I concur with Carl Dahlhaus's assertion that "the recourse to imagined dissonances should be understood as a speculative hypothesis, not as a description of musical reality." In a sober analysis of this difficult issue, Dahlhaus goes on to state that the implied dissonances are not to be "jointly heard," by which he means that they are not to be part of the real-time experience of music. Rather, he argues, they "need only be taken into consideration during analysis," adding later that "it [the notion of implied dissonances] appears as a speculative hypothesis meant to explain *why* they [triads] cohere." But Dahlhaus, too, has difficulty disengaging experience from speculation, stating that the "tacitly implied dissonances" may be "simultaneously conceived," by which he means that they may be part of an actual experience of music.[43] The "speculative hypothesis" of implied dissonances, it turns out, is highly mobile, surreptitiously displacing itself from analysis to some kind of "simultaneity" with phenomenological experience.

In the end, Dahlhaus does not settle the issue, although he hints at a plausible explanation when discussing the nature of essential dissonances in Kirnberger, a key figure in Rameau's reception in Germany. "Kirnberger," says Dahlhaus, "underestimates that the category of harmony-peculiar dissonance is a function, and not a substantive concept—in the sense of Ernst Cassirer."[44] In his own exegesis of the fundamental bass, Dahlhaus argues for a functional role, referring to notions such as latency and possibility, but never equivocating the abstract with the "real." Dahlhaus's shortcoming is, then, that like other commentators he does not question the order of reality, or as he might say, the concreteness of music itself, be it a chord or the continuo. An uncomfortable polarity between the real and the nonreal emerges in which the latter is believed to be the less dependable element in the binarism. This belief reflects the suspicion with which Western epistemology has long held the imaginary and the imagination, on the one hand, and how it has valorized the real, on the other. And although it seems commonsensical, closer examination of this belief will find it to be plagued by a myriad of internal contradictions and to be supported by a misplaced reliance on the abilities of one sense (sight) over all others. This will become apparent in the following overview of the epistemology of the imagination in Plato and Aristotle.

3.3. The Imaginary and the Imagination in Epistemology: Plato and Aristotle

At the root of the problematics of the imagination lie competing notions of immanence and originality, on the one hand, and evanescence and secondariness, on the other. As the faculty that enables secondary presentations—or, more properly, re-presentations—the imagination becomes a disputed faculty of human cognition. This is first thematized in Plato's dualistic epistemology, which focuses on the nature of imaginary phenomena.

In contrast to the immutable universe of ideas, Plato proposes the existence of a realm of images, sensory impressions, and shadows. One universe is intelligible, the other empirical and sensorial. The former contains the archetypes according to which the visible objects we commonly associate with reality are formed by means of either imitation (*mimêsis*) or participation (*methexis*), processes that predetermine the secondariness of the empirical and the sensible. It is to this secondary, evanescent realm that *phantasia* belongs.[45]

In the *Republic* (ix), *phantasia* comes uninvited into epistemology, as it were, considered only so that we can ward off its shadowy designs. Earlier, however, in the memorable simile of the line (*Republic*, vi), *phantasia* figures prominently. Plato discusses the relation between the intelligible and the sensorial orders, setting up four hierarchically organized ontological domains and four corresponding epistemological operations. The intelligible realm includes the region of science—which goes beyond sensorial elements and includes most prototypically mathematical postulates—and the highest level, the universe of ideas (*eidos*)—accessible to pure reason (*logos*) without any intervention whatsoever of sensorial vision or empirical experience. The latter is accessible by means of intelligence (*noêsis*), the former by discursive thinking (*dianoia*). The sensorial order also has two levels. Closest to the border separating the two realms are those objects that are directly visible (e.g., living beings and things).[46] Farthest from it are those which are only indirectly visible (e.g., shadows and images of living beings and things). The sensorial order is accessible by means of belief (*pistis*), in the case of the directly visible, and by means of imagination (*eikasia*), in the case of the indirectly visible.[47]

As epistemological operations, belief and imagination offer a weak scaffold to the edifice of knowledge when compared to the solid foundation provided by knowledge of ideas and the lesser but cognitively reliable operations of discursive thinking. In terms of ontological status, the indirectly visible has almost none. As Plato reminds us in the celebrated allegory of the cave, images are secondhand impressions, shadowy reflections that keep us in the dark, preventing us from being able to "see" the real world; *phantasia*, which relies on images, is classified as the lowest form of being.

Tightly constructed though his arguments may seem, in the end Plato cannot keep images out of his model for knowledge. He conspicuously allows images for their unique capabilities in helping to outline mathematical postulates:

> [A]lthough they [students of geometry and calculation] use visible figures and make claims about them, their thought is not directed to them but to those other things that they are like. . . . These figures that they make and draw, of which shadows and reflections in water are images, they now in turn use as images, in seeking to see those others themselves that one cannot see except by means of the eye of reason.[48]

In this brief concession the imagination comes into contact with intelligence (*noêsis*), since Plato recognizes that abstract thought is not possible in the absence of images. Images are, in other words, necessary components of the operations of discursive thinking, in particular, and of the intellect, in general.[49] But any suggestion that there might exist a series of inductive inferences originating in sensorial experience and at play in the pursuit of the ultimate level of intellection would be mistaken. Plato sets a strict limit on where images may infiltrate the highest intelligible realm. Imagination and intellection are thus uneasy accomplices. Images, if they are to be of the higher type, have to be suprasensible, corresponding as they must to the transparent images of the mind's eye, eternal, immutable, and self-contained, and not to those available to the body's eye, temporary and mutable.[50] This higher-type image, furthermore, is not merely a reproduction or a copy; it is rather the product of a reduction to atemporal postulates of images distinct from those forming part of the sensorial domain. In an important notion for later epistemological systems, the Platonic Idea remains prehypothetical.

In the *Philebus* Plato discusses the notion of the reproductive imagination in the context of memory, perception, and phantasy. A twofold scheme results in which perception is conceived as presentative imagination, on the one hand, and memory and phantasy are conceived as reproductive imagination, on the other. This reproductive imagination is close to the highest mental functions, but not identical to them, and on final analysis (in the *Timaeus*) the human imagination remains tied to laws of matter and so, again, can never aspire to the level of the Idea.

With its demands for immanence and immutability, Plato's exacting epistemology automatically casts out the ephemeral world of sensations which serves as source for the imaginary. Furthermore, the very act of vision in human reality and experience is defined as being intrinsically insufficient, a distorting obstacle to truth. It is no surprise that metaphors of images and shadows are used to describe what the body's eye can see. The problem is compounded by Plato's insistence on conflating adjectives with nouns, with the result that the imaginary is bound to the imagination; this also means that ontology becomes entangled with epistemology. In the end, the material form of the imaginary is secondary to a reality existing elsewhere (i.e., the Idea or scientific formulations). At stake remains the very definition of the real, for as Plato argues, as long as we insist on hanging onto our immediate world we shall remain blind to the realities hidden there.

In the course of thinking through the question of imagination Plato outlines the two main issues concerning the relation between the knowledge afforded by sensible experience and by pure thinking. First, the transcendental status of the Idea means that the imagination, at whatever cognitive level (i.e., *eikasia* or *dianoia*), and the imaginary, on whichever ontological order (i.e., visual or scientific images), are relegated to secondary status. Second, the restricted role he allows images manages to open a space that, however narrow, enables the imagination to find a place among other mental powers and to gain a bearing in the problem of knowledge. These issues will inform other philosophical attempts to define the nature of the imaginary and the peculiar cognitive capacity of humans that will be named the imagination.

It is Aristotle who, in the psychology outlined in *De Anima*, first locates the imagination explicitly as part of human intellection.[51] The soul, he claims, features a tripartite arrangement: vegetative, sensorial, and intellectual. The sensorial faculty is responsible for motion and sensation. Responsible for thinking, the intellectual faculty is subdivided into passive (i.e., receptive) and active (i.e., productive). The passive intellect constitutes a gateway for the sensorial part of the soul, functioning as a receptacle for memories, perceptions, and sensations.

With this outline in place, Aristotle is able to include sensible experience as part of the broad domain of knowledge. Sensorial experience makes possible the phenomenal awareness of things, an awareness which becomes, so to speak, the content fueling the doings of the passive intellect. Now, this awareness does not belong to a pure intellectual domain, for the intellect remains the sole property of the cognitive faculty that, in contrast to the sensitive faculty, operates at the level of abstraction, principles, and universal causes.[52]

By including sensorial awareness as a form of cognitively available reality, Aristotle cleverly shifts the Platonic emphasis on the *content* of the imaginary toward a view of it as a temporal *process* occurring within the human soul, by which sensory impressions are both retained and re-presented.[53] He focuses, in other words, on the *imagination*, and less so on the *imaginary*. Hereby the imagination emerges as a uniquely human capacity to transform sense perception into an intellectualized sensation: that is, the imagination interprets the data of sense perception, and as such functions in the manner of a conduit between the sensorial and intellectual faculties. The product of this interaction constitutes a new kind of knowledge, what might be termed sensorial cognition.

Perception is itself reconfigured. Aristotle divides perception into two types corresponding to the external and internal senses. The imagination belongs to the internal senses, which also include memory and the common senses (i.e., combinations of the external senses of sight, hearing, and so forth). In contrast to the common senses, which may produce a composite image of an object known through direct perception, the imagination, like memory, does not require the object to be present. Consequently, the imaginary representation of an object is, like a phantasm, not really there.[54] An important caveat, then, is that the imagination requires a prior sensible experience of an object, and that in consequence its imaginary objects (e.g., mental representations) are ultimately derivative of sensory perception. Two issues follow from this: (1) the Aristotelian imagination is reproductive in that it produces a kind of weakened sensation; (2) given its reproductive nature, the powers of imagination are intimately connected to reminiscence. (Memory, Aristotle reminds us, subsists on the persistence of images.)

The notion that the imagination is essentially reproductive carries two of the most important repercussions for future philosophical explanations of the imaginary: (1) that it is temporally secondary to some prior reality or experience, and (2) that its ontological status is indeterminate. These Aristotelian tenets will resurface in Hobbes's celebrated claim that "all fancies [imaginings] are motions within us, relics of those made in sense."[55] The priority Hobbes grants sense perception obscures the fundamental role that Aristotelian epistemology ascribes to the imagination. Nowhere is this role more clearly stated than when Aristotle affirms that "for the thinking soul images take the place of direct impressions . . . and for this reason the soul never thinks without phantasms." Aristotle releases the imagination from its moorings in sense perception, securing for it a place in intellectual activity. Key here is his turn toward thinking, that is, to an intrinsically temporal human activity.[56] Hobbes's claim, it follows, rings hollow in the present context, for Aristotle focuses on how the imagination makes possible thought, and not on the fact that the "relics" (images, memories, etc.) are by necessity derivative or cognitively unreliable. Images become cognitively processed sensations, in an apparent trade-off in which the loss of immediacy in sensation represents a gain for cognition with the assistance of the imagination. Philosophy must then contend with Aristotle's notion that sense perception must be negotiated in a temporal span other than that in which it occurs. In a way, the immediacy of sense perception does not give intellection space for reflection.[57] The imaginary is the fruit of that reflection. In the end, Aristotle's conception of the imagination asserts that direct impressions must become representations in order for them to be the subject of intellection.

Hobbes's use of the term "fancies" speaks to a problematic association the imaginary has with prior experiences, perceptions, and sensations, one closely tied to dreams. Briefly, in their ability to lead the mind astray, dreams become the shadowy side of Aristotle's imagination, an obscure activity of the soul that humans must guard against.[58] Furthermore, Hobbes's expression "within us" highlights the possibility that the imagination may be an agent for radical subjectivity. Post-Aristotelian philosophy had viewed the problem positively with Augustine's introduction of the "combinatory imagination" by which he proposed that the imagination has the ability to bear images or thoughts that no single faculty or sense by itself can.[59] The combinatory imagination established an important relationship between imagination and intentionality; the human mind, Augustine recognized, possesses the ability to manipulate willfully the imagination to produce an imaginary to suit many purposes, cognitive or creative.

Our survey of Aristotle's discussion of the imagination and the imaginary leaves us with a family of concepts that grant to the imagination near-Protean capacities for productive knowledge and deception. There emerge, however, three main issues from his seminal work which, if in no way conclusive, will inform further discussion of the imagination: (1) Attempts to secure for the imaginary a secure ontological foundation seem doomed to failure. The imaginary remains immersed in a radical indeterminacy, and it would not be an exaggeration to say that its peculiar materiality, such as it is, will prove a most undisciplinable element among human sensitive and cognitive capacities. The imaginary will resist attempts to circumscribe it within paradigmatic physiognomies. In consequence, propositional claims about the imaginary fall short of the adequacy criteria of indubitable existence. Nonetheless, Aristotle posits that the ontology of the imaginary ought not to be cast in dual opposition against the real and the feigned. (2) Aristotle skirts the problem of the imaginary's ontological instability by emphasizing the imagination as intellectual activity and thus turning away from Plato's adjective/noun ascriptions to the imaginary toward the verb form, that is, from *eikôn* (image) to *eikazô* (to make like). He assigns the imagination its own epistemological domain, which, however ungraspable, can, as Hume will pronounce, act as a "completing power." (3) The imagination becomes participatory.[60] This shift leads to a drawing together of thinking subject and object or sensation thought. But because Aristotle develops neither a theory of subjectivity nor a theory of consciousness, the imagination will remain isolated from the particular interaction between the subject and the activity of representation.

We may at this point provisionally compare the positions on the imagination by the philosophical tradition of Plato and Aristotle to the critiques of implied tones by Dahlhaus and Lester. For instance, Dahlhaus's interpretation of implied dissonance as a *Funktionsbegriff* might be said to follow the Aristotelian conception of the imagination as activity. By contrast, Lester's calls for the concrete acoustical expression of implied dissonances reflect an attempt to attenuate the disruptive force of the imaginary, understood as the not-real. Furthermore, echoing Plato's classification of the imaginary within the shadowy world of the indirectly visible, Lester seeks to bring the implied dissonances into the realm of the directly "audible." The move, for Lester, must be away from the metaphysical uncertainty (or even falsity) that characterizes one side of the imaginary.

As we moved from antiquity to the present day, our discussion of the imagination and the imaginary has suggested how and why the stakes for cognitive claims made by appeal to the power of the imagination have been so high. At best, such claims have contended with the rectifying attempts by some to anchor the ontological instability of the imaginary onto some concrete, empirically verifiable reality; at worst, these rectifying attempts may be seen as a wholesale dismissal of the imaginary. Narrowing our focus to Rameau's more immediate intellectual background, that of seventeenth-century philosophy, we find a more complex picture, however, particularly when we consider the role played in his theory by the binary semiotics we saw at work in Descartes (Chapter 2). We now return to Rameau (by way of Descartes), taking a close look at the representational constraints he faces when formulating the semiotics of the fundamental bass. Once this semiotics is clarified, the imagination is taken up again to conclude this chapter.

3.4. Compound Representation: The Ternary Semiotics of the Fundamental Bass

We have seen in Chapter 2 how the semiotic protocols through which the analysis of measurement and order represents its object sanction a transparent relation between signifier and signified. This transparence is cognitively upheld by the "fact" that representation is the product of subjective reflection, recorded linguistically by consciousness. Representation and consciousness fold onto one another, and so the question of how consciousness has the capacity to form representations is pointless, for all consciousness is intrinsically representative. Accordingly, representation constitutes the unmediated *form* of the subject's consciousness, not the *object* that gives form to consciousness. In consequence, nothing precedes or prefigures representation. At that moment in the early eighteenth century in which Rameau was to begin his trying efforts to theorize harmony, the conditions were ripe indeed for the rise of the subject—defined as self-consciousness—to unprecedented prominence as the main protagonist of human negotiations of music. Joining this emerging subject are the new cognitive-linguistic conquests of what we have been calling classical semiotics, after Foucault. Or so we may think. After all, why is it that Rameau, a rightful heir to this semiotics, appeals to the ambiguous, even anonymous, agency of implication? And why is it that, armed as he would have been with the powerful logic of Port-Royal grammar, he avoids giving to the predicate of "implication" an explicit subject when he says that the "fundamental bass is implied"?[61] To answer these questions we need to examine the semiotic coordinates at which Rameau positions the fundamental bass itself.

Descartes's concept of intuition and its associated semiotics would seem to have provided the revolutionary theoretical argument of Rameau with a secure cognitive enclosure. Accordingly, Rameau's conception of harmonies as unitary entities represented by the fundamental bass stands for an intuition of the subject, that is, a cognitive act of grasping a multiplicity of sounds as one.[62] In Book 1 of the *Traité*, analysis of the *son fondamentale* provides the terms that define the fundamental bass, the elements that constitute it (i.e., the sounds of a chord), and the relationship between these sounds and the fundamental bass. And as part of a semiotic system that, like intuition, is self-contained, the fundamental bass constitutes a sign insofar as it unmediatedly represents (i.e., stands for) the series of inferences that result from the linear analysis of the fundamental sound into the *accord parfait*.

According to this reading, the analysis and eventual synthesis of the fundamental sound into the fundamental bass would parallel Descartes's account of intuition in Rule 3. The tight correspondence between, on the one hand, Cartesian intuition and the system of representation that it entails and, on the other, Rameau's conception of harmony and its associated semiotics ideally manifests the cohesiveness in the binary foundation of classical representation. Further analysis, however, reveals that vestiges of musical practice in the fundamental bass render opaque the otherwise transparent representation of intuition.

Foucault describes three variables in the signifier-to-signified relation in the classical conception of the sign: (1) the certainty of relation (whether a sign is accurate or probable), (2) the type of relation (whether a sign belongs to the whole it denotes or is separate from it), (3) the origin of relation (whether the sign is natural or conventional).[63] In all three variables, probability, separatedness, and conventionality are the favored terms, reflecting the privileged status of human agency in the knowledge of the world and its representation.

Under the first variable the fundamental bass constitutes a probable sign, since at the time of the *Traité* there is no clear and evident proof that it can denote the totality of sounds that Rameau claims it represents.[64] Under the second variable the fundamental bass, as signifier, holds a metonymical relationship with a harmony, as signified; that is, the fundamental bass is a part of the whole that represents an essential aspect of the whole (i.e., its foundation in a natural order). It would seem as though this metonymy simultaneously plays a semiotic function *and* expresses the ontological continuity between fundamental bass and *accord*. This ambiguity, which might be semiotically disruptive, is only apparent. "In order to function," Foucault writes, "the sign must be simultaneously an insertion in that which it signifies and also distinct from it."[65] As an object of knowledge, the fundamental bass is indeed an element of perception, but it is also differentiated from the total impression and given epistemological priority over the total impression by means of analysis. Out of this differentiation arises the fundamental bass as a separate sign (in Foucault's typology), independent from the intervallic aggregate it expresses, and superior, in fact, to this aggregate. The fundamental bass represents an intuition, a radically distinct expression—as sign—from that ontological entity which it designates, the chord.

Matters become more complex under the third variable. Given that traces of musical practice (i.e., its appearance as musical notation) and cognitive abstraction (i.e., its status as intuition) intermingle in the fundamental bass, the origin of the relation of signifier to signified cannot be said to be either natural or conventional. More specifically, three issues arise: (1) Rameau advances the fundamental bass as a transparent representation of nature's organization and regulation of harmony; (2) this transparent representation is carried out unmediatedly—hence naturally—by the subject's intuition; (3) Rameau defers to the conventional code of musical notation to express this representation.

In connection with the first two issues we must note that given the transposition of things from an order of being to an order of knowledge, the subject's intuition forms an unbroken continuation of nature, not simply a medium for the apprehension of principles that reside in nature. In this important sense the "reduction to natural principles" adduced by Rameau's title corresponds in equal measure to the fact that the sounds making up a major triad reside in nature and are given in the *son fondamentale,* and to the fact that this realization is the result of analysis by the subject.[66]

The third issue concerns what Allan Keiler, discussing the uneasy relation between musical notation and the fundamental bass, believes to be the result of Rameau's use of "analytical tools not suitable or not properly clarified in the new analytical context."[67] Keiler explores two questions: (1) how does Rameau use musical notation? and (2) what does he aim to represent? First, Rameau's use of musical notation to describe music constitutes a metalinguistic deployment: musical notation acquires the character of paraphrase, an analytical clarification or expansion from which generalizations can be made about chord inversion, chord progression, and dissonance treatment.[68] It is erroneous, Keiler reminds us, to interpret Rameau's notation itself as though it were music. For instance, when Rameau, in the case of *double emploi,* gives two fundamental bass notes to a single bass note in the continuo, the resulting rhythmic distortion does not substitute a composer's intention. Second, according to Keiler, Rameau confuses the representation of a structural ambiguity in the way a chord relates to what precedes it and what follows it and the representation of this ambiguity as perceived by a hearer, "which is to revise hypothetical readings of the input as he receives more information."[69] The semiotic residuum here is found in the cognitive discrepancy between an objective representation of structure and a perception of this structure as it moves to and from other structures. The tension, in any case, results from superimposing within the same sign (e.g., the fundamental bass) a phenomenological perspective onto a structural one.

With characteristic accuracy Keiler's interpretation diagnoses the metalinguistic symptom afflicting Rameau's representation of harmonic progressivity. But it overlooks a crucial historical question: why would Rameau choose to use a notation so susceptible to misunderstanding? Part of the answer lies in the assumption Rameau makes about the solid semiotic foundation of the fundamental bass as a representation of chordal structure. Conceived as intuition, we have seen, the fundamental bass serves a dual function as representation of objective and subjective domains, in accordance with classical epistemological protocols. What is misunderstood, then, is the semiotic function of the musical notation. Keiler concludes that Rameau's predicament results from a divergence between theoretical awareness and the language used to represent such awareness: "An analytic language can very often be pressed into the service of representing new attitudes and novel solutions for which the language was never intended."[70] He suggests that Rameau's theory of harmony appears at a "preparadigmatic" moment, a historical moment in which, according to Thomas Kuhn, knowledge exists in unmarked form but no controlling metaphor has yet emerged that might permit the formulation of theoretical generalizations and the articulation of a coherent vocabulary through which to express these generalizations.[71] Keiler's Kuhnian interpretation of history means that the tension between the conventional and the natural sign might be seen to belong to the sociology of semiotics: as a conventional code, musical notation carries signifying duties determined by a community of users made up of composers, performers, and theorists. We may consider, for instance, how to the community of figured-bass users the interval count of figured-bass notation would have expressed a natural relation between signifier and signified; that is, in their eyes, hands, ears, and minds, what one saw is what one played and heard, no more and no less.[72] In contrast, for this community the fundamental bass would have been emblematic of the potential semiotic excesses (i.e., arbitrariness) of conventional signs, particularly at those moments in which it does not coincide with the continuo or, worse yet, where it indicates something not "in the music." In this shift the defamiliarization of musical notation in its new guise as fundamental bass characterizes two phenomena associated with semiotic reinscriptions: (1) a sign traditionally associated with one presumably unfigural function comes to play a role as a trope (in this case a metonymy), and (2) this new role is met with resistance.

The issue intersects also with something akin to epistemological capital (to adapt Pierre Bordieu's useful terminology), for if the "natural" signs of the figured bass help to preserve the conceptual heritage of a community of musicians, semiotic changes would likely hold the potential that their knowledge may become attenuated, if not altogether extinct. Rameau claims the opposite; namely, that the conventional codes of figured-bass notation obscure the principles of nature and manifest intuitionless, and therefore crude, representations.[73] For example, he believes that by having a particular interval migrate indiscriminately from sonority to sonority—which is how figured-bass manuals most often organize the presentation of chords—figured-bass practitioners indulge in the worst kind of dispersive knowledge (his critique of this feature of figured-bass manuals is particularly strong in Book 4 of the *Traité*). From this perspective the fundamental bass is an attempt to arrest the raving polysemy of figured-bass representation, which Rameau does by grounding representation in the double order of nature and the subject's intuition. In the final analysis the fundamental bass holds a natural relation to its origin while depending upon a conventional code for its expression. This duplicity acquires particular force in the semiotic domain of implied dissonances.

In the case of implied dissonances we find two types of signs superimposed: the fundamental bass and figured-bass numerals. We may easily distinguish Rameau's representation of implied dissonances by comparison with Foucault's idea of "duplicated representation" in classical semiotics (the idea, again, refers to the unquestionable capacity of the sign to unite signifier to signified and therefore paradigmatically to represent the act of representing). The representation of implied dissonances suggests the opposite from classical representation: not only is one signifier (e.g., 7) unable to represent a clear and evident signified (e.g., an implied dissonance), but also its very presence foregrounds the inadequacy of another, supposedly self-sufficient, sign, the fundamental bass, to represent in the plenitude guaranteed by classical semiotics. This particular semiotic quandary entails what I will term *compound representation*.

I am not the first to discuss the incompleteness of Rameau's semiotic system. Brian Hyer explains the notion of implied dissonances by appeal to Derrida's logic of the "supplement" and to the critique of the metaphysics of presence.[74] Hyer points out that implied dissonances are necessary supplements to Rameau's system of three main chord functions (*tonique, dominante,* and from the time of the *Nouveau système* on, *sous-dominante*) in order to clarify their status as signs and in relation to one another. Without "supplemental dissonances" (Hyer's term) "the dominant and subdominant signifiers would amount to no more than ambiguous triads, incapable of signifying anything on their own."[75] Most problematic to Rameau's system is that the very center of a mode, the signifier tonic—an *accord parfait*—is signified only by the dissonances literally present or added to other perfect chords located either a fifth above the tonic (to which a seventh is added) or below (to which a sixth is added). Were it not for these "supplemental dissonances," the tonic would be an empty sign, wholly without functional meaning. In Hyer's reading, Rameau's chord types and the relations ascribed to them in the grammar of permissible progressions are characterized by a perpetual deferral of meaning. Tonics are signified by subdominants and dominants. Reciprocally, subdominants and dominants are themselves not self-sufficient because, in spite of their having been given individual characteristics in the supplemental dissonances, each always constitutes already a referral to the tonic.

Hyer's probing analysis highlights the nature of the relations between the chord types, moving away from their structural descriptions (i.e., as collections of consonant and dissonant intervals) as the basis of meaning. He proposes that these relations be understood in terms of desire: in the desire for dissonance resolution he perceives a parallel with the "yearning of the signifier for the signified." He frames supplemental dissonances as "the mechanism responsible for this desire," a mechanism that, moreover, depends ultimately on the human agency that ascribes to harmonies characters, ways of behaving, even speaking powers. Such characteristics, guaranteed in Rameau's system by the humble supplemental dissonances, encapsulate the human need to inscribe the aural in legible terms: "[F]or an aural inscription to be decipherable, it must bear some hint or trace of human intention, something obliging it to move to the tonic, and that something is a dissonance, a letter, a name."[76] Human intention, Hyer submits, finds expression in linguistic terms, prosopopoeia in this case, for we, he says, compulsively pass music "through the conceptual net of language" in our attempts to make sense of it.

Hyer's detailed poststructuralist methodology foregrounds the contingent nature of Rameau's theoretical language and the essentially discursive nature of music-theoretical entities. It does not, however, raise any questions about the radical indeterminacy of implication—Hyer refers to "a mechanism responsible for this desire"—or how desire might form part of the sign itself, particularly within the binary semiotics available to Rameau. Most significantly, although Hyer refers to the fact that "the intuitions of tonics and dominants, not to mention sub-dominants, were intuitions that Rameau had to encourage in listeners," he pays no heed to the epistemology of such intuitions beyond his deconstructive exegesis. It remains a puzzle that these supplemental dissonances have a questionable ontological status but somehow are key to the functioning of the theory of harmonic progression.

To supplement Hyer's account of "human intention," it will be necessary to examine the intervention of the subject in the binary structure of classical representation. My thesis is that this intervention carries two significant consequences: (1) the vaunted powers of the classical sign are uniquely challenged by the representation of harmonies in motion, and (2) the representation of this motion requires that we reconfigure our understanding of the classical sign from a binary structure to a ternary structure.

The challenge for Rameau is to open up a conceptual space for the question of temporal perception of harmonic progressivity by the listener in the narrow confines of the classical sign, and, moreover, to do so within a binary semiotics which is ideally suited to represent things objectively. This objectivity, we remember, results from an analysis of measure and order in which the presence of the very subject carrying out the analysis is abrogated. Three points must be considered: (1) whether the recognition of a subject (Keiler's "hearer," Hyer's "listener") as active participant in the cognitive process by which harmonies are said to connect to one another requires that the very conception of the Cartesian subject as a self-effacing presence in representation be revised; (2) whether the insertion of the subject in the process of representation pries open the closed binary structure of the classical sign, revealing the possibility of a ternary arrangement; (3) whether this new arrangement is closely tied to the consideration of time in music, which in itself demands a revision of the concept of Cartesian intuition.

First, implied dissonances mark the irruption of relational thinking into music theory, that is, thinking prompted by the emergence of harmony as the preeminent structural determinant in music. This relational thinking lies outside of the representation of intuition provided by the fundamental bass and is dependent upon the perceiver, a point made by Hyer's notions of "desire" and "human intention." Over and above this, we may think of this phenomenon as a reinsertion of an explicit subject into the transcendental and reductive process of intuition. Accordingly, insofar as the logic of the supplement operates in the notion of implication, it does so by planting human consciousness right in the middle of the binary semiotic system—that is, from a more localized semiotic perspective, the supplemental agency is located not in the signifier of the figure "7," for instance, but in the agency of mental consciousness that must now intuit which harmonies are to be considered unstable in spite of their apparent intervallic stability as triads (as in Example 3.1) and which are not. The subject's agency provides the missing grammatical element, so to speak, that is absent when a series of harmonies share identical structural descriptions as triads.

Second, the unmediated relationship between signifier and signified in the binary semiotics of classical representation does not function equally well in all domains. In the case of harmonic progressivity, the subject mediates the signifier-to-signified relation. Hence there are three terms in the representation of harmonic progression: the signifier (i.e., the compound representation of fundamental and figured bass), the signified harmony that is said to move, and the subjective agency that wills this motion. In fact, as part of a reconfiguration of the protocols of classical semiotics, the implied dissonance may not need to be explained as a compound representation juxtaposing natural and conventional signs. That is to say, the figure by which it is expressed does not constitute a sign in the way the fundamental bass does. The reason for this is that it designates neither a dissonance nor the act of representation; instead, it designates the presence of the subject in the act of representation. It is as though the representation inserts agency into intuition. The move here is from a binary and unmediated semiotics to a ternary and mediated semiotics in which the subject emerges as an equal term.

Third, the concept of transcendental intuition subtending binary representation necessarily integrates the temporal domain into its virtual space of simultaneity. This constitutes, in essence, a linearization of the otherwise spatial structure of classical analysis. But it is not simply that the analytical steps leading to intuition, outlined in Rule 7 of *Rules,* are traversed backwards (such a process would lead to a state of cognitive want, in classical epistemology). More precisely, this linearization deals with the successive ordering of simple natures (e.g., intuitions), establishing the way they relate to one another. This entails giving continuity to that which analysis renders discontinuous, which, as Foucault notes, "implies . . . a certain power of the imagination that renders apparent what is not, but makes possible, by this very fact, the revelation of that continuity."[77] Just as grammar emerges as the science of the signs through which humans group individual perceptions and pattern their thought, the theory of harmony emerges as a science (i.e., knowledge) of the progressive combination of chords individually perceived. Put another way, the verticality of intuition is rendered horizontal when Rameau unfolds the intuition of sound (i.e., a single harmony founded on an acoustical phenomenon) into a new kind of intuition of music (i.e., harmonies combined in their succession). This new kind of intuition is informed not by the analysis of measure and order, not by hearing deep inside the fundamental sound the murmur of nature, but by bringing musical experience, or practice as it is often called, to bear in the understanding of music. This new intuition entails an imaginary recreation of conditions arising in musical situations in which explicit dissonant content is the norm rather than the exception. These situations intersect with the systematization of Rameau's theory and with the semiotics of classical representation.

We witness here a move from the epistemology of sound toward the epistemology of music.[78] Sound fits within the space of Cartesian intuition, music does not. Although I think that the call for implied dissonances invokes an intuition, it is an intuition unlike that guaranteed by Descartes's transcendental subject. Rather, it is an intuition born out of an empirical subject: Rameau. I mean Rameau in his dimension as a composer and performer with vast knowledge of the chordal practices of his contemporaries and predecessors. And, so, the vicissitudes of musical practice reenter our argument. The call for implied dissonances, which we initially considered as a blatant disregard for musical reality, results in fact from a process of reconfiguring features of musical practice itself: the perfect cadence and sequential progressions as cadences writ large. This process of reconfiguration I will term *counterinduction*. Counterinduction, in turn, functions with the help of the imagination and the imaginary, to which we now return.

3.5. Imagination and Counterinduction, or the Practice of Theory

The imagination holds a peculiar place in seventeenth-century epistemology, not least because of its multifarious applications. Descartes's thought exemplifies this situation particularly well. We saw in Chapter 2 how Descartes inherits a productive conception of the imagination from Aristotle. Early in his work we learned that Descartes ascribes to the imagination unheard-of cognitive functions. In both his analysis of the perception of time in music and his use of images to represent proportions, the imagination is advanced as nothing less than the process of consciousness and thought itself. Further, I argued that by moving the imagination to the forefront of intellection and perception, Descartes takes a decisive step toward articulating a subjectivity defined largely by the agency of the perceiver in shaping the object of perception. This process, I suggested, is inseparable from the fundamental distinction between subject and object which will govern claims of (and disputes about) epistemology after Descartes, although it is true that within the metaphysics of his later thought (e.g., the *Meditations*), Descartes will famously demote the imagination because it is seen as an extension of sensorial perception and can be conducive to self-deception.

Chameleon-like, the imagination emerges from under a reason-driven epistemology in various guises: it encompasses fantasies in which self-contained, delusory worlds may be created; it can conjure up images of objects and of experiences which can then be analyzed and modeled, and about which generalizations can be made; and, through its powers, absence can be summoned into presence. At once unavoidable and refractory, no single definition can circumscribe its domain. As a creative endeavor it deals with fictions, dreams, and possibly hallucinations. As a modeling operation it mediates between perception and ideas. As an invocatory power it facilitates memory and representation. It may be more fruitful therefore to acknowledge that to some seventeenth-century philosophers no concept mediates what is seen as a complex relation between sense and intellect more effectively than the imagination (one could superimpose the "dialectics of theory and practice," or perception and conception onto this scheme). In the words of Francis Bacon,

> It is true indeed that the imagination performs the office of an agent or messenger or proctor in both provinces, both the judicial and the ministerial. For sense sends all kinds of images over to imagination for reason to judge of; and reason again when it has made its judgement and selection, sends them over to imagination before the decree be put in execution. For voluntary motion is ever preceded and incited by imagination; so that imagination is a common instrument to both— reason and will; saving that this Janus of imagination has two different faces; for the face towards reason has the print of Truth, and the face towards action has the print of Good; which nevertheless are faces—*quales decet esse sororum* [such as sisters' faces should be].[79]

Understood as a mediator between sense and intellect, the imagination participates in a triadic relationship, providing an alternative to the binary model of classical representation.[80] In this triadic relationship the imagination must be understood as an operation (i.e., something that is done, an activity), and the imaginary as an evident or visual realization of this operation rather than as an entity that opposes the real (or the sensed). Bacon's colorful analogy itself presents the imagination as an active participant of a fundamental cognitive process, a mobilizer of particular, if peculiar, cognitive powers.[81]

In however many guises it may have appeared at this point in history, the imagination ceased to pass for an ontologically stable concept; philosophy was quick to recognize this and relented in trying to give it an ontological foundation. In our time Wolfgang Iser summarizes the difficulties inherent in dealing with the imagination by identifying three predominant paradigms in the history of its reception: (1) the *foundational discourses* which attempt primarily to define the imaginary in relation to something that belongs to the real; (2) the view that it constitutes a *combinatory activity* that ameliorates deficiencies of sensorial experience and overreaches the bounds of reason; (3) its status as a *faculty.*[82]

Foucault attributes to the imagination in the classical episteme the power to complement representation by making it responsible for the linking of individual impressions, which means that representation depends on the possibility of imaginative recall given *by* and *in* the imagination: this happens, for instance, in the intuition-driven reduction and representation of temporal experience in the *Compendium*. Similarly Iser wonders "whether the imagination was always invoked when the reason had reached its limits, or whether imagination needed deficiencies in order to come into operation."[83] One such deficiency exists in epistemology's failure to satisfactorily account for the domain of experience. And so when, beginning in the seventeenth century, epistemology aspires to incorporate this domain, claims about knowledge have to invoke the imagination. This appeal too carries connotations for an emerging subject. "With the self-fashioning of the subject," writes Iser, "the imagination advanced to the head of the faculty hierarchy."[84] The intense interest in the imagination in the seventeenth century provides a perfect occasion for an inquiry into its practical deployment. For, as I have suggested, one may superimpose the binary theory/practice onto the imaginary/real opposition. Descartes himself takes this approach in his self-described scientific fable *Le monde* (1632).[85] There we witness an extravagant liaison between reason and the imagination.

Le monde is a treatise in physics and light advancing a theory of the origins and workings of the solar system.[86] *Le monde* is unique for the way in which Descartes casts his formulations in the manner of a fable: "Allow your thought for a little while to go out beyond this world, in order to come to see another completely new one, which I will cause to be born in its presence in imaginary spaces."[87] The experiment is a curious one. There, in the name of knowledge, Descartes deploys the imagination as a cognitive medium that both enables and sanctions the fabrication of an imaginary world parallel to our own. Most significantly, he elevates the imaginary to the level of an entire text. This radical move results from a shift in the way Descartes relates images to the world. No longer are the objects of the imagination specific and localized images (e.g., the string lengths in the *Compendium*); instead, these images are now conceived in terms of spaces that are considered to be isomorphic with those that our senses are actually capable of perceiving in motion.

At the root of Descartes's method lies a simple reconfiguration of sensorial perception. In his earlier work Descartes upheld the doctrine of internal senses and the common sensibles to explain corporeal phenomena.[88] In *Le monde*, by proposing that motion is all that is absolutely necessary to establish the existence and explanation of these phenomena, he supplants the internal sense/common sensible matrix with the imagination, thereby constructing a conceptual space where these phenomena can be "observed" in motion.[89] Motion emerges as the efficient cause of phenomena existing within these spaces. Thus, images arise as extension in motion, and the spaces of the imagination allow this motion to be carefully analyzed, as though in a controlled experiment. Some spaces, it follows, are rendered "visible" exclusively by the imagination, and the continuity of motion in space can be "seen" and truly grasped not in the immeasurability of the actual world or the universe but in the more manageable dimensions of imaginary representation.

Now, none of this would be acceptable were it not for the underlying premise that perceptual images need not resemble what they represent, in accordance with classical semiotics. Descartes locates knowledge in his own representation, transferring control of unruly domains such as vast spaces to the makings of the imagination.[90] In short, the imaginary of *Le monde* enables concepts to be comprehended which perception alone cannot grasp. Any cognitive deficiency, it transpires, occurs in the domain of reasoning and also in perception. In the end, all of this constitutes a conceptual gambit by means of which Descartes postulates that the imaginary world of the fable is more knowable than the real world, that is to say, it is subject to cognition in ways that the realm of empirical observation cannot be.[91] More significantly, in advancing this proposition he would be adopting the imaginary not simply as a parallel model (let alone the opposite) of the real, but as a more accurate version of it.

The important moment in the conception of the imaginary marked by *Le monde* was not to inspire further similar "scientific" work. Newton, a paragon of the scientific aspirations in the new century, could think of no more acerbic attack on Descartes's fable than to proclaim it a "romance" of nature, a fanciful fabrication with no empirical, scientific, or, ultimately, epistemic value. Yet the liaison between sense perception and intellect effected by means of the imagination may be seen to illuminate the relation between the generalizations of music theory and the particularities of musical practice, in the case of Rameau.

As a domain of human activity, music surely lies far apart from the vast and ungraspable spaces of the solar system. But as a field of inquiry within the protocols of classical knowledge, it too presents cognitive challenges of its own. First, music demands a more focused epistemology of the aural. Second, any generalized cognitive (i.e., theoretical) claims about music have a duty to negotiate with practical traditions (i.e., composition and performance) and their intrinsic "messiness." With this the Descartes of *Le monde*, for instance, did not have to contend, and, strictly speaking, neither for that matter does the Descartes of the *Compendium*.

By "the aural" I do not mean the study of sound beyond Renaissance Neoplatonic and Pythagorean constraints, as, for instance, in the work of Benedetti, Galilei, or Beeckman.[92] Rather, I mean that epistemology must take account of the position of the subject as privileged locus of perception in the act of hearing. We have seen how Descartes places sound perception at the center of music theory. I noted the striking correspondence between the emergence of a new concept of subject with the cognition of sound and discussed the role that the imaginary and the imagination play in this connection. However, I also noted that Descartes abandons the study of sound precisely because he saw that once applied to the level of music (i.e., understood as organized sound with affective and expressive content) the tenets of mathesis universalis would have to yield to the nonmeasurable passions of the soul. Furthermore, except for the intervention of the imagination in the comprehension of musical time, Descartes relies on a traditional transposition of perceptual cognition from all the other senses to that of vision, as exemplified by his use of images. In contrast, Rameau must deal with the aural as such, particularly when confronting the delinearization of cognitive intuition into a succession of chords. In other words, he must give ideational content and formal representation to the notion that whatever happens between two successive chords obeys a causal link between two harmonic intuitions. In short, Rameau will have to correlate cognition (which is objectively guaranteed by Cartesian intuition) with the aural perception of moving "things" (which has no objective referent at this point in history). The move is from subject to listener, and from listener to interpreter, albeit one with a set of tightly regulated interpretive options.

As for the second of Rameau's challenges, that of negotiating the vicissitudes of practice within the context of an avowed scientific enterprise, it should suffice to note the tension that he faces in formulating an epistemologically closed system that would explain natural—hence immanent—principles of harmony against the intrinsically temporal—hence changing—space of a historical field.[93]

In light of these challenges I will propose similarities and differences between Descartes's and Rameau's appeals to the imagination. First, like Descartes, Rameau avails himself of the imagination as a resource for giving conceptual form to previously nonexistent questions of aural perception and cognition. Second, unlike Descartes, Rameau negotiates the presence of a body of practical evidence by adopting an alternative method to deductive and inductive enterprises. Whereas Descartes's theoretical practice moves along a single deductive path, imagining unseen things for us to grasp, Rameau's traverses a two-way path: he adopts elements from musical practice, theorizes them, and then projects these theorized elements back onto the practice which they now inform. Following Feyerabend, I term this procedure "counterinduction."[94] More precisely, counterinduction refers here to the process by which a theory generalizes from singularities of practice even if these generalizations contradict other aspects of practice. The process is most effective in the way it *prefigures* the practice it first analyzes, that is, how it explains potential manifestations of musical practice not just by modeling or systematically explaining existing practice but also by envisioning how such practice may take shape in accordance with principles the theory has advanced. Also included in counterinduction is the set of relations between practice, theory, and the practice of theory that emerges from the traversal of this two-way path.

As an example of counterinduction, we may consider Rameau's move in the *Traité* from his initial reduction through intuition of harmonic structures (Book 1) to his first attempt to theorize the concatenation of these structures (Book 2). Cartesian intuition yields for Rameau a unitary conception of the triad: an instant of perceptual-cognitive plenitude in which its materiality as a congeries of intervals is represented by a single tone. Measured and ordered, the triad—a musical reality of harmonic practice—enters into a correspondence with the fundamental bass—the representational reality of epistemological practice. A series of triads—which stand closer than the single triad to the realities of musical practice—does not allow for a similar reduction, however. At the very moment in Book 2 of the *Traité* that Rameau theorizes the temporal unfolding from harmony to harmony, the reductive process enabled by intuition unravels. It is there that we witness the irruption of the realities of musical practice into Rameau's system, in this case the perfect cadence as a prototype of harmonic progressivity. (This reality is to be understood as that which musicians would handle without much reflection about how or why it works.) Rameau reinscribes the perfect cadence as a set of voice-leading moves (i.e., intervallic progressions). Most importantly, these moves are only partially regulated by the relationship of the chords' fundamental basses, since nothing in a fifth relation guarantees that one chord should proceed to the next. Rameau, in other words, takes a topos of musical activity (in both the literal sense of closing clausula being a common practice, and the figural sense of its being a paradigmatic motion-to-rest gesture) and tropes it as an ideal of musical motion. Troped, this gesture will henceforth accompany the perception *and* cognition of other progressions like a spectral presence, a vestige of the perfect model in the less-than-perfect instances sometimes found in practice. By virtue of the counterinductive model these "imperfect" progressions reflect in their concatenation the theoretical principle Rameau extracts from practice.

The effectiveness of counterinduction does not reflect the failure of Cartesian intuition as a cognitive operation; however, it reflects the fact that intuition and its epistemological support system are not sufficient to explain fully the temporality of harmonic practice. We encounter here a paradox of the perception of harmonic progressivity: just when Rameau had at his disposal a self-reflective epistemology that would make it possible to submit the world to the tribunal of classical representation, he had to make an urgent appeal to a court headed by that most elusive of faculties, the imagination. I am referring to implied dissonances, a paradigmatic manifestation of the *prefigural* function of counterinduction: how it predetermines the way a particular aspect of musical practice must be cognitively perceived.

The proposition that the relation between two chords a fifth apart must be mediated by a dissonance and that this dissonance does not need to be acoustically present is difficult to accept on two accounts. First, in musical practice many chord-to-chord successions do not have dissonances, as Lester notes in his critique of Rameau.[95] Second, the notion of implication demands that we abandon the correspondence between signifier and signified, a demand hard to satisfy according to the epistemological dictates of classical semiotics: that is, the representation signifies something that does not form part of the acoustical "reality" of a harmonic succession. Any perceived tension between this acoustical "reality" and its theoretical representation would grossly simplify a more subtle relationship between signifier and signified in implied dissonances. By the protocols of counterinduction, implication demands an ideational ascription onto the perception of chord successions of one voice-leading feature (i.e., dissonance) that is common to the chordal chain that we call "sequence." This ascription is logically preceded by the observation that in composition a sequence by fifths occurs at moments where the harmonic syntax seems most fluid, an observation that is in no way intuitional (in Descartes's sense) but in every way musically *intuitive* (in its common sense). This intuitive observation, of course, resonates with the more formal account of the perfect cadence model as well as with the principle of necessary dissonance, given that sequences in the music known to Rameau most often do feature dissonances. What I am describing, in other words, sounds very much like an inductive method. But because Rameau goes on to make of chordal dissonance a *principle* of harmonic progression and because this notion of chordal dissonance could not come into being were it not for the initial intuition that yields the fundamental bass, the deductive impulse of his system must be integrated into the inductive impulse.

Why the particular chord succession we call "sequence"? At the time of the *Traité*, Rameau had especially kind words for the series of seventh chords related by descending fifth. In Book 4 he describes this succession as having an ideal connectedness, which he calls "the bond of the most natural harmony."[96] The presence of acoustically real dissonant sevenths in most actual versions of this progression might have given Rameau sufficient reason to call this a "most natural harmony," particularly in the way in which dissonances generate the necessary instability for his musical intuition of harmonic progression.

By featuring the conditions of the perfect cadence at the level of a multichord chain, the otherwise unremarkable "sequence" might be seen to emerge as a paradigm for noncadential harmonic concatenations. The homogeneity among chords in the sequence guarantees that no chord other than the cadential goal, the point of equilibrium, may assert hierarchical superiority over the others. Considering that in the *Traité* the chordal taxonomy consists of only two main chord types, the sequence can be seen to reflect accurately the order of harmonic things. Thus, with the sole exception of the closing progression, the sequence reduces harmonic content, particularly function, to pure motion. (This is in itself a necessity in a system devoid of an underlying matrix of harmonic scale degrees other than *tonique* and *dominante-tonique*.)

Considered as motion, the sequence might seem to constitute a locus of immediacy in the experience of music, a locus free, for instance, from the dialectics of absence that Hyer identifies in Rameau's system of chord types. However, this immediacy would not have been tenable within a system in which things could be neither known as unmediated perception nor known outside of representation. As pure motion the sequence would be semiotically empty, negating representation and therefore intuition, as defined by Cartesian epistemology. It would belong, in other words, to a realm of unmediated temporal consciousness, one which classical semiotics would not sanction. Accordingly, an unmediated perceptual experience would be no experience at all. In this sense no object of perceptual experience could be said to be real unless it is mediated by analysis. The most urgent consideration here is that without this mediation no index of reality could be determined; reality needs analysis to assert its existence. In turn, analysis needs the imagination to perform the work of connecting individual impressions, the chords. We may compare the situation to what Socrates calls a "provocative," a report of perception on which the judgment of sensation does not offer a trustworthy verdict and therefore invites the intellect to reflection.[97] As a domain of perception the notion of harmonic progressivity is Rameau's "provocative." What it provokes is a chain of dependencies between perceptual experience, musical intuition, and cognitive intuition. This chain is crucial for assigning a particular position to the subject as a conscious participant in acts of cognition (and, as we saw earlier, in the semiotic relationships through which cognition is expressed). Implied dissonances are a willful ideational ascription by the subject to the object it claims to cognize: I think, therefore I hear—*cogito ergo audio*. But the relationship between subject and object here is dialectically entangled within the counterinductive method insofar as the subject becomes a cognizing being by borrowing from its object (i.e., the sequence) precisely that which it contributes to the understanding of harmonic progression in general: I hear, therefore I am—*audio ergo sum*. We must remember that in Cartesian intuition the object is separated from the subject precisely by virtue of its being brought under the controlling gaze of the subject's mind; here, by contrast, the two come together.

Now, because the relation between subject and object is articulated in terms of something that is implied, we may very well consider Rameau's subject as Aristotle's "thinking soul," that particular entity among beings for whom "images take the place of direct perceptions." From this perspective it is important to recognize that the imagination is deployed to act upon the real: the analytic of intuition does not set up an opposition between a false reality of unmediated sense perception and the reality of thought and mental images. Their relationship is based on a mutual borrowing rendered unequal solely because the subject is the willing and conscious entity that performs the operation and the object is not.

My thesis, then, is that the subject is a semiotic agent mediating between the signifier "7" and the signified "harmonic succession"; in consequence, the subject is that which guarantees meaningful harmonic concatenations as it actively enters a kind of phenomenological semiosis. Rameau's "[I]t is implied" stands for "I imply." And yet one must question the role of nature in this formulation. How can Rameau balance the naturalistic premise of the *Traité* and the presence of a compositional idiom at a foundational level of the system? Could it not be that in the experiential immediacy of a chain of dominants Rameau is able to position the listening subject? And could it not be that in seeking to emulate this plenitude and extend it to the experience of hearing harmonically he stipulates that all other harmonic progressions aspire to the conditions of a chordal chain? There is no external evidence to demonstrate that these were deliberate actions by Rameau, and no theory of the subject as locus of nature exists outside of the definition of the subject as cognizing being.

For Rameau the conflict appears at the level of narrative structure: the deductive arrangement of the *Traité*, which resonates with classical cognitive ideals of intuition-based foundations, precludes the incorporation of compositional idioms at a foundational level near the beginning of the treatise. It is not quite the case, then, that the aim of the theoretical structure of Rameau's treatise is, as Daniel Chua puts it, "to represent the practical reality of music in the principles of nature—book three, 'on composition,' book four, 'on accompaniment.' "[98] In Chua's Foucauldian interpretation, the first two books perform typical representational functions of the classical age, namely,

> to measure the object of its nominations, to order its being, tabling its identities and differences and displaying its progression from simple to complex structures. First, the "relationship between harmonic ratios and proportions" to establish the fundamental base (bass) from which music can be measured; then—book two— the ordering of the "nature and proportions of chords" by arranging their identities and differences along the lines of consonance and dissonance as states of equilibrium and motion.[99]

The model of counterinduction suggests an alternative, though not mutually exclusive, outline in which the narrative structure of the *Traité* is not rigorously linear. We might do well indeed to conceive of the presence of musical practice at foundational levels in the *Traité* as a manifestation of the inconspicuous character of counterinduction. In this sense counterinduction operates at a meta-narrativic level, deeply informing what happens in the *Traité* but not driving its more apparent plot.[100]

A more general conclusion is that Rameau's theory of harmony keeps within its recesses a vivid memory of the musical practice it seeks to explain. Memory is meant literally as that on which imagination feeds: the cognition of harmonic progressions by means of implied dissonances carries with it the spectral presence, the memorial vestiges of those progressions in which the dissonances are explicit.[101] This spectral presence is tied in to remembrance, but remembrance made actual, remembrance of that which, without being there, *would have been there*. As readers of Rameau we face the challenge of accepting that this spectral presence in no way contradicts the musical reality it seems to distort. Indeed, as part of the process of counterinduction, the imaginary may seem to ignore or contradict undeniable phenomenal facts. The reason it appears to do so is to generate a new kind of experience, a predetermined, organized, and therefore informed way to hear how chords relate to one another. Hearing harmonically, Rameau implies, is hearing actively, informing perception with mechanisms of cognition that are grounded in theory that we must, he says, deploy in the production of harmonic intelligibility (we have seen the conflict between this subject-based epistemology and the nature-based focus of his actual discourse). An asymmetrical relationship is established between the structure of musical phenomena (i.e., triads) and our cognition. Put differently, what can be said about structure becomes now dependent on what we say it is, a situation consonant with classical representation and evident in Descartes's statement in Rule 12; again, "when we consider things in the order that corresponds to our knowledge of them, our view of them must be different from what it would be if we were speaking of them in accordance with how they exist in reality."[102]

What would otherwise be habitual knowledge (what I have also called "musically intuitive" knowledge) is now grounded on a conceptual frame. And within this frame the imagination works as the mechanism of cognition that the human mind must deploy in the production of harmonic coherence. I would assert that from the perspective of cognitive perception the deployment of counter-induction as a system is inseparable from an awareness of the limitations of practice—what some might term "reality." For Rameau, the perceptual activity of hearing and the palpability of performance practice are incomplete without the reflective activity of music theory. At this point in the history of music theory an unavoidable dialectic between practice and theory emerges that reflects how "[reality] can neither justify nor enrich itself through any other image of reality," as philosopher Clément Rosset puts it.[103] Rameau's theoretical practice, then, outlines a relationship to musical phenomena that is dependent on a double reflection, a looking glass in which practice reflects theory and theory reflects practice. By this I mean that at a point in the practical application of theory, a principle (i.e., harmonic progression) may supersede the practice that the theorist seeks out to understand. This superseding encompasses the description and prefiguration of musical practice by means of counterinduction. Methodologically this means that the meaningful comprehension of musical practice occurs under the aegis of the imaginary representation of practice by theory. The subject's imagination constitutes the agency behind this process, for as Josué Harari puts it, this representation is "a construct that is the product of self-enclosed reasoning."[104]

Questions of method were very much at the forefront of epistemology in Rameau's more immediate eighteenth-century intellectual milieu. In his *Traité des systèmes* (1749) the Abbé de Condillac presents a critique of methods, questioning the assumptions of thinkers as diverse as Bayle, Descartes, Malebranche, Leibniz, and Spinoza, among others.[105] As Thomas Christensen notes, Condillac rejects both a purely deductive project based on the establishment of a governing principle (*esprit de système*) and one that first presents hypotheses which are then tested in a variety of cases; instead, he favors the *esprit systématique*, in which empirical data are evaluated in order to arrive at a set of underlying principles.[106] Christensen highlights the importance of Condillac's awareness of "the dialectical relation between reason and experience" for his classification of systems. A similar, albeit more balanced, dialectic is evident in Rameau's *Traité*, as the quotation at the beginning of this chapter attests. We witness in Rameau an attempt to strike a balance between the narrative structure of the *esprit de système* and the lure of the *esprit systématique* calling for the incorporation of musical practice. He wants to have it both ways. In the end we are left with the question of the role of the imagination within the system(s), for as we have seen, the recourse to a first principle (e.g., that all harmonic progressions must have dissonances) entails a willful blockage of "reality" in the name of system.

Condillac himself had much to say about the imagination:

> The ability we have to revive our perceptions in the absence of objects gives us the power to reunite and connect the most disparate ideas. There is nothing that cannot take a new form in our imagination. By the readiness with which it transfers the qualities of one subject to another, it puts together in a single subject what

would naturally suffice to embellish many subjects. At first nothing seems more contrary to truth than the way in which the imagination manages our ideas. In fact, if we do not become masters of this operation, it will invariably lead us astray, but if we know how to control it, imagination becomes one of our chief sources of knowledge.[107]

The passage echoes two themes we have explored before, namely, the topoi of the imagination-as-transgression in place since the Greeks (of which Condillac accuses the Descartes of *Le monde* in Chapter 12 of the *Traité des systèmes*), and of the imagination as something that contributes toward knowledge. More useful are Condillac's categories of the reproductive and productive imagination. The reproductive imagination retraces temporary perceptions, combining perceptions but inventing nothing. The productive imagination is engaged when the force connecting the present to the absent assumes new forms, supplying something to that which is perceived. In reflecting about the possible truths and falsehoods of the productive imagination Condillac's ideas help us to observe the theoretical practices outside science, for as he writes in the *Traité des systèmes*, "there is [a] difference between the principles of physics and those of politics. Physical principles are facts that experience does not allow us to doubt; political principles do not always have this advantage." And, furthermore, "imagination is . . . the name of the mental process that combines the properties of various objects to create groupings for which there are no models in nature."[108] Contemporary theoretical practices around areas of human endeavor— Rousseau's theory of education and Montesquieu's theory of government— deploy the productive imagination to produce explanatory models in ways that provide useful parallels to and distinctions from Rameau's own.[109]

Rousseau and Montesquieu advance inaugural theories of education and government which, like Descartes's efforts in *Le monde*, appeal to conjectural fictions.[110] Rousseau's *Émile* is a philosophical tract, but its subject is a practical one: the education of a fictional character, Émile. A widely influential writing, it defined the parameters of the field of education, articulated the nature of the object of study, and provided a methodology by which to explore these parameters. *Émile* presented, in short, a theory of pedagogy, a discipline belonging to the domain of the then nascent social sciences.[111] Theory, fiction (i.e., the imaginary), and practice hold a complex relation made explicit by Rousseau himself. "With regard to what will be called the systematic portion of the book . . . it is here that the reader will probably go wrong," Rousseau writes, adding, "you will tell me 'this is not so much a treatise on education as the visions of a dreamer about education.'" Advocating nothing less than the authority of the imaginary over other realms, Rousseau announces in the Preface, "[E]ven if my method is fanciful and unsound, my observations may still be of service," and later, "people are always telling me to make *practical* suggestions. You might well tell me to suggest what people are doing already. . . . [T]hese are matters with regard to which a suggestion is far more chimerical than my own."[112]

By willfully ignoring observable practice, *Émile's* fiction sets out to supersede available reality as a guarantor of truth. In the final analysis the presentation of theory constitutes the raison d'être for the fictional account; no competition between the imaginary and the real exists for Rousseau, and so there is no need to invoke standards of verisimilitude and verification.[113] Theory gives *Émile* structural coherence and conceptual significance over and above its more apparent and immediate literary appeal as a story. It is testimony to the power of Rousseau's prefigurative move that *Émile*'s fictional world would eventually become factual: his reverie became a "reality," as *Émile* inspired a revolution in the pedagogical field.

At roughly the same time Rousseau advanced a theory of education, Montesquieu used a similar approach to tackle government, a domain of human activity perhaps more intractable than education (or music). In *Les lettres persanes* (*The Persian Letters*, a vivid commentary by two fictional travelers on the socio-political life in France) and *De l'esprit des lois* (*The Spirit of Laws*) he presents theories of law and government. Like Rousseau, the kind of knowledge that Montesquieu advances does not depend on empirical facts, and like Rousseau and Descartes before him he also met vociferous resistance. Voltaire, for one, accuses Montesquieu of "mistaking his imagination for his memory," pointing out that citations are "faulty" and facts "falsified" in order to fit his theses.[114] Ever the "positivist," Voltaire would not comprehend that, insofar as they "exist," empirical facts exist to provide an arena in which Montesquieu could carry out theoretical activity. Ironically, these facts, as Harari notes, enable the articulation of concepts characteristic of scientific systems such as "principles" and "general causes."[115]

The subject matter these two theorists tackle imposes itself on the particular approach they follow. According to Montesquieu, for example, laws and government depend on innumerable economical, historical, political, and social factors. Each one of these factors is itself variable with respect to time and place, making nearly impossible the formulation of general principles. He makes a conscious choice to formulate general principles of law and government from the perspective of a fictional account of a virtual reality. And while Montesquieu gambles that this virtual reality may resonate with features of his readers' actual lives, he places the highest stakes on the disparity between those features and the ideal setting of the feigned account. This disparity, he expects, might induce in the reader a vision of how things could be. At the very least, Montesquieu's fictional account, in a reversal of the Socratic provocative, might incite the reader's reflection on existing economical, political, and social practices. In the end, out of Montesquieu's theoretical reflection emerges a single principle explaining the relationships at play in the practice of government, relationships that, in his theory, should inform the formulation of laws.

Theory and the imaginary are deployed to attenuate the variables of existing realities, or what we may term "social practice"; more importantly, together they prefigure a possible and desirable practice. It is the function of the imagination to mediate between the poles of theory and the imaginary. The imagination performs this function both for the theorists who must conjure up the details of their accounts as well as for the theories that they want to advance. But it also performs a function for the readers of these theories, being their responsibility to transform the imaginary by means of the imagination into a productive encounter with actual experience. We may say that the theoretical imaginary is not something that determines meaning (we would call this the hermeneutic imaginary); rather, the imaginary makes meaning possible (a poetic imaginary) and ought to be part of the poetics of interpretation, whether of political life or education.

But what of musical practice? On the surface Montesquieu, Rousseau, and Rameau might seem unlikely bedfellows. But their differences, on closer examination, are more in degree than in kind. To be sure, Rameau did not write a musical fable to account for the ratios of the monochord, nor did he couch his theories in the rhetoric of literary fiction. Quite the contrary, as Christensen has shown, his theoretical work was singularly marked by scientific aspirations, or as Duchez has cogently argued, his theory is founded on an "epistemo-musical" epistemology. But Rameau does rely on the imagination and the imaginary to make his theory of harmonic progressivity both possible and understood; this is hardly a scientific process in the manner that he himself would have envisioned. Consider, for instance, the parallel between Montesquieu and Rameau. Both use the imaginary to organize or stabilize a seemingly unruly reality. Montesquieu proclaims, "I have laid down the first principles, and have found that the particular cases follow naturally from them; that the histories of all nations are only consequences of them."[116] Rameau's invocation of implied dissonances reflects a similar reliance on theoretical principles. The perfect cadence and the fifths sequence are expressions of the principles of chordal dissonance and harmonic progressivity, but as theoretical models they are a consequence of these very same principles. The same can be said then of the principle of *liaison en harmonie,* which is formulated according to consideration of its presence in musical practice. In any event, unlike the observers through which Montesquieu presents his theories in *The Persian Letters,* the story of the *Traité* begins after Rameau has observed practice.

My claim is that like Montesquieu and Rousseau, Rameau and Descartes before him share an operative attitude toward the ordering of knowledge by looking, hearing, and thinking outside the coordinates of perceived reality.[117] This going outside corresponds to an operation of the imagination; in the end the imagination acts as a kind of interface between theory and practice, between the incomplete given and the complete created, between uninformed fact and informed possibility. We may profitably situate such attitude historically as reflective of the fact that these theorists, *pace* Hume, Newton, or Voltaire, are cognitively strongest when they are metaphysically most secure, manifesting the powers the classical episteme grants to representation.[118] In the specific case of Rameau, I will suggest that theory and practice are like the proverbial "two sides of the same coin": even when hidden from view, the other side is always there. (The relationship of music theory and practice, one would hope, should not be reduced to a "heads or tails" contest.) In his thought the imagination and the imaginary occupy the area between the two sides, inhabiting spaces that neither pure theory nor pure practice can alone fill. Example 3.2, for instance, shows a harmonic prototype as it may appear in actual practice, yet Rameau does not present it until the last book of the *Traité*, keeping accompaniment— the lowest-ranking activity of musical practice in his hierarchy of knowledge— apart from model. By the same token, the cadential prototype, unproblematically introduced in Book 2, becomes less of a presence as the more practical considerations of Books 3 and 4 arise. The fact remains, however, that in the counter-inductive model there are traces of practice and theory at both inductive and deductive ends.

We must identify this complex epistemological situation as a reflection of a unique moment in the history of music thought. Rameau faced a formidable challenge in conceiving and explaining for the first time notions such as harmonic order and progressivity. It would be no exaggeration to say that Rameau is inventing harmony from the ground up, like Descartes's "world." "After Rameau," writes Brian Hyer, "theories of music become much less concerned with musical practice *per se* (with how one *copes* with music as a performer or composer) and more obsessed with ontological questions, questions about what music (or musical phenomena) can be said to be."[119] This is indeed a perceptive reading of Rameau's contribution and can be accepted with the provision that we understand that "what music can be *said* to be" defines the priority of the epistemological field in defining the ontological. In the most extreme version of the priority of the epistemological, Rameau implies that unmediated hearing is nearly deaf, or worse yet, idiotic.[120] The emphasis on epistemology, I have proposed, parallels Descartes's shift of representation from an order of being to an order of knowing. Furthermore, I would add that understood as a form of practice, hearing—"how one *copes* with music" as a *listener*—is radically reconfigured by the insertion of the subject in representation. By the protocols of the classical episteme, thinking (saying, writing) is representing, and representing is intuiting. This is the practice of theory signified by the heading of this section of the chapter. Rameau's challenge: to teach his readers how to hear the familiar (the triad) in unfamiliar ways (as a unitary entity whose order is determined by the fundamental bass) and so to reconfigure the experience of hearing successive chords, to render the perceptual cognitive, to reclaim hearing from nature by becoming one with it, to order musical things by making everything in music *be* harmonic. The theory of harmony demanded new ways of hearing, transforming established perceptual norms implicit in figured bass. Such transformation provided a unique opportunity for the imagination to participate as mediator between practice and theory, because the imagination was recognized as possessing the capacity to enter spaces that left to their own devices neither sense nor reason could safely reach. Rameau's early theory of harmonic progressivity needs the imagination to bridge the boundaries separating practice (accompanying, composing, listening, performing) and understanding. As long as we insist on seeing Rameau's imaginary as widening the gap between sense and concept, we will not do justice to the claims he makes on behalf of implied tones or the fundamental bass. For, if theory brings about an interaction between the given and the imagined, then what it produces must be more than a difference between the two. Like a bridge, it does not matter from which direction it is traveled. To my mind this is a compelling heuristic justification for conceiving theory and practice alongside the imagination in a triadic relation. The theorizing act by which Rameau asks us to understand the progression in Example 3.1 as being unstable transforms represented practice into a sign (i.e., the implied dissonances expressed by the figures above the fundamental bass) and casts the imagination in a form that allows us to conceive what it is that the sign designates. To paraphrase a statement I made earlier, the imagination is a form of consciousness, not the object that shapes consciousness. In a radical assertion of the epistemological value given to conventional and probable signs, this particular sign (i.e., to imply) points toward a cogent explanation of music's harmonic logic and progressivity made possible by and carried out by the subject. The imaginary, acoustically empty implied dissonance should not be condemned to the epistemological limbo of the neither here nor there, and Rameau's theory should not be demeaned because it relies on the imagination. It should be valued for that relationship. For that is its connection to music, to the thing it seeks to explain and understand. The notion of implication constitutes not so much a negation of reality but part of the operation through which theory calls attention to its own power to signify. The imaginary performs what Harari calls "a semiotic operation": it constitutes a means to translate, and thus to make comprehensible, a "text" that it resembles but of which it is not a copy. As a key element in the act of representation, the imaginary and the imagination claim respectively to be the medium of reflection and the operation by which the "text" is made understood, known, or, more precisely re-cognized, as I have argued in my discussion of classical analysis (see the previous section above). Rameau's theory is not an inadequate or distorted replica of musical practice but a way of enabling reflection on music itself. Theory and practice intersect at the imagination.

And just as I argue that at the dawn of Descartes's emerging conception of the early modern subject stands music, here at the dawn of modern music theory stands the subject. It is indeed a mark of Rameau's accomplishment as a thinker that from now on the subject—defined as a willful, conscious agent of understanding, that is, as a listener—will constitute the locus of negotiations with sound reconfigured as chords in motion. Of course, Rameau's enterprise is characterized by overconfidence, ignoring sometimes the limits of its cognitive claims. In adding the "correct" figures to a figured bass by Corelli, for example, he falls victim to the narcissism of one who, not unlike the author of *Le monde*, becomes a kind of (re)creator, not interpreter.[121] No doubt, Rameau's implied dissonances raise important questions about the relation between sense and concept, theory and practice, and object and representation. As modern readers we ought to remember that in the end, as W. J. T. Mitchell once wittily remarked, "there is no representation without taxation."[122] And as we contemplate once more the relation of Rameau (and music theory) to the classical episteme, we ought to keep in mind that it is precisely by partaking of the confidence in the subject and its powers of representation that his conjuring the imagination and advancing a ternary structure for the music-analytical sign unwittingly levies a tax on the binary transaction of classical representation.

4 Gottfried Weber and Mozart's K. 465: The Contents and Discontents of the Listening Subject

Rameau's music-theoretical ideas found fertile soil in Germany, where his conceptual innovations were disseminated during his life and following his death in 1764. As is amply known, the Frenchman's theories were argued over at great length and with various degrees of perspicuity, understanding, and misunderstanding equally by zealous advocates (Marpurg) and moderate followers (Kirnberger). Meanwhile detractors (C. P. E. Bach, most notoriously) proclaimed in no uncertain terms those theories to be simply wrong. In the dissemination of Rameau's ideas in Germany during the second half of the eighteenth century we may more generally observe a coincidence with the emergence of a German "version" of the French Enlightenment. To give one example, a project such as Sulzer's *Allgemeine Theorie der schönen Kunst* (1771/1774) reflects a rapidly growing sense that encyclopedic thought and systematic taxonomies learned from the French could not only organize previously existing knowledge in orderly fashion but could actually produce new knowledge. This new knowledge was valued precisely because of the systematic foundation and consistent methodology it introduced to the study of a hitherto unsystematically approached domain of human endeavor. What is more, the German *Hochaufklärung* may be characterized as being preoccupied less with thorny epistemological premises per se than with more practical matters of knowledge adaptation, production, and translation. In a way, that practical attitude was made possible by the fact that German intellectuals were in a position to survey in hindsight the vast intellectual labor and struggles of their neighbors to the west. (Thus, the question of "Was ist Aufklärung?" could have been raised only in Germany, as did the editors of the *Berlinische Monatschrift* [1793], with famous responses by Kant and Moses Mendelssohn, among others.) Based on that labor and those struggles, writers could adopt this or that position wholesale (e.g., Marpurg), or else they could adopt some ideas but not all (e.g., Kirnberger).

The latter approach, of partially adopting ideas, is very much in evidence in the music-theoretical work of Gottfried Weber (1779–1839). Against the musical soundscape provided by, among others, his fellow Mannheimer Stamitz and Mozart (his favored composer), Weber developed a formidable theory of music in which order and system take the form of numerous tabular taxonomies but in which he also renounces the need for explicit foundations on mathesis. I say "explicit" pointedly, because Weber makes implicit use of concepts that were developed at great epistemological effort by his predecessor Rameau. Chordal roots, to give but one example, are taken by Weber to be part of the way things are. A similar attitude informs his analytical practice, which he frames in the manner of "observations" and against "theoretical demonstrations."

Best known today for having formalized and popularized the analytic use of Roman numerals, that ubiquitous metalanguage for explanations of harmony in tonal music, Weber concluded the third volume of his *Versuch einer geordneten Theorie der Tonsetzkunst zum Selbstunterricht* (*Attempt at a Systematic Theory of Musical Composition for Self-instruction*) by analyzing the opening excerpt, shown in Example 4.1, from the Adagio introduction to Mozart's String Quartet in C major, K. 465.[1] In thirty densely argued pages Weber presents an exhaustive note-by-note, sonority-by-sonority interpretation of just four measures plus the downbeat of the fifth measure—which he calls "a particularly remarkable passage" (*eine besonders merkwürdige Stelle*)—out of the twenty-two comprising the introduction. The following excerpt is characteristic of the interpretive density of the analysis, here in response to the first two simultaneously heard notes (C and A♭) in the cello and viola on the last quarter of m. 1:

> This [dyad] leaves the ear with a new element of uncertainty: is this latter note to be heard as g♯ or a♭? . . . If [however] it is heard as a♭, much ambiguity remains, in that the ear still has the choice of regarding the dyad as belonging
>
> | | |
> |---|---|
> | to the chord of | A♭, |
> | thus as the chord on the sixth scale-degree in C minor | c: VI |
> | or as the tonic chord of A♭ major | A♭: I; |
> | or as belonging instead to the minor triad | f, |
> | thus as the chord on the fourth scale-degree in C minor | c: iv; |
> | or perhaps as the tonic chord of F minor | f: i. |
>
> Initially, the ear must await more precise specification, in what follows, of the intended key—of which there is as yet no intimation (164/204–205).[2]

Through a narration of his encounter with Mozart's passage, Weber goes on to articulate a contentious argument in which each new note is an opportunity for dissension and an occasion for jostling expectations against disappointing contradictions; this mode of interpretation is fueled by doubt, in a manner redolent of what Paul Ricoeur terms a "hermeneutics of suspicion."[3]

The discourse generated by the interpretive anxiety in this excerpt suggests that the epithet "particularly remarkable" fits Weber's analysis comfortably; his analysis "transforms" an experience that lasts approximately twenty-five seconds in performance into a significantly longer version of that experience. To be sure, transformations of this kind are a characteristic feature of narratives,[4] reflecting the difference that exists, in Barbara Herrnstein Smith's words, between "the formal properties of a linguistic event and the set of conditions conventionally implied by the occurrence of an event of that form."[5] Yet the radical

Example 4.1
Mozart, String Quartet in C Major, K. 465, first movement, mm. 1–4. Gottfried Weber, *Versuch einer geordneten Theorie der Tonsetzkunst zum Selbstunterricht* (1832: III, 204). Reduction by Weber.

difference between the two time spans in Weber's analysis brings to the fore something more. It introduces a yawning gap (some may consider it an existential abyss) between the experience of music and the cognitive apprehension of that experience through a theory-driven representation. This results from the particular way in which Weber brings together the consciousness of a subject in the act of listening, a particular structure of knowledge that subtends that consciousness, and the linguistic and metalinguistic mechanisms that help give material form to these two characteristics. Assuming momentarily that this initial critical diagnosis may be correct, one might still wonder of what is this analysis a symptom? Or, taken as an index of action by a listener in response to a musical experience, what can Weber's analysis tell us about how this action may have been framed by cognitive, epistemological, and representational contingencies historically available to him?

This chapter addresses these questions by exploring, first, what theory of consciousness is available to Weber's listening subject that is able to divide itself into subject of experience and object of inquiry? Second, how does this theory of consciousness participate in Weber's theory of harmony? And, third, what can be said to constitute the empirical evidence of the act of listening when we are engaged in it at the same time that we wish to examine it?[6] These are fundamental questions that emerge from an urgent awareness of the intrinsically temporal and unavoidably ephemeral nature of human existence at the turn to the nineteenth century. My interpretation of these matters resorts to versions of the subject and subjectivity proposed by late-eighteenth-century philosophy (Kant and Fichte), as well as responses to these by the Romantics (particularly Friedrich von Schlegel and Novalis).[7] Their responses are then connected to the role of language in mediating the temporal alterity of the listening subject.

Before moving to Weber's analysis, a word about the place of this analysis within the overall trajectory of the book. I have mentioned the presence in this analysis of a "listening subject." The reader may wonder why I do not simply refer to "the listener." The answer is that this simpler and widespread designation would exclude the dialectic that I argue exists between the listener and that to which he or she listens, a dialectic that I have framed in terms of a subject/object relationship. And what is more, it excludes various other cognitive postures, linguistic protocols, and culturally determined contingencies. In my reading, "listening subject" will therefore designate four distinct, albeit interrelated senses: (1) the bearer of linguistic predicates (i.e., Weber's "das Gehör"), (2) the bearer of psychological states and processes (i.e., what I read as the anxious interpreter in Weber's narrative), (3) the cognitive subject in dialectic to the object of cognition, and (4) the agent behind the activity of analysis (i.e., Gottfried Weber as theorist and introspective listener). In fact, I will make a case to propose that the coexistence of these various senses of "listening subject" crystallize in Weber's concept of multiple meaning (*Mehrdeutigkeit*). This, I will argue, marks a key moment in the trajectory of the history of the dialectic between musical subject and its representations and functions apart from incipient empirical accounts of tonal perception at the beginning of the nineteenth century.[8]

The emergence of the figure of the listening subject is best seen against the general background that I have drawn in the preceding chapters. To summarize, early modern subject/object relations were announced by Descartes's assertion at the beginning of his *Compendium musicae* that "its [music's] object is sound" (*Huius objectum est sonus*).[9] With this terse statement, Descartes had announced at the dawn of the seventeenth century that an adequate knowledge of music was no longer possible under the dispersive epistemology of the Renaissance, with its admixture of Pythagorean mathematics, Neoplatonic metaphysics, and numerological analogies (Zarlino's thought is characteristic in this regard). Instead, music (i.e., as sound) had to be brought into the fold of the *cogito* by the analysis of perception. This was made possible by understanding the natural physico-acoustic materiality of sound, newly established as "object" of knowledge. In opposition to this object, the human mind was located as subject, and as the cognizing and perceiving locus in the constitution of knowledge. Knowledge, however, was structured around intersubjective, universal values of order and measurement: mathesis universalis. Rameau, whose epistemology was, like Descartes's, grounded on an omniscient *cogito*, had sought the appeal of nature to provide his theory of harmony with an unshakable foundation (along with numerous appeals to mechanistic and gravitational theories, among others).[10] But as discussed in Chapter 3, Rameau faced the vexing problem of accounting for the way in which harmonic concatenations were perceived by a "listener" as they unfold. Rameau's solution was to postulate that dissonances were understood as participating in all progressions, a responsibility which, however, he never explicitly assigned to the listener. In Weber the responsibility for understanding is openly (and exhaustively) assigned to the listener. Without anticipating my arguments, I would say here that the conditions for the possibility of such assignation and, indeed, for the emergence of the figure of the listening subject result not from the epistemological triumph of a rationality untrammeled from the axioms of mathesis or from the discovery of the capacity of linguistic discourse to faithfully represent human experience, but from the

Example 4.2
Outline of Weber's analysis.

recognition of limitations in the structure of representation: in this recognition the subject itself becomes object of its own representation. First then, Weber's account.

4.1. The Analysis

As outlined in Example 4.2, Weber organizes his analysis into six sections, framed by an introduction and a conclusion. Together, Sections 1 through 5 form the first part of the analysis. Section 6 constitutes the second part.

In the first part Weber's account is intensely preoccupied with the here and now, elaborating a third-person narrative around the main character, a figure he calls "the ear" ("das Gehör").[11] No mere witness to events occurring outside of itself, this character is the locus of subjective experience, the intensity of which, I would submit, is vividly felt by the reader of Weber's discourse. Considering the music on the downbeat of m. 3, for example, Weber writes, "the ear now yearns for a G major chord simple and unadorned, or at most embellished by an A_5 suspension. But that this $C\sharp_4$ should forcibly displace the harmony note D_4, that it should mar its arrival, indeed subvert the entry of the long-desired G major chord . . . —the likes of this it [the ear] never expected" (177/217).

In contrast to the first part of the analysis, the account in the second part has an objective tone, with the past tense controlling the narrative as Weber turns toward a discussion of what he calls the composer's "intentions." Here the narrator is distanced from the unfolding of the "piece," and the narrative dislodges the subjective immediacy that characterizes Sections 1 through 5. For the first time in the analysis a single underlying musical idea is shown in toto.[12]

"The intention (*Intention*) behind this entire passage," explains Weber about Example 4.3, "was unmistakably the following pattern of imitation in which the figure (*Gesang*) in the voice that enters at the end of b. 1 (viola)—$A\flat_3$-$A\flat_3$-G_3-$F\sharp_3$-G_3—is imitated note for note an octave (double octave) higher by the upper voice (first violin) entering one bar later—A_5-A_5-G_5-$F\sharp_5$-G_5" (179/220).[13]

Lengthiest among all sections, Sections 1 and 5 deal with the question of harmonic meaning in music that, as Sections 2, 3, 4, and 6 help to explain, engages in all sorts of rhythmic displacements, contrapuntal imitations, and sharp juxtapositions of tones of figuration (e.g., neighboring and passing tones) with

Example 4.3
Weber's analysis of the intention (*Intention*) behind Mozart's passage: pattern of imitation. Weber, *Versuch* (1832: III, 220).

chordal notes. Weber begins by describing how in the first two measures the ear "encounters a succession of interesting, aurally intriguing and highly agreeable ambiguities of key and chord progression." He proposes that the solitary C in the bass voice releases two possible contexts: as tonic of either C major or minor.[14] A new set of uncertainties arises with the entrance of A♭ (quoted at the beginning of the chapter). The ear, he maintains, "must await more specific information."

A complete A♭ triad forms in m. 2; with this, the ear experiences "the pleasant sense of relief which it always associates with the gradual resolution of ambiguities." Relief is short-lived, however, as the ear soon faces further choices. Weber asks whether this chord is VI in C minor or I in A♭ major, adding that, "as yet there is still no good foundation on which to base a decision. For all we know, the A♭ may turn out to be merely a passing tone to G, and the chord [may] come to rest on a C minor triad," as Example 4.4 illustrates.

The arrival of A♮ on the second beat of m. 2 contradicts all expectations. Weber proposes the interpretations shown in Example 4.5. Although the interpretation at the bottom—as ii°[7] in G minor—is closest to the "ear's previous assumption," the ear continues in doubt and eagerly awaits clarification.[15] Only with the arrival of the G-major chord on the second beat of m. 3 does the ear seem somewhat satisfied. But still, the ear contemplates two choices, could this be the dominant of C minor . . . or major?

The $B♭_5$ in the uppermost voice on the third beat of m. 4 most strongly challenges the interpretive efforts of the subject. This "foreign" note, Weber says, "forces the ear to interpret this dyad [G_2–$B♭_5$] as some other chord, belonging to a different key." Example 4.6 reproduces his interpretations. First, he considers a succession of a G-major triad and a D^7 chord (represented by the letters immediately beneath the music). Second, he regards the dyad G_2–$B♭_5$ as part of a G-minor triad and as the tonic in that key. Next, he presents four possible interpretations for the measure as a whole.

Whatever the explanation, he notes, the modulation to G minor is rather uncommon, so that "[the ear is] disinclined to tolerate [it] in this manner." In effect, the deviation in m. 4 prompts Weber to claim that the ear is justified in feeling that there must be something wrong.[16] In a particularly vivid passage, he then remarks,

Example 4.4
Possible interpretation of
A♭ as a passing note to G.
Weber, *Versuch* (1832: III,
205).

Example 4.5
Possible harmonic inter-
pretations upon arrival of
A♮. Weber, *Versuch* (1832:
III, 206).

...the chord [c g e♭' a"], which considered as a four-note chord
with diminished fifth..°a⁷

...the chord [c g e♭' a"], which considered as a four-note chord
with diminished fifth...$^\circ a^7$
can be heard as the seventh scale-degree in B♭ major.............B♭: $^\circ vii^7$
or - closer to the ear's previous assumption - as the second
scale-degree in G minor, [...]..g: $^\circ ii^7$
(trans. Bent, 165)

Example 4.6
Harmonic interpretations
of m. 4. Weber, *Versuch*
(1832: III, 208).

...forces it [the ear], indeed, for reason of coherence to take it
initially as a G minor triad..g
and as the tonic chord of G minor...g:i.
The chord progression of this bar is thus:

```
          G    -      D    -        g
    G:    I    -      V    -    g:  i
or  C:    V    -  G:  V    -    g:  i
```

or otherwise, if the F♯ and a" are considered purely as passing notes:

```
    G:    I    -    g:  i;
or  C:    V    -    g:  i.
```

(trans. Bent, 166-167)

So revolutionary a move [the first voice] tries to foist upon the ear not only at
a point of such weak stress but also in bare two-part texture. . . . On its own authority, and without any apparent motivation, it takes the law into its own hands
and seeks to overthrow the G major triad which has been in force as the result of
the combined efforts of all four voices, . . . [and transforms] it now unilaterally
into the triad of G minor. (168/209)

Here the ear quarrels with the music and appears to come dangerously close to
falling into a cognitive abyss: "[The ear is] left in some doubts as to whether
to believe, whether to take seriously, what it has heard."

Following a brief discussion of the B_{b2}–D_{b6} dyad in m. 5 which, according to the ear, brings two utterly distant keys (G minor and B♭ minor) next to one another, Weber concedes that although the ear could further assume that D_{b6} might be a chromatic passing tone $C_{\#6}$ to D_6, "this hypothesis is no more borne out than was the earlier one of A_5 for B_{b5}." Seemingly exhausted by his interpretive efforts, he casually remarks that mm. 1–4 are restated a whole tone lower in mm. 5–9. But before moving on to Section 2, Weber declares that his analysis will become clearer during a "consideration of the interaction (*Verflechtung*) of the piece's melodic lines" (171/213).

Indeed, Section 2 explains the interaction of sharply dissonant neighboring and passing tones with notes that hold harmonic status. In the next two sections, briefer than Section 2, Weber simply draws attention to cross-relations and parallel progressions at the interval of a second as noteworthy features of the passage. In contrast to Section 1, he makes no effort to interpret the harmonic content.

Under the heading "Review of the grammatical construction of the passage as a whole," Section 5 promises to bring together the interpretation of harmonic content with passing tones, cross-relations, and parallel progressions, aspects to which Weber devotes individual chapters elsewhere in the *Versuch* (Vol. 2, Section VI, "Tonal shaping of entire pieces"; Vol. 3, Section VII, "Passing notes"; Vol. 4, Section X, "Movement by leap," and XI, "Merits of particular parallel progressions"). The disturbing ambiguities in the Mozart passage are said to arise from the multiple intersections of cross-related notes, passing tones, and the like. For instance, the cross-relation A_{b3}–A_5 between the viola and first violin in mm. 1–2 occurs as the viola itself introduces the passing tone G, and the resulting chord (C_3–G_3–E_{b3}–A_3) "doubles the disturbing effect to the ear" (175/215). By metrically realigning dissonances, Weber offers six alternative versions in which these disturbing effects disappear. This exercise, he maintains, validates his preceding analytical observations. At the end of the passage he concedes an important point: "the transition from the fourth to the next bar, with the emergence of the dyad [B_{b2}–D_{b6}], brings with it the remote and *unaccountable* conjunction, already mentioned, of the keys of G minor and B♭ minor" (178/219, emphasis mine). In the end, in this section he restricts himself to spelling out the pitch-class content of chords, but the analysis sheds no new light on their intriguing harmonic relationships. It appears then that his promise of a comprehensive account of the whole falls short of its mark, or better yet, that his idea of the "whole" bears no direct relation to the original experience of the passage as it unfolds before the ear. In his account, that is, the otherwise persuasive contrapuntal analysis does not yield a harmonic synthesis.

No admission in the analysis is more startling than that found in the conclusion. There, after reiterating a common theme throughout the account, namely, that the music presents intensely disturbing features to the ear, Weber writes,

All that technical theory could have done, it has here done. . . . But does the accumulation of simultaneities and successions of notes ever overstep the limits of harshness that can be tolerated by the ear? Or does it not? In all the preceding discussions this question has received no categorical answer, although it has been much illuminated. . . . In the last resort, it is the *musically trained ear alone* that must be the judge, and in this respect a *supreme* judge has already decided *in favour* of the passage—I refer to *the ear* of a *Mozart*. . . . As to what is acceptable to *my* ear, I freely admit that with tonal constructs such as these it does *not* feel comfortable. And this I can say openly and in defiance of those fools and jealous ones, because I believe I have the right to declare with pride: *I know what I like in my Mozart.* (182–83/225–26, emphasis in original)

Like the expression "unaccountable conjunction," expressions such as "all that technical theory could have done, it has here done," and "no categorical answer" immediately raise suspicions about the motivation behind Weber's conclusion. Why would he, after thirty pages of detailed, note-by-note analysis, end on a note of peculiarly mixed decision and resignation? What is the nature of Weber's resistance to "categorical answers," and what the agency of the "*supreme* judge" in his determination of "*my Mozart*"?

4.2. (Im)possibilities: Weber's Concept of *Mehrdeutigkeit*

In his conclusion Weber is placing limits not so much on the kinds of knowledge that analytic interpretation affords, but on those which music theory (i.e., what he calls "technical theory") can generate. This betrays no false modesty, for in the introduction to the analysis he states that

anyone who is acquainted with my theory and knows its way of working will be aware that clear-cut directives and prohibitions, declarations as to whether this or that conjunction of pitches, sequence of notes, chord progression, etc., etc., is or is not admissible, is simply not my forte. . . . [My theory] amounts in essence purely to *observations* upon that which sounds well or badly . . . and in no way deals in *a priori* and dogmatic theoretical *demonstrations*. (162/200, emphasis in original)

He pushes the envelope even farther, virtually surrendering rights to final arbitration: "nobody should expect from me a verdict as to whether and how far this or that feature of the Introduction in question *should be admitted or prohibited and categorically forbidden*" (163/202, emphasis in original).

Weber's disclaimers enable his analysis to assume the guise of description and thereby avoids any suggestion that he might be advancing a prescriptive mode of listening. Indeed, the rejection of "systems" runs like a motive in his thought. In a telling moment, Weber had declared that "Music (*die Tonkunst*) is, after all, not a science endowed with mathematical consistency and absoluteness" (162/202). The position here echoes Weber's clearly spelled methodological philosophy in the Foreword to the *Versuch* (1st edition):

My *Versuch einer geordneten Theorie* is in no way intended . . . to be a system in the philosophical-scientific sense of the word, in no way an assemblage of truths, all derived in a logically consistent manner from one supreme fundamental principle.

On the contrary, it is a principal feature of my view that our art is in no way suited to such systematic demonstration, or at least until now has not yet been suited to it. . . . Thus this is not a work in the form of a strictly systematic foundation and derivation, but only one carried out in the most orderly possible fashion, an "attempt towards a systematic theory." I do not pretend to use the title, "system," which sounds much too grand to me.[17]

Weber's indictment of deductive methodologies and of systems in general deserves closer scrutiny (more on this below). For now, suffice it to note that he does not renounce order altogether: his title refers to what he sees as a systematic (i.e., properly organized) progression in the presentation of the treatise contents. During the Mozart analysis, furthermore, he often hints at notions of musical order that subtly depart from the self-assured programmatic statements in the Foreword.[18] For instance, what legal foundations would sanction the invocation of "authority" and "law," made in reference to the entrance of the B_{b5} in m. 4 in the first violin? When Weber levies charges against, of all things, the note B_{b5}, he unwittingly reveals that this note might be breaking an order of things that, although abrogated from the analytical discourse, nonetheless subtends his interpretation.

The kind of order Weber has in mind is dictated by his principal theoretical formulation: the theory of harmonic scale steps (*Stufentheorie*).[19] This well-known theory conceptualizes the quality and harmonic function within a key of any and all chords in terms of the position they may hold within the fixed order given in a major or minor scale. As a primary conceptual order *Stufentheorie* is itself animated in Weber's analytical practice by another concept: *Mehrdeutigkeit* (multiple meaning). Weber introduces the concept thus: "Multiple meaning is what we call the possibility of explaining a thing in more than one way, or the quality of a thing, whereby it can be considered sometimes as this, sometimes as that" (1832, 1:42).[20] With its slippery conjunction ("or"), ambivalent demonstrative pronouns ("this," "that"), and the grammatically multivalent "as," Weber's definition revels in ambiguity, resisting facile interpretation. Such discursive elusiveness forms part of an opacity integral to the concept's designation of a subject and its cognitive choices, on the one hand, and the choices offered, so to speak, by the object of cognition, on the other.

In a way, this indeterminacy with regard to knowing subject (i.e., the one explaining) and known object (i.e., the thing) makes it a definition like no other in harmonic theory up to Weber's time. This indeterminacy, however, is grounded on three preconditions, which the definition presumes and links together: (a) sensory certainty—as the immediate awareness of sense-objects (i.e., "things"), which we saw in the Mozart analysis; (b) perception of these objects—as the mediated knowledge of things on the basis of recognizing some properties (i.e., "qualities"); (c) understanding—as knowledge of things (i.e., "explanation") that manifest some underlying order. And while it is obvious that Weber's introductory definition is not committed to saying either that any such underlying order inheres to the object or that the subject produces the understanding of that order, he is nonetheless making a large claim for the way in which the subject, independent of first principles, has unheard-of jurisdiction over its encounter with things. This can be observed in comparison with, for instance, Descartes's deployment of mathesis universalis or, closer to Weber's critical aims, Rameau's appeal to the authority of a nature inherent both in the materiality of sound and in the mechanisms of human cognition. By assigning the jurisdiction of multiple meaning to the subject's cognition (i.e, as a domain of explanation) *and* designating it as a quality inherent in the musical object, Weber shifts the epistemological balance further away from an order of things dictated from without. This is an epistemological gesture that could only have happened in the wake of Kant's "second Copernican revolution": the fundamental conditions for both understanding and the order of knowledge are conceived by Weber from the perspective of the consciousness that attains it. It is the subject who may explain a thing "as this" *or* who may instead consider the thing "as that." The control of the conjunction "or," in the definition of multiple meaning, is in the hands, or rather the ear, of the listener. Listening had never been more interpretive.

In Weber, the decisive turn toward the subject as locus of cognition of music is more markedly delineated within the context of what he calls "multiple meaning of position" (*Mehrdeutigkeit des Sitzes*). Most prominent among the various types of multiple meaning, this particular type deals specifically with the identity and variable function of harmonies within several keys. "Every harmony has multiple meaning," writes Weber, "in that one can underlay it sometimes with this, sometimes with that Roman numeral, and can therefore regard it as belonging to more than one key" (1832, 2:50).[21] To outline the possible tonal (i.e., key) contexts for any given chord, Weber draws a series of exhaustive tables, such as that reproduced in Example 4.7 indicating every possible location for any major triad within potential keys.

In their quality and localization, and in the possibility of their interpretation, chords in the table might be profitably analyzed according to a mutually complementary distinction made by Foucault between *empiricities* (*empiricités*)—particular objects of study determined by a given field of knowledge (e.g., economics)—and *positivities* (*positivités*)—strategies for determining relationships established to posit, affirm, distribute, organize, and explain the empiricities within a space of knowledge.[22] At the level of empiricity (i.e., the concept of chord), the table in Example 4.7 represents a more or less permanent and predetermined space distributed and organized according to a simple analysis of (1) identities established among a set of chord types (major, minor, etc.), and (2) differences among the harmonic functions determined by the location of chord types within the scale. (In Weber's theory, the scale itself emerges as a key empiricity.[23]) Combined, these identities and differences would correspond to "the quality of a thing" in the definition of multiple meaning of position. Along the axes of positivities, the table offers a grid of cognitive possibilities from which to affirm and explain its contents, be it a chord or a key. These cognitive possibilities exist for the active consciousness of the listening subject to scan

```
                    Db        Eb   Fb  F   Gb      Ab  Bb  Bb  Cb
                    C,  C#,  D,  D#,  E,  E#,  F#,  G,  G#,  A    A#,  B

In        C      :I.....................IV..........V.............................
major     Cb, B  :.....................IV.......V.............................I..
keys      Bb     :.................IV.......V.............................I.........

          A      :...........IV........V...............................I.............
          Ab, G# :....IV.........V.....................................I...............
          G      :IV.......V...................................I....................
          Gb, F# :.....V.............................I...............................IV
          F      :V.....................................I.............................IV......
          Fb, E  :...................I...............................IV..........V.
          Eb     :...................I...........................IV..........V........
          D      :.............I...........................IV.........V.......
          Db, C# :.....I.........................IV..........V..................

In        c      :..................................V...VI.....................
minor     b      :..................................V...VI.....................
keys      bb, a# :..............................V...VI.....................
          a      :.........................V...VI.....................
          ab, g# :.....................V...VI.....................
          g      :.............V...VI.....................
          f#     :......V...VI.....................
          f      :V...VI.....................
          e      :VI...............................................V.
          eb, d# :...............................................V.....VI
          d      :.............................................V...VI.......
          c#     :...........................................V....VI.............
```

Example 4.7
Table of Multiple Meaning of Position (*Mehrdeutigkeit des Sitzes*) for major triads.
Weber, *Versuch* (1832: II, 52).

adjacencies and discontinuities among these empiricities. Choices among those possibilities are made by the subject in an effort to achieve a sort of tonal localization, which corresponds to the "possibility of explanation" in the definition of multiple meaning. (The spatial metaphor of *Sitz*—literally "seat"—strongly suggests Weber's notion of localization.) In the principle of simplicity and the law of inertia Weber does offer syntactic protocols by which to determine relationships among the empiricities posited. However flexible, these protocols nonetheless help to direct the kinds of questions the listener asks.

We may at this point make two general observations about Weber's table. First, an internal matter: In the connection existing between empiricities and positivities, the mode of knowledge and the objects of knowledge hold a dialectical relation. For instance, as an empiricity, the identity of a chord is not guaranteed by its ontic ground, that is, as an array of the pitch classes it contains. Its identity is inscribed, instead, in the musical context, not independently but as determined by a listening subject. Reciprocally, any such determination depends on the traces given to the subject by the objects themselves, whether a single tone, a dyad, a triad, or any other such sonorous accumulation. A great part of Weber's virtuosity in defining multiple meaning resides in his ability to place this dialectic at the center of his theory of harmony. Second, an external matter: the relation of Weber's conception of order to that of the classical age. Weber's table immediately bears resemblance to the great taxonomies of Linnaeus, for example, and echoes the classifying spirit that evinced, in Foucault's analysis, classical knowledge's interest in order and measurement following analysis of identities and differences in a field of objects. Indeed, just as Linnaeus availed himself of precise classificatory criteria (form of objects, their quantity, the manner of relation to one another, and relative size), Weber too follows a systematic order establishing first the form of chordal types, then dividing them according to size, and finally ascribing to them relations in the space of the scale. "[I]n Classical terms," writes Foucault, "knowledge of empirical individuals can be acquired only from the continuous, ordered, and universal tabulation of all possible differences."[24] Both in the classification of plants and in the classification of chords, empirical individuals are determined by observation and audition, respectively. In fact, the exclusive reliance on audition and his cognitive faith in audibility help explain Weber's disinclination to embrace fundamentalisms that may be in any way redolent of a system builder such as Rameau. Likewise, his metonymy of hearing ("das Gehör") to describe the cognitive activity of a listener bespeaks a residual interest in the facultative aspects of listening, an interest that, however, he would not have the opportunity to incorporate systematically into his theory. Epistemologically Weber lies on the acoustic divide of the study of musical perception, and not on the side of *Tonpsychologie* that would take hold later in the nineteenth century. But returning to the comparison with the analysis of objects and their tabular display, it ought to be noted that (1) the objects in his table are grounded in the link between a set of pitch classes and the verb *to be* (this relation revels in its binary exactitude, according to protocols we have seen in classical representation); (2) the taxonomy of the table is a direct consequence of his refusal to consider chords as simple elements (i.e., the way Rameau, for instance, considered the intuitions of his chordal categories and that made possible their quantitative analysis) and choosing instead to treat them as complex elements (i.e., objects encountered in experience that must be approached qualitatively); and (3) his rejection of system and mathesis is counterbalanced by his embrace of classification and taxonomia.

This admittedly superficial comparison to Linnaeus's classical taxonomies suggests that Weber's thought keeps the residue of a mode of ordering things dating to a much earlier time. But if in the totality of order expressed in the taxonomy of chords he might reveal the empirical positivistic spirit of a Linnaeus, in upholding the unconditionally necessary cognitive input of a listener he departs sharply from such epistemology. After all, the listener decides just what it is that a chord *actually is,* severing the presumed bond that exists between the object in the table and the verb "to be." Any given representation in the table is no longer the being of thought, for as we see in the Mozart analysis, representation has been made subject to thought. Similarly, representation is no longer the mode of the subject's interiority; instead, that interiority has become the staging area for contending representations. In Kantian terms the subject determines the formal conditions of experience in relation to any given object. The verticality of the virtual space of knowledge of empiricities in the table of chords must now come to the encounter of the horizontality of human experience, one which is manifest, in Weber's analysis, in an urgent concern for localization along a temporal continuum.

Assigning to the listening subject the task of navigating the paths by which the empiricities may be interconnected does not, however, end the relationship between empiricity and positivity. Because the grid of the table provides an a priori referent for a listening subject, the subject is dialectically defined in relation to the music, around the question "where do I stand?" "We are selves insofar as we move in a space of questions," maintains Charles Taylor, and the same can be said of Weber's listening subject, that peculiar being whose self is intimately bound with tracing an experience of music.[25] However, it is one thing to move in a space of self-questioning, and quite another to live in a modality of experience marked by suspicion, as Weber does in relation to Mozart's introduction. Even in those all-too-rare moments when an instant is affirmed by the analysis, it is expected that what follows might contradict it. For example, when in m. 2 Weber reveals a progression from A♭ to D^7, the dominant of the dominant of C minor, followed in m. 3 by the expected G chord, he declares, "the ambiguity that has prevailed hitherto is now at last sufficiently eradicated for the ear to hear the chord as an established dominant chord, or fifth scale-degree, of C minor or C major" (166/207). Temporary relief immediately gives way to still greater ambiguity, though, when the much noted B♭5 appears in the upper voice "contradicting this [G] chord."

Expectation, contradiction, and reinterpretation play a crucial role in Weber's interpretive method. Weber himself addressed the matter by giving conceptual space within his theory to a processual understanding of harmony. This space is occupied by what he termed "multiple meaning of harmonic progression" (*Mehrdeutigkeit der Modulation*). The notion helps to explain harmonic meaning in context and includes, significantly, the possibility that in some passages even context may not clarify meaning, "leaving the matter undecided" (1832, 2:155). In such cases Weber proposes that "true multiple meaning of harmony" (*eigentliche oder wirkliche Mehrdeutigkeit der Harmonie*) occurs. We might say that in that event Weber's theory sanctions a kind of harmonic noumenon. This is not meant in the sense that there exist passages whose harmonic content somehow transcends either the Kantian a priori forms of time and space or the categories, and are therefore conceivable only through pure understanding (in this regard Weber's theory operates within a phenomenal epistemology). Rather, this harmonic noumenon is meant as a parallel space along the explicit positivities of the table, a space marking off a content without form, the Kantian "unknown something," or simply that which Weber believes to lie beyond the explanatory powers of "technical theory."[26]

Interpreting true multiple meaning this way makes sense if we consider the quadrant of the table figuratively, as the representation of a constructed space, as a *Darstellung*. Literally a "placing there," *Darstellung* designates in the exalted lore of the Romantics (the members of the *Athenäum* circle during the late 1790s—August and Friedrich von Schlegel, Caroline and Dorothea von Schlegel, Novalis, Schleiermacher, and Tieck—but for the present purposes mainly Novalis and Friedrich von Schlegel) the materiality of figural representation in discourse. The emphasis given in *Darstellung* to external representation suggests that the space of the table has a counterpart to which it does not give material form. This counterpart is, I submit, time.[27] As an a priori form of sensible intuition, Kant's time is not subject to representation; it is, rather, a condition of the possibility of all representation. Not so for the Romantics, for whom time is associated with a form of internal representation, *Vorstellung*, a suprasensible representation that brings an image before the subject's mind.[28] In Weber's theory listening becomes intrinsically interpretive, interpretation becomes a hermeneutics of suspicion, and this suspicion is experienced by the consciousness of a subject (i.e., self-consciousness) as it navigates the coordinates of the tables. The time of analysis emerges, therefore, as the arena in which the encounter between interpretation and self-consciousness takes place. And analysis is the linguistic staging of that encounter, which helps explain why language gains unprecedented importance as a mediation of temporality in Weber's account and as the material by which he attempts to give form to the internal representation of *Vorstellung*.

4.3. Troping Temporality:
The Romantic Representation of Time

When Kant lodged time within the subject as an a priori form of the internal sense, he unwittingly posed a formidable challenge to those who wished to give temporality any sort of substantial presentation[29]—all the more so at a time in which temporality's relation to existence had become a central critical concern. "Time is undetermined finitude," said Novalis, who also recognized that it "passes in accordance to representations."[30] The conflicted relationship between finitude and indeterminacy articulated here may have had a paralyzing effect on Weber's reading of Mozart. "Weber," writes Brian Hyer, "insists on an impossible division between past and future in which what appears to be an openness towards the future emergence of the music is, rather, a near permanent indecision with regard to the musical present. . . . By the time the ear gathers enough information to make a decision about a given moment in the music, the moment is long gone."[31] Gone indeed. In Weber's analysis causal connections hardly matter, and later events seldom illuminate the meaning of earlier ones.[32] The time of Mozart's remarkable passage does not sit still awaiting Weber's analytic portrait, which creates ontological and epistemological challenges for his analysis: If time constitutes in fact the ground of being and a condition of lived experience, how can the objects of this experience be known? Caught in this predicament, Weber presents the perfect picture of a reluctant Kantian—that is, a subject who, while recognizing that time is available and necessary to individual consciousness as a condition for its existence in the world and for its representation, is all too aware that the experience of it (and its substantial presentation) is ephemeral and so eludes synthesis.[33]

Still, given the positivities at play in the structure of multiple meaning, we may provisionally conclude that for Weber cognition is temporal and temporality is cognitive. In an analytical practice that deploys multiple meaning, transcendental time is represented empirically as *temporality*, or lived time. This temporality is always already entangled with the succession in which a subject addresses things through a self-conscious cognitive effort.[34] Just how difficult this interrelation and the task of self-consciousness are becomes apparent in the following fragment by Novalis: "In a broad sense, self-consciousness is a task—an ideal—it would be a condition in which time does not advance, a timeless but steadfast, always unchanging condition. (A condition without past or future and still changeable.)"[35] The tension between what Novalis sees as an action (this task is given the urgency of the present tense "is") and what it should be as a condition or state of being (framed by the conditional "would") is one between the now and the ever, and it encapsulates a desire for immanence and progression that can only be articulated dialectically. (Note how Novalis's rhetorical contortions sagaciously engage the reader in the self-conscious task his fragment articulates.) I believe that Weber pursues this task, but not, I would submit, with a full critical awareness of the complications suggested by Novalis. That is, in the Mozart analysis this task assumes the form of consciousness of a psychological subject (i.e., "das Gehör") for whom change, however, conjures up incessant alienation created by the steadfastness of musical time itself. Despite being aware of the evanescence of musical time, this subject tries nonetheless to apprehend its experience as well as to understand what of it can be grasped and how this may be done. And "tries" is the appropriate expression, because for Weber it is one thing to reconstruct the past and to prefigure the future, and quite another to construct a present constantly impelled by the un-remitting force of time. We must feel compelled to ask, therefore, why would Weber advance an analysis that could easily be read as working within what is in essence a poetics of self-doubt and suspicion? Moreover, if the analysis so quarrels with the "musical present," as Hyer notes, then what, if anything, does it adequately address and how does it do that?

Addressing the last question first, we recall that what we may call a Romantic "practice" of Representation was available to Weber. Romantic Representation had a pragmatic end. As Novalis offered, "One understands something most easily when one sees it represented (*repräsentiert*)," namely, by granting it material and figural form.[36] This figural form is paradigmatically given in discourse. In the face of the ephemeral quality of Weber's temporal experience of music, Representation assumes the unenviable task of ameliorating as best it can a seemingly irremediable condition of existence. Thus, the internal representation of temporality (i.e., *Vorstellung*) assumes external form in Representation. These internal and external forms of representation hold a complex relationship. It is not the case that an external representation of temporality (i.e., discourse) *stands in* for an internal one (i.e., the experience of time represented in *Vorstellung*), as a more convenient duplication. Rather, these forms share succession as a basic ordering principle, without the two being equivalent.[37]

We may sum up the relation of one temporality to another, or rather, of their representations, by considering their different contributions to the constitution of subjective experience. In a "first" temporality the subject constituted is aware of some way in which time provides the grounds for its being. Let us call this an "existential field." In a "second" temporality the representation of this awareness as discourse provides the grounds for an "epistemological" assessment of the existential field. The linguistic discourse proper constitutes a "practical" synthesis of the existential and the epistemological. It is a staging of the troping of one temporality for another.

In a more general context such troping of temporalities resonates with the emerging consciousness of the indispensability of time as a defining modality for the empirical existence of beings in the world. This has been dubbed "The Age of History" by Foucault, who has in mind particularly the episode beginning around 1775 in which History, the "mode of being that prescribes their destiny to all empirical beings," is recognized to constitute "the depths from which all beings emerge into their precarious, glittering existence."[38] Indeed, in the account of his encounter with Mozart's introduction Weber addresses his very own empirical condition within this History as the subject of a fractured temporal existence. And yet this interpretation, which might otherwise gibe with the "existential" and "epistemological" claims outlined above, does not fully account for Weber's distended linguistic *practice* in his analysis of Mozart.

A suitable explanation for Weber's linguistic practice may be found in the poetics of the Romantics. In late-eighteenth-century Germany, heightened re-alization of the aporia of the representation of temporality forms part of a renewed interest by the Romantics in arresting linguistic figures which, in mediating between language and time, make manifest the compromising maneuvers humans perform to account for their precarious temporal existence. These figures are allegory and irony.[39] Each provides a way to understand how Weber negotiates the question of temporality at two levels: (1) the level of the single moment (irony), and (2) the level of the entire analytic narrative (allegory). First, irony and the particular version of subjectivity it subtends.

4.4. The Ternary Sign of Romantic Irony

The semiotic structure of irony is uniquely suited to negotiate the elusive immediacy of time, which it does in dialectical fashion. As the trope in which a single signifier sanctions multiple and simultaneous signifieds, irony is a propositional statement that asserts by negating and negates by asserting.[40] By sanctioning a semiotics of the "may be," irony heightens the process of its construction, injects distance and difference into signification, and demands constant interpretive suspicion. Its structure challenges any uncomplicated binary connection posited between things and signs because neither things nor the signs that designate them are or mean what they may seem. Whatever substantiality the ironic sign may hold, it calls into question the original unity presumed to exist in other signs and in other tropes.[41] This questioning gives rise to the negativity of a doubling effect in which self-contradictory meanings coexist, contravening the traditional analytic proposition that a thing cannot simultaneously be and not be (which Kant terms the "law of contradiction"). To cancel out or resolve this negativity would simply mean that irony ceases to exist.

Novalis and Schlegel might have sensed the existential nature of irony; for them, it is not something that is, a rhetorical device; rather, it is something one does. Taking a cue from the structure of the trope, Novalis and Schlegel thematized irony dialectically by requiring the negation of the asserted negation, and did so most radically by refusing to arbitrate in favor of any final proposition at all. Thus, when Schlegel proclaimed that "irony constitutes an analysis of thesis and antithesis," he explicitly omitted synthesis, and with it its conciliatory intent, as he would put it. Romantic irony, as it is known, more than a rhetorical trope, encompassed for Novalis and Schlegel an attitude informing our encounter with the world.[42] This attitude could in turn be expressed by means of a discursive activity that questioned linguistic referentiality with its vaunted capacity to apprehend the world. Thus, despite believing in the clarifying powers of Representation, Novalis warned against having absolute faith in the transparency of language: "all the superstition and error of all times and peoples and individuals rests upon the confusion of the symbol with what is symbolized— upon making them identical—upon the belief in true complete representation —and relation of the picture to the original—of appearance and substance—on the inference from external similarity to complete inner correspondence and connection—in short on the confusion of subject and object."[43] From Novalis's caution about a transparent referential theory of representation it can be seen how the linguistic incompatibilities built into irony allowed its emergence as a paragon for an alternative theory of representation. Irony would have legitimized the representation of phenomena in terms of possibilities rather than fixed objects.

We would do well at this point to consider elements of Romantic irony in the use of the Roman numeral. The first and most obvious is that as a grapheme it does not bear an iconic resemblance to musical notation. Being explicitly a nonmusical metalanguage, the sign of the Roman numeral does not mean what it "says," but instead is made to mean something else. It is what semioticians might call an "unmotivated" sign.[44] But for Weber the Roman numeral does not seem to have any associations with abstract ciphers in the manner in which Leibniz, for example, might have thought of symbols. If anything, it would have a common link to Kant's meaning of symbol as a mode of intuitive representation. Thus, when introducing Roman numerals, Weber simply displaces the descriptive mark of the "German letters" (*deutsche Buchstaben*), which up to that point in the *Versuch* has designated chords without reference to a definite scale or key.[45] In its uncomplicated manner Weber's displacement projects an aura of cognitive neutrality, openly adopting a conventional sign, not even bothering with historical references to his predecessors (e.g., Vogler). Yet this semiotic transformation does not operate unidirectionally (i.e., from numerical symbol to marker of harmonic identity and function), for even after it has been firmly established as a metalanguage in its new music-theoretical surroundings, the Roman numeral carries with it remnants of previous significations as ordinal number. In fact, without these remnants it could well have lost credibility. Indeed, known across Germany as conveyors of authority and tradition, Roman numerals presented a logical norm and outlined a systematic arrangement of objects.[46]

Above and beyond this ironic aspect, the Roman numeral is tangled up with the conceptual model of multiple meaning within which it constitutes a medium of reflection on chords. A material transcription neither exclusively of chords nor of an experience of them by a listener, the Roman numeral, like the conceptual model of which it is a part, is both. In this particular condition as sign, the Roman numeral signals a shift in the nature of representation of music by music theory. By compromising the notion of a univocal materiality in the objects it names, the Roman numeral relaxes the correspondence theory of representation found in previous analytic metalanguages, as, for example, in Rameau's fundamental bass.[47] Whereas the fundamental bass engaged in a mimetic representation of harmony that aimed to make the musical object it designated present to the hearing subject, the Roman numeral makes the subject present to a particular harmony, if it can. The signifying space that Rameau so valiantly fought for on behalf of his subject when he injected the imagination into the tightly constructed binary structure of classical representation is now available to the listener. It is, however, so radically reconfigured by Weber as not to constitute the same space at all. In the Roman numeral, opposite a pitch-class collection (the signifier) stand a number of signifiers. And outside this one-to-several binary stands the listening subject, but not, however, as Rameau's *tertium quid*. Rather, the subject stands as the legislative term (i.e., the decision-making member) in a reconstituted ternary sign: pitch-class content, Roman numeral designating possible tonal relations, and listener. This legislator, however, must first deal with a signifier that acquires depth before the ears, so to speak, a signifier that offers differentiated signifieds at every turn, each one of which holds mutually exclusive relational attributes. As I see it, the Roman numeral points to an increasingly debilitated classical binary representation: it signals the encroachment of interpretation into the structure of representation. The encroachment of interpretation brings to the fore the conditions under which it produces knowledge and understanding of the harmonic content of a composition—keeping in mind, however, that the many semiotic gains of the classical sign of the fundamental bass (e.g., the reductive intuition of chordal inversion) are co-opted in the process. To return to the issue of irony, then, Roman-numeral analysis of the kind exemplified by Weber's analysis of the Mozart passage constitutes a tool for a mode of critical interpretation that, like irony, is structured around semiotic doubting and disputing, achieved by teasing out potential meanings. In the process the analytic sign effects a mediation (and at times a separation) between logical norm and aesthetic form, that is, between the cognitive complex of empiricities and positivities, on the one hand, and the intricate musical context of Mozart's music, on the other.

In *Stufentheorie* the logical norm of Roman numerals corresponds to the order of the scale and the a priori cognitive choices available in Weber's theory. But in the Mozart analysis we find this logic altered by Weber's hermeneutics of suspicion. And even though Novalis, for instance, argued on behalf of a need for systemlessness (*Systemlosigkeit*) within systems, it would be erroneous to conclude therefore that Weber engages here in a systematic undoing of the ordinal predeterminations of his taxonomies. For although the conditions of its creation and possible dissolution (as in irony) are inscribed onto the loose anchoring of Roman numeral to an acoustical correspondence, it is the activity of interpretation by a subject that most benefits from the dialectic of Romantic irony. This, however, goes well beyond the level of semiotic interpretation that I have offered thus far, for in order for the subject to account for its interpretive activities, it must position itself as subject of self-analysis, the nature of which is implicated in the possibility of self-consciousness.

4.5. Versions of the Self: Subjectivity and Self-consciousness

In considering the semiotic deferral made possible by irony, I have offered an explanation for the productive tension between music-theoretical metalanguage and individual linguistic propositions in the Mozart analysis, as well as for *Mehrdeutigkeit* in general. Irony participates in the production of the analytic text and is constitutive of a semiotically multiplied subjectivity that enunciates that text. Likewise, my discussion of *Mehrdeutigkeit* has noted the analytical urgency to distinguish between subject and object equally in Weber's explanatory model and in the musico-cognitive analytic acts in which he deploys the model. In his theoretical formulation Weber unproblematically presumes the binary opposition of subject and object. However, his Mozart analysis reveals a more complex, tripartite distinction between (1) listening subject, (2) listened-to musical object, and (3) self-observed listening subject (i.e., the narrator of the relation between 1 and 2). Can this division be simply regarded as the result of actions by a naive self-positing "I"? At first, that may seem to be the case, particularly since in its attempts to exercise its legislative powers over the musical object, the subject accentuates an orientation of the self toward itself. On second look, though, Weber's ironist does not fit the picture of the Cartesian *cogito* meditating on the agency of suspicion in order to confirm a certain and undoubtable *audio* ("I-hear"). We may, in fact, preliminarily note that if Weber's "ear" affirms the *cogito,* then its vacillations disconfirm the Cartesian predicate *ergo sum.* In all, the peculiar self-alterity in Weber's analysis intensifies the need to explain the agency of the subject in the encounter between "das Gehör" and Mozart's remarkable passage.

Irony offers a point of departure for investigating the capacity of the subject for self-reflexivity. It reveals and addresses counteracting forces by which the self shapes reality and is in turn shaped by them. With recourse to irony, Novalis and Schlegel outlined a self-reflective activity: *ironic consciousness.* Similar to the way in which the interpretive activity of irony probed the criteria for linguistic evaluation and arbitration, so ironic consciousness questioned the presumed unity and challenged the identity of the interpreter (e.g., Weber's "das Gehör"). Ironic consciousness carried unprecedented consequences for the understanding of subjectivity. It granted an opportunity for the momentary suspension of the contiguous identity of a subject who could then engage in self-interrogation. This corresponds to Novalis's "timeless condition" of self-consciousness. In our case the Roman numeral functioned as part of an ironic linguistic act that may have helped define the place and movement of musical objects. Similarly, as Romantic ironist, the analyst engaged in a self-reflective act through which a position and a clear sense of self-as-listener might be attained. With this proviso in place, the subject was seen as a *cogito* capable of immediate self-knowledge insofar as it could constitute itself as the predicate of linguistic discourse. Linguistic mediation, in other words, made it possible for the subject to posit itself (and its temporal existence, *pace* Kant) as self-reflection.

For the Romantic ironist, subjectivity was mediated through Representation. Self-knowledge and linguistic representation were bound in this mediation, with the latter providing the staging grounds for the former. Self-reflection was made possible by narration in the third person, posited as a kind of second self. In this important sense Weber's analysis of Mozart may be understood as an analysis to the second power, a self-analysis of the activity of cognition—in brief, an exercise in self-doubling. As corollary to Novalis's distinction between symbol and thing, cited before, we may say that from the activity of self-doubling there emerges an empirical subject (say, Gottfried Weber as he hears Mozart's introduction) and a narrated self, or "symbolic" self in Novalis's terms (e.g., "das Gehör"). Neither of these two versions of the subject, empirical or symbolic, corresponds uniquely to any of the four categories of "listening subject" I gave in the introduction to this chapter; rather, these two versions accentuate the interdependence among the four categories. Indeed, the separation between these two versions functions in accord with the ironic logic of productive self-contradiction, not as negation of one term by another nor as assertion of one over the other, but dialectically, by the establishment of a mutually critical relationship between the two terms.[48] It is crucial, furthermore, initially to see this self-division not as producing two objects, but rather as creating an opportunity in which, by means of language, the subject is enabled to act upon itself. This action consists of a mutual reflection of a doubled self. "[This] reflective disjunction," writes Paul de Man, "not only occurs by means of language as a privileged category, but it transfers the self out of the empirical world into a world constituted out of, and in, language—a language that it finds in the world like one entity among others, but that remains unique in being the only entity by means of which it can differentiate itself from the world."[49]

What de Man outlines here goes to the heart of an interdependence of language and human subjectivity voiced in Herder's pronouncement that we are a "linguistic creation" (*Sprachgeschöpfe*). Herder's idea forms a key part in the poetic background for a broadly defined Romantic subjectivity. Indeed, this "linguistic turn" was to be explored by the Romantics in counterpoint to the cognitive structures (and strictures) put in place by Kant's epistemology.[50] For if Kant's epistemology gave light to the "lamp" that enabled the subject to forgo its former cognitive image as "mirror" of the world, this light was felt to be insufficient to illuminate the subject itself, paradoxically leaving it in the shadows of its all-encompassing transcendental powers of cognition.[51] In the form of self-commentary, linguistic discourse becomes in turn the mirror for the lamp (or another lamp itself). Linguistic discourse allows the subject to see itself as if it were "world," permitting its differentiation from a post-Kantian world it presumably regulates. Furthermore, for the Romantic ironist (and for Weber, as I will argue), the matter of differentiation and illumination is ultimately ethical, a dialectical corrective to the omniscient knowledge of the self and the world that forms part of the two dominant versions of the subject at the end of the eighteenth century: Kant's transcendental ego and Fichte's Absolute I. It will be necessary to consider their postulates.[52]

Kant inherits a Cartesian picture of the subject defined as a thinking thing (*res cogitans*) whose consciousness may transparently survey its own mental contents. In Chapter 2 we find intuition to be the analytic reduction of a succession of temporal episodes by a subject who perceives the totality of that succession thanks to an intellectual effort which it alone controls. This Cartesian *cogito,* that well-rehearsed figure whose awareness of its mental contents constitutes the beginning and end of consciousness, and whose being is itself grounded on self-intuition, is drastically reconfigured by Kant.[53] In the first *Critique*, Kant alters the isomorphic relationship between thinking and being of Descartes's pithy *cogito ergo sum* argument. For Kant, the subject's capacity for thought as well as the consciousness of this capacity needs to be determined before its nature as a thinking *being* can be established. The nature of this capacity turned out to be elusive, as the following excerpt attests:

> Through this I or he or it (the thing) which thinks, nothing further is represented than a transcendental subject of the thoughts = X. It [I, he, or it] is known only through the thoughts which are its predicates, and of it, apart from them, we cannot have any concept whatsoever, but can only revolve in a perpetual circle, since any judgement upon it has always already made use of its representation. And the reason why this inconvenience is inseparably bound up with it, is that consciousness in itself is not a representation distinguishing a particular object, but a form of representation in general, that is, of representation in so far as it is entitled knowledge; for it is only of knowledge that I can say that I am thereby thinking of something.[54]

This passage from the Transcendental Dialectic begins by affirming a point Kant makes earlier, in the Transcendental Deduction: "[T]he empirical consciousness, which accompanies different representations, is . . . without relation to the identity of the subject."[55] This is so because the identity of the subject is transcendentally (not empirically) dictated to it by the a priori forms of intuition (time and space) and the categories of understanding. These forms of intuition and categories of understanding give objective shape to all representations but not to the subject. Thus, the subject is limited to know what it thinks (its representations) and how it thinks (by means of the forms of intuition and the categories). But it lacks the capacity for self-representation, not being able to know itself outside of its thoughts. Kant's I does not think: "it thinks a thinking of thinking."[56] In other words, the I-think could not stand outside itself because that standing outside constituted already a representation of the I.[57] This constricted subject is Kant's "transcendental subject of the thoughts = X." The transcendental subject "I" is given in its "predicates," but ends up being caught in a "perpetual circle," moving back and forth from *its representations* to *itself as a representation.* Like all else, the "I" may intuit this circle but only as appearance. According to Kant, the "I" is not an intuition. Lacoue-Labarthe and Nancy note that self-presence is not guaranteed in the absence of an *intuitus originarius;* in consequence, the subject is dealt a defeating blow, since "all that remains of the subject is the 'I' as an 'empty form' (a purely logical necessity) . . . that accompanies my representations."[58]

Kant's epistemology, which made of things objects of the subject's apperception, also made of this subject merely a function of synthesis, a presupposition to representations. Anything ascribed to the self by the "I" is already an object or predicate of the "I." But the one predicate that remains out of reach is the "I" itself. Consciousness is equally qualified in Kant's thought. While Kant's "I" allows for an awareness of its changing conscious states and for the recognition that those states are borne by the "I," these states cannot remain outside synthesis by categories such as "causality" if they are to be recognized as being "mine." As Andrew Bowie remarks, Kant had "a difficulty in explaining the consciousness which must be already there for our multiple representations to be representations of an 'I.'"[59] In the end, the aporia of the Kantian subject may be characterized by the subject's limitation in being able to account only for the results (synthesized intuitions) of its consciousness.

The aporia of Kantian self-representation (i.e., Kant's "perpetual circle") had two consequences. First, the Kantian subject could not be an object of its own contemplation. Second, consciousness was assumed and deemed a spontaneity, not something that could be looked at. In fact, looking at consciousness carried for Kant the threat that the I might come undone, for what would sanction the synthesis of consciousness itself when consciousness was that which allowed all syntheses in the first place? As for temporality, the I was aware of its appearance *in* time but not, significantly, *as* time. In the end, consciousness could articulate only what it produced (i.e., its syntheses or its contents or thoughts "as its predicates"), but it could not articulate itself.

The successful rendering of phenomena into products of the syntheses of the I by Kant's epistemology carried profound ontological implications. There was, for instance, a division between phenomena and things themselves. Fichte detected this, but more urgently, he thought it contradictory that Kant's successful epistemology made gains on the world on behalf of the subject at too great a cost: it kept the subject at an unnecessarily cautious distance. In the deep schism between knowable and unknowable elements within Kant's subject, Fichte saw a problematically compounded self. His theory of knowledge fought to restore the unity of an untrammeled and originary self-consciousness to the I. But there could be no return to the Cartesian *cogito* with its sharp distinction between the mind and all else. Instead, Fichte veered off Cartesian and Kantian dualisms by proposing an I that might precede all distinctions between the I (i.e, subject) and the not-I (i.e., object). This self-conscious and self-positing I he termed "Absolute," a sort of I-itself.[60] First, to avoid what he saw as a potentially devastating division within the subject, Fichte established that a consciousness that makes of itself an object could be neither an object nor an appearance to begin with.[61] Second, he made a distinction between the *facticity* of the Kantian I and the I defined as an *activity*. Third, he claimed that the activity of self-reflection did not require it to be determined by an a priori, for such activity already constituted evidence that the I could think itself (i.e., present itself to itself and be the subject of its own contemplation). To designate this activity, Fichte coined a term, *Tathandlung*. The term refers to "an activity which presupposes no object, but itself produces it, and in which, accordingly, the acting (*Handlung*) immediately becomes the deed or fact (*Tat*)." This self-constitutive activity is a precondition of all knowledge (*Wissen*). In Fichte's words, "we do not act because we know, rather we know because our vocation is to act." As Frederick Neuhoser claims, "Fichte must be understood as holding that the I just *is* the activity of referring diverse representations to a single possessor of those representations."[62] The sole evidence necessary for the I is its action of thinking itself, which really means that the act of thinking is anterior to any empirical evidence of the thought "I." Fichte frames this notion most dramatically in the proposition "I am I": "because the subject of this proposition is the absolute subject, the subject purely and simply, then (in this single case) the proposition's inner content is posited along with its form: 'I am posited *because* I have posited myself. I am, *because* I am.'"[63] Here it is manifest that self-positing and Being are one and the same thing. The inseparability of Being from self-consciousness follows from Fichte's proposition. Self-consciousness, he argued, could not be defined strictly in the cognitive terms of pure reason (as Kant dictated) but as practical reason (which he called the root of all reason). In sum, Fichtean self-consciousness was an activity of an I always already immediately present to itself.

By positing the Absolute I as an unconditional point of origin for all consciousness, Fichte restores to the subject something like the powers of self-intuition of the Cartesian *cogito*. Indeed, in an effort to elaborate the process by which this Absolute I can reflect on itself, he posits the notion of intellectual intuition: "one can still raise oneself to a consciousness of an intuition of the pure I (an inner intuition, of course)."[64] This leaves, however, a subject so tightly wound up in its unity that it cannot explain how the pure self-positing I can intuit an empirical I without having to reintroduce a dangerous split in the Absolute I. Fichte's solution is to reinstate a dualism, but one that adopts the form of a pronounced dialectic in the structure of the self: "Suppose that the highest concept is the I, and that a not-I is opposed to this I. It is clear that the not-I cannot be placed in opposition to the I unless it is *posited*, and indeed, posited within the highest thing we can conceive of, that is, posited within the I." Having introduced the not-I as a self-negation regulated by the I, Fichte proposes a further division. "It would be necessary to consider the I in two different aspects," he concedes, "as that *in* which the not-I is posited, and as that *which* is posited in opposition to the not-I, and which, consequently is itself posited in the absolute I."[65] Here we find, then, a divided I: first, an I defined as *action* ("the I *in* which the not-I is posited") and, second, an I defined as *object* ("the I *which* is posited in opposition to the not-I"). But this division reintroduces the schism within the subject that Fichte sought to reconcile in the first place. How Fichte reintroduces this division can be explained in three steps: (1) the synthesis of I and not-I in the Absolute I reflects the unlimited nature of the Absolute I, (2) the Absolute I needs the opposition of a not-I to "intuit" itself to itself, and (3) in this need the Absolute becomes determined by the not-I, which makes it self-limiting (i.e., not Absolute). Still, this self-limitation was something that Fichte willingly allowed by theorizing the existence of two opposing drives that regulate the subject. He called these drives theoretical, which drives the subject to reflect upon itself, and practical, which incites endless striving toward infinity, toward the Absolute.

Fichte's conciliatory gesture toward a divided self conceals an inherent contradiction in his foundational proposition "I am I." The aura of total self-identity surrounding this proposition masks a profound difference. Together with the initial negativity that undoes the unity of the Absolute I, the tension between identity and difference within the constitution of the subject forms a central concern for Romantic subjectivity. The Romantics' criticism of Fichte transposed the subjective self-alterity of the theoretical and practical drives to a mediating poetic field. This is, of course, a story that bears on the oft-discussed Romantic turn toward subjective poetry, in particular.[66] But it is also a story that bears on more general issues of representation as the mediating element. Schlegel, for one, perceived in the subjective idealism of the Absolute I a self-alienating estrangement from the phenomenal world, and sensed as well an excessive subjectivization and formal abstraction of all encounters between the I and the world, including, most importantly, the encounter with art, and ultimately with its truths.[67] And hardly any truth could have been more elusive than that of time, for in it the subject became aware of its finitude. This subject is, of course, not the subject of a *cogito;* it is an empirical self whose defining characteristic is its operative function in reflection.[68] Against the finitude of the subject stood the infinite with its eternal but never fully graspable truths. Aware of its limitations, Schlegel postulated a subject who might experience the Absolute (which he included in the notion of the infinite), however vicariously. First, he had to cast the Absolute in terms of relations, as "an infinite fullness" that by definition could never cease. Second, he had to outline an action by the subject that would enact for its consciousness the relations that Schlegel believed to be inherent in the Absolute. With its ceaseless oscillation, irony approximated a representation by the subject *and* to the subject of these relationships.

Lest it be thought that Schlegel simply recapitulated the Absolute I under the premise of representation, it should be noted that his conception of representation placed exacting constrictions on its claims to knowledge. First, in no sense did irony represent the Absolute; rather, it enacted the experience of it, reminiscent of Fichte's I as an activity, but different from it in being an act of reflection, a representation. Second, this representation did not seek a transcendental union of the subject in the Absolute; Romantic irony simply enacted their interdependency. Third, as a result of this interdependency, there was no final synthesis for the subject. Schlegel believed that the subject ought to remain in a state of becoming, forever moving in ironic self-reflection: "irony is the clear consciousness of eternal agility, of an infinitely teeming chaos."[69]

Schlegel's thoughts have, no doubt, loud, strong, transcendentalist overtones. But true to his ironist creed, they give voice to a practical program: the Romantic ironist is a subject defined by action. This action, which begins with a self-positing I, contains also the possibility of its annihilation in the form of the non-I. But unlike Fichte's negative dialectic, the Romantic ironist's self-alienation constitutes a source of productive self-reflection precisely because of its awareness of the devastating potential of self-alterity.

Without making causal connections between Weber and the Romantics or Fichte, we can see Weber's interpretation of Mozart as a field of subjective action and understand this action as operating under the logic of irony. Weber's compounded subject who writes itself hearing is a product of action too. The ceaseless vacillations of "das Gehör" constitute acts of self-reflection. And nowhere else is the ironic spirit of such acts better exemplified than in the refusal to reach final decisions. In the end, the outcome of this mediation in Weber's analysis is the realization that neither a fixed position nor an absolute sense of self is prescribable. As a whole, the analysis would be in line with Schlegel's pronouncement that "[irony] is the freest of all licenses, for by means of it one transcends oneself,"[70] allowing the analyst to come to terms with the limitations and possibilities for the representation of harmony by theory. This posture would make of the Mozart analysis testimony of a productive condition of being in the world that is critical (in a Kantian sense) through and through. Consider, for instance, the shattered images of time Weber unwittingly offers: when he fills every moment with thick descriptions and suffuses the temporal with the spatial, he is in fact prying open the structure of consciousness. "Das Gehör" seeks to slow down the passing of time, and in a way accomplishes its goal, but not without giving rise to two temporalities: that of analysis, and that of a musical performance of the introduction.[71] Like other binaries, this one suggests a hierarchy in which the temporality of performance is placed over that of analysis. Indeed, although the analysis constitutes a whole (with a classical Aristotelian structure of beginning, middle, and end), it attends to the larger original totality of Mozart's introduction by means of an allegorical relation. Mozart's introduction constitutes the third term in Weber's tripartite division of the subject that must be understood allegorically.

4.6. Between Fragment and Totality: The Allegorical Mediation of Analysis

Weber's analysis is fragmentary in two ways: first, in the way the conceptual poetics of its harmonic interpretation tear apart the musical instant, leaving for the reader nothing but shards of time, and second, in the way in which its discursively elongated duration relates to the continuity and totality that Weber presumes Mozart's passage to be. These two fragmentary characteristics are summed up in the underlying discrepancy of a temporal-spatial nature that exists between the experience of the passage and the cognitive apprehension of that experience. Smith's thoughts on the anisochronies of narrative help us make sense of this discrepancy. To recapitulate her words from the introduction to this chapter, there is an inherent difference between the linguistic form of an event and the events represented by that form. To supplement Smith's distinction, we may consider Weber's analysis tropologically, giving its discursive totality a sharper profile. For, although the analysis is a fragment, it also forms a totality on its own. And for this totality to represent another (larger) totality, it must relate to the larger totality as a displaced temporality: allegorically.

Allegory, said Schlegel, "is the mediating term between unity and multiplicity." [72] Like irony, allegory operates under a logic of disjunction. Its disjunction is markedly temporal, for it is with time itself (to which it seeks to restitute some continuity) that allegory maintains a fundamental relationship. Basically its structure foregrounds the disparity between the totality of the time told—taken as a moment of origin—and the time of the telling—taken as a representation of that originary moment. Allegory (from Greek, *allos*, "other," and *agoreuein*, "to speak") does speak of other time, expresses the other "in other words," which makes it the paragon of temporal alterity in discourse.

To be sure, Weber's analysis appears to fold these temporalities into one another in an attempt to mediate the temporal experience of the musical passage (i.e., unity) and its cognition in time (i.e., the multiplicity of instances that he recounts). I have suggested that the narrative of Section 1, in particular, elaborates in discourse a presumed homology between time-consciousness and something like the structure of time itself as it is expressed in the music. Out of that homology, Mozart's introduction emerges as a trace of the subject's consciousness. But the homology conceals a series of temporal disjunctions. We have, first, an experience that precedes the analysis, and second, Weber's representation of that experience (through analysis). This process, by which events experienced are given figural form in narrative a posteriori, I will term *postfiguration*. Hereby events are refigured, but in the sense of being constructions in the present that deal with experience, not as it may have existed in a prior and ideal form but rather with the active process of their production through the intervention of "technical theory." In this sense allegory bears within itself the marks of the time of its production. It is key to understand here that, similar to the relationship between an empirical and a linguistic subject, the "I-hear" of Weber's analysis (i.e., "das Gehör") is a linguistic effect standing for an "I-have-heard." The analysis, like allegory, submits experience to the materiality of the telling, as a written or spoken account of some other time. In other words, this "I-have-heard" comes to be as a result of analytic discourse, and comes into being as a result of constituting itself through self-reflection in its very effort to apprehend music. We may borrow Heidegger's notion of "having been in the world" to frame the relation between narrative and temporality in Weber's discourse. Following such formulation, we may further note that the narrative expresses the dialectic between immediacy (of "having been") and endlessness (of not being there anymore). This dialectic, in turn, speaks to the dynamic tension between the subject of the telling ("das Gehör") and the subject telling (Weber), on the one hand, and between these subject(s) and the musical object, on the other.

But Weber's analysis is no solipsistic meditation on the flux of time. Apprehending music means also apprehending something of the empirical subject behind it, Mozart. [73] And it is in relation to "*a Mozart*" that there appears a third allegorical temporality: the listening experience that will follow the analysis (an "I-will-hear"), including all subsequent hearings of the passage which the analysis *prefigures*. [74] Ultimately, this temporality is extra-analytical and exceeds the enclosures of allegory proper, for it is indicative of an infinite domain similar to the Absolute of Romantic irony. The analysis shares with irony the critical separation of sign and concept (irony) and of ephemeral experience and eternal being (allegory). With this observation we can begin ascribing an identity to the "*supreme* judge . . . *the ear* of *a Mozart*" that "has already decided *in favour* of the passage," as Weber writes in his conclusion (183/225; emphasis in original). A good place to start is by aligning the infinity of all time with the infinity that is available to Mozart as a musical "poet," using Schlegel's favorite designation for paradigmatic artists: "[T]he ear of *a Mozart*" sanctioned nothing less than the Absolute, that dimension of existence of which only a listener engaged in the oscillation of irony can catch a glimpse. As for Mozart and his remarkable passage, Schlegel's words about Romantic poetry might suit: "The romantic kind of poetry . . . can be exhausted by no theory and only divinatory criticism could dare try to characterize its ideal. It alone is infinite, just as it alone is free; and it recognizes as its first rule that the whim of the poet can tolerate no law above itself."[75]

Read this way, Weber's analysis cannot be simply considered as an attestation or externalization of an originary experience by an originary and absolute (Fichtean) consciousness. The linguistic, subjective, and cognitive dynamics at stake are more involved than that. Thus, my allegorical interpretation neither juxtaposes nor nests two temporalities. Rather, it points toward temporal vectors variously emerging from the musical experience, the consciousness of that experience, and the consciousness that examines the consciousness of that experience. Neither one of these, in the end, can be absolutely determined to mark a point of origin. Each one can set off a chain of temporal relations along a particular vector. It may be the musical passage, which then enters a particular relation with the analysis; or it may be the analysis, in turn, as we read it, that frames a particular relation to the passage, and so on. In any event, the peculiar mode of representation in Weber's analysis provides a mediating linguistic structure that examines the very nature of temporal consciousness, a mediating structure that begins as representation of that consciousness and turns into a critical production of it. It would be hard to fault Weber for trying this, I believe, and a grave mistake to read the analysis as an ontological incarceration of the musical object (be it the passage or an individual chord) in the field of positivities of *Mehrdeutigkeit*. Surely one of the most telling ironies to emerge from my reading of Weber's analysis is this: how the analyst's indulgence in the plenitude of an interpretive existence manifests the emptiness of being of a subject who in the hollow spaces of harmonic identity tries to find the bearings for its existence as listener. In this analysis the lack of certitude and fixity coincides with the subjective striving for self-identity. This is, however, an endeavor that cannot but remain in a constant race against itself, trying to come to terms with some inadequacy, revealing that listening—whether retrospectively or prospectively—must find legitimacy in its own writing, writing which itself then reinitiates the race against itself.

The multiple temporal disjunctions and conjunctions of allegory resonate with the poetics of Romantic irony that I have pursued. In both, a dialectical interdependence between subject and object serves a cognitive purpose: to enable self-reflection, which at the same time critically brings to the fore the limitations of such enterprise. But irony, in particular, serves also an argumentative role, which we may relate to the specific context in which Weber's analysis appeared. During the 1820s a number of critics including Carl Cramer, François-Joseph Fétis, Giuseppe Sarti, and the anonymous "A. C. Leduc" were engaged in heated public debate about the correctness of Mozart's introduction. The predominant opinion among these critics, which Weber did not share, was that Mozart must have somehow erred. I take Weber to be playing the simultaneously self-deprecating and knowing *eiron* to the critics' pretentious *alazon* who thought Mozart was wrong.[76] How, then, to read his stance (i.e., his interpretive indecision and his final verdict) in this debate? An interpretation could feasibly consider his attitude as that of the ironic hero. "If inferior in power or intelligence to ourselves, so that we have the sense of looking down on a scene of bondage, frustration, or absurdity," writes Northrop Frye, "the hero belongs to the *ironic* mode."[77] Accordingly the *eiron* succeeds when the reader is made into an implicit *alazon*, which certainly would have included any of his adversaries. And to some degree that would include also ourselves. Indeed, it may seem reasonable for us as readers to question Weber's frustration when the musical present thwarts his efforts to grasp it, or to become frustrated when he ignores feasible causal connections between chords, or, in the worst of cases, even to think it absurd to hear a single dyad in three possible keys (e.g., C–A♭ in m. 1).[78] Weber, I think, is content in that particular analysis to disperse the totality of being and experience of the listener among subject, object, "das Gehör," "*my Mozart*," and "*a Mozart.*"

And yet we can detect in Weber's ironic hero a sophisticated listener communicating from beneath the debilitating weight of analytic paraphrase. We may do so because there we can recognize perhaps the story of anyone who has ever felt the tension between an imaginary theoretical reality and some other reality of musical experience. For Weber, as for anyone who analyzes a piece of music, discourse becomes the only possible habitation for the burden of the consciousness of our own listening practices.[79] From a historical perspective, the matter of multiple and simultaneous subject positions forms part of a productive strategy (inherited from the Romantics) to provide an alternative to the discontinuity of the subject in time. If nothing else, this reading has shown that insofar as the representation of the self is consubstantial with both a particular narrative and an interpretation, it is in effect inseparable from them. In the end, the self-negation (*Selbstvernichtung*) of the ironic analyst is an index of action, and the narrative in which this action is carried out is itself an "act performed in response to conditions given by circumstantial and psychological variables of which every utterance is a function."[80] In spite of the fact that there is no final redemption in the conclusion to Weber's analysis, there is no radical alienation in the lack of final synthesis, no yearning for a Hegelian *Aufhebung*. For Weber, analytic closure with respect to Mozart's passage can exist only ironically; any other conclusion would be considered an artificial device that would arbitrarily block off the subject's self-questioning. And yet he is presenting a system (e.g., the "Systematic Theory" of his title). His entire analysis is therefore attuned to Schlegel's dictum that "it is equally fatal for the mind to have a system and to have none. It will therefore have to decide to combine both."[81]

Weber's analytical contents and discontents speak to complex representations of time and temporality, to the relational nature of his analytical metalanguage, and ultimately to the open-ended possibilities of his theory within a Romantic framework. Were his versions of subjectivity and their representations to operate under a logic of identity, this logic would halt the very possibility of representational expression because any sign (e.g., "das Gehör," "IV," or "Gottfried Weber") would have been consummated once and for all. This would mean that as the implementation of an all-encompassing logical mandate, theory would reduce to itself anything beyond itself and would therefore assume a technical character. Such logic of identity would make of Weber's theory something of a technology, an activity exclusively controlled by the logic of *technē* (Greek: artifice), and analysis simply the product of its application. Interpretation would become a mechanical activity that the Romantics would have considered not just the opposite of the organic but its negation, because it would be the negation of art as the locus of the truths of the Absolute. "If the character of a given problem is insolvability, then we solve it by depicting its insolvability," said Novalis, adding that "we know enough of *a*, when we understand that its predicate is *a*."[82] Art is "the presentation of the unrepresentable," and analysis might well then be the representation of the unrepresentable. But at least this way we know what art or analysis may or may not be. In his encounter with Mozart, Weber appeared to have realized this as well, although doubtfully with full authorial awareness and intention.

Surely this analysis is an isolated case within Weber's analytical oeuvre. As we know, Weber's interpretive model became the dominant analytical metalanguage in Anglo-American music theory for a set of reasons that run counter precisely to the spirit of his Mozart analysis. No doubt, the discursive space of Weber's theory (i.e., the empiricities of his chord tables) encourages the instrumental use of the Roman-numeral cipher in analysis and thus the objectification of the harmonic content of tonal music. Such use is made, however, at the expense of the subjective positivities along the axis of interpretation that ought to be inseparable from the presumably objective empiricities. That is a problem for both Weber's theory and his followers. The reception history of Weber's work loudly attests to the preference for final conclusions and the appeal of the fixed musical object represented by the Roman numeral. Further, such instrumental and technological application forms part of the background of an increasing commodification of knowledge in social, cultural, and economic spheres throughout the nineteenth century and into our day.[83] Viewed as cognitive currency, the Roman numeral does reduce the "chord" to a semiotic essence, exchanging the chord and its associated experience for the satisfaction of capturing that chord and that experience in a grapheme. It might be said, furthermore, that Weber encourages the reduction of music to distended harmonic states. But here I use the word "state" pointedly, to designate what I see as one of the most fundamental aspects of Weber's interpretive endeavors: that of placing the listening subject on the page, not merely as an empirical inscription, but as a linguistic locus of an interrelation between itself and the putative musical object that transcends that inscription. These states designate the space of being for the listener and ultimately, as I have repeatedly remarked, belong fully neither to the music nor to the listener. Weber's definition of *Mehrdeutigkeit* brilliantly frames this simultaneity of belonging (no irony here). The divided subjectivity that emerges is not that of the positive sciences, which, following developments in the psychology of perception, would usher the study of harmony into a stage of self-assured rationality. Weber may not have been aware of the tension between the disjointed musical experience his theory made possible and the staging of a contiguous self-consciousness of which his analysis was evidence (this in itself would reflect a tragic element alongside the ironic one). But I wish, in closing, to suggest that neither the rational metaphor of an analytical and theoretical instrumentality nor the theatrical metaphor of a linguistic staging exists in Weber at the exclusion of the other. No irony is greater than the coexistence, within a single "work," of these metaphors. Whatever its ambiguities and inadequacies, Weber's thought had the merit of placing the debate of interpretation into an arena where experiential tensions could coexist.

Epilogue

From the full embedding of human agency in a holistic world in Zarlino to the often contentious interior negotiation of listening by Weber's "das Gehör," my readings have shown music theories to participate in a transhistorical process whereby the figure of the subject (the knower) vies for or asserts for itself a particular position within the space of possible thought. Indeed, a common theme throughout the preceding chapters has been the analytical premise that particular conceptualizations of the subject are productively intertwined—that is, dialectically—with the cognitive enclosures and discursive formations that make these conceptualizations possible in the first place. I say "productively" because the concept "subject" has been presented positively, as an instrument in the production of music-theoretical knowledge and as part and parcel of music theories' inescapable "textuality." By "intertwined" I suggest the existence of a negativity at the center of the concept, which I locate in the subject's circular agency in its own articulation and constitution. Namely, any of the particular relations we define with ourselves as subjects hinges on cognitive dictates of our own design at the same time that these dictates are outlined in the act of defining those relations. To sum up this circularity, in the conceptualizations of the subject and in the kinds of musical thought that have accompanied these conceptualizations, we are at once elements and agents of a single process, we constitute center and periphery, *arche* and *telos*.

Combined, the two elements in my adjectival construction "productively intertwined" designate a dialectic relationship that exists at the core of the concept of the subject. In my account the production of various versions of the subject has been made possible by the self-reflective processes that have allowed the subject(s) to think themselves as musical hearers and listeners. Reciprocally, the degree of cognitive clarity in each act of self-reflection has been equally determined by the type of subject produced and by the degree of transparency of its representations. Seen as a game with profound ontological and epistemological outcomes, it might appear as if the cards have always been stacked in favor of the subject. As a cognitive proposition, the subject has been the fundament on which all that is said is grounded, a *sub-jectum* in the strictest sense of the word. In Descartes, to take a paradigmatic example, what the subject pronounces—the "I"—becomes the sub-ject of a *cogito* defined as first principle. In short, the subject of this *ego cogito* holds absolute control over the legislative powers governing its own design but is paradoxically unaware of its powers precisely because there exists no distance from which to observe them. Descartes's subject grounds all predication concerning the object of music—sound—and constitutes the unique locus of the most concentrated form of knowledge of experience—intuition. In interpreting Rameau, I drew a profile of the subject that too was seen against the background of its capacity for objective analysis of nature vis-à-vis harmony and its capacity to ground an inseparable relation between sense and concept. But there too, the absence of any cognitive distance in the act of representation was the occasion for ambivalence in the semiotics attending to the temporal dimension of chordal succession.

Even a cursory glance at the trajectory of the subject that I have registered reveals that it has been marked since its inception by the repeated probing of its self-legislating powers. Thus, Descartes, whose version of the subject as an *ego cogito* was founded on such powers, would arrive at his tantalizing realization of subjective self-transparency by submitting doubt to a methodic process. Once the subject could be certain that doubt originated in the *cogito*, it could be demonstrated that the subject was indeed present to its thought, in turn defining the subject by its capacity for self-presence. Constituted at bottom by a total relation to Being, the Cartesian subject surged forth from the transformation of the negative form of knowledge as *dubito ergo cogito* into the positive proposition *cogito ergo sum*.

Such doubt was not an exclusive feature of the airy abstractions of Cartesian metaphysics. It formed part of Rameau's concerns with the place of harmony in musical practice. My reading of Rameau proposed that the ultimate assertion of the subject's cognitive authority be located not just positively in his objective analysis of nature, or in his having placed the subject's musical experience on the precise coordinates given by that analysis. Rather, in an inversion of the positive terms of the analysis of nature, I suggested that Rameau's subject be recognized in the more indistinct contours of *sous-entendre* ("implication"). There, at the threshold of what would have been considered silent by the day's acoustical and psychological standards, I heard the noisy intervention of the subject's imagination. I argued that this intervention denoted an excess of meaning at a cognitive register not available in the classical sign, indeed, a cognitive register not available to the Cartesian subject. Explained by Foucault as a transparent mark of analysis and as a self-sufficient union of signified and signifier, the classical sign and the representation of harmony it contained could not, in my account, adequately account for the temporal element that Rameau intuited in harmonic successions. Needing to give form to its consciousness of the interconnection of harmonies, Rameau's subject wrestled the classical sign into yielding space for the subject to actively participate in the cognition of harmonic interconnection. Rameau's cognitive gesture carried two important consequences. First, it opened up the possibility of a ternary semiotics, with the subject as a third, albeit indistinct, term added to the classical sign's binary structure. Second, Rameau made of the agency of the subject a fundamental condition of musical thought, where "musical thought" is reduced to the idea of harmony. Radically departing from the idea that knowledge should collapse the product of analysis into the cognitive *punctum* of Cartesian intuition, Rameau constructs his version of the modern subject in his efforts to recuperate time for the subject, so to speak, which allows for its active participation in the cognition of music. At the same time modern musical thought, in my account, is demarked by the way in which theory demands and constructs a new kind of subject.

Returning to epistemology, we found that Kant's subject too emerged out of a questioning of its self-legislative powers, in fact encasing their domain within the a priori forms of sensibility (time and space) and the categories of understanding. The Kantian subject, however, came at considerable expense, since it lost what Merleau-Ponty pointedly calls its capacity for "psychological intimacy":[1] that is, Kant's subject could not present itself to itself as it really was, but only as a mediated cognition—as representation. To recall my discussion in Chapter 4, the Kantian subject was advanced as a logical necessity that accompanies our representations. It was one representation among many, and one that, crucially, no longer held a direct relation to being. We may thus think of Kant's subject as having disjoined the Cartesian copula *cogito ergo sum*, maintaining the subject's privileged position as *cogito*, but separating the *cogito*'s causal relation to being (i.e., *ergo sum*). In turn, my interpretation of Weber's analysis of Mozart brought to the fore the increased tension caused by the separation between knowing and being. There I argued that Weber's analytical discourse should be read as an attempt to mediate between knowledge and being. This mediation consisted in the simultaneous assertion of the listener's presence in the experience of music and in the cognitive apprehension of that experience. Of this mediation, however, the subject was dependent, appearing as the main figure of an empirical consciousness that evaded it. Further, Weber's listening subject contained within it multiple points of articulation. To begin with, like Descartes's subject, Weber's listener was the subject of predicates. But it also delineated a cognitive and psychological category bearing analytical processes and emotional states, and an empirical subject producing the analysis. It was too a subject of enunciation addressing itself, addressing interlocutors (i.e., the critics to whom the analysis conclusion was partly directed at), and implicitly addressing the composer. Furthermore, it was the subject of address by "events" in the music and ultimately by something like the Absolute of the early Romantics. In the end, it was a subject who identified the traces of its own consciousness in the act of listening, a listening subject constituted in the very act of contemplating—if not confronting—its own experience.

Keeping this last observation in mind, we may now say that Weber's analysis expresses a reversal of the Kantian loss of "psychological intimacy" identified by Merleau-Ponty. "Das Gehör," in the analysis, believed itself to be fully in touch with its cognitive and psychological processes, laying bare for the reader to see, even and specially when all that was revealed were the suspicions accompanying the question "where am I?"

Psychological intimacy, in the form of a phenomenology of interiority, could not have returned in the form one finds it in Descartes. No matter how decisively the responsibility for knowledge was delegated to the listening subject, the kind of knowledge Weber's listening subject pursued—the knowledge of what this or that harmony was—became elusive. In Weber, the elusiveness of the object of knowledge is most pronounced in the fact that it came to be defined as a set of possibilities. This brings me to the question of the "object."

Weber offers a suitable starting point to evaluate the object as a supplement (in Derrida's sense) of the subject. It surely would not escape the reader's attention that in his version of the subject the gain of "psychological intimacy" coincided with a compromised relation with its objects. I made sufficiently clear that I do not consider Weber to be an unrepentant Kantian for whom "the world emerges from the subject," as Alfred North Whitehead put it.[2] Instead, I concluded, "the subject determines the formal conditions of experience in relation to any given object." But I also noted that such determination by the subject often does not exhaust the meaning of its objects of experience, even with the subject legislating the nature of that meaning. For Weber, for instance, the ontology of objects of experience constituted a privileged locus of meaning. That particular ontology turned out to be rather complex, lying at the intersection of the musical object's ontic ground as pitch-class aggregate and the interpretive acts of the listening subject.

Part of me wants to say that the musical object, in Weber, is somehow external, that it designates an experiential reality, and to say, further, that it is therefore objective in an elemental sense: the object is a chord and its transparent signifier, the Roman numeral. Such assertions would not be entirely wrong, but they could hardly be said to be right. Risking sounding redundant, I ought to repeat here that in my reading of Weber's analysis and my teasing apart of his conceptual model of *Mehrdeutigkeit,* object and subject are so fully interdependent that the distinction we make between them is more heuristic than anything else. Such distinction, that is, helps us understand the relation between a theoretical notion and its coming to be in analysis. I should say, then, that insofar as musical object bears on the being of the subject, the object is more process than substance. Or, to bring back Kant one last time, that Weber's analysis must be seen as mediating knowledge and being, and that in this sense "knowledge" constitutes knowledge of oneself as a listener. Thus, analysis constitutes an action whereby being is in some way reinserted into the definition of what constitutes knowledge. In making this connection between knowledge and being in language, I am not suggesting that the subject is fully self-present in language or that it captures the objects of its experience fully in language. Neither am I suggesting that the subject and its objects are subjected to the linguistic system in which they appear. For while I spoke of Weber's discourse as "the only possible habitation for the burden of the consciousness of our listening practices," I also pointed to the multiple vectors of temporality emerging from analysis that extend beyond the circumscriptions of the analytical narrative.

Rameau deals with its object differently than Weber. The anxieties associated with interpretation are reduced in Rameau, for whom, simply put, there are fewer analytic choices. We may want to note that even in the case of a chord that may serve two functions, according to how it is approached and left, Rameau resolves the problem with the heavy hand of an authoritative subject that determines the presence of *double emploi.* Rameau's music-analytical choices are not really interpretive, being instead given a priori by the analysis of nature. However, as my analysis of signs indicated, the semiosis communicating the analysis of nature could not contain the fact that, as acoustic objects, harmonies were not grounded in nature alone. Most extremely expressed in the case of *sous-entendre*, the nature of the object was premised less in a substance-based ontology than in a relational-based one. The object was thus fully embedded in the cognitive activity of the subject who must understand as being there "things" that are not, by traditional definitions of "being," "there."

The object, in Descartes's pithy motto "of this [music] the object is sound" in conjunction with the set of Preliminaries to the *Compendium,* asserts at once an order of things that strategically assigns the subject a separate position in relation to all else. In Chapter 2 I described the Cartesian "knower" (and "hearer") as "a cognitive construction, the privilege of which is to hold a particular and generalizable perspective *of* and *over* that which it perceives." I might here adapt Whitehead's notion of "superject" with regard to Descartes's "hearer" to mean that condition in the structure of the subject that allows it to survey all things as if from above, including its own perception. Descartes's gesture epitomizes the "productive intertwining" of the subject that I referred to above, and likewise encapsulates the idea that subject and object exist in a state of absolute embedding. In the simultaneous separation and bringing together of object and subject, knowledge becomes objectively *of* the subject. Compared to a previous way of thinking, the human presence in the world according to which humans were fully embedded within the world, Descartes's subject extricates itself from it, albeit only in a very restricted sense. Having brought the cosmos into the fold of the *cogito,* we could equally say that never before had the subject been so deeply ingrained in it. And yet we must recognize in his methodological separation of subject from object a strategic deployment of a belief in our ability to know that is markedly different from that represented, in my account, by Zarlino's thought.

To conclude, I wish to note that my emphasis on Descartes throughout this Epilogue is motivated by my belief that in some sense the Cartesian idea of self-staging constitutes the dominant form of subjectivity in music theory and analysis. I say this in full awareness that my own case studies have argued for the presence of other forms of subjectivity. But I am also aware that any of these other forms has emerged from a more or less direct encounter and subsequent negotiation with the Cartesian model. As for music theory and analysis, it is not difficult to see why the Cartesian subject should prove so enduring. Whether one's project entails systematic formal generalizations of musical objects or experiential accounts of encounters with music, Cartesian subjectivity, in its dialectical commitment to the subject-object interrelation, can be pressed into serving the objectivity of formalism or the subjectivity of experience-based analysis. After all, if the subject is a sort of conceptual arm of subjectivity, it is also a cognitive prerequisite for the object and for any claims to objectivity. It can be found in Forte's objective mapping of intervallic sets, and in Lewin's formalization of a Husserlian phenomenology made to register our perceptions of intervallic transformations. It makes possible the pedagogical staging of the pupil who inhabits Beethoven's compositional practice in A. B. Marx's Hegelian subject of *Bildung,* and it grounds the objectivity of Stumpf's psychological efforts. It hovers over Riemann's ambivalence about whether functions designated chords, relations, or both, and sanctions the perceptual activity of his mature conception of *Tonvorstellung* and the objectivity of the *Tonnetz.* And what are Hanslick's controversial "tonally moving forms" if not the apotheosis of Cartesian objectivity? Of course, in each of these diverse models Cartesian subjectivity stands next to other, often more crucial, contingencies (intellectual, cultural) that have shaped these modes of thought. Thus the emergence of a science of mind in nineteenth-century German empirical science is decisive for an objectivity that is radically different from Weber's. Helmholtz's psychological concept of *Tonempfindung,* for instance, reactivates the idea that the contents of sensation can be grasped and mapped with an accuracy unthinkable by Descartes, Rameau, or Weber.

With a present still made in the image of Cartesian subjectivity, what is, then, the position of the subject in music theory today? In recent years, as Slavoj Žižek notes, "all academic powers have entered into a holy alliance to exorcise this spectre [the specter of the Cartesian subject]." To cite some of the attacks he lists:

> [T]he postmodern deconstructionist (for whom the Cartesian subject is a discursive fiction, an effect of decentred textual mechanisms); the Habermasian [and Bakhtinian] theorist of communication (who insists on a shift from Cartesian monological subjectivity to discursive intersubjectivity) . . . the cognitive scientist (who endeavors to prove empirically that there is no unique scene of the Self, just a pandemonium of competing forces) . . . the feminist (who emphasizes that the alleged sexless cogito is in fact a male patriarchal formation).[3]

The subject, we have been made well aware of, is no longer arbiter or source of meaning. It is, instead, a linguistic effect perennially under construction, or a product at the mercy of overwhelming forces of class, culture, ethnicity, gender, race, and society. It is, furthermore, no longer a unified, self-present concept, being rather a collection of assorted positions, or at best a crossroads where multiple concepts intersect before moving on. Abstract rationality, in these critiques, gives way to critical understanding; Heidegger supersedes Descartes. In these critiques we easily recognize some of the polemics associated with attacks on abstract rationalism, formalism, and objectivism, which, critics often say, remain the main cognitive fountainheads of much music theory and analysis. These things many want to exorcise. Fine. This is no place to engage in polemics about the ideological virtues of the modern or the postmodern or the contested hegemony of structuralism (which, by the way, remains a much misunderstood notion) over hermeneutics. Nor could I. For one, my readings of the subject in music theory have come dangerously close to asserting a sort of postmodern critical transcendentality—for instance, in the attention I paid to representation as a condition of possibility for the concept of the subject, to say nothing of my

Foucauldian methodological predilections. Nonetheless, I hope I have been able to suggest how even at its most objective and "rational," subject, object, and representation have been dialectically (not dualistically) founded in the inherent excess by which they, within the self-assigned space of modern knowledge, have carried an often "unacknowledged kernel of the *cogito*" in the irrepressible force of the imagination. Moving beyond the subject of musical thought I have outlined will require more than revealing the (presumed) misguided values of autonomy, interiority, centrality, and self-presence. It will require listening back, way back, by the sounding beacon of our recent critical and cognitive gains but without allowing that sound to deafen us, to the recesses of history where the subject, the object, and the complex of representation that enabled them came to exercise the most daring of rights: the freedom to imagine how music may sound.

Glossary of Greek Terms

aisthetikon	αἰσθητικόν
alazôn	ἀλαζών
archê	ἀρχή
dianoetikon	διανοητικόν
dianoia	διάνοια
eidos	εἶδος
eidôlon	εἴδωλον
eikazô	εἰκάζω
eikasia	εἰκασία
eikô	εἴκω
eikôn	εἰκών
eirôn	εἴρων
eirôneia	εἰρονεία
epistêmê	ἐπιστήμη
gnôsis	γνῶσις
idiôtês	ἰδιώτης
logos	λόγος
mathêma	μάθημα
mathêsis	μάθησις
methexis	μέθεξις
mimêsis	μίμησις
noêsis	νόησις
nous	νοῦς
onomata	ὀνόματα
pathos	πάθος
phainô	φαίνω
phantasia	φαντασία
phantasma	φάντασμα
pistis	πίστις
sêmeia	σημεῖα
technê	τέχνη
telos	τέλος

Notes

Introduction

1. The works to which I refer are *The Order of Things* ([1966] 1971) and *The Archaeology of Knowledge* ([1969] 1972). Two other widely read texts from that period are *Madness and Civilization* ([1961] 1965) and *The Birth of the Clinic* ([1963] 1973).

2. Foucault (1972: 15, n2).

3. Both in the scheme of historical discontinuities and ruptures in the fabric of knowledge, as well as in the idea that historical knowledge should be about the articulation of objects, concepts, and theories in specific sciences, Foucault follows Gaston Bachelard and Charles Canguilhem. Gutting (1989: 9–54) offers a helpful introduction to Bachelard's and Canguilhem's formative influence on Foucault.

4. Throughout the book I use "it" as the pronominal referent for subject (or the plural "they"). Impersonal and objectifying as this is, the choice allows the reference to a depersonalized subject and subjectivity that can then be historically contextualized against the more existential, personalized "self"; it has the further advantage of avoiding the unnecessarily restrictive gendered designation (he) or the more inclusive, albeit clumsier, "he/she." As will become clearer from Chapter 2 on, the subject indeed becomes increasingly objectified, as a spatial and privileged position in relation to other objects.

5. Heidegger (1971: 213). Compare with an early denunciation of the potentially deceitful capacities of language, Bacon's "idols of the market": "For men believe that their reason governs words; but it is also true that words react on the understanding"; Francis Bacon, *Novum Organum* (1620: 80).

6. The binary pair of music as a "cultural trope" and as "disciplinary object" appears in Kramer (1995: 61). My use of the term "statement" here corresponds to Foucault's use.

7. My sense of "statement" here preserves some but not all of Foucault's sense. For Foucault, statements are not reducible to sentences (which are governed by grammar rules and are bound to written texts) or to propositions (which are governed by logic rules). A statement constitutes, rather, a set of signs to which status of knowledge may be ascribed: it is not so much a structure of signification as a function of the existence of signification available in what is written (said, enacted). This function spreads along a network that includes a subject position (conceived as a space potentially filled by individuals other than the author), a referential field (i.e., a statement has as its correlate domains in which objects appear and relations among them may be assigned), an associated field (e.g., other statements), and a material situation (e.g., the possibility of reinscription and transcription and institutional sources of its

stability). See Foucault ([1969] 1972), chapter 3, "The Statement and the Archive."

8.   The notion of representation as a "cognitive protocol" is Hayden White's (1978: 239). It will become increasingly clear that this book is not about the representation of mental imagery as viewed by cognitive studies or by scholars inclined toward analytical philosophy. From the extensive bibliography on the subject, I have in mind here DeBellis (1995), Gødoy, Inge, and Jørgensen (2001), Howell, West, and Cross (1991), Lerdahl (2001), and Raffman (1993).

9.   This threefold classification of listening appears in Barthes's "Listening" (1991: 245–46).

10.   In this arrangement—the subject as object—lies the possibility that a history of the subject of music theory might parallel a history of the phenomenology of interiority, which the book touches upon as a subsidiary theme. Barthes (1991) suggests a parallel between the history of listening and the history of the phenomenology of interiority but pursues the idea along different lines than I do.

11.   See Aristotle, *Metaphysics* 983a30, and for the latter meaning, *Physics* 189a31.

12.   Subjectum est prima substantia, quod ipsum nulli accidit alii inseparabiliter, etc. (*The Marriage of Philology and Mercury*, Book IV, Ch. 361, trans. John Bauschatz).

13.   Individual expression, write Gunter Gebauer and Christoph Wulf, "does in fact begin to appear from about the twelfth century on." However, they note after Paul Zumthor (*Oral Poetry: An Introduction*, 1990) that "the I in the texts does not designate a potentially individual and certainly not an empirical person"; see Gebauer and Wulf (1995: 85–86).

14.   Starobinski (1986: 223).

15.   Here it is worth remembering that Descartes does not "invent" the modern subject, he merely gives it the most thorough articulation. Despite its title, the Cartesian "subject" is itself a unit of order of knowledge (*savoir*), and so it evades authorial determinations in Foucault's reckonings.

16.   Descartes (1985: 39).

17.   Latour (1993: 136).

18.   Kramer (1995: 9).

19.   Kramer (1995: 9–10).

20.   This list of meanings for "subject" adapts and modifies one given in Inwood (1992: 280).

21.   A tripartite semiological analysis of music and musical discourse is advanced in Nattiez (1990). The model I follow is less concerned with questions of meaning, as Nattiez's is, though there are overlapping interests in matters of metalinguistic representation.

22.   Scott Burnham (1992b: 75–76) discusses the limitations and possibilities of what he calls "mediating generalizations" learned through musical training. Admitting the difficulty of not resorting to these generalizations, he warns

the reader not to mistake "forms of theoretical and pedagogical discourse for musical content," or to confuse these "textbook categories of musical experience" as substitutes for the "experience itself." My inquiry begins, so to speak, at a level at which those "forms of theoretical and pedagogical discourse" are made possible prior to their deployment in pedagogy.

23.　White (1978: 239).

24.　My choice also reflects Foucault's undermining of the "event" as a category for analysis of the episteme. According to Foucault, the complexity inherent in any such events cannot explain the consciousness of an age; in fact, for the consciousness of an age no single event holds the status of "fact" independently of its own (epistemically regulated) mechanisms of representation.

25.　Rameau (1722: xxi); translation mine.

26.　Feyerabend (1993: 20–23, 61–64).

27.　My analysis views the local ideas about implication and harmonic succession articulated in the *Traité* archaeologically, as symptoms of an epistemological attitude that no single intellectual trend or ideological attachment of Rameau's can fully explain. My focus on the imaginary and the imagination in the *Traité* should not be taken to mean either that other notions are of less importance for Rameau's thought or for musical thought in general or, worse still, that all the aspects of his music theory are dependent on this single notion. As Christensen's study of Rameau's relation to the intellectual milieu of the Enlightenment has shown, understanding the ideas coming in and out of Rameau's work during and after the *Traité* is indispensable for a full appreciation of the conceptual flexibility of his music theory (Christensen 1993a). For an exposition of his historiographical agenda, see Christensen (1993b), especially 16–17.

28.　Gottfried Weber (1832, I:42).

29.　A concise account of the interaction between natural science and history in Riemann (with insightful references to Helmholtz) appears in Burnham (1992a). More recently Rehding (2003) explores a wide range of ideological implications in Riemann's thought, including natural sciences, German nationhood, and technology.

30.　Christensen (1993a), David E. Cohen (2001), Duchez (1986), Hyer (1994, 1996a, and 1996b), and Saslaw (1990, 1991, and 1992). Also Ian Bent's erudite introductions to the two volumes of *Music Analysis in the Nineteenth Century* (see Gottfried Weber [1832] 1994 for bibliographical information).

31.　The following glosses Foucault's critique in Chapter 1 of *Archaeology of Knowledge* (1972: 21–30).

32.　Alex Rehding, in a personal communication, jokingly suggested that I should name this project "The Birth of the Listener," keeping the Foucauldian motif (after "Birth of the Clinic") but hoping to erase the suspicion of readers (and potential publishers) more accustomed to linear narratives.

33.　Blasius (2002).

34.　Foucault ([1966] 1971: xi).

1. Zarlino

1. Havendosi adunque a ragionare della compositione del Contrapunto, bisogna avanti di ogn'altra cosa conoscere gli Elementi, di che si compone: imperoche niuno saprà mai per modo alcuno ordinare, o comporre alcuna cosa; ne mai conoscerà la natura del composto, se primieramente non conosce le cose, che si debbono ordinare, o porre insieme; & la natura, o la loro ragione (Zarlino [1558] 1965: Part 3, Ch. 3, "The Elements That Make Up Counterpoint," 149/6). Hereafter, all references to *Le istitutioni harmoniche* (Zarlino [1558] 1965) will be to the 1558 facsimile and will indicate first the part (in Roman numerals in the notes), followed by chapter number, and page references to the translation (when available) and the original, in that order. The present citation would read III, 3, 149/6. Translations from Parts 1 and 2 are mine. For a translation of Part 3, see Zarlino ([1558] 1983).

2. By "values" I mean the worth assigned by a particular author or a community of authors (in Kuhn's sense) to a single idea (notion, concept) or groups of ideas (notions, concepts) advanced by other authors. "Values" include, in the present context, things that we may anachronistically consider to be matters of belief; they also include ideas as they are accumulated through secondary commentary, a prevalent intellectual phenomenon throughout Western Europe up to Zarlino's time.

3. The latter includes the *compositore* and *sonatore* as well (Zarlino [1558] 1965: Ch. 11). There Zarlino echoes Boethius's Pythagorean definition of *musicus* as one whose judgments are formed "according to speculation or reason" (Boethius 1989: I, 34). Erich Reimer (1978) provides an overview of the distinction from the Middle Ages to the mid-eighteenth century.

4. For reception of Aristotle in Venice, see Olivieri (1983). More general examination of Aristotle in the Renaissance appears in Charles Bernard Schmitt (1983, 1984). Schmitt (1976) also discusses Platonism.

5. By "cognitive" is meant that which pertains to knowledge in general (intellectual or otherwise).

6. The rational impetus of method is made evident by Cicero's rendering of *methodus* as *ratio*.

7. Not included, for instance, are examples from *Le dimostrationi harmoniche* (1571). The account here is limited in scope and does not aim to offer either a comprehensive overview of Zarlino's thought or to take his thought to stand for musical thought in late Renaissance Italy. I would note that the general overview I present is carried with a modicum of apprehension about offending specialists, but also with the belief that legitimate historiographical concerns will otherwise go unexpressed.

8. Zarlino's thought is enormously complex and his cultural, intellectual, musical, political, and social reach extends well beyond the limits of my analysis. Although I touch briefly on humanistic principles, I do not engage that aspect of Zarlino in detail; other topics traditionally addressed, such as the compositional principles articulated in Parts 3 and 4 (e.g., contrapuntal rules, text setting), his polemics against the chromaticists, and the ever-contentious issue

of tuning (admittedly of great importance in Zarlino's thought), are not considered. The scholarship on Zarlino (or addressing Zarlino indirectly) is vast and includes penetrating studies of some of the issues I do not address. The following are noteworthy: Feldman (1995), Haar (1971), Judd (2000), Moyer (1992), Palisca (1985, 1989, 1994), Reiss (1997), Tomlinson (1993), Walker (1978).

9. In examining these correspondences, my analysis recapitulates and expands that of Foucault ([1966] 1971: Ch. 2).

10. [T]utte le cose create da Dio furno di lui col Numero ordinate (Zarlino [1558] 1965: I, 12, 21).

11. See Zarlino ([1588] 1966).

12. Ma ben si connoscerà poi l'udito esser molto piu necessario & megliore . . . nelle cose che appartengono all'intelletto (Zarlino [1558] 1965: I, 1, 3). James W. McKinnon (1978) offers a detailed account of the historiographical issues involved in the competing traditions of musical genesis by Pythagoras and Jubal.

13. Et è tanta la certezza di dette scienze, che col mezo de numeri si fa infalibilmente il rivolgimento de cieli, le congiuntioni de i pianetti, il far della Luna, il suo Eclisse, & quello del Sole, & infiniti altri bellissimi secreti, senza a esser tra loro punto di discordia. Resta adunque che la Musica sia & nobile & certissima, essendo parte delle scienze mathematiche (Zarlino [1558] 1965: I, 1, 4).

14. See Aaron ([1523] 1970: Book 1, Ch. 1, 4–11). For a rather different attitude, see Girolamo Cardano ([c. 1546] 1973: Part 1, Ch. 1). There Cardano tersely states: "I do not consider that music should be esteemed for its antiquity or its glorious inventors." (De Musica was written c. 1546 but was not published until 1663.) Cornelius Agrippa ([1530] 1998) goes much further, writing against music, in what Gary Tomlinson titles a "dispraise of music" (Strunk 1998: 289).

15. Aaron ([1523] 1970: 9).

16. Zarlino's praises of music are translated in Strunk (1998: 293–99). The opening passage to which I refer is omitted there, however: Avegna che per l'origine & certezza sua le laudi sue siano chiaramente manifeste, tuttavia quando considero niuna cosa ritrovarsi, la quale con questa non habbia grandissima convenienzia, non posso di lei in tutto con silentio trapassare (Zarlino [1558] 1965: I, 2, 4).

17. Tomlinson (1993: 99); emphasis mine.

18. Cicero (De Divinatione: Book II, 15, 34). The entire passage reads: Concedam hoc ipsum, si vis, etsi magnam iacturam causae fecero, si ullam esse convenientiam naturae cum extis concessero. Elsewhere in De Divinatione he states that "for either a certain divine power makes the signs of our dreams counselors for us, or [it makes] conjectures from a certain convenientia and association of nature, which they [Greeks] call sympatheia" (Book II, 60, 124). In both instances Cicero, a critic of divination, makes a concession to convenientia. Other senses in which he uses the term include convenientia and the preservation of nature, convenientia of parts, and of times (all in De Officiis: I, 28, 100, I, 4, 14, and II, 21, 54, respectively), convenientia of things pertaining to

friendship (*De Amicitia,* 27, 100), and in explicit reference to the Stoics' notion of *homologia* (*De Finibus,* III, 6, 21).

19.   Foucault ([1966] 1971: 17). Foucault, after P. Grégoire (*Syntaxeon artis mirabilis,* 1610), gives the following partial list: "Amicitia, Aequalitas (contractus, consensus, matrimonium, societas, pax, et similia), Consonantia, Concertus, Continuum, Paritas, Proportio, Similitudo, Conjunctio, Copula." In historical terms more precise than Foucault's, this symbolist tradition is inaugurated by Stoic semiotics, which considered signs to be *semeia,* "natural events which can be taken as the symptoms of something else," and not words (*onomata*). In medieval culture, this semiotics is made manifest by the assignation of symbolic meaning to things, which sees the rise of the "universal symbolism" that Foucault associates with the sixteenth-century episteme. In the interim, though, two events would have intervened. First, Aristotelian naturalism would challenge these impulses. In turn, Neoplatonism (greatly influenced by interest in the Kabbalah and the *Corpus Hermeticum,* as Umberto Eco remarks) would reignite the interest in a cosmology imbued with magic, the belief in an absolute correlation among things, and the acceptance of such belief as a basic foundation for the search for knowledge. This account of "Hermetic semiosis" summarizes Eco's discussion (1990: 13–22). For further discussion of Stoic semiotics, see Todorov (1982: 22). Among the many writings on the Hermetic tradition, Daniel Pickering Walker (1958, 1985) and Frances Yates ([1964] 1991) are useful, as is, particularly for the musician, Tomlinson (1993). The sharpest criticism of Foucault's historical generalization about the doctrine of correspondences is given by George Huppert, who proposes that Hermetic practices were often scorned "by the *hommes moyens instruits* of the sixteenth century" (1974: 206). His overall argument, that these practices coexisted with others that we may consider "rational," is well taken, although his judgment both that the latter is intellectually superior to the former and that Foucault's analysis cannot tell us anything about the "fundamental codes of [a] culture" (207) bespeaks his own biases. A similar rejection of Hermetic thought appears in Brian Vickers (1984).

20.   See Foucault ([1966] 1971: 29). Foucault makes a distinction between *semiology* and the more common term *semiotics.* The former is specific to his analysis of signs in the sixteenth century. The latter, in its most general sense, refers to the study of signs and their interpretation *tout court.* Combined, however, Foucault's semiology and hermeneutics may be said to correspond to a kind of general sixteenth-century semiotics.

21.   [C]he è harmonia, la quale si scorge tra quelle cose, che si veggono & conoscono nel cielo. Et soggiunsi, che anche nel legamento de gli Elementi si comprende: conciosiache essendo stati creati dal grande Architettore Iddio (si come creò ancora tutte l'altre cose) in Numero, in Peso, & in Misura (Zarlino [1558] 1965: I, 6, 14).

22.   In Ptolemy's syntonic diatonic tuning followed by Zarlino ([1558] 1965: II, 39), each tetrachord presents the order: minor whole tone (19:9), major whole tone (9:8), and major semitone (16:15).

23.   [C]ome due numeri Quadrati convengono in uno mezano numero propor-

tionato, cosi due di essi elementi in uno mezano si congiungono. Conciosia che al modo che il Quaternario, & Novenario numeri quadrati si convengono nel Senario, il quale supera il Quaternario di quella quantità, che esso è superato dal Novenario; in tal modo il Fuoco & l'Acqua, che sono in due qualità contrarij, in uno mezano elemento si congiungono: Impero che essendo il Fuoco per sua natura caldo & secco, & l'Acqua fredda & humida, nell'Aria calda & humida mirabilmente con grande proportione s'accompagnano. . . . [D]i modo che sono con tanto maraviglioso ordine insieme uniti, che tra essi non si ritrova più disparità (Zarlino [1558] 1965: I, 6, 14). Aristotle outlines his theory of change in *Physics* and the particular account of the elements appears in *On Generation and Corruption* (1922: II, 1). Zarlino ([1558] 1965: II, 45, 136) cites this doctrine again in the midst of a discussion concerning the natural intervals of the human voice and the artificial ones of instrumental music: opposite things can be brought together, but in the end, only natural ones preserve their perfection.

24.   For a critique of the reductive nature of Foucault's taxonomy, see Tomlinson (1993: 52–61). Tomlinson observes that Foucault gives no rationale, either internal to his analytic method or external by the historical evidence he provides, for reducing to four the many terms for correspondences available and recognized by sixteenth- and early-seventeenth-century authors. Further, Tomlinson remarks that by ignoring the term *consonantia* Foucault renders the system of correspondences deaf and mute, which, of course, excludes music from active participation in the Renaissance episteme. (Tomlinson counters with arguments for an auralist orientation in Agrippa and Ficino.) Foucault's analysis gives exclusive rights to written signs (he speaks of "the prose of the world") which had to be somehow engaged visually ([1966] 1971: Ch. 2). In fact, he speaks not of "correspondences," as I do, but of "similitudes" and "resemblances." My change aims to de-emphasize the visual.

25.   Note that in Cicero's use of the term, spatial proximity does not constitute a conceptual determination, as it does in Foucault's analysis.

26.   The reason for using "sign for" instead of "word" (or "symbol") is that it better expresses a fundamental relation for the semiotics of Zarlino of linguistic signs to nonlinguistic signs and all things in general, as will become clearer later on. Suffice it to note for now that in the system of correspondences, words, and languages, however descriptive of the world, constitute themselves images of the world. See Foucault ([1966] 1971: 36–37).

27.   The reader ought not to confuse a sign such as "diapason" in its function as signature with its function as linguistic sign proper. Zarlino, for example, offers an etymological account for that particular name explaining that it combines the words "through" (δια) and "everyone" or "universality" (πασα) to form the expression "universally harmonious" ([1558] 1983: 26). Of course, in its combined meaning, the sign becomes signature.

28.   See Zarlino ([1558] 1965: III, 3, 8/150).

29.   "It seems most distinctive of substance that what is numerically one and the same is able to receive contraries" (Aristotle 1963: 5, 4a10).

30.   Zarlino ([1558] 1965: III, 38, 80–81/189).

31. Analogy, from αναλογια, was rendered in Latin as *proportionalitas* (proportion).

32. Proportionality is not meant here solely as well proportioned or rational, for irrational things too have their own proportion.

33. Foucault ([1966] 1971: 23). As described by Foucault, sympathy relies heavily on the Aristotelian notion of potentiality, which he overlooks.

34. Here, the circular graphic representation in Example 1.1 is fundamental to the understanding of correspondences. Zarlino ([1558] 1965: Part 1, Ch. 30) represents the "principle of inequality" (*Principio della inequalità*) as a sort of open-ended downward ladder that proceeds to infinity.

35. See Foucault ([1966] 1971: 28–29).

36. See Foucault ([1966] 1971: 40).

37. See Eco (1990: 24). Eco uses the expressions "hermetic drift" and "unlimited semiosis" to connote a negative aspect of "the interpretive habit which dominated Renaissance Hermetism." On the practical (and positive) use of "drift" in sixteenth-century thought, see Yates (1966).

38. "Unity, although not itself a Number, nevertheless is the source of number, and everything, whether it be simple, compound, corporal, or spiritual, comes from this Unity" (La quale Unità, ben che non sia Numero, tuttavia è principio del Numero; & da essa ogni cosa, ò semplice, ò composta, ò corporale, ò spirituale che sia, vien detta Una) (Zarlino [1558] 1965: I, 12, 22). In the music-theoretical tradition, the metaphysics of unity figures prominently in Boethius, under the decisive influence of Nicomachus of Gerasa. But the idea can be traced back to Neoplatonic ontotheological doctrine, in which the Divine was Unity itself. For a useful discussion of the main issues of the idea, see David E. Cohen (1993: 19–22, 35). For discussion of Boethius's indebtedness to Nicomachus, see Bower (1978).

39. In the *Arithmetic,* Boethius defines unity as the "mother of all number" (1.14, 1.17, 2.8) and number as a "collection of unities" (13.11–12); cited by Bower in Boethius (1989, I:6, n58). The metaphysics of unity are inseparably bound to conceptions of God as Being, that is, to ontotheology. David Cohen (1993: 10–11, 18–25) traces some of the intricacies of this doctrine.

40. Quanto sia necessario il Numero nelle cose; & che cosa sia Numero; & se l'Unità è numero (Zarlino [1558] 1965: I, 12, 21–22).

41. Il Numero essere moltitudine composta di più unità (Zarlino [1558] 1965: I, 12, 22). (Compare with Boethius's definition in n. 39 above.)

42. See Nichomachus of Gerasa (1926: II, Ch. 6).

43. Per qual cagione la Musica sia detta subalternata all'Arithmetica, & mezana tra la mathematica, & la naturale (Zarlino [1558] 1965: I, 20, 30).

44. Zarlino ([1558] 1965: I, 20, 30–31). The role of musical writings in associating mathematics and the physical phenomena are considered in Rose (1975). A broad overview of how music participated in the rise of a rational aesthetics (about which more in Chapter 2) appears in Reiss (1997: Part 3). Stillman Drake (1970) establishes a direct correlation between Vincenzo Galilei's work on music and the scientific developments of Galileo Galilei.

45. Et si come nelle cose naturali, niuna cosa è perfetta, mentre che è in potenza: ma solamente quando è ridutta in atto; cosi la Musica no può esser perfetta, se non quando co'l mezo de i naturali, o artificiali istrumenti si farà udire: la cual cosa non si potrà fare co'l Numero solo, ne con le Voci sole: ma accompagnando & queste & quello insieme; massimamente essendo il Numero inseparabile dalla consonanza. Per questo adunque sarà manifesto, che la Musica non si potrà dire ne semplicemente mathematica, ne semplicemente naturale; ma si bene parte naturale, & parte mathematica, & conseguentemente mezana tra l'una & l'altra. Ma perche dalla scienza naturale il Musico hà la ragione della materia della Consonanza, che sono i Suoni & le Voci, & dalla Mathematica hà la ragione della sua forma; cioè della sua proportione; però dovendosi denominare tutte le cose dalla più nobile, più ragionevolmente diciamo la Musica essere scienza mathematica, che naturale: conciosia che la forma sia più nobile della materia (Zarlino [1558] 1965: I, 20, 31).

46. See Fend (1991: 210).

47. Here Zarlino must ignore Aristotle's sharp critique of Pythagorean doctrine in *Metaphysics* (Aristotle 1924: Book Alpha, 5), where he outlines the fundamental opacity of the status of number as either material or formal cause for the world.

48. Cosi della nostra scienza della Musica i posteri mostrando gli errori de passati, e aggiungendovi la loro autorità, la fecero talmente chiara e certa, che la connumerorno, e fecero parte delle scienze Mathematiche; e questo non per altro, salvo che per la sua certezza; percioche questa con le altre insieme avanza di certezza le altre scienze, & tiene il primo grado di verità; il che dal suo nome si conosce: poi che mathematica è detta de μάθημα parola greca, che in latino significa Disciplina, e nella Italiana nostra lingua importa Scienza, o Sapienza; la quale (si come dice Boecio) altro non è che una intelligenza; o per dirla piu chiaro, capacità di verità delle cose che sono, e di loro natura non sono mutabili (Zarlino [1558] 1965: I, 1, 4).

49. I owe this observation to Giuseppe Gerbino (personal communication).

50. See, for example, Palisca (1985: 247–50), Wienpahl (1959).

51. Francisco de Salinas, who lived in Italy from 1538 until 1561, also invoked the senario to determine the forms of simple consonances (*De musica libri septem*: Lib. II, Cap. 12).

52. The formula is $1 + 2 + 3 = 1 \times 2 \times 3 = 6$ (Zarlino [1558] 1965: I, 13, 22–23).

53. [I]l gran Profeta Mose, nel descrivere la grande et maravigliosa fabrica del mondo, eleggesse il numero Senario; non havendo Iddio nelle sue operationi mai havuto di bisogno di tempo: percioche, come colui, che d'ogni scienza era perfetto maestro, conoscendo per opera del Spirito divino l'harmonia, che in tal numero era rinchiusa; et che dalle cose visibili et apparenti conoscemo le invisibili d'Iddio, la sua onnipotenza, et la divinita sua; volse col mezo di tal numero in un tratto esprimere et insieme mostrare la perfettione dell' opera, et in essa la rinchiusa harmonia, conservatrice dell' esser suo, senza la quale a patto alcuno non durarebbe: ma del tutto, o si annullarebbe, overamente ritornando le cose nel loro primo essere . . . di nuovo si vederebbe la confusione dell' antico Chaos (Zarlino [1558] 1965: I, 13, 23).

54. "Che dal numero Senario si comprendeno molte cose della natura"; the verb *comprendere* holds a dual meaning as intellectual understanding and physical inclusion, which suits Zarlino's explanatory agenda: as form is subject to intellectual understanding, so matter is subject to physical inclusion.

55. Non è adunque maraviglia, se da alcuno vien detto Segnacolo del mondo (Zarlino [1558] 1965: I, 14, 24). See 14, 23–24.

56. Virtue was a central notion of artistic, intellectual, cultural, and social life in the Italian quattrocento and cinquecento. "The conception of virtù," writes Alistair Crombie, "embodied a program for relating man to the world as perceiver and knower and agent in the context of his integral moral, social, and cosmological existence. The program presupposed the stability of nature and mankind and of their relations" (1986: 49).

57. Zarlino ([1558] 1965: I, 16, 27).

58. In his deployment of the *ottonario* (i.e., number 8), Zarlino evades the question of making this the source for consonances: he would have to justify the exclusion of the ratio 7:5, which might have proven more difficult than the appeal to the doctrine of potentiality. For readers today, these may be glaring inconsistencies, leading commentators to say, for example, that "Zarlino offered a number of ad hoc explanations to account for . . . embarrassing discrepancies" (Christensen 1993a: 74). Zarlino's example of the minor sixth is a favorite of contemporary criticisms of Zarlino's explanatory "fabrications." See, for example, Palisca (1985), H. Floris Cohen (1984).

59. Onde si come il Binario hà quasi la istessa natura, che hà l'Unità, per esserle vicino; cosi la Diapason hà quasi la natura istessa dello Unisono; si per essergli vicina; come si scorge ne i termini delle loro forme; come etiandio, perche gli estremi delle lor proportioni non sono composti di altri numeri, che della Unità: Di modo che imitando lo effetto la natura della sua cagione; & essendo i numeri harmonici cagioni de gli harmonici suoni; è cosa ragionevole, che il suono imiti anco la natura loro; & che li detti due suoni della Diapason parino un suono solo (Zarlino [1558] 1965: III, 3, 8/150). Claude Palisca notes that Zarlino chooses among authorities in his theory of origin of intervals: the theory that intervals begin in the diapason is Plato's (*Epinomis*, 991a), as transmitted by Marsilio Ficino. Zarlino thus rejects "the principle that musical intervals are built from an indivisible unit" (Palisca 1985: 245–46).

60. Et tanto più sono vaghe, quanto più si partono dalla semplicità, della quale i nostri sentimenti non molto si rallegrano, & si accompagnano ad altre consonanze; poi che amano maggiormente le cose composte, che le semplice (Zarlino [1558] 1965: III, 3, 19/155).

61. There appears in his discussion of *musica mondana* a comment to the effect that the sensorial limitations of humans keep us from actually hearing the music of the spheres (Zarlino [1558] 1965: I, 6, 12). Concerning Zarlino's awareness of developments in perspective, there is no sufficient evidence that he would have known Alberti, though it is highly improbable that he did not; Part 1, Chapter 20 makes explicit reference to the science of perspective.

62. See Zarlino ([1558] 1965: III, 71, 263/278). Aristotle's distinction among sense objects appears in *De Anima* (1968: II, 6, 418a–418b).

63. I quali Oggetti tanto più sono grati al propio sentimento, & tanto più soavi, quanto più sono a lui proportionati: Et cosi per il contrario; come si vede dell'Occhio nostro, ilquale riguardando nel Sole è offeso: perche tale Oggetto non è a lui proportionato (Zarlino [1558] 1965: III, 71, 263/278).

64. La natura odia le cose senza proportione, & senza misura; & si diletta di quelle, che hanno tra loro convenienza (Nature hates things without proportion [and measure] and delights in those that have propriety between them) (Zarlino [1558] 1965: III, 36, 76/185; translated in Martha Feldman 1995: 186, n104). Note that Marco and Palisca render *convenienza* as "proportion" (Zarlino [1558] 1983).

65. Horace, *Ars Poetica:* III, Ch. 26, 333–34; cited in Palisca, introduction to Zarlino ([1558] 1983: xvii, n10).

66. See Zarlino ([1558] 1965: III, 26, 51–52/171–72; Ch. 26, "What Is Required in Every Composition: First, the Subject").

67. [C]onciosiache [gli Antichi] molto ben sapevano, che l'Harmonia non può nascere, se non da cose tra loro diverse, discordanti, & contrarie; & non da quelle, che in ogni cosa si convengono (Zarlino [1558] 1965: III, 29, 59/176).

68. Questo bello, & utile avertimento conferma esser vero, & buono le operationi della stupenda Natura, la quale nel produrre in essere gli Individui di ciascuna specie; mai li produce di maniera, che si assimiglino in tutto l'uno all'altro; ma si bene variati, per qualche differenza (Zarlino [1558] 1965: III, 29, 60/177).

69. Debbe adunque ogni Compositore imitare un tale, & tanto bello ordine: percioche sarà riputato tanto migliore, quanto le sue operationi si assimiglieranno a quelle della Natura. . . . Non dovemo adunque per alcun modo porre due Unisoni l'uno dopo l'altro immediatamente, ne due Ottave, ne due Quinte; poi che naturalmente la cagione delle consonanze, che è il Numero harmonico, non contiene nel suo progresso, overo ordine naturale due proportioni simili (Zarlino [1558] 1965: III, 29, 61/177; translation slightly modified).

70. Feldman (1995: 171–72). Zarlino introduces Willaert as a figure central to his treatise in the Proemio to the *Istitutioni*.

71. On this point, see Feldman (1995: 172–73).

72. The summary of Zarlino is from Palisca, s.v. "Zarlino, Gioseffo," in *The New Grove Dictionary of Music and Musicians,* 2nd ed. (London: Macmillan, 2001), vol. 27, 752. Tomlinson (1993: 55) makes a similar but more general point in connection to the bricolage of the "Renaissance magus," who he notes, citing Lévi-Strauss (1966: 16ff.), was "pursuing his 'science of the concrete,' his knowledge of reality, across a landscape of tools and materials that are found 'at hand,' readily perceived and connected to one another in patterns of likeness." My point differs from Tomlinson's in that I associate Zarlino's *bricolage* with the construction of myth, after Lévi-Strauss's formulation. This view echoes Venetian myths of Willaert. Ellen Rosand (1977) provides commen-

tary on Venetian mythology. Martha Feldman (1995) offers an overview of the network of literary, artistic, rhetorical, civil, social, and political elaborations of Venetian myths, outlining some of their tensions.

73. See Lévi-Strauss (1964).

74. The sociopolitical picture of Venice at the time of Zarlino is extremely complex. A thorough examination of Zarlino's thought within this picture goes well beyond the purposes of this chapter. Suffice it to note here in relation to the notion of myth construction that Willaert was indeed elevated to mythical status during his lifetime as well as following his death in 1562. See Einstein (1949, 1:321–24); cited in Feldman (1995: 174). To date, the most detailed musico-sociological analysis of Cinquecento Venice appears in Feldman's work, which focuses on text and poetics of the madrigal and makes only passing comments about Zarlino's "idealist Neoplatonic leanings" (1995: 186).

75. Judd (2000: Ch. 7) notes that publication of the *Istitutioni* coincided with its author's membership in the mathematical section of the Accademia Veneziana, whose members "comprised the intellectual and social elite of Venice." She also proposes that with the publication of the *Istitutioni* Zarlino sought to position himself as a likely successor to Willaert at San Marco.

76. Zarlino ([1558] 1965: II, 7, 71). Perhaps not coincidentally, Zarlino's discussion of the well-disposed subject moves from passions to military matters, recounting ancient lore about the power of music to move men into battle. It is significant that Zarlino's discussion does not delve into questions of aesthetic empathy between music and listener by appeal to the Aristotelian psychology available to him. In Chapter 2 we will see how different Zarlino's attitude is from that of Descartes.

77. Feldman (1995: xxvii) remarks that "Willaert was . . . an arm of the state whose position [at San Marco] demanded unfaltering loyalty to the republic's self-image and its long-standing ideals," and that "despite his northern origins . . . Willaert was wholly assimilated to a Venetian image." Elsewhere she notes that "It may be all the more significant . . . that one of the few [among Willaert's pupils] from a Venetian dominion, a native of nearby Chioggia, became the foremost explicator and apologist for the Venetian idiom. Gioseffo Zarlino, theorist, teacher, and later chapelmaster, played a crucial role in clarifying for later generations the aesthetic impulses and compositional habits of contemporaneous Venetian musicians" (xxviii).

78. Palisca, s.v. "Theory, Theorists," in *The New Grove Dictionary of Music and Musicians*, 2nd ed. (London: Macmillan, 2001), vol. 25, 374.

79. In the syntonic diatonic tuning system—which Zarlino thought was applicable to vocal music only—each interval within the tetrachord corresponds to a superparticular ratio (i.e., 9:10, 8:9, 15:16). The scale formed from this tetrachordal arrangement contains the consonances given by the senario. For an overview of Galilei's polemics, see Palisca (1989: Ch. 6), Galilei (1989a, 1989b). Galilei's arguments in favor of equal temperament (for fretted instruments) appear in *Dialogo della musica antica et della moderna* ([1581] 1967), to which Zarlino responds in the *Sopplimenti* ([1588] 1966). Galilei would in

turn eventually propose that no numerical limits be imposed on intervals, in *Discorso intorno all'opere di messer Gioseffo Zarlino da Chioggia* ([1589] 1934). Palisca's progressivist reading of Galilei's endeavors argues for a triumph of a nascent empiricism over numerological speculation. For a contrasting interpretation of these developments, see Walker (1978: 14–26).

80.   Benedetti's arguments are examined by Palisca, who first brought to light letters written by Benedetti to Cipriano de Rore (c. 1563), in "Scientific Empiricism in Musical Thought" (1994: 200–35). See Palisca (1985: 261–65) for a discussion of Benedetti's refutation of Zarlino's tuning. (Benedetti's attacks on Zarlino's tuning system appear also in *Diversarum speculationum mathematicarum et physicarum liber,* 1585.) For a cautionary reading of Benedetti's success in what Palisca considers to be a "potential blow to number symbolism" (1994: 216), see H. Floris Cohen (1984: 76–77).

81.   Galilei would have the last word in his polemics with Zarlino, writing a retort to Zarlino's *Sopplimenti* in his *Discorso intorno all'opere di messer Gioseffo Zarlino da Chioggia* ([1589] 1934). Here I address Zarlino's response to the question of method, not the details of his mathematical arguments against Galilei.

82.   L'Verità . . . [è] che le Forme delle consonanze & d'altri Intervalli che usiamo à nostri tempi nelle Cantilene vocali & naturali, non sono cosa dell'Arte, ne inventione dell'Huomo, ma della istessa Natura primieramente prodotte, collocate & registrate tra molte cose, & specialmente tra le parti del primo Numero perfetto (Zarlino [1588] 1966: 8).

83.   Nello scrivere poi & ragionar delle cose della Prattica, hebbi sempre pensiero, com'anco al presente hò, d'insegnare il modo, che si tiene hoggidi nel comporre le Cantilene, & mostrar la diversità de i Modi ò Tuoni, non già secondo'l costume de gli Antichi . . . ma secondo l'uso de' Moderni (Zarlino [1588] 1966: 9).

84.   Ne fu mai ne anco è mia intentione di scriver l'uso della Prattica secondo'l modo de gli Antichi, ò Greci, ò Latini, se bene all fiate la uò adombrando; ma solamente il modo di quelli, c'hanno ritrovato questa nostra maniera, nel far cantar insieme molte parti, con diverse Modulationi, & diverse Aria, & specialmente secondo la via & il modo tenuto d'Adriano Willaert . . . nelle cose della Prattica mio Precettore (Zarlino [1588] 1966: 9). Zarlino's claims here do not suggest more than a modest historical consciousness, that is, a keen interest in establishing with exactitude the chronological trajectory of this or that phenomenon. McKinnon (1978: 10–18) discusses this issue.

85.   Viewing polyphony as a triumph is a highly contested issue in the poetics of Renaissance humanism. Nicola Vicentino (*L'Antica musica ridotta alla moderna prattica*, 1555), for one, considered modern polyphony to represent the unfortunate triumph of the lowly *senso* over the more elevated *ragione* of ancient monody.

86.   [L]a cognitione perfetta della Musica s'acquista da due parti, l'una dellequali chiamaremo Historica & l'altra Methodica (Zarlino [1588] 1966: 10).

87.   See Zarlino ([1558] 1965: I, 12, 21). For the notion of wisdom, Zarlino cites Plato (*Epinomis*).

88. A rather different attitude toward ancient knowledge is evident in Galilei's demonstration of the falsity of the myth of the Pythagorean hammers.

89. See Galilei (1989a: 183): "[T]he diapason may be said to lie between the half and the whole, or, if we wish, the one and the two. However, these must not be considered simply as cardinal numbers, but as numbers measuring only those portions of the strings capable, when struck, of producing a pitch. For what Zarlino says in Chapter 15 of the first [book] of the *Istitutioni,* maintaining that number is sonorous, cannot stand in any case, for, not having in itself body—and sound is not produced without the percussion of some body capable of rendering a sound—a simple number, consequently, cannot be sonorous, although it is divisible, just as time and a line, which also lack body, are divisible."

90. See Jardine (1985). Not to leave the impression that there was a wholesale rejection of a prior way of thinking about the world, it was Bacon (1620) himself who cataloged 130 different topics for history, ranging from "Histories of Sounds in the upper region (if there be any), besides Thunder" (#13) to "History of Music" (#70) and "History of Cookery, and the arts thereto belonging, as of Butcher, Poulterer, etc." (#81). Alistair Crombie (1986) discusses the role of experimentation in shaping a belief in the "rational anticipation of effects" around the end of the sixteenth and beginning of the seventeenth century.

91. Cardano ([c. 1546] 1973) argued that study of music ought to consider "the way proportions are perceived," as Ann E. Moyer put it (1992: 61). He had also suggested that ancient authority be questioned (see n. 14 above).

92. See Yates ([1964] 1991: 403).

2. The Representation of Order

1. See Descartes ([1618] 1987). Page references will be to the French translation with cross-references to the modern edition (Descartes [1618] 1986). All translations are mine, with the assistance of John Bauschatz, who cross-referenced my translations with the Latin original. An English translation (Descartes [1618] 1961) is not altogether reliable. Frédéric de Buzon (Descartes [1618] 1987) bases his translation on the original edition (Utrecht, 1650), but takes into account subsequent editions (1656, 1683, 1695) and translations into English (1653), Dutch (1661), and French (1668).

2. André Pirro (1907: 1–2) notes that the title "Compendium" was commonly used in philosophy and theology schools to designate summaries used by pupils. He cites the *Compendium* of Cassiodore (sixth century) as an early example and remarks that during the sixteenth century a great number of such writings had appeared with music as their subject: Lampadius (1539), Adrian Petit Coclicus (1552), Adam Gumpeltzhaimer (1591), Sethus Calvisius (1594), Henricus Faber (1596), and Laurentius Stiphelius all wrote *Compendia musicae.* Lorenzo Tigrini summarized Zarlino's teachings in his *Compendio della musica* (1588).

3. François F. Fétis ([1836] 1972: III, 292) proclaims the *Compendium* to be "peu digne du nom de son auteur." Hugo Riemann recognizes the *Compen-*

dium as being "among the ablest musical writings of its time" but bemoans that its author "left nothing more comprehensive on the theory of music"; cited in Augst (1965: 119). Incidentally, Descartes intended the *Compendium* as a private present to Isaac Beeckman, going as far as to ask Beeckman to keep it in the "shadow of your archives" and not to display it "for the judgment of others."

4. Compare, however, to the following: "Si je ne meurs que de viellesse, j'ai encore envie quelque jour d'écrire de la théorie de la musique" (letter from Descartes to Constantijn Huygens, 4 February 1647; AT, IV, 791). Aside from the *Compendium,* Descartes's thoughts about sound and music are scattered in letters to Beeckman (1619) and Mersenne (1629–34) (Descartes 1991). Surprisingly, there is no specific mention of affections brought about by music in the valedictory *Les passions de l'âme* (1649).

5. For these topics see Augst (1965)—scientific aspects; Gaukroger (1995: 74–80)—philosophical issues; Sepper (1996: 37–46)—single-issue approach; Pirro (1907)—historical and methodological aspects of the treatise; H. Floris Cohen (1984)—invoking mathematics to confirm Zarlino; and Christensen (1993a: 77–80)—generating intervals from the monochord.

6. Henry Klumpenhouwer (1992) examines Descartes's derivation of dissonant relationships and discusses analytical applications to the music of Lassus. Wilhelm Seidel (1970) discusses issues of meter. Pirro (1907) focuses on rules of composition.

7. On Descartes's aesthetic and psycho-perceptual innovations, see Racek (1930), Manuel (1957), Revault d'Allonnes (1951). De Buzon (in Descartes [1618] 1987: 5–18) identifies and gives a brief but insightful introduction to methodological and conceptual issues in the *Compendium.* To date, the most comprehensive analysis of the *Compendium* appears in Van Wymeersch (1999). Van Wymeersch is the only other commentator to apply Foucault's ideas to Descartes. I obtained a copy of her book too late to include it in my research, but there are similarities between her argument and mine. A key distinction is that Van Wymeersch regards "aesthetics" mainly as a theory of beauty, while I focus on questions of cognitive perception and representation. Reiss (1997) gives the *Compendium* an unusually privileged place in the integration of mathematics within the arts and aesthetics. His argument circles around the emergence of what he calls "rational aesthetics," the place of mathematical logic in "debates about the passions, the functioning of the senses, what is and is not beautiful, moving, attractive, and why and how" (155). Sweeping in its conclusions and thoroughly researched, Reiss's book constitutes an important and largely unsung contribution to the understanding of Descartes. Reiss, however, does not address the question of representation. Heinrich Besseler (1959: 41) identifies in Descartes a decisive turn toward the listener as the ground for a new stage in the history of hearing; however, although he identifies the articulation of a "subject," he refers to the "subject" of the *Meditations* from 1641, missing the important methodological steps established in Descartes's earlier work. Johannes Lohmann (1979) considers the question of the "object concept" as it appears in Descartes, discussing as well what he calls a "space of representation" (*Darstellungs-*

Raumes) and the analytical implications of Descartes's mathematics, all of which he uses to argue a broad historical point: how Descartes's treatise heralds the consciousness of the modern age. Finally, Helga de la Motte-Haber and Peter Nitsche (1982) provide a useful, though unfortunately brief, analysis of perceptual subjectivity.

8. Compare to de Buzon: "le est donc question, dans ces *Praenotanda*, d'une intelligibilité, d'un sensible ainsi articulé qu'il paraisse proportionné sans que l'esprit doive faire effort de compréhension" (Descartes [1618] 1987: 12).

9. Descartes does not use the term "subject" to designate the perceiver. Following Aristotelian usage (*hypokeimenon:* that which underlies), subject (*subjectum*) describes, in Descartes, that of which attributes are predicated.

10. I do not discuss what some may consider the bulk of the treatise, that dealing with consonances. That section is divided into three parts: the first pertains to consonances proper, the second to "degrees or musical tones," and the third to admissible dissonances. Throughout the chapter I will refer to the "Preliminaries" to designate the Preliminary notes.

11. References to the text will read *Rules,* while individual Rules will be nonitalicized (e.g., Rule 2, or Rules 7 and 12). Page references will be given in the following order: first, the individual Rule; second, the page number in the English translation (Descartes 1985); third, the page number in the Latin text as edited by Charles Adam and Paul Tannery (Descartes [1618] 1986). "Rule 2, 13/AT, X, 366" refers to second Rule, p. 13 in the English translation, and p. 366 in vol. X of Adam and Tannery. The dating of the *Rules* is highly contested. I follow the division outlined by John A. Schuster (1980), who identifies three sections: a first section dating from the fall of 1619 in which Descartes discusses the idea of mathesis universalis in the final paragraphs of Rule 4 (these paragraphs are known as Rule 4B); a second section (Rules 1–3, 4A, and 5–11) focuses on the question of method in areas such as rhetoric, psychology, and dialectics during 1619–21; third, the remaining Rules, which are taken up in 1626 and completed by 1628 (Rule 8, begun in the second section, is finished in this last section). Revision of dates for the *Rules,* thought to have been written in 1628, was begun by Jean-Paul Weber (1964).

12. Among commentators on the *Compendium*, Reiss (1997) distinguishes himself for aligning the document with the early modern. Kate van Orden (2002) discusses Descartes's writing from a cultural history perspective, considering in particular the intersections between the senses and the body. My thanks to Professor van Orden for providing a précis and bibliographical information for her essay before publication.

13. A useful account of Beeckman's musical doctrines appears in H. Floris Cohen (1984: 116–61).

14. See Besseler (1959). According to Palisca (1994: 189–99), Aristoxenus had undergone a revival in Renaissance Italy, mainly through the work of Galilei and Artusi, as well as "literary humanist" Carlo Valgulio.

15. See Gaukroger (1995: 58).

16. Descartes (1985: 81/AT, XI, 4).

17. Compare with Lohmann (1979: 82–83), who argues that the radical separa-

18. Augst (1965: 120) positions *Le monde* along a continuum in Descartes's intellectual development that begins with the *Compendium*: "its [the *Compendium*'s] value is enhanced by the fact that the theory of sound partially formulated in it is the first in a series of geometrical models leading to the design of the cosmic machine described in the 'Fable' of *Le monde.*"

19. More specifically, Rule 12 concerns the perception of color: each color can be represented uniquely in the imagination. In *Le monde,* by contrast, he skews appeals to object qualities such as color, advancing instead a conception of matter based on the kinds of corpuscles and the laws by which they move.

20. Zarlino, we remember, referred to voice (*voce*), which he considered different from and superior to sound (*suono*). His account in the *Istitutioni* defines sound as an exterior phenomenon that does not possess harmony (*concento*). By contrast, voice is a meaningful, internally produced phenomenon (Zarlino [1558] 1965: Part 2, Ch. 10, 92–93).

21. De Buzon (Descartes [1618] 1987: 9).

22. We must not overlook the fact that although the bulk of the *Compendium* is devoted to practical issues of counterpoint, these matters neither are foundational nor constitute Descartes's most original contribution. It is significant, nonetheless, that he chooses counterpoint as a kind of goal of his deductive approach, and that in the end he positions it outside of the Neoplatonic cosmologies of his immediate predecessors and contemporaries, and of the more practical compositional concerns of seventeenth-century Italian counterpoint manuals that appear after Zarlino, for example. For discussion of the similarities and differences between the arrangement of sections in the *Compendium* and the *Istitutioni,* see de Buzon's introduction to Descartes ([1618] 1987: 7–9).

23. H. Floris Cohen (1984: 163) portrays Descartes as "Zarlino, *more geometrico,*" noting, for instance, that "while Kepler [*Harmonices mundi libri,* V, 1619] rejected the arithmetical analysis of consonance in order to replace it by original geometric considerations, Descartes, much less radically, merely transformed Zarlino's numerical magnitudes into segments of given lengths." I will offer a different interpretation of these "segments" later in this chapter.

24. Pirro (1907: 3) cites Cicero: "Ars enim quum a natura profecta sit, nisi naturam moveat ac delectet nihil sane egisse videatur" (For as art started from nature, it would seem to have done nothing if it should not stir nature and give pleasure) (*De Oratore,* III); he suggests that Descartes places this near the beginning of his writing as a sort of presupposition for art. Zarlino had invoked the Horatian maxim as well. See also Reiss (1997: 159), and compare to Giulio Caccini's humanistic claims in *Le nuove musiche* ([1602] 1970). Upon hearing Caccini sing, someone told him of "not having heard such harmony in a single voice . . . that had such power to move the affect of the soul" (tanta forza di muovere l'affetto dell'animo) (ibid.: 45); translation modified. Hitchcock, editor of this volume, notes that the word *animo* designates spe-

cifically a part of the soul (*anima*) where feeling, as well as the intellectual and moral faculties, lie.

25. The astrolabe was a device used by astronomers and navigators for taking the altitude of celestial bodies. The *mater* was a plate engraved with a web of crisscrossing circles indicating altitude, and the *rete* was a rotatable circular ring of the stars.

26. 1. Sensus omnes alicuius delectationis sunt capaces.

2. Ad hanc delectationem requiritur proportio quaedam obiecti cum ipso sensu. Unde fit ut, v.g., strepitus scloporum uel tonitruum non videatur aptus ad Musicam: quia scilicet aures laederet, ut oculos solis adversi nimius splendor.

3. Tale obiectum esse debet, ut non nimis difficulter & confuse cadat in sensum. Unde fit ut, v.g., valde implicata aliqua figura, licet regularis sit, qualis est mater in Astrolabio, non adeo placeat aspectui, quam alia, quae magis aequalibus lineis constaret, quale in eodem rete esse solet. Cuius ratio est, quia plenius in hoc sensus sibi satisfacit, quam in altero, ubi multa sunt quae satis distincte non percipit.

4. Illud obiectum facilius sensu percipitur, in quo minor est differentia partium.

5. Partes totius obiecti minus inter se differentes esse dicimus, inter quas est maior proportio.

6. Illa proportio Arithmetica esse debet, non Geometrica. Cuius ratio est, quia non tam multa in ea sunt advertenda, cum aequales sint ubique differentiae, ideoque non tantopere sensus fatigetur, ut omnia quae in ea sunt distincte percipiat. Exemplum: proportio linearum facilius oculis distinguitur, quam harum, quia, in prima, oportet tantum advertere unitatem pro differentia cuiusque lineae; in secunda vero, partes ab & bc, quae sunt incommensurabiles, ideoque, ut arbitor, nullo pacto simul possunt a sensu perfecte cognosci, sed tantum in ordine ad arithmeticam proportionem: ita scilicet, ut advertat in parte ab, verbi gratia, duas partes, quarum 3 in bc existant. Ubi patet sensum perpetuo decipi.

7. Inter obiecta sensus, illud non animo gratissimum est, quod facillime sensu percipitur, neque etiam quod difficillime; sed quod non tam facile, ut naturale desiderium, quo sensus feruntur in obiecta, plane non impleat, neque etiam tam difficulter, ut sensum fatiget.

8. Denique notandum est varietatem omnibus in rebus esse gratissimam. (Descartes 1987: 55–58/AT, X, 91–92)

27. De Buzon (Descartes [1618] 1987: 10).

28. Pirro (1907: 26) cites Plato (*Philebus*), Aristotle (*Poetics*), Quintillian (*Institutionum Oratoriarum*), and Augustine (*De Pulchro et Apto*). In "Of Beauty" [1625], Bacon (1948) offers a different take on the idea of proportionality: "There is no excellent beauty that hath not some strangeness in proportion." While not the place to pursue Bacon's statement, suffice to say here that his idea may be more representative of a general aesthetics (in the eighteenth-century sense of the term) at play in art than Descartes's ideal of absolute proportionality.

29. Aristotle (1968: III, 2, 426a27; II, 10, 422a20, 424a28). Alan Towey (1991) has

suggested that Aristotle's doctrine that the sense faculty is a proportion may have reflected the "then recent discovery in acoustics that certain pairs of musical notes which mix together to produce a pleasant unity (i.e., a consonance) can be expressed as proportions of simple rational numbers." A useful account of the relationship between *sensus* and *ratio* beginning with Boethius is found in Klaus-Jürgen Sachs (1991). The comparison between sight and hearing appears in Zarlino ([1558] 1965: Part 1, Chs. 6 and 12), and in Boethius (1989, I:9). De Buzon interprets Preliminaries 1–6 as a rewriting of Aristotle's passage.

30. This is not to imply that the perceiver gains the capacity for constructing proportions that are not already "there" in the object. The priority I refer to here is given in the order of discussion of proportionality in the notes.

31. Besseler (1959: 30, 41) points out the emphasis Descartes placed on the hearer: "Es ist bedeutsam, daß Descartes zum erstenmal in der Geschichte des Musikschrifttums nicht von der Musik selbst ausgeht, sondern vom Hörer . . . und der Einbildungskraft, so kennzeichnet sich damit die neue Lage." There exists, of course, a long tradition in thought about music that concerns the effect of music on the listener, a tradition as old as music theory itself. The centrality of the hearer identified by Besseler may be best regarded as the result of a growing concern with the place of the listener as locus for understanding music's effect, which for him marks a broader historical transition from music as a "'umgangsmäsigen' Kunst" (before 1600) to a "Darbietungskunst" (after 1600) (1959: 26, 44). As I will argue, what is truly original to Descartes is the epistemological foundation on which he places the listener.

32. I should note here that "object" means interval, not pitch, and that "parts" refers to the proportions by which an interval is defined as the relation between two pitches.

33. Augst (1965: 122).

34. Reiss (1997: 159). Reiss (189) rightly critiques Augst for claiming that Descartes's application of quantitative measure to a hitherto qualitative domain was original.

35. See Descartes ([1618] 1987: 11).

36. According to Gaukroger (1995: 59–60), Descartes would have been familiar with Aristotle's *De Anima* from his studies in metaphysics at La Flèche. Other sources known to him would have also presented sensation as having a proportional basis (e.g., Augustine's *De Musica*). De Buzon notes the relationship between Descartes and Aristotle but does not pursue its implications (Descartes [1618] 1987: 11).

37. Aristotle (1968: III, 2, 426b8); emphasis mine. This doctrine is influenced by Aristotle's archaic position on the physiology of perception which held that particular organs consisted of particular elements (e.g., the eye of water) and that therefore their objects would be related to the particular qualities associated with these elements. See Aristotle, *De Sensu:* Ch. 2, 483a13–24.

38. Likewise, the intellect (*nous*) can grasp the universal form from the particular.

39.   Aristotle (1968: III, 2, 426a9). For Aristotle's use of *pathos* see Aristotle (1994b: Gamma, 5, 1010b–1011a).

40.   Later I examine the relation between sensation, imagination, and intellection. Suffice it to say that in order to think the soul needs images given to it by sensation. For Aristotle on sight, see Aristotle (1968: III, 2, 425b12–425b25).

41.   Compare, however, with my discussion below (Sec. 2.2) of Aristotle's process for mentally inspecting sensations stored in memory and recreated in the imagination.

42.   This is not to say that sensations cannot participate in the formation of knowledge. I will return to this point. Quotation from Aristotle (1986: 192); see also D. W. Hamlyn's notes in Aristotle (1968: 122).

43.   For a different account of the distinction between subject and object, see Lohmann (1979: 86–87). Lohmann pursues the intellectual continuity between Descartes and the Thomist analysis (after Arabic Aristotelian commentators Avicenna and Averroes) of *intensio* (concept) as *intentio prima* (i.e., the act of addressing oneself to a thing) and *intentio secunda* (i.e., the act of addressing reflectively one's cognitive act). Descartes would have known Thomist precepts from his studies at La Flèche, although Gaukroger (1995: 52, 60) believes that, given the ambiguous position of the Jesuits with respect to Aquinas, Descartes did not become well acquainted with his writings until as late as 1628.

44.   It should come as no surprise that Descartes chooses to address first the subject of time in music; after all, the temporal aspect of music allows for a purely quantitative analysis of its proportions and enables close examination of how a perceiving subject is to negotiate the question of representing proportions. Significantly, Descartes believed that such was the power of "time in music" that it alone could bring pleasure. "The question of rhythm is anterior to that of consonance," writes de Buzon (in Descartes [1618] 1987: 12), adding that "the correspondence between the *affectiones* of sound and the *affectus* of the body is easy enough to obtain."

45.   Wilhelm Seidel (1970: 299) critiques Descartes for offering only the simplest of examples (*proportio dupla*) and for failing to comment on the implication of nonperiodic arrangements. Pirro (1907: 86) cites Thoinot Arbeau's (*Orchesographie*, 1589) definition of the "chanson commune et régulière" as a reference for Descartes's example. Such a "chanson" consisted of sixteen measures, which, repeated, formed the first part; this was followed by a middle part of sixteen measures and then by another sixteen measures, also repeated. According to Arbeau, this formal arrangement had fallen out of fashion forty or fifty years before.

46.   Haec autem divisio notatur percussione, vel battuta, ut vocant, quod fit ad juvandam imaginationem nostram; qua possimus facilius omnia cantilenae membra percipere, & proportione quae in illis esse debet delectari. Haec autem proportio talis servatur saepissime in membris cantilenae, ut possit apprehensionem nostram ita juvare, ut dum ultimum audimus, adhuc temporis, quod in primo fiut & quod in reliqua cantilena, recordemur; quod fit, si tota cantilena vel 8, vel 16, vel 32, vel 64, &c., membris constet, ut scilicet omnes divisiones a proportione dupla procedant. Tunc enim, dum duo prima

membra audivimus, illa instar unius concipimus; dum tertium membrum, adhuc illud cum primis coniungimus, ita ut sit proportio tripla; postea, dum audimus quartum, illud cum tertio iungimus, ita ut instar unius concipiamus; deinde duo prima cum duobus ultimis iterum coniungimus, ita ut instar unius illa quatuor concipiamus simul. Et sic ad finem usque nostra imaginatio procedit, ubi tandem omnem cantilenam ut unum quid ex multis aequalibus membris conflatum concipit (*Compendium*, 14/AT, X, 93–94).

47. Robert Gjerdingen cites passages from John Locke's *Essay concerning Human Understanding* (1690), where Descartes's analysis seems to be taken for granted. Locke, Gjerdingen says, "takes up auditory imagery, the holistic nature of a melody, attention, and performance, and memory by association: 'sounds . . . are modified by diversity of notes of different length . . . which they may make that complex idea called a tune, which a musician may have in his mind when he hears or makes no sound at all [Book II, Ch. 18, Sec. 3].' 'Thus a triangle, though the parts thereof compared one to another be relative, yet the idea of the whole is a positive absolute idea. The same may be said of a family, a tune, etc.' [Book II, Ch. 25, Sec. 6]"; see Gjerdingen (2002: 958).

48. Sepper (1996: 44–46).

49. This process brings together the two parts of the soul: the sensitive part (*aisthetikon*) and the thinking part (*dianoetikon*). Quotation from Aristotle (1968: III, 7, 431a14).

50. Non quidem in quantum ad aliquod genus entis referuntur, sicut illas Philosophi in categorias suas diviserunt [; rather,] monet enim res omnes per quasdam series posse disponi . . . sed in quantum unae ex alijs cognosci possunt (Rule 6, 21/AT, X, 381).

51. Si igitur, ex. gr., per diversas operationes cognoverim primo, qualis sit habitudo inter magnitudines A & B, deinde inter B & C, tum inter C & D, ac denique inter D & E,: non idcirco video qualis sit inter A & E, nec possum intelligere praecise ex jam cognitis, nisi omnium recorder. Quamobrem illas continuo quodam imaginationis motu singula intuentis simul & ad alia transeuntis aliquoties percurram, donec a prima ad ultimam tam celeriter transire didicerim, ut fere nullas memoriae partes relinquendo, rem totam simul videar intueri; hoc enim pacto, dum memoriae subvenitur, ingenij etiam tarditas emendatur, ejusque capacitas quadam ratione extenditur (Rule 7, 25/AT, X, 387–88, emphasis mine).

52. We have here a case of self-doubling which is made possible by abrogating the empirical self (the one doing the narrating) from the activity of cognition itself. The point is that Descartes does not see a division. We will return to this matter in connection with the classical sign in the third section of the chapter, and in much greater detail in Chapter 4, regarding a contrasting attitude toward self-doubling in the early nineteenth century. For a critique of this aspect of Descartes's self-representation, see Judovitz (1988).

53. For a discussion of the empirical basis of Descartes's notions of order, deduction, and intuition, see Judovitz (1988: 59–60).

54. Jones (2001: 61) discusses this passage from the *Rules*, commenting on the

issue of intuition, the question of "evidence," and method. Jones notes a connection between this passage in the *Rules* to the methodological orientation in the *Geometry*. He does not, however, mention the *Compendium*.

55. For detailed discussion, see Van De Pitte (1988).

56. Descartes's disclaimer: "In case anyone should be troubled by my novel use of the term 'intuition' . . . I wish to point out here that I am paying no attention to the way these terms have lately been used in the Schools" (Rule 3, 14/AT, X, 369). *Nous*, in Aristotelian thought, is often rendered as "intuition," meaning a sort of intellectual perception of mathematical individuals, or the definitions of first principles. Jonathan Barnes (Aristotle 1994a) notes that to many the distinction between induction and intuition posited by this translation introduces a distinction between demonstrative and empirical knowledge (induction), on the one hand, and intuitive rationalist knowledge, on the other, which is, I believe, the distinction that Descartes wants to make. In Book B, Chapter 19 of the *Posterior Analytics* (Aristotle 1994a), where this division may first be noted, Aristotle seeks to answer the question of "what is the state (*hexis*) which gets to know principles?" (99b18–19). By "state" Aristotle means a mental disposition, or as Barnes puts it, "havings" or graspings. Aristotle believes that *nous* is the state of comprehending a principle, for *nous*, as he states in the *The Nicomachean Ethics* ([1925] 1980: 43a35–b5), is a perception of "primitive definitions." Conceiving of *nous* as intuition, as a sort of perception, is justified on these grounds. However, Aristotle does not consider *nous* to be a method of acquiring knowledge, in the way induction is. Barnes: "*nous*, the state or disposition, stands to induction as understanding (*epistêmê*) stands to demonstration. Understanding is not a means of acquiring knowledge. Nor, then, is *nous*" (Aristotle 1994a: 268).

57. Richard Rorty (1979: 47–48) comments on a related and pertinent issue. The Greeks, he writes, paraphrasing Wallace Matson (1966), had "no way to divide 'conscious states' or 'states of consciousness'—events in an inner life—from events in an 'external world.' Descartes, on the other hand, used 'thought' to cover doubting, understanding, affirming, denying, willing, refusing, imagining and feeling, and said that even if I dream that I see light 'properly speaking this in me is called feeling, and used in this precise sense that is no other thing than thinking' [*Meditations*, Second Meditation]". "Once Descartes had entrenched this way of speaking," he continues, "it was possible for Locke to use 'idea' in a way that had no Greek equivalent at all, as meaning 'whatsoever is the object of understanding when a man thinks' or 'every immediate object of the mind in thinking' [John Locke, *Essay Concerning Human Understanding*, and 'Second Letter to the Bishop of Worcester']." Rorty concludes that "immediacy as the mark of the mental (with the criterion of immediacy being incorrigibility) became an unquestioned presupposition in philosophy because of such passages as these."

58. Judovitz (1988: 62). Gaukroger (1995: 120–24; 1997) traces Descartes's interest in the clarity and vividness of mental images to rhetoric, where bringing something before the mind of the listener is of paramount importance. According to Gaukroger, Descartes would have been familiar with the rhetorical-psychological ideas of the Roman rhetorical writers. Reiss (1997: 119–20)

points out that in sixteenth-century France the idea that arithmetic as an art of reckoning, in opposition to dialectics and rhetoric, which remained as arts of disputing and persuading, was widely circulated. This idea is directly tied to the emergence of mathematics as the basis for discovery and knowledge, one that sanctioned conceptual elements, method, reasoning processes, and certain modes of representation. What I call "figural" in Descartes's approach to representation (which includes actual images as well as algebraic descriptions of them, as in the Preliminaries) may be considered to appeal to both rhetorical goals of evidential vividness and mathematical method.

59.   "Figural" ought not to be taken to suggest that which stands against a background, as is used in discussions of visual perception. Descartes uses the term "figures" (*figuras*) for the visual representation of objects of perception by the imagination. I will be using the term "images" (*imagines*) to accentuate the relation of "figures" to the imagination. In my discussion of Rule 14 below, I return to Descartes's use of "figures."

60.   See Judovitz (1988: 64–65).

61.   Here one sees in Descartes a strong tendency to "image" the world in order to render it comprehensible to the reader, a trend that culminates in the scientific fable *Le monde*. I discuss *Le monde* at greater length in Chapter 3.

62.   Plato (1992: 1147–48 [VII, 532]).

63.   Comparing Descartes to Zarlino, Christensen (1993a: 77) claims that "the string divisions he [Descartes] plotted were *real physical entities*" (emphasis in original) and "string segments were now the true foundation of sounds, and numbers were only a description." Zarlino "had considered string divisions only *images* of the numerical ratios he believed to be the cause of musical consonance" (emphasis in original). I think that what takes place is not so much an ontological reversal, as Christensen states, but a leveling of sense with intellect.

64.   Comparing Descartes's approach to the apprehension of time in music to that of sound, it is interesting to note that he feels that merely describing the principle of proportionality of sound is insufficient—this is what he does when explaining time—and that he must complement his linguistic representation (i.e., the postulates themselves) with visual representation, albeit conjured linguistically.

65.   Rules 12–18 mark Descartes's return to questions of method. Rule 12, in particular, "sums up everything that has been said before, and sets out a general lesson the details of which remain to be explained as follows" (Rule 12, 39/AT, X, 411). Gaukroger (1995: 157) explains that Rules 12–18 deal "with how to solve problems when we know the simple natures concerned," saying that overall the main concern of these rules is with "the mechanistic construal of cognition" (112, 146–47, 152–72). (A final set, which Descartes never wrote, were to deal with cases where the relevant simple natures are not known.)

66.   For example, images feature prominently in the hydrostatics manuscripts written around the same time as the *Compendium*.

67.   Gaukroger (1995: 158–59).

68.   Here Descartes is focusing on what he calls "simples": "those things which we

know so clearly and distinctly that they cannot be divided by the mind into others which are more distinctly known" (Rule 12, 44/AT, X, 418). Shape, extension, and motion are all examples of simples.

69. When referring to the part of the mind where imagining takes place, Descartes prefers the term "phantasy" (*phantasia*).

70. Gaukroger (1995: 172).

71. This is most radically expressed in *Le monde*, where Descartes will invite the reader to join him in a "fable" in which the world would be indeed constructed. Fears that this constructivist attitude would be interpreted as a direct challenge to God's authority prompted Descartes to halt publication of that writing. For discussion of Descartes's attempts to delimit the range of knowable things, see Jones (2001: 67–68).

72. See Reiss (1997: 86–131, 11, 155–87).

73. Born in Germany, Christoph Clavius (1537–1612) was the foremost Jesuit mathematician during the sixteenth century, working in Rome. On the education of Descartes, see Gaukroger (1995: 58–59, 74).

74. See Isaac Beeckman (Journal, 1604–34; cited in H. Floris Cohen 1984: 117), Giovanni Battista Benedetti (1585), Vincenzo Galilei ([1581] 1967). These authors' contributions are discussed by Cohen (ibid.: Chs. 3–5). Palisca (1985: Ch. 10) discusses Galilei and Benedetti at some length. See also Palisca (1989) for translations of Galilei's writings. On early-sixteenth-century authors, see Lodovico Fogliano, *Musica Theorica* (1529), Girolamo Cardano, *De Musica* (in Cardano [c. 1546] 1973). Moyer (1992: 161) writes that "the originality [of Cardano's theories of sound perception] lies in shifting the cause of music's effects on the emotions away from the proportions themselves, towards the ways those proportions are perceived." For further discussion of Fogliano and Cardano, see Reiss (1997: 169–87), Palisca (1985: 235–44), Moyer (1992: 141–47, 158–68). Reiss also includes Gaffurio's ideas (*Theorica Musice*, 1492) about the "proportional analogy of senses to their objects as reason to numerical quantity" as an important precedent to the work of later authors, but notes his dependence on cosmological and theological considerations (171). A strong Neoplatonic bent is also evident in Cardano. Although tempting, a historical interpretation that considers the work of Cardano and Fogliano as precedents for ideas about sound perception and transmission developed by the scientists later on in the century must overlook the different epistemological ground upon which each "group" stands. Palisca (1994: 200–235) offers a summary of scientific efforts, which he terms "scientific empiricism," during the latter part of the century.

75. Compare with the following: "[T]he subject position is the site to which music is addressed as something meaningful and the site from which the meaning of the music is enunciated. The historical appearance of these processes might roughly be given a double date of origin, one around the close of the sixteenth century and one around the close of the eighteenth century, both historical moments that consolidate a gradually developing identification of subjectivity with a sense of inwardness. . . . [M]usic quickly comes to the fore as a means of forming and cultivating inwardness because of the seemingly direct relationship between music and emotion, and again between music and

the interior of the body that hears, plays and responds to music" (Kramer 2001: 158).

Kramer follows the traditional account of subjectivity that locates inwardness in the emergence of monody and opera but does not pursue the matter from an epistemological perspective. Tomlinson (1999: 34–40) explores the relation between Cartesian subjectivity and early modern opera. Descartes's subject is defined there according to the dualistic terms outlined most explicitly in the *Meditations.*

76.   I will henceforth not italicize the expression "mathesis universalis."

77.   Mathesis universalis is not, however, mathematics itself. The Greek term *mathêma* designates ordered knowledge, with mathematics being an exemplary, albeit particular, case. The best available discussion of the idea of mathesis universalis is that of Giovanni Crapulli (1969). A similar term, *mathesis universa,* commonly designates throughout the sixteenth century all the mathematical disciplines taken together as a unified whole. The term does not indicate, however, a particular "science" (ibid.: 8). Crapulli recognizes Descartes's claim in the *Rules* about the role that mathesis universalis plays in the formation of his method. He notes that a similar sense is already in evidence by 1597 in the work of Jesuit-educated Belgian mathematician Adriaan van Roomen in his *Apologia pro Archimede* (Ch. 6): "geometriae et arithmeticae communis est scientia quae quantitatem generaliter uti mensurabilem considerat . . . ad quam spectant affectiones communes omnibus quantitatibus . . . non abstractis tantum ut numeris et magnitudinibus, sed concretis etiam, uti temporibus, sonis, vocibus, locis, motibus, potentiis . . . proportiones eas quae spectant ad analogias . . . ad scientiam aliquam universalem iure merito pertinere existimandum est" (Common is the science of geometry and arithmetic, which considers quantity, in general, as measurable . . . to which feelings common to all quantities look . . . not only in abstract numbers and magnitudes, but also in concrete things, such as time(s), sounds, voices, places, movements, abilities . . . these proportions which look to analogies . . . one ought to consider that it [they], quite deservedly, pertains to a certain universal science); cited in Crapulli (1969: 146; see also 101–23), translated by John Bauschatz. Van Roomen, Crapulli notes, "remains rigidly within the institutional field of mathematics and leaves out of his exposition all considerations of a philosophical order" (153).

78.   Descartes does not claim to coin the term, but neither does he specify where he may have first encountered it. Van Roomen is the most likely source, according to Crapulli.

79.   Crapulli (1969: 145).

80.   I have in mind the otherwise admirable study by H. Floris Cohen (1984).

81.   See Foucault ([1966] 1971: 56–57).

82.   Reiss (1997: 120) gives a detailed account of arguments in sixteenth-century France concerning the connection between the logic of discourse and that of mathematics. Thinkers such as Ramus and Bovelles argued for an epistemological equivalence between dialectic and arithmetic, governed as these were by the corresponding ideas of syllogism and logism, respectively. Ramus: dialectic is the "art of disputing well" while arithmetic is the "doctrine of reckon-

ing well." Descartes, on the other hand, quickly distances himself from this tradition, dismissing their claims that inference chains "regulate human reason" (Rule 2, 12/AT, X, 365).

83. Tomlinson (1993: 190–94) discusses the Foucauldian critique of resemblance.

84. Foucault ([1966] 1971: 72).

85. Foucault ([1966] 1971: 69).

86. Foucault ([1966] 1971: 70).

87. This is a crucial point that Foucault's analysis overlooks.

88. Foucault ([1966] 1971: 64).

89. An important caveat here is that although the sign represents representation itself, this representation is not open to analysis. At this level the representation of representation is an action carried out by consciousness, not the product of self-reflection.

90. Tout ce qui est tellement en nous, que nous en sommes immédiatement connaisants: in Descartes ([1641] 1984); see also 113/AT, VII, 160. Tout ce qui se fait en nous de telle sorte que nous l'apercevons immédiatement par nous-mêmes: from *Principles of Philosophy* (1644), in Descartes (1985: Part 1, Sec. 9); see also 195/AT, VIIIA, 7.

91. See, for example, Carter (1995), Kurtzman (1993), Tomlinson (1993: particularly Ch. 7, "Archaeology and Music: Apropos of Monteverdi's Musical Magic").

92. The emphasis here is different from the well-known notion of social and political identity self-fashioning articulated by Stephen Greenblatt (1980). Any connections that may be made between these senses of identity construction and the kind of representational self-designation that I have discussed would nonetheless be said to operate at the level of episteme.

93. Judovitz (1988: 82); Husserl (1970: 81). Benveniste (1971) influentially argued that language is the medium in and through which the subject is constituted. This medium, however, divides the subject into what is uttered and the utterance itself. As a result, the "I" is in constant shift between these two levels. Critics like Judovitz adopt a poststructuralist position characterizing the "subject" as a linguistic effect: "the 'I' does not refer either to a concept or an individual, but to the locutionary position within an utterance" (1988: 4).

94. See Descartes ([1618] 1987: 54); 62/AT, X, 90, 95. See also de Buzon (1983), Clark and Rehding (2001: 1–2).

95. See Gaukroger (1995: 101–103). Descartes declared that the idea for the "foundations of a marvelous science (mirabilis scientiae fundamenta)" came to him in three dreams(!).

96. On author function and discursive practice, see Foucault (1984: 108–17) and ([1969] 1972: 215–37).

3. The Complicity of the Imagination

1. Throughout this chapter I draw a distinction between *tones* and *notes*. Implied *tones* include those *notes* that we see written on a separate staff below a

score, or indicated by means of figures over the fundamental bass, or that we find sheltered within the confines of parentheses in analyses. This distinction is articulated by William Rothstein (1991: 293–94), who identifies tones as "not what we 'hear' in the literal sense of that word"; "rather," he states, "they are a way of representing to ourselves what we have heard already." Tones have definite pitches but may, for example, lack register specificity. In contrast, notes are the actual sounds heard as the result of a performance, mental or actual, of a passage; they possess pitch, register, timbre, and duration. I will make more problematic the question of whether or not tones have a place in the listening experience, and thus whether or not tones operate exclusively at the analytical level. Rameau himself provides a distinction in the "Table of Terms" in the *Traité* between *Ton* and *Son*. *Ton* designates both "the space between two sounds that are compared to one another" and the sense of our modern concept of "key." *Son* refers to an acoustic phenomenon (which he considers the domain of physics) but, most importantly for the present discussion, it also signifies for Rameau actual and conceptual sounds, that is "notes" *and* "tones."

2. [S]i l'on retranche la Basse fondamentale, & que l'on mette alternativement à sa place l'une des autres parties, l'on trouvera tous les Accords renversez de ceux-cy, dont l'Harmonie sera toûjours bonne, parce qui si la Basse fondamentale en est retranchée, elle y est toûjours sous-entenduë (Gossett, 67/*Traité*, 57). On appelle Cadence *parfaite*, toutes les conclusions de Chant qui se sont sur une Notte tonique précédée de sa Dominante; cette Notte doit être toûjours entenduë dans le premier Temps de la Mesure, pour que la conclusion puisse se faire sentir, & la Dominante qui la précéde en ce cas, doit porter toûjours l'Accord de la *Septiéme*, ou au moins le Parfait, parce que la *Septiéme* peut y être sous-entenduë (Gossett 235/*Traité*, 216). References to the *Traité* give first page numbers in Philip Gossett's translation (Rameau [1722] 1971), followed by the corresponding pages in Erwin Jacobi's edition (Rameau [1722] 1967a). Translations from the *Traité* are by Gossett, unless otherwise indicated. I have maintained original spellings.

3. I discuss Rameau's concept of *sous-entendre* in "The Complicity of the Imaginary: The Case of Rameau's Implied Dissonances," unpublished paper read at the 21st Annual Meeting of the Society for Music Theory, Chapel Hill, N.C., 2–5 December 1998. Brian Hyer (1994) examines what he calls "supplemental dissonances" in Rameau. Taking Derrida as a point of departure, Hyer offers a subtle semiotic account of Rameau's concept that suggests the need for an intentional action by the listener. I return to Hyer later in the chapter. David Cohen (2001: 71–74) also addresses Rameau's concept, but in a different context and from a very different perspective. Cohen's essay appeared after I had written the bulk of this chapter, but there are overlapping themes between his work and mine regarding issues of "agency" and "cognition."

4. The context of my discussion in this chapter should make clear that my sense of "implication" is different from that commonly associated with the work of Leonard Meyer and Eugene Narmour. The better alternative, using Rameau's original expression *sous-entendre*, would force me to use an English verb (to imply) in combination with the French verb, a less economical option.

5. My analysis views the local ideas about implication and harmonic succession

articulated in the *Traité* archaeologically, as global symptoms of an epistemological attitude that no single intellectual trend or ideological attachment of Rameau's can fully explain. My focus on the *Traité* should therefore be taken to mean neither that subsequent writings are of less importance for Rameau's thought or for musical thought in general nor, worse still, that all the basic notions of his music theory are manifest there in full or "embryonic" form. As Thomas Christensen's expansive study of Rameau's relation to the intellectual milieu of the Enlightenment has shown, understanding the ideas coming in and out of Rameau's work during and after the *Traité* is indispensable for a full appreciation of the conceptual flexibility of his music theory (Christensen 1993a).

6. Rameau's fundamental impact on musical thought has also been explored by Brian Hyer (1996a). The fundamental study of Rameau's cognitive framework is that of Marie-Elisabeth Duchez (1986). Duchez's work engages Rameau's scientific spirit in a way different from mine, but her ideas of cognitive modeling and her penetrating analysis of Rameau's appeals to nature are relevant to my discussion.

7. An exception occurs in Book 2, Chapter 9: "en remarquant que *si nous sous-entendons* un accord de Septiéme dans le premier Son d'un intervale de Quinte en descendant, cette progression doit être égalment sous-entendue après un accord de Septiéme" (Gossett, 83/*Traité*, 69); emphasis mine, translation modified.

8. Feyerabend (1993: 20).

9. My analysis of Rameau's theory of representation will differ from Allan Keiler's interpretation in his classic "Music as Metalanguage: Rameau's Fundamental Bass" (1981); see p. 170.

10. A related offshoot of my analysis consists in juxtaposing against the rational coordinates of Rameau's science—"notions of causality, belief in universality of laws, determinism, mechanism, and the immanent rationality of the natural order, and a holistic vision of the world"—a less rational element in the form of the imagination. The summary of the rational coordinates of classical science appears in Duchez (1986: 91).

11. The question of how much in Rameau is old and how much new is best summed up by Carl Dahlhaus (1989: 10): "Und daß Rameaus Harmonielehre sowohl ein Ende als auch einen Anfang markiert, ist eine Trivialität, deren Diskussion erst dadurch, daß man sich angesichts von Details, in denen 'der Teufel steckt,' über die relative Bedeutung oder Irrelevanz des Alten und des Neuen verständigen muß, überhaupt lohnend erscheint." Duchez (1986: 99) considers Rameau's work to unite two other types of theoretical discourse: didactic and scientific.

12. See Duchez (1986: 93).

13. See Duchez (1986: 93).

14. Rameau's account traces each part of the cadence separately, much in accordance with Zarlino ([1558] 1965: Part 3, Chs. 10 and 38), to which he adds a fundamental bass, figures, and even additional parts. A thorough account of

the theory of intervallic progression appears in Dahlhaus (1990); see also Dahlhaus (1989: 81–82). Derrida's notion of reinscription is used to indicate the revalorization of a less-valued term in a traditional opposition in a way that permits it to redefine the dominant term (Derrida 1978). Here I use it to describe Rameau's reuse of preexisting phenomena in order to constitute his own explanatory system.

15. See Christensen (1993a: 111–13) for a discussion of contradictions in Rameau's formulation of the seventh as a fundamental dissonance. Christensen notes that it is according to its function as a basic dissonance in the perfect cadence that we must interpret Rameau's attempts to incorporate the seventh as derived from the fundamental bass. This is an instance of practical considerations forcing Rameau to accommodate a phenomenon into his scheme of first principles.

16. The subdominant does not form one of the basic chordal categories in the *Traité*; Rameau will, however, identify it on a par with the tonic and the dominant, in *Nouveau système de musique théorique* ([1726] 1967b).

17. David Cohen (1993) offers an extensive overview and critique of the notions of consonance and dissonance. Dahlhaus places Rameau's concept of harmonic progression in the context of the theory of intervallic progression (1990: 29; 1989: 77, 81). Dahlhaus (1989) overstates his case, calling Rameau a traditionalist.

18. [S]i nous pouvons donner une progression à la partie que nous represente cette corde entiere, ce ne peut être qu'en la faisant proceder par ces intervales consonans que nous rendent les premieres divisions de cette corde, ainsi chaque Son s'accordera toûjours avec celuy qui l'aura précédé (Gossett, 60/*Traité*, 50); translation modified.

19. Christensen (1993a: 132). For an in-depth discussion of the idea of cognitive model, see Duchez (1986).

20. La suite de l'Harmonie n'est autre chose qu'un enchaînement de *Nottes toniques* & de *Dominantes,* dont il faut bien connoître les dérivez, pour faire ensorte qu'un Accord domine toûjours celuy qui le suit (Gossett, 288/*Traité*, 269); emphasis in original, translation modified.

21. Rameau makes a distinction between *dominante-tonique,* the dominant seventh chord that participates in a perfect cadence, and *dominante,* the dominant seventh chord which does not (in a diatonic progression there is only one *dominante-tonique*). In terms of its relative instability, the dominante is nonetheless conceived as an analogue of the *dominante-tonique.*

22. Il se trouve une si grande liaison dans cette suite d'Accords, qui est le noeud de l'Harmonie la plus naturelle, que l'habitude s'en acquiert souvent avant la connoissance (Gossett, 410/ *Traité*, 397); translation mine (Gossett omits the reference to *liaison*). Christensen (1993a: 129) refers to one such progression as "a sequence of 'dominants.'" I use the term "succession" because the term "sequence" does not figure in Rameau as such. In places Rameau uses the expression *enchaînement de Dominantes* (e.g., Gossett, 224/*Traité*, 204). For discussion of the status of knowledge of figured-bass practitioners, see Duchez (1986: 98–102), David Cohen (2001).

It is important to note that Rameau's example is not presented as an expression of an incipient concept of harmonic tonality based on the cycle of fifths (the use of minor mode here constitutes telling evidence). The emphasis here is on the chord-to-chord progression, and this is important because it reflects Rameau's concern with the temporal unfolding of chords in a *Modulation*, not with a spatialization of the concept of scale steps. Dahlhaus (1984: 25) makes a related point: "Im Begriff der Basse fondamentale ist strenggenommen nicht der geringste Ansatzpunkt für die Etablierung einer Tonart enthalten: Reguliert werden ausschließlich die Fundamentschritte von Akkord zu Akkord, nicht die Gruppierungen um tonale Zentren."

Alexander Rehding suggests that critics such as Dahlhaus (1990: 35) and Kurth (*Die Voraussetzungen der theoretischen Harmonik*), who regard this example by Rameau and other examples by Sechter as representatives of a tradition that juxtaposes "Riemannian function harmony with harmonic relations based on the cycle of fifths," overstate their case. Rehding remarks that the "sequence" example appears only once in the *Traité* and that it does so relatively late, diminishing its importance to Rameau (1999: 202, n65). Indeed, the relative insignificance of the harmonic model of fifth progression is seen when measured (in Whiggish fashion) according to its explanatory capacities and presence within a system against the fully developed cadential model of functions as it figures in Riemann. Dahlhaus (1989: 10–11) calls the issue an "awkward problem" in Rameau, saying that it is a matter of emphasis, even with Rameau, who gives more emphasis to the relationship of the subdominant to the tonic in the works following the *Traité*.

23. To the best of my knowledge, Rameau is the first theorist to single out the progression by fifths as a prototype of harmonic mobility. Until this time the figured-bass tradition neither refers to the chain of seventh chords as a pervasive idiom in the literature, nor describes it as a particularly unstable phenomenon. Nonetheless, in figured-bass treatises c. 1700 a series of seventh chords is summarily prescribed to realize unfigured basses proceeding by fifths, suggesting its wide use. In our century Wilhelm Fischer (1915: 33) singles out this progression, aptly identifying it as "the engine behind *Fortspinnung*."

24. I will use the French *liaison en harmonie* instead of the cumbersome translation "interconnectedness within harmony." Robert Gjerdingen uses the expression "harmonic connection" in his translation of Dahlhaus (1990: 34).

25. The most expansive discussion of *liaison en harmonie* appears in the *Nouveau système* (Rameau [1726] 1967b: Ch. 16); see also there (p. 56) and, for a comparison between *modulation* and *discours,* pp. 40–41.

26. Or rien ne peut mieux faire sentir une *Liaison* en Harmonie, qu'un même Son qui sert à deux Accords successifs, & qui fait souhaiter en même tems le Son, pour ne pas dire, l'Accord qui doit suivre immediatement (Rameau [1726] 1967b: 57); translation mine. Rameau's emphasis of the harmonic (e.g., "not to say the chord") over the contrapuntal (e.g., "makes one desire the tone") is in line with his reinscription of intervallic progression. (I will return to the trope of "desire" in Sec. 3.4.)

27. Implication figures prominently in the case of *double emploi*, the term that

Rameau coins in *Génération* to explain how a single chord may yield two different fundamental basses in the event of an irregular succession. A common case is the use of scale degrees two and four as basses for a chord "built" on the second scale degree (i.e., d–f–a in the key of C major): when explaining its progression *from* the tonic chord, Rameau gives this chord the fundamental bass note F, considering d as a dissonant sixth [*sixte ajoutée*]—like the implied seventh, a supplementary dissonance; when explaining its progression to the dominant chord, Rameau gives D as the fundamental, with c as a dissonant seventh. Allan Keiler (1981: 100) provides an excellent analysis of *double emploi*: "Rameau confuses the problem of structural ambiguity (a chord may function differently in relation to what precedes and what follows), which is an aspect of structural description, with the problem of the perceiver, which is to revise hypothetical readings of the input as he receives more information." Similar to other commentators (to be reviewed shortly), Keiler identifies the problem but offers no reasons as to why Rameau may have deployed the representational model he used. Keiler considers this a problem resulting from Rameau's use of analytical musical notation, or as he puts it, with Rameau's "metalanguage."

This is Rameau's explanation of motion other than by fifth (or fourth) and third: "whenever it is permissible to have a fundamental bass ascend a tone or a semitone, the [root] progression of a [descending] third and a[n ascending] fourth is always implied" (s'il est permis de faire monter la Basse-fondamentale d'un Ton ou d'un semi-Ton, la progression d'une Tierce & d'une Quarte y est toûjours sous-entenduë) (Gossett, 234/ *Traité*, 214).

28. On appelle *Cadence parfaite,* toutes les conclusions de Chant qui se sont sur une Notte tonique précédée de la Dominante; cette Notte tonique doit être toûjours entenduë dans le premier Temps de la Mesure, pour que la conclusion puisse se faire sentir, & la Dominante qui la précéde en ce cas, doit porter toûjours l'Accord de la *Septiéme,* ou au moins le Parfait, parce que la *Septiéme* peut y être sous-entenduë (Gossett, 235/ *Traité*, 216, emphasis in original). A variation of this point is made in *Génération harmonique* (Rameau [1737] 1968: 173); cited in full in n. 43 below.

29. Sous-entendre. On regarde dans la Musique les termes de *Sous-entendre* & de *Supposer* presque comme synonimes; cependant leur signification y renferme un sens bien different l'un de l'autre. Par le mot de *Sous-entendre* on doit être prévenu que les Sons ausquels on l'applique, peuvent être entendus dans les Accords où ils ne se trouvent point; & même, à l'égard du Son-Fondamental, il faut s'imaginer qu'il devroit être pour lors *entendu au dessous* des autres Sons, lorsqu' on dit qu'il est *Sous-entendu* (Gossett, xlv (Table of Terms)/ *Traité*, xxi (Table des Termes); emphasis in original, translation mine. Gossett renders "il faut s'imaginer" as "we imagine," an ascription to the first person plural that actually occurs only once elsewhere in the *Traité* (Book 2, Ch. 9).

30. See Christensen (1993a: Ch. 5).

31. The Greek word *synkoptein* means to hit together or collide. The notion and principle of collision are central to fourteenth-century impetus theory, a theory that reconfigured the field of mechanics. This model holds that the continuing motion of a body is due to an internal power implanted by a

projector that initiates the motion, as in a pendulum. For useful discussions see Kuhn (1970: 118–22) and Gaukroger (1995: 57–58). In Book 2 Rameau cites the etymology of syncopation from Brossard's *Dictionnaire de musique* (1703). It should be noted that the section of the *Traité* in which this appears was part of Rameau's Supplement to his treatise. Gossett's translation (Rameau [1722] 1971) interpolates this appendix within the main text. I am grateful to David Cohen for bringing this to my attention.

32.   Christensen (1993a: 129). Christensen renders *sous-entendre* as "impute," making it clear that he believes Rameau to be implicating the listener as intentional agent in the process of implication.

  This proclivity leads Rameau ([1726] 1967b: Chs. 20 and 23) to refigure continuo parts by Corelli and Lully; Lully is critiqued also in *Observations sur notre instinct pour la musique* (1754) and *Code de musique pratique* (1760). In "Examples of errors found in the Figures of Corelli's Opus 5" (Rameau [1726] 1967b: Ch. 23), Rameau seeks to demonstrate how the Italian's figures obscure "the true chords that must be found as a consequence of the interconnection that the fundamental progression of a fifth must naturally effect in each modulation" (les veritables Accords qui doivent s'y trouver, en consequence de la *Liaison* que le progrès fondamental de *Quinte* doit entretenir le plus naturellement dans chaque *Modulation*) (95); emphasis in original. I will not delve into these revisions other than to say that they reflect discrepancies between theory and practice that Rameau resolves in favor of theory. I am not interested in the charges of dogmatism that may fairly be levied against Rameau, agreeing with Christensen that Rameau's revisions cannot always be justified, and that they reflect Rameau's overgeneralizing impulses. For discussions of these "revisions," see Christensen (1993a: 129–31), Albert Cohen (1992), Lester (1992: 305–19), Mitchell (1963: 230–31).

33.   Lester (1992: 137), Denis Delair, *Traité d'accompagnement pour le théorbe et le clavessin* (1690). Car si chacun de ces Sons portoit un accord parfait, l'on peut dire que l'ame n'ayant plus rien à desirer après un tel accord, seroit comme incertaine du choix qu'elle auroit à faire de l'un de ces deux Sons pour son repos (Gossett, 62/*Traité*, 53); translation modified.

34.   Lester (1992: 119).

35.   According to Christensen (1993a: 115–16), the model of harmonic progression displays the harmonies of a mode, such that all nontonic harmonies are compelled to resolve to the tonic, evidently a claim for long-range projection of the two-chord perfect cadence model to the level of key.

36.   Burnham (1992a: 7–9). Christensen (1993a: 114) identifies as characteristic of French Baroque music "precise articulations of phrase structure delineated by frequent cadential caesuras." This he contrasts to the motoric Italian style, a style that corresponds more closely to Burnham's reference.

37.   For further discussion of this shift, see Christensen (1993a: 185–90). Note, however, that the idea of a relative tonic remains in place in *Génération harmonique* (Rameau [1737] 1968); cf. n. 43 below.

38.   Lester (1992: 136).

39.   Lester (1992: 138).

40. The preface to the complete works characterizes the 1730 edition as sparse, logical, rational (German) [*sparsam, logisch, rational (deutsch)*] in contrast to the phantastic, sensuous overabundance of seventh chords, ninths, chord inversions, and so on (French) [*phantastisch sinnlich in der Überfülle von Septimenakkorden, Nonen, Akkordumkehrungen usw. (Französisch)*] of the 1736 French edition; see Telemann (1965), vii. Note that the revised edition does not indicate a 7 at the end of the second phrase in m. 8, in contrast to its parallel point in m. 4. This suggests that the editor paid attention to the musical context: the first cadence needs to be made more unstable than the second one.

41. Lester (1992: 156).

42. Austrian composer Wolfgang Ebner had expressed some reservations about the series of sixth chords, observing that "[T]here is a way in which one can both ascend and descend in three parts. Although the manner in question is far from agreeable, I nevertheless include it as the result of considerable experience, because it is nowadays much in vogue among sundry musicians of standing": rule thirteen in *A Short Instruction and Guide to Thoroughbass* (1653); quoted in Francis Thomas Arnold (1931: 133). The question of "taste," a central topic in eighteenth-century French aesthetics, might have some relevance to the issue of added dissonances, in particular in relation to musical practice. It is beyond the scope of this study to address this issue.

43. Dahlhaus (1990: 28). Dahlhaus may have had in mind a passage from *Génération harmonique* (Rameau [1737] 1968: 173), in which Rameau writes "a tonic note can become whatever one wishes relative to that which follows it; so that when it is approached as a tonic, it can immediately be called dominant or subdominant of that which follows it, adding the dissonance appropriate in that instance, although that is not necessary: it need only be implied" (Une Note-tonique peut devenir ce qu'on veut, relativement à ce qui la suit; de sorte qu'y étant arrivé comme à une Tonique, on peut l'appeller sur le champ Dominant ou Soudominante de ce qui la suit, en y ajoutant même la Dissonance qui lui convient pour lors, quoique cela ne soit pas nécessaire; il suffit de l'y sousentendre); translation mine. Rameau's expression *sur le champ* suggests a phenomenological understanding of the process of imputing dissonances.

44. [W]urde von ihm [Kirnberger] verkannt, daß die Kategorie der harmonieeigenen Dissonanz ein Funktions- und nicht ein Substanzbegriff (im Sinne Ernst Cassirers) ist (Dahlhaus 1984: 11). The reference is to Ernst Cassirer (1910, [1910] 1923).

45. By *phantasia* the Greeks understood what we call imaginary. Initially the term signifies the capacity "to be like" (*eikô*), imitation being the dominant trope. The noun form (*eikôn*) indicates the state of being like, an image, or copy, the verb (*eikazô*) signifies the activity of making like or copying, and *eikasia* denotes the process by which such copying occurs (i.e., imagining). This signifying complex relates both to the material and to the means of expression, but does not distinguish between them; in other words, it conflates ontology and epistemology (we will see some of the difficulties created by later attempts to separate these). A more closely related term to imagination, *phantasia*, derives

from *phainô*, "to appear" or "to come to light." From this term springs *phantasma*, a noun that indicates both the appearance (i.e., the result of the "activity" of the verb *phainô*) as well as a mental state that stands opposite reality.

The etymology of the word "imagination" comes from the Latin *imago*, meaning "imitation," "picture," or "simulacrum." The objects described by the term are considered derivations and copies of a given object. Ultimately, the term epitomizes the representation—and thus a secondary manifestation, if not, in a sense, the opposite—of the real. From its inception, it follows, the concept of *phantasia*/imagination depends on an implicit definition of reality, yet efforts to describe its ontological foundation against this definition of reality run into considerable difficulty. This occurs because the imagination encapsulates an opposition that has marked Western metaphysics from its inception, namely, the relation of mind to matter.

Phantasia and imagination coexist until the seventeenth century, at which time the former becomes more closely associated with mental creativity and license, and the latter remains rooted in the more or less concrete evidence of sense data. However, Hobbes ([1651] 1996)—who tries to make a clear distinction between the two concepts—upholds their synonymy. Nowhere are the difficulties in separating the two more evident than in the variety of terms that appear in Germany during the nineteenth century, to witness, *Einbildungskraft, Fassungskraft, Phantasie,* and *Perceptionsvermögen,* among others.

46.   Why an ocular metaphor became inseparable from human knowledge is not known. John Dewey speculated that the act of vision—which relates a subject to an object—serves as a model for a theory of knowledge in which, according to pre-Socratic notions, objects refract light to be seen. The distinction lies, then, in that this makes no difference to the object seen but a great deal to the eye and the subject. A theory of knowledge of universals, therefore, is comparable to a theory of seeing the unchangeable, and theory itself signifies "contemplation" of universals (Dewey [1929] 1960: 23; cited in Rorty 1979: 39). Here we witness the inception of what may be called the tyranny of the visual as the trope for imagination and the mind (Aristotle calls sight "the most highly developed sense"). The ocular metaphor of the mind's eye inaugurates the notion that knowing something has its equivalent in "looking at it," and not, as Rorty (1979: 39) puts it, "rubbing up against it, or crushing it underfoot, or having sexual intercourse with it." This assumption carries debilitating consequences for notions of aural imagery; thus, Mitchell (1986: 9–10), for instance, does not list "aural" as one of the members of the "family of images."

47.   I render *eikasia* as "imagination" to denote its dual meaning as noun and verb.

48.   Plato (1992: *Republic* VI, 510d3–511a1).

49.   In the letter to Dion, Plato (1961: 1589, letter VII [trans. L. A. Post]) specifies four stages on the way to knowing an object: "first, a name, second, a description, third, an image, and fourth, a knowledge of the object."

50.   Plato distinguishes betwen *eidos* and *eidôlon.* The former refers to a "suprasensible reality," the latter to the sensorial impression that affords a phantasm of the "Idea" (*eidos*).

51. See Aristotle (1968). Some of the following discussion of Aristotle echoes points discussed in Chapter 2, Sections 2.1 and 2.2. The emphasis here, however, is on the epistemological value assigned to the imagination.

52. Aristotle divides forms into two categories (he predicates cognition on the basis of the existence of forms in substances): first, the "essential form," which is the nature of a thing that makes it the species it is; second, the "sensible form," which identifies the nature of a thing that is accessible through the external senses (1968: II, 12, 424a17–424b21). For their connection in sense perception, see Chapter 2, Section 2.1.

53. As noted in Chapter 2, Section 2.1, Aristotle uses a single term—*pathos*—to refer to the experience of sense perception and the quality of the object experienced.

54. The expression "not really there" is, of course, suspect, since the spatial metaphor in "there" constitutes an inappropriate transposition of the Platonic spectator theory of knowledge. When Aristotle refers to the imagination as a process and to the imaginary as a special kind of transformed immaterial content of the mind, there is no "there" in the imagination.

55. Hobbes ([1651] 1996: 38). Hobbes's phrase captures the predominantly Aristotelian outlook on the imagination which will influence Locke's and Hume's influential positions: that it is a faculty of perception *and* a power of representation.

56. Aristotle (1968: III, 7, 431a–431b19). This effects a shift from the Platonic understanding of temporality in the cognitive use of images. Plato allowed images into epistemology insofar as they facilitated the mind to reveal truths always already present in objects of knowledge.

57. This is not to say that Aristotle's hylomorphic argument, by which the substantial forms of objects are transported to the intellect, is abandoned. Rather, his theory of the imagination points to a necessarily temporal account of how a particular kind of perception—sensation—is made contemplatable. For a discussion of hylomorphism that does not consider the role of the imagination, see Rorty (1979: 45).

58. The imagination, Aristotle says, is most active when our senses are suspended, that is, during sleep, and dreams are susceptible to images that have no correspondence with sensible realities.

59. See Augustine (1979: epistola, vii, 225–26).

60. Here we see Aristotle rejecting the idealistic extravagances of his master: "Above all one might raise the problem of what the [Platonic] Forms of perceptibles might contribute to the eternal things or to things that come into being and are destroyed. For they are the cause neither of change nor of any modification for them. And indeed they do not contribute in any way either to the science of the others (for these are not substance . . .), nor to their being, not being present in the *participants* [things that Forms are a model for]" (1924: I, 9, 991a9–14); emphasis mine.

61. Strictly speaking, the proposition "the fundamental bass is implied" satisfies the logical distinction that Port-Royal grammarians make between objects of thought (e.g., the fundamental bass) and operations (e.g., the copula "is")

that undoubtedly joins such objects to either a verb, as happens here, or to a subject, as I am claiming Rameau could have done.

62. See also Duchez (1986).

63. See Foucault ([1966] 1971: 58).

64. Rameau's discovery of Sauveur's work on the harmonic series (dating to 1701–1702) prompts him to advance the *corps sonore* (in *Nouveau système* and especially *Génération harmonique*) as proof that the fundamental sound does represent the sounds of the *accord parfait,* a move betraying empiricist tendencies that are far more attenuated in the epistemology of the *Traité.* Christensen (1993a: 137–39) provides a useful account of Rameau's encounter with Sauveur's discoveries. Duchez (1986: 104) finds that Rameau's discovery of Sauveur catapults his thought with singular force in *Génération,* arguing that the *corps sonore* validates his empirical commitments: with its phenomenal validity it brings together a "triple correspondence between an acoustical series of frequencies, a perceptual series of pitch 'heights,' and a mathematical series of numbers." Further, she explains, the *corps sonore* both demonstrates Rameau's claims about the "natural" capacities of perception advanced by his theory of the *Basse fondamentale* and transforms music theory into a "physico-mathematical science" (Rameau [1737] 1968: 30) with a broad foundation on perception (Duchez 1986: 108–109). I argue, however, that the physical reality that Rameau seeks is counterbalanced in his epistemology by the nonphysical reality of implied dissonances. Likewise, I offer an alternative view of the correspondence between "perception," "mathesis," and "sound," providing a semiotic reading not available in Duchez's study, and I outline the presence of a dialectical tension in the physico-acoustic and mathematical certitude, which for Duchez confirms Rameau's psycho-physiological hypothesis.

65. Here I paraphrase Foucault ([1966] 1971: 60–61).

66. Compare, however, to this startling claim from *Nouveau système* (Rameau [1726] 1967b: iii): "In fact, there exists in us the seeds of harmony of which we are apparently not aware: however, it is easy to perceive it in a cord, in a pipe, and so on, and in whatever one finds whose resonance makes three different sounds heard at once" (Il y a effectivement en nous un germe d'Harmonie, dont apparament on ne s'est point encore apperçû: Il est cependant facile de s'en appercevoir dans une Corde, dans un Tuyay, & c. dont la resonance fait entendre trois Sons differents à la fois). From the *Traité* onward Rameau will progressively locate the natural principles of music in a believed correspondence between a natural predisposition of human perception and cognition and the nature of sound. See Duchez (1986), David Cohen (2001).

67. Keiler (1981: 84).

68. Keiler (1981: 92).

69. Keiler (1981: 100).

70. Keiler (1981: 84).

71. See Kuhn (1970). Another feasible explanation might consider such knowledge as a form of "tacit knowledge," after Michael Polanyi's formulation (1958).

72. Here I am thinking of figured-bass notation in terms of the figures them-

selves, putting aside the fact that there is room for variation within any realization and for adding figuration not given explicitly in the figures.

73. For discussion of Rameau's distinction between various kinds of knowledge, see also David Cohen (2001).

74. See Hyer (1994: 16-29, 37-38). Derrida develops the notion of *supplement* from Rousseau, who argues that writing is a parasitic supplement to natural spoken language. Derrida claims that if speech needs this supplement, then speech cannot be naturally self-sufficient and is therefore marked by an absence or lack. All representation, he proposes, requires a supplementary element, and can never feed merely upon that which is represented. "Writing," remarks Derrida, "is dangerous from the moment that representation there claims to be presence and the sign of the thing itself . . . the sign is always the supplement of the thing itself" (Derrida 1976: 144).

75. Hyer (1994: 29).

76. Hyer (1994: 30, 38).

77. Foucault ([1966] 1971: 72).

78. "Rameau . . . placed music in the realm of sound," writes Daniel Chua, explaining the shift away from a conception of music alongside "the domains of fable, medicine, astrology." According to him, "music by the middle of the eighteenth century became only that which was heard," and "from now on music was to be audible." Chua's point is that Rameau, like Descartes, consciously sets out to explain "sound" (Chua 1999: 77-78). By emphasizing implied dissonances I highlight the intervention of the inaudible in Rameau's enterprise.

79. Bacon (1623: 405-406). Bacon's quotation at the end of the passage is to Ovid, *Methamorphoses*, ii, 14.

80. I am not suggesting that during the seventeenth century there exists a uniform response to the question of the imagination. G. W. von Leibniz, for example, distinguishes the intelligible, "the *object of understanding alone*," from the sensible and the imaginable. Perpetuating the duality of classical conceptions of the imagination, he maintains that the "*imagination contains the notions of the internal senses*, which are *clear but confused*, and the *notions of the common sense*, which are *clear and distinct*"; see "Letter to Queen Sophie Charlotte of Prussia, On What is Independent of Sense and Matter, 1702" (Leibniz 1989: 187).

81. The passage's rhetorical force resides of course in the fact that Bacon effectively causes the reader to oscillate between the process of imagining the imagination performing its judicial duties and the realization that without the imagination itself that process would not be possible; the reader mandates, so to speak, the imagination into action to form a reasoned account of what Bacon is saying.

82. See Iser (1993: 180-81).

83. See Foucault ([1966] 1971: 69-70), Iser (1993: 181).

84. Iser (1993: 182).

85. See Descartes (1985: 79–98/AT, XI, 3–48). See also my discussion in Ch. 2, Sec. 2.1.

86. Relevant literature on *Le monde* and on Descartes's use of fable includes Dalia Judovitz (1988: 87–97), Timothy J. Reiss (1976: 19–27).

87. Descartes (1985: 90).

88. To recall our earlier discussion of Aristotle, the internal senses include memory and the imagination, while the common sensibles include combinations of external senses of sight, hearing, etc.

89. David Hume takes up this idea in *A Treatise on Human Nature* (1739–40) (Hume 1826: Part II, Chs. 2–3, 54–57). In explaining how we have an idea of space, even in the absence of direct impressions of it, he suggests that by means of the senses of sight and touch, impressions may be arranged as points in a line. The imagination then transforms these impressions into a "compound impression, which represents extension," that is to say, the abstract idea of space (the same applies, *mutatis mutandis*, to our idea of time). Going beyond what the senses or reason alone can accomplish, the imagination complements and, in a sense, supplants them.

90. This epistemological position does not, however, demote the centrality of God; on the contrary, it is believed that God's creation is reflected in the perfection of the imagined world. For an insightful critique of the relation between "man" and the idea of the infinite, see Foucault ([1966] 1971: 316).

91. In *Rules* Descartes had made explicit the role of fable as a device for giving life, as it were, to the facts of his method. As Harriet Stone (1996: 173–74) points out, "the imaginary, or poetic, dimension is thus consciously intended by Descartes to convey the truth of his science, to translate it to the reader."

92. These writers are discussed in Chs. 1 and 2.

93. The tension between music theory's claim to capture immanent elements of music and unavoidable historicity of theoretical inquiry is given attention in Dahlhaus (1984), Christensen (1993b).

94. The term was introduced by Paul Feyerabend (1993: 20): "[W]e may use hypotheses that contradict well-confirmed theories and/or well-established experimental results [or facts]. We may advance science by proceeding counterinductively." As he argues, if the empiricist dream is to have absolute agreement between facts and theories, and the inductive scientist's to produce hypotheses that are in agreement with facts, the counterinductivist must introduce disagreements between facts, hypotheses, and theories. My own usage refers to a kind of reversal of induction, but not to deduction per se. In this case it may be more accurate to refer to Feyerabend's sense as "contra-induction." I do adopt his position that the introduction of contradictory hypotheses permits a theory to "progress," in the sense of moving away from previously established knowledge, particularly knowledge that, like musical practice, is "used": "How can we possibly examine something we are using all the time? How can we analyze the terms in which we habitually express our most simple and straightforward observations, and reveal their presuppositions? . . . [W]e need a set of alternative assumptions or . . . an entire alternative world[,] . . . we must invent a new conceptual system that suspends, or

clashes with, the most carefully established observational results, confounds the most plausible theoretical principles, and introduces perceptions that cannot form part of the existing perceptual world" (Feyerabend 1993: 22–23).

95.   See Lester (1992: 136).

96.   Gossett, 410/*Traité*, 397. See n. 22 above for French original.

97.   See Plato (1992: *Republic* VII, 523b). A provocative in Plato is already an image, in contrast to the intuitive experience of a sequential passage in Rameau, which is unmediated perception. See also Mitchell (1986: 93).

98.   Chua (1999: 79).

99.   Chua (1999: 78–79). Note that in its basic progression from foundation to practice, my outline at the beginning of Section 3.1 parallels Chua's Foucaldian account here; however, the introduction of counterinduction makes that outline less linear.

100. Rameau, like Descartes before him, is blind to the effect discourse has on the constitution, let alone construction, of knowledge, and not just on its presentation.

101. My interpretation differs from Duchez's idea that Rameau considered "music theory as an experimental science of his time in the sense that it tried to describe, understand, to create a portion of human experience—the musical experience of his time—by means of prevision." Furthermore, Duchez notes, Rameau's theory has the peculiar advantage of knowing its results in advance: the music he knew (Duchez 1986: 92). Closer perhaps to the idea of counterinduction is the following remark by père Castel: "il [Rameau] va de la pratique à la regle, de la regle au raisonnement, du raisonnement au principe," in *Journal de Trevoux* (October and November 1722); cited in Duchez (1986: 92, n6).

102. Descartes, *Rules*, Rule 12, 44/AT, X, 418. Duchez articulates a different relationship between objective and subjective values in Rameau. In her reading, subjective values are psycho-physiological and are based, as Rameau himself insists, on the ear (*l'oreille*): the ear selectively occupies itself with the fundamental bass, the ear supplies what is missing and inexact [in music], the auditive sense that realizes the "rights" held by harmony. The primordial character of the fundamental bass is that it is not really heard but, rather, inferred or implicit in a given musical context. ("[L]e caractère primordial de la basse fondamentale est le fait qu'elle n'est pas réellement entendue mais elle est implicite dans un contexte musical, ou qu'elle peut en être inférée; non entendue, mais sous-entendue par l'oreille") (Duchez 1986: 123). However, Duchez does not delve into questions of *le réel* or into the difference in status between fundamental bass and implied dissonances. See also David Cohen (2001) for discussion of "the ear" in Rameau.

103. Rosset (1989: 83).

104. Harari (1987: 54).

105. See Condillac ([1749] 1982: 1–153).

106. This gloss of Condillac's taxonomy of systems summarizes Christensen's

account (Christensen 1993a: 36–37). The remainder in the discussion of Condillac is mine.

107. Condillac ([1746] 2001: Part I, Ch. 2, Sec. 75).

108. Condillac ([1749] 1982: 146, 259).

109. I owe these examples, and much of their analysis, to Harari (1987: 45–66).

110. See Rousseau ([1762] 1961), Montesquieu ([1721] 1964, [1748] 1989).

111. Rousseau's concerns in *Émile* include, among others, faith, family, morality, and, perhaps most importantly, the place of the subject in society.

112. Rousseau ([1762] 1961: 2, 1–2).

113. There are past pedagogical practices that Rousseau implicitly argues against. But in contrast to the theories of Rameau, for instance, in which there is a deliberate attempt to codify existing practice, Rousseau chooses for the most part to ignore available practices.

114. Voltaire, "Idées républicaines par un membre d'un corps" (*Mélanges*); quoted in Harari (1987: 51).

115. Harari (1987: 54–55).

116. Montesquieu ([1748] 1989: Pref., 91); quoted in Harari (1987: 52–53).

117. This does not mean "innovation" as a mark of ingenuity or "progress." The various appeals to the imagination and the imaginary by writers of disparate fields would lend credibility to a more strictly archaeological study of French thought during the mid-eighteenth century. Such inquiry, however, extends beyond the aims of the present chapter.

118. I take the expression "metaphysically most secure" from Hayden White's gloss on Foucault: "The important point for Foucault is that the eighteenth century was strongest where it was *metaphysically* most secure, not where it was *empirically* full" (White 1978: 242). My reference to Hume, Newton, and Voltaire is intended to counter the impression that Foucault's sweeping generalization holds for the *âge classique* as a whole.

119. Hyer (1996a: 81).

120. The Greek *idiôtês* stands here for a singularity without replica, an irrepresentable entity. See also Rosset (1977).

121. A strong case could be made for pursuing the relation between theory and the concept of the natural in Rameau as a transference, explicit in Descartes, of God's creative powers to man. Stone (1996: 181–89) discusses Descartes in this connection.

122. Mitchell (1990: 21).

4. Gottfried Weber and Mozart's K. 465

1. The analysis appeared in the third edition of the *Versuch*—Weber (1832). Weber first published a version of the analysis in two installments in his journal *Caecilia: eine Zeitschrift für die musikalische Welt*, 14/53 (1831): 1–49; 14/54 (1832): 122–29. Citations throughout will be to Weber ([1832] 1994),

followed by page numbers corresponding to the *Versuch*. Translations are Bent's unless otherwise noted. Bent's translation interpolates portions of the *Caecilia* version, as well as references to the Mozart passage that appear elsewhere in the *Versuch*. Register designations have been changed to ASA standards (middle C = C_4).

2. Weber uses Gothic letters to designate chordal roots, Roman letters to label keys, Roman numerals to indicate chords built upon scale degrees, uppercase letters to denote major keys and chords, and lowercase letters to denote minor keys and chords.

3. Ricoeur, says John B. Thompson, distinguishes a brand of hermeneutics the task of which is to demystify a "meaning presented to the interpreter in the form of a disguise." This type of interpretation is "animated by suspicion, by scepticism towards the given, and it is characterized by a distrust of the symbol as a dissimulation of the real" (Ricoeur 1981: 6). By "hermeneutics of suspicion," Ricoeur (1970: 32) describes an interpretive activity that looks upon the contents of consciousness as being in some sense false. I adopt the term not to indicate a falsity in the contents of consciousness in Weber's analysis or an illusory ideology behind his analytic practice, but to frame what I see as an overwhelming doubt informing his account of listening to Mozart's introduction.

4. In this respect, there are no isochronous analyses, as there are no isochronous narratives. Gérard Genette, who calls isochronous narrative a "hypothetical reference zero," remarks that such equality between the duration of an event and the duration of its representation "would thus be a narrative with unchanging speed, without accelerations or slowdowns, where the relationship duration-of-story/length-of-narrative would remain always steady" ([1972] 1980: 88). Genette's observation is, however, grounded in a structuralist separation of story (signified) and discourse (signifier) that my reading of Weber's analysis will avoid. I see the narrative and the experience as being inseparable, for reasons that will become clear as I proceed. I ought to note that I do not intend here to pursue a narratological analysis of Weber's account.

5. Smith (1981: 220).

6. Several commentators have discussed this analysis from a number of perspectives. Bent (Weber [1832] 1994: 158) divides the analysis into "experiential" and "intentional" sections. Hyer (1996b: 92–94), discusses the issue of time perception (which I view from a different angle). Saslaw (1992: 275) comments on the analysis as part of a comprehensive examination of Weber's theory of harmony. I do not intend to advance this particular analysis and its particular interpretive procedure as representing all of Weber's analytical and theoretical work. I do, however, propose the analysis to reflect limitations and possibilities of music theory in general. These limitations and possibilities will be seen, archaeologically, to partake of concerns about the nature and representation of subjectivity in circulation during the decades prior to the publication of his work.

7. Throughout this chapter the term "Romantics" refers to the early Romantics— who, incidentally, did not give themselves this name.

8. Marvin (1987: 72–76) discusses Weber's theory as an anticipation of early-twentieth-century *Musikpsychologie*. She briefly mentions the analysis of K. 465. Saslaw (1991) presents an analysis of "hearing" in Weber's theory of harmonic progression and harmonic relations, relating it to contemporary work on cognition by Lerdahl, Krumhansl, and Kessler (pitch space), and Dowling and Harwood (cognitive schemata). Besseler (1959), in a wide-ranging study of the history of hearing, makes no mention of Weber.

9. Descartes ([1618] 1986: 89).

10. See Van Wymeersch (1999) and Chua (1999: 78); see also Descartes (1985: 19). For historical background on mathesis universalis, see Crapulli (1969); Foucault ([1966] 1971: 56, 71–76) discusses Descartes's conceptual deployment of mathesis universalis; Judovitz (1988) presents a critique of the representational role given to the notion by Descartes. See also Christensen (1993a).

11. A literal translation of the German "das Gehör" is "hearing." For the present summary of the analysis, I maintain Bent's translation as "the ear." However, in the discussion following Section 4.1, I offer a critical interpretation of Weber's term.

12. Weber provides a score of the entire introduction (the score appears at the beginning of the analysis and Example 4.1). Example 4.3 reproduces his first *analytical* illustration in which elements of more than one or two measures are shown.

13. Weber overlooks here the change of A♭ to A♮.

14. Weber is applying here the notion that when attuning itself to a key, the ear would be inclined to understand the opening chord or pitch of a piece as a tonic. This basic principle ("simplicity"—*Einfachheit*) constitutes one of his two primary mechanisms for the understanding of harmonic progressions in the context of a key. The other principle is termed "the musical law of inertia" (*das musikalische Gesetz der Trägheit*): once attuned to a key, the ear will consider any other diatonic chord existing within that key as belonging to that key, and in the case of a digression the ear will consider that chord as belonging to the closest related key. See Gottfried Weber (1832: II, 110). Saslaw (1992: 197–203) provides detailed commentary.

15. The interpretation favoring G minor is in accordance with the principles of simplicity and inertia, for this key lies closest to C minor in Weber's chart of key relations.

16. Weber's strong response to the introduction of B♭ has to do with the fact that he considers the harmonic scale to be normative, in which case this pitch class cannot be easily assimilated within the context of C minor.

17. This passage comes from the foreword to the first edition (1817). It is reproduced in the third edition (1832: x–xi). Cited in Saslaw (1992: 24).

18. We ought to keep in mind that the analysis of Mozart was added to the 1832 edition. This may explain the methodological discontinuity between the foreword to the first edition and this, his final analysis in the third edition, save for the fact that in it Weber preserves his earlier forewords with slight alterations. In other words, he could have tailored his statements to correspond bet-

ter to the analysis. But as we have seen, in his preamble to the analysis proper Weber chooses instead to echo his antisystematic philosophy.

19. Strictly speaking, the conceptualization of chord types using the major and minor scales is not original in Weber, having been articulated by Vogler, and is present in greatly attenuated form in Kirnberger and Koch. The popularization of the model and its rapid dissemination, however, stem from Weber's work.

20. "Mehrdeutigkeit nennen wir nämlich die Möglichkeit, Eine Sache auf mehr als Eine Art zu erklären, oder die Beschaffenheit einer Sache, wonach sie bald für Dieses, bald für Jenes gelten kann" (translated in Saslaw 1992: 94). This definition appears within the context of explaining note names at the keyboard (i.e., enharmonic notes), but will inform other versions of multiple meaning. Georg Vogler, who anticipated Weber in the use of Roman numerals, had defined *Mehrdeutigkeit* only in relation to chords: "In the language of music just as in rhetoric, cases present themselves in which one can attribute several meanings to one idea. The doctrine of Multiple Meaning determines once and for all, all possible cases in which either the same harmonies strike the ear as different, or the same harmonies strike it as the same" (*Handbuch zur Harmonielehre und für den Generalbass, nach Grundsätzen der Mannheimer Tonschule zum Behuf der öffenlichen Vorlesungen im Orchestrions-Saale auf der K. K. Karl-Ferdinandeischen Universität zu Prag* [Prague: Barth, 1806], 6); cited in Saslaw (1992: 72).

21. [U]nd so ist jede Harmonie, und in soweit mehrdeutig, dass man ihr bald diese, bald jene römische Ziffer unterlegen, sie folglich als, mehr denn Einer Tonart angehörig, betrachten kann (translated in Saslaw 1992: 158).

22. Contrary to what their name may suggest, empiricities are not to be understood principally as things given in experience. For example, Foucault (1973: 218–19) considers "wealth" as the empiricity addressed by economics of the classical episteme, one superseded in the nineteenth century by another, rather distinct empiricity, "production." A putative stable "empirical" entity (let us call it "goods") would not be relevant to an archaeological analysis: the corresponding positivities organizing and indeed dictating our knowledge of these empiricities formalize this "entity" to consciousness in radically incompatible ways in accordance to particular postulates (i.e., conceptions of order, systems of signs, and sanctioned modalities of representation): whereas the classical age might have valued goods according to what could be exchanged or paid for them, labor is, beginning in the nineteenth century, the measure and source of their value. See Foucault (1973: 253–63). A more elaborate articulation of positivity appears in Foucault ([1969] 1972: 31–41, 125–31). There Foucault outlines the extent to which discursive formations produce for the nexus of empiricities and positivities: objects of study, subject positions, concepts to articulate objects and subjects, and interpretive and explanatory strategies that account for them.

23. The scale provides a useful example of the difference between empirical entity and empiricity (which I illustrated, after Foucault, with the entity "goods"). Doubtlessly available as an empirical entity much before *Stufen-*

theorie ever entered consciousness (e.g., in figured bass), the scale exists in Weber as an empiricity insofar as it constitutes a matrix for all relations among chords, a material form in accordance with which chords are distributed in their elementary singularity and equivalence.

24.   Foucault (1973: 144).

25.   Taylor (1989: 34).

26.   Kant ([1787] 1965: 272 [A255/B 311]) notes that "the concept of a noumenon is merely a *limiting concept*" (emphasis in original).

27.   The concept of *Darstellung* is of fundamental importance to Romantic aesthetics, criticism, and poetics. Studies pursuing that connection include Benjamin ([1919] 1980, [1924–1925] 1985), Frank (1989a), Helfer (1996), Lacoue-Labarthe and Nancy (1988), and Seyhan (1992). To be sure, Weber's principle of simplicity and the law of inertia, along with what he calls "habits of the ear" ("New Beginning," "Position of the Harmony," "Customary Progression," "Half-reattunement," and "Return of Passages Already Heard") and his network of key relations, are essentially temporal aspects of his theory. My point is that all these are sanctioned by a particular notion of temporal representation, and that this notion is historically contingent upon ideas of representation in circulation during the decades prior to the publication of the *Versuch*.

28.   In its reflexive form, *sich vorstellen* signifies the activity of (re)presenting something to oneself.

29.   See Lacoue-Labarthe and Nancy (1988: 30).

30.   Zeit ist das unbestimmte Endliche . . . Zeit geht auf die Vorstellungen (Novalis 1957b, 433, no. 2943).

31.   Hyer (1996b: 94).

32.   There are instances in the analysis where this is not the case, as for example in m. 3, where Weber writes that "thanks to the emergence of this G major triad, the ambiguity that has prevailed hitherto is now at last sufficiently eradicated for the ear to hear the chord as an established dominant chord . . . of C minor or major" (170/207). But, as I have already noted, even here the doubt about the mode reveals that the interpretive clarification is only partial.

33.   Kant defined synthesis as "the act of putting different representations together, and of grasping what is manifold in them in one [act of] knowledge" ([1787] 1965: 111 [A 77/B 103]); synthesis, furthermore, is "an act of the self-activity of the subject" ([1787] 1965: 152 [A 130/B 130]). Less exacting in their cognitive reach, representations are "inner determinations of our mind in this or that relation of time" ([1787] 1965: 224 [A 197/B242]).

34.   I wish to note that my expression "lived time" bears no relation to *Erlebnis* (lived experience) or to the phenomenological tradition of Husserl or, more particularly, Heidegger. The latter's categories of "within-time-ness" (*Innerzeitlichkeit*)—which expresses a kind of temporality of action—and "temporality" (*Zeitlichkeit*)—which refers to a kind of totality of past, present, and future—might provide tempting but ultimately inappropriate comparisons to the Romantic elaboration of time I discuss. See Husserl (1964) and Heidegger (1962). The classic application of phenomenological insights

to music analysis is Lewin (1986). Other work deploying phenomenological ideas appears in Clifton (1983), Lochhead (1980, 1995), and Ferrara (1991). Saslaw (1991: 128) notes that "[t]hroughout his discussion of harmonic progression, Weber speaks of the ear considering 'each harmony as it occurs,' making it clear that these mechanisms work only *within a framework of time*" (emphasis mine).

35. Selbstbewußtsein im größern Sinn ist eine Aufgabe—ein Ideal—es wäre der Zustand, worin es keine Zeitfortschreitung gäbe, ein zeitloser-beharrlicher, immer gleicher Zustand. (Ein Zustand ohne Vergangenheit und Zukunft und doch veränderlich.) (Novalis 1957a: 334, no. 1232). Translations from Novalis and Schlegel are mine unless otherwise noted.

36. Man versteht eine Sache am leichtesten, wenn man sie repräsentiert sieht (Novalis 1957a: 448, no. 1694).

37. This external Representation does not constitute a return to *Darstellung*, for *Darstellung* would have been an initial staging area for an experience, for instance, the tabular representation of chord relationships.

38. Foucault (1973: 217–19).

39. Other characteristic expressions of the Romantics' concern with linguistic mediation of time include the aphorism and commentary of the "second power"—in Friedrich von Schlegel's formulation—such as "reproductions of imitations, critiques of reviews, postscripts to addenda, [and] commentaries on notes" (1967: 181, no. 110). (Es ist ein erhabener Geschmack, immer die Dinge in der zweiten Potenz vorzuziehn. Z. B. Kopien von Nachahmungen, Beurteilungen von Rezensionen, Zusätse zu Ergänzungen, Kommentare zu Noten.) Incidentally, Foucault (1973: 221) singles out the years 1795–1800 as the turning point within the "Age of History," during which remnants of classical thought are finally jettisoned; he makes no mention of the *Frühromantik*, however, betraying his exclusive reliance on developments taking place in France.

40. Several authors have commented on the relation of irony to music, including Bonds (1991), Chua (1998), Hatten (1994), and Longyear (1970).

41. For instance, metaphor, metonymy, and synecdoche operate by the logic of substitution, cause and effect, and whole-to-part relation, respectively.

42. Ironie ist Analyse der These und Antithese (Schlegel 1981: 155, no. 809). Between 1800 and 1801 Schlegel replaced the term "irony" with the more explicitly subject-oriented word "conscience." On this shift, see Handwerk (1985: 18).

43. Auf Verwechselung des Symbols mit dem Symbolisierten—auf ihre Identisierung—auf den Glauben an wahrhafte, vollständige Repräsentation— und Relation des Bildes und des Originals—der Erscheinung und der Substanz—auf der Folgerung von äußerer Ähnlichkeit auf durchgängige innre Übereinstimmung und Zusammenhang—kurz auf Verwechselungen von Subjekt und Objekt beruht der ganze Aberglaube und Irrtum aller Zeiten und Völker und Individuen (Novalis 1957b: 93, no. 2084).

44. The term appears throughout Todorov (1982) to designate arbitrary signifier-signified relations.

45. See Gottfried Weber (1832: II, 44).

46. The esteem with which Roman numerals were held in Germany can be evinced by the fact that during the sixteenth century they were "defended as *de düdesche tall* (the German numbers), as against the Hindu [-Arabic] place-value notation" being adopted in Europe at the time; see Menninger (1969: 281).

47. Rameau's concept of *double emploi* is a good example of the difference between the semiotics of the early eighteenth century and those available to Weber. Rameau appeals to *double emploi* to account for the bivalency of a single chord; in such case, a chord *has* two functions. For Weber, in contrast, a chord *may have* one of several functions. Keiler (1981) offers a detailed examination of the question of Rameau's analytic metalanguage.

48. This notion of "empirical self" is to be differentiated from the self-evident (though no less epistemologically implicated) narrator who enunciates the analysis in the first place. In any event, that authorial voice is fettered by the dialectical character of the analytical narrative. Biddle (2001: 187–88) discusses what he calls "an excessive empirical self" from a different perspective.

49. De Man (1983: 213). De Man's indebtedness here is to Heidegger and, most specifically, to Hölderlin.

50. See Herder ([1770] 1965: 722). By "poetic background" I refer to the productive (i.e., as *poiesis*) aspect of Romantic subjectivity, not to the role of poetry per se in the matter. The Romantics' literary response to Kant is subject to extensive discussion in Lacoue-Labarthe and Nancy (1988).

51. This metaphor, famously voiced by Yeats ("that soul must become its own betrayer, its own delivered, the one activity, the mirror turn lamp"), is best known now through Abrams's (1973) classic on Romantic criticism, *The Mirror and the Lamp*.

52. I call the Romantics' response a "dialectical corrective" because in the end they too aspired to gain control over their lack of control, by recognizing it and by incorporating that recognition in their critical practice. Such dialectical turns can, of course, become endlessly meaningless, but not so for the Romantics, as my discussion has intimated. The complex history of the Romantic subject, which merits extended analysis, goes well beyond the scope of this chapter. At the risk of oversimplifying and hardening the contours of this figure, suffice it to note that besides Novalis and Schlegel many other influential characters stand out, including Hölderlin, Schelling, Schleiermacher, and, as a key thinker of German Idealism, Hegel. Novalis and Schlegel, however, articulate the fundamental tenets of the early Romantic subject. On this question, see Lacoue-Labarthe and Nancy (1988: 27–36). Bowie (1990) provides an elaborate account of developments of Romantic subjectivity, beginning with Kant's third *Critique*, which he sees as ushering in the move toward aesthetics by the Romantics (Lacoue-Labarthe and Nancy begin with the first *Critique*). Frank (1995) discusses the Romantics' Kantian reception, which was shaped by Friedrich Jacobi's elaborations of Kant.

53. Strictly speaking, Descartes's subject had been critiqued by Berkeley (in *Prin-*

ciples of Human Knowledge) and, most relevant for Kant, by Hume (in *A Treatise on Human Nature*).

54. Kant ([1787] 1965: 331–32 [A 346/B404]).

55. Kant ([1787] 1965: 153 [B133]). Powell (1990: 79) notes a distinction obscured by Kant's terminology of the "self": "the 'I' of such thoughts as 'I think that it is snowing' or 'I ache all over' is the 'I' of empirical apperception, and the 'I' of the 'I think'—as the logical form of consciousness—is that designated by the transcendental unity of apperception. . . . [T]he 'I think' need never occur as a thought itself, but only as a formal constraint on thoughts." In Kant's words, "this proposition ['I think'] is not itself an experience, but the form of apperception, which belongs to and precedes every experience"; Kant ([1787] 1965: 336–37 [A354]).

56. The expression is Fichte's (*Vocation of Man,* 1800), quoted in Bowie (1990: 63).

57. There exists a difference between the I (*Ich*) of the philosophers, with its transcendental nature, and what I have been calling the subject, an empirical being or self (*Selbst*). The connection between the I and the subject is crucial for the Romantics, but is articulated in terms of an aesthetic relation between an experiencing subject and the Absolute. A key distinction, however, is that the Romantics bring language into (conflicting) contact with Kant's epistemology, not as its practical arm, but in order to question correspondences between things, language, and art.

58. See Kant ([1787] 1965: 369 [B408]); Lacoue-Labarthe and Nancy (1988: 30).

59. Bowie (1990: 59).

60. Whereas for Kant the Absolute (*das Absolute*) referred to an unconditioned reality, for Fichte it refers to the total unity of subject and object under the action of the I, as will be explained shortly. For discussion of the notion of "Absolute," see Lacoue-Labarthe and Nancy (1988), Bowie (1997: 75–80), and Neuhoser (1990: 111). Fichte announces the "unconditionally and absolutely" self-positing I in "Concerning the Concept of the *Wissenschaftslehre*" [1st ed., 1794] in Fichte (1988: 125). For publication details, see Daniel Breazeale's "Editor's Preface" in Fichte (1988: 87–93).

61. These three points summarize an account of Fichte's theory of the subject given by Andrew Bowie (1990: 58–67).

62. Fichte (1988: xiv); Bowie (1990: 62), citing Fichte (*Werke,* ed. Immanuel Hermann Fichte [Berlin, 1971], II, 263); Neuhoser (1990: 113); emphasis mine.

63. Fichte (1988: 124–25) ("Concerning the Concept of the *Wissenschaftslehre*"); emphasis in original.

64. Fichte (1988: 205) ("Concerning the Difference between the Spirit and the Letter").

65. Fichte (1988: 134) ("*Wissenschaftslehre*"); emphasis in original.

66. Seyhan (1992: 35–48) traces the poetic turn from Fichte's subjectivity through Novalis and Schlegel with particular acuity. The locus classicus where the emergency of the "literary" out of Kantian (and a severely under-

played Fichtean) philosophy is elaborated is Lacoue-Labarthe and Nancy (1988). For an earlier and decisive study of the Romantics' relation to Fichte, see Benjamin ([1919] 1980). I ought to note that many important developments follow Fichte that weigh heavily in Romantic aesthetics and the philosophy of consciousness. Notable among them is Schelling's proposal for an *Identitätsphilosophie* that considers that in consciousness subject and object are identical. Bowie (1990: Ch. 4) offers a useful discussion of various aspects of Schelling's philosophy. The Romantics, however, are unique in their focused commitment to a language-centered response to Fichte.

67. Benjamin ([1919] 1980) remains the classic study of the Romantics' relation to Fichte.

68. Lacoue-Labarthe and Nancy cite Benjamin, who believes Fichte to postulate the primacy of the substantial self over thought, whereas the Romantics "hold the primacy of reflection, of the self-reflection of everything, over the self"; Lacoue-Labarthe and Nancy (1988: 135, n26). See also Benjamin ([1919] 1980: 24).

69. Ironie ist klares Bewußtsein der ewigen Agilität, des unendlich vollen Chaos (Schlegel 1967: 263, no. 69). In Romantic aesthetics, the trope of "endless reflection" is a complex one. Lacoue-Labarthe and Nancy: "It is the scheme of irony, if one recalls that irony, insofar as it addresses the poet himself, reveals to the poet that his truth—from the point of view of the infinite—is his own limitation, or in other words, his finitude" (1988: 78); also: "The finitude of the poet, however, is understood at once as the annihilation or dissolution of the subject in the absolute Subject *and* as the limiting condition of the form imposed on the author no less than on the work" (ibid., 140, n44, emphasis in original).

70. Sie [Ironie] ist die freieste aller Lizenzen, denn durch sie setzt man sich über sich selbst weg (Schlegel 1967: 160, no. 108). Incidentally, an ironic reading would compromise an interpretation of Weber's analysis in terms of Schleiermacher's hermeneutic circle. Schleiermacher's demands for absolute whole-to-part integration as a necessity for proper understanding and cognition cannot accommodate the partial closure that Weber's conclusion offers, although, as Manfred Frank (1989b: 445) notes, Schleiermacher accepts as a "consequence of the infinitude of interpretation that 'noncomprehension will never entirely be dissolved.'" Frank's citation is to Schleiermacher's speeches for the academy in Berlin, *Über den Begriff der Hermeneutik* (in *Hermeneutik und Kritik*, ed. Manfred Frank, 1977, 328).

71. One thinks of the notion of "close reading" so often invoked to describe analytic practice, and how a spatial metaphor of nearness is deployed to account for a particular kind of temporality that differs from the common-sense temporal modality associated with so-called "real-time" experience.

72. Friedrich Schlegel, *Transcendentalphilosophie*, 41; cited in Bowie (1997: 68). It should be clear from the following that the Romantics' relation to allegory is unlike Goethe's and the critical tradition that follows him. For Goethe, allegory stood beneath symbol as a less preferred form of imaginative expression. The symbol, in Goethe's well-known categorization, could see the gen-

eral in the particular, whereas allegory could only deploy the particular as an instance of the general. By this account, allegory advertised a separation between the abstract concept and the image it portrayed. In contrast, the symbol presented a total unity between concept and image. Following this line of thought, Hegel would consider allegory to empty out the subjectivity of the characters in the allegorical telling. These characters served as hollowed-out individuals in the service of a concept against which they remained dialectically discontinuous. For a critique of the symbol in relation to allegory, see Benjamin ([1924–25] 1985: 159–67).

73. By empirical subject I do not mean merely the subject that Weber makes explicit in Section 6 of the analysis, in which he refers to Mozart's intention.

74. Weber discusses the decaying effect of repetitions within a composition as well as repeated hearings in a section entitled "Return of Passages Already Heard" (1832: II, 149). His discussion of K. 465 suggests, however, that some passages (or pieces) are unaffected by this. Granted, few pieces in the literature may fall under this category. For a different interpretation of Weber's ideas about rehearing, see Hyer (1996b: 95–97).

75. Die romantische Poesie . . . kann durch keine Theorie erschöpft werden, und nur eine divinatorische Kritik dürfte es wagen, ihr Ideal charakterisieren zu wollen. Sie allein ist unendlich, wie sie allein frei ist, und das als ihr erstes Gesetz anerkennt, daß die Willkür des Dichters kein Gesetz über sich leide (Schlegel 1967: 183, no. 116).

76. A thorough discussion of the debates appears in Vertrees (1974). See also Weber (1994: 159–60). In Greek comedy the *eiron* was the underdog, weak but clever dissembler, who regularly triumphed over the boastful *alazon* by bringing conflicting and contrasting views into focus. In the *Nicomachean Ethics* Aristotle conceives of *eironeia* as "the contrary to boastful exaggeration; it is a self-deprecating concealment of one's own powers" ([1925] 1980: 1108a19–a23). While Weber does not exactly conceal his powers, his doubts and struggles present him as a vulnerable analyst.

77. Frye (1957: 34); emphasis in original.

78. See Hyer (1996b: 94): "Weber never draws on his experience of the present to imagine a possible future, but rather dwells obsessively on the past. His cursor movements leave the ear hanging on the edge of a phenomenological cliff without the slightest idea of what is to come, and it is this cognitive precipice that he identifies with the musical present."

79. This notion of language as the carrier of the burden of consciousness bears a connection with Heidegger's reading of Hölderlin in the chapter ". . . poetically man dwells . . ." in Heidegger (1971).

80. Smith (1981: 221).

81. Es ist gleich tödlich für den Geist, ein System zu haben, und keins zu haben. Er wird sich also wohl entschließen müssen, beides zu verbinden (Schlegel 1967: 173, no. 53).

82. Wenn der Charakter des gegebenen Problems Unauflöslichkeit ist, so lösen wir dasselbe, wenn wir seine Unauflöslichkeit darstellen. Wir wissen genug

von a., wenn wir einsehn, daß sein Prädikat a. ist (Novalis 1957a: 288, no. 1043).

83.   This view was suggested by Brian Hyer (personal communication).

Epilogue

1.   Merleau-Ponty (1964: 152).
2.   Whitehead ([1929] 1941: 88).
3.   Žižek (1999: 1).

Bibliography

Aaron, Pietro. [1523] 1970. *Toscanello in musica*. Trans. Peter Bergquist. Colorado Springs, Colo.: Colorado College Music Press.

Abrams, Meyer Howard. 1973. *The Mirror and the Lamp: Romantic Theory and the Critical Tradition*. Oxford: Oxford University Press.

Agrippa, Henry Cornelius. [1530] 1998. Excerpt from *Declamation of the Uncertainty and Vanity of the Sciences and Arts*. Ed. and trans. Gary Tomlinson. In *Source Readings in Music History*, rev. ed., ed. Oliver Strunk; Leo Treitler, general ed., 304–308. New York: W. W. Norton.

Aristotle. 1906. *De Sensu*. In *Greek Theories of Elementary Cognition from Alcmaeon to Aristotle*, trans. John I. Beare. Oxford: Clarendon Press. Public domain version available online at http://www.pastmasters2000.nlx.com

———. 1922. *Aristotle on Coming-to-Be and Passing-Away (On Generation and Corruption)*. Trans. H. H. Joachim. Oxford: Clarendon Press. Public domain version available online at http://www.pastmasters2000.nlx.com

———. 1924. *Metaphysics*. Rev. with intro. and commentary by W. D. Ross. Oxford: Clarendon Press.

———. 1963. *Categories*. Trans. with notes by J. L. Ackrill. Oxford: Clarendon Press.

———. 1968. *De Anima*. Books II and III, trans. with intro. and notes by D. W. Hamlyn. Oxford: Clarendon Press.

———. [1925] 1980. *The Nicomachean Ethics*. Trans. with introduction by W. D. Ross; rev. ed., ed. J. L. Ackrill and J. O. Urmson. Oxford: Oxford University Press.

———. 1986. *De Anima*. Trans. with intro. and notes by Hugh Lawson-Tancred. London: Penguin Books.

———. 1994a. *Posterior Analytics*. Trans. with commentary by Jonathan Barnes. Oxford: Clarendon Press.

———. 1994b. *Metaphysics*. Books Γ, Δ, and E, trans. with commentary by Christopher Kirwan. Oxford: Clarendon Press.

Arnold, Francis Thomas. 1931. *The Art of Accompaniment from a Thorough-Bass as Practised in the 17th and 18th Centuries*. London: Humphrey Milford.

Augst, Bertrand. 1965. Descartes's Compendium on Music. *Journal of the History of Ideas* 26 (1), 119–32.

Augustine. 1979. *Works. Selected Library of the Nicene and Post-Nicene Fathers of the Christian Church*. Vol. 1, ed. Philip Schaff, letters trans. J. G. Cunningham. Grand Rapids, Mich.: Eerdmans.

Bacon, Francis. 1620. *Preparative toward Natural and Experimental History: Description of a Natural and Experimental History Such as It May Serve for the Foundation of a True Philosophy*. Public domain version available at http://www.constitution.org/bacon/preparative.htm

———. 1623. *De Augmentis Scientiarum*. In *Works*, vol. IV. Link through the Bibliothèque Nationale de France web site, http://gallica.bnf.fr

———. 1948. *Selected Essays of Francis Bacon*. Trans. and ed. John Max Patrick. New York: Appleton-Century Books.

Barthes, Roland. 1991. *The Responsibility of Forms: Critical Essays on Music, Art, and Representation*. Trans. Richard Howard. Berkeley: University of California Press.

Benedetti, Giovanni Battista. 1585. *Diversarum Speculationum Mathematicarum et Physicarum Liber*. Turin: Haeredes N. Bevilaquae.

Benjamin, Walter. [1919] 1980. Der Begriff der Kunstkritik in der deutschen Romantik. In *Gesammelte Schriften Werkausgabe* 1, ed. Rolf Tiedemann and Hermann Schweppenhäuser, 7–122. Frankfurt am Main: Suhrkamp.

———. [1924–25] 1985. *The Origin of German Tragic Drama*. Trans. John Osborne. London: Verso.

Benveniste, Émile. 1971. *Problems of General Linguistics*. Trans. Mary E. Meek. Coral Gables, Fla.: University of Miami Press.

Besseler, Heinrich. 1959. *Das musikalische Hören der Neuzeit*. Berlin: Akademie Verlag.

Biddle, Ian. 2001. The Gendered Eye: Music Analysis and the Scientific Outlook in German Early Romantic Music Theory. In *Music Theory and Natural Order from the Renaissance to the Early Twentieth Century*, ed. Suzannah Clark and Alexander Rehding, 183–96. Cambridge: Cambridge University Press.

Blasius, Leslie David. 1996. *Schenker's Argument and the Claims of Music Theory*. Cambridge: Cambridge University Press.

———. 2002. Mapping the Terrain. In *The Cambridge History of Western Music Theory*, ed. Thomas Christensen, 27–45. Cambridge: Cambridge University Press.

Boethius. 1989. *Fundamentals of Music*. Trans. with intro. and notes by Calvin M. Bower. New Haven, Conn.: Yale University Press.

Bonds, Mark Evan. 1991. Haydn, Laurence Sterne, and the Origins of Musical Irony. *Journal of the American Musicological Society* 44 (1), 57–91.

Bower, Calvin M. 1978. Boethius and Nicomachus: An Essay concerning the Sources of the "De Institutione Musica." *Vivarium* 16, 1–45.

Bowie, Andrew. 1990. *Aesthetics and Subjectivity: From Kant to Nietzsche*. Manchester: Manchester University Press.

———. 1997. *From Romanticism to Critical Theory: The Philosophy of German Literary Theory*. London: Routledge.

Burnham, Scott. 1988. Aesthetics, Theory, and History in the Works of A. B. Marx. Ph.D. dissertation, Brandeis University.

———. 1992a. Method and Motivation in Hugo Riemann's History of Harmonic Theory. *Music Theory Spectrum* 14 (1), 1–14.

———. 1992b. The Criticism of Analysis and the Analysis of Criticism. *19th-Century Music* 15 (1), 70–76.

Buzon, Frédéric de. 1983. Sympathie et antipathie dans le "Compendium Musicae." *Archives de Philosophie* 46, 647–53.

Caccini, Giulio. [1602] 1970. *Le nuove musiche*. Trans. and ed. H. Wiley Hitchcock. Madison, Wis.: A-R Editions, 1970.

Cardano, Girolamo. [c. 1546] 1973. *Writings on Music*. Trans. and ed. with introduction by Clement A. Miller. Rome: American Institute of Musicology.

Carter, Tim. 1995. Resemblance and Representation: Towards a New Aesthetic in the Music of Monteverdi. In *"Con che soavità": Studies in Italian Opera, Song, and Dance*, ed. Iain Fenlon and Tim Carter, 119–34. Oxford: Oxford University Press.

Cassirer, Ernst. 1910. *Substanzbegriff und Funktionsbegriff: Untersuchungen über die Grundfragen der Erkenntniskritik.* Berlin: Bruno Cassirer.

———. [1910] 1923. *Substance and Function and Einstein's Theory of Relativity.* Trans. William Curtis Swabey and Marie Collins Swabey. Chicago: Open Court.

Christensen, Thomas. 1993a. *Rameau and Musical Thought in the Enlightenment.* Cambridge: Cambridge University Press.

———. 1993b. Music Theory and Its Histories. In *Music Theory and the Exploration of the Past,* ed. Christopher Hatch and David W. Bernstein, 9–39. Chicago: University of Chicago Press.

Chua, Daniel K. L. 1998. Haydn as Romantic: A Chemical Experiment with Instrumental Music. In *Haydn Studies,* ed. W. Dean Sutcliffe, 120–51. Cambridge: Cambridge University Press.

———. 1999. *Absolute Music and the Construction of Meaning.* Cambridge: Cambridge University Press.

Cicero. *De Divinatione,* Book II. Available online at http://www.thelatinlibrary.com

Clark, Suzannah, and Alexander Rehding. 2001. Introduction. In *Music Theory and Natural Order from the Renaissance to the Early Twentieth Century,* ed. Suzannah Clark and Alexander Rehding, 1–13. Cambridge: Cambridge University Press.

Clifton, Thomas. 1983. *Music as Heard: A Study in Applied Phenomenology.* New Haven, Conn.: Yale University Press.

Cohen, Albert. 1992. Rameau on Corelli: A Lesson in Harmony. In *Convention in Eighteenth- and Nineteenth-Century Music: Essays in Honor of Leonard G. Ratner,* ed. Wye J. Allanbrook, Janet M. Levy, and William P. Mahrt, 431–45. Stuyvesant, N.Y.: Pendragon Press.

Cohen, David E. 1993. Metaphysics, Ideology, Discipline: Consonance, Dissonance, and the Foundations of Western Polyphony. *Theoria* 7, 1–85.

———. 2001. The "Gift of Nature": Musical "Instinct" and Musical Cognition in Rameau. In *Music Theory and Natural Order,* ed. Suzannah Clark and Alexander Rehding, 68–92. Cambridge: Cambridge University Press.

Cohen, H. Floris. 1984. *Quantifying Music: The Science of Music at the First Stage of the Scientific Revolution, 1580–1650.* Dordrecht: D. Reidel.

Condillac, Etienne Bonnot de. [1749] 1982. *Traité des systèmes.* In *Philosophical Writings of Etienne Bonnot, Abbé de Condillac,* trans. Franklin Philip, with the collaboration of Harlan Lane. Hillsdale, N.J.: Lawrence Erlbaum.

———. [1746] 2001. *Essay on the Origin of Human Knowledge.* Ed. and trans. Hans Aarsleff. Cambridge: Cambridge University Press.

Crapulli, Giovanni. 1969. *Mathesis universalis: Genesi di un'idea nel xvi secolo.* Rome: Edizioni dell'Ateneo.

Crombie, Alistair. 1986. Experimental Science and the Rational Artist in Early Modern Europe. *Daedalus* 115, 49–74.

Dahlhaus, Carl. 1984. *Die Musiktheorie im 18. und 19. Jahrhundert, Erster Teil: Grundzüge einer Systematik.* In *Geschichte der Musiktheorie,* Band 10. Darmstadt: Wissenschaftliche Buchgesellschaft.

———. 1989. *Die Musiktheorie im 18. und 19. Jahrhundert, Zweiter Teil: Deutschland.* In *Geschichte der Musiktheorie,* Band 11. Darmstadt: Wissenschaftliche Buchgesellschaft.

———. 1990. *Studies on the Origins of Harmonic Tonality.* Trans. Robert O. Gjerdingen. Princeton, N.J.: Princeton University Press.

DeBellis, Mark. 1995. *Music and Conceptualization.* Cambridge: Cambridge University Press.

De Man, Paul. 1983. The Rhetoric of Temporality. In *Blindness and Insight: Essays in the Rhetoric of Contemporary Criticism,* rev. with introduction by Wlad Godzich, 187–228. Minneapolis: University of Minnesota Press.

Derrida, Jacques. 1976. *Of Grammatology.* Trans. Gayatri Chakravorty Spivak. Baltimore: Johns Hopkins University Press.

———. 1978. Form and Signification. In *Writing and Difference,* trans. Alan Bass, 1–30. Chicago: University of Chicago Press.

Descartes, René. [1618] 1961. *Compendium of Music.* Trans. Walter Robert. Rome: American Institute of Musicology.

———. [1641] 1984. *Meditations on First Philosophy.* In *The Philosophical Writings of Descartes,* vol. II, trans. John Cottingham, Robert Stoothoff, and Dugald Murdoch, 3–62. Cambridge: Cambridge University Press.

———. 1985. *The Philosophical Writings of Descartes.* Vol. I, trans. John Cottingham, Robert Stoothoff, and Dugald Murdoch. Cambridge: Cambridge University Press.

———. [1618] 1986. *Compendium musicae.* In *Oeuvres de Descartes,* vol. X, ed. Charles Adam and Paul Tannery, 89–141. Paris: J. Vrin.

———. 1986. *Regulae ad directionem ingenii.* In *Oeuvres de Descartes,* vol. X, ed. Charles Adam and Paul Tannery, 359–488. Paris: J. Vrin.

———. [1618] 1987. *Abrégé de musique.* Trans. with introduction and notes by Frédéric de Buzon. Paris: Presses Universitaires de France.

———. 1991. *The Philosophical Writings of Descartes.* Vol. III, trans. John Cottingham, Robert Stoothoff, Dugald Murdoch, and Anthony Kenny. Cambridge: Cambridge University Press.

Dewey, John. [1929] 1960. *The Quest for Certainty: A Study of the Relation of Knowledge and Action.* New York: Putnam.

Drake, Stillman. 1970. Renaissance Music and Experimental Science. *Journal of the History of Ideas* 31 (4), 483–500.

Duchez, Marie-Elisabeth. 1986. Valeur épistémologique de la théorie de la basse fondamentale de Jean-Philippe Rameau: Connaissance scientifique et représentation de la musique. *Studies on Voltaire and the Eighteenth Century* 245, 91–130.

Eco, Umberto. 1990. *The Limits of Interpretation.* Bloomington: Indiana University Press.

Einstein, Alfred. 1949. *The Italian Madrigal.* 3 vols. Trans. Alexander H. Knappe, Roger H. Sessions, and Oliver Strunk. Princeton, N.J.: Princeton University Press.

Feldman, Martha. 1995. *City Culture and the Madrigal at Venice.* Berkeley: University of California Press.

Fend, Michael. 1991. The Changing Functions of "Senso" and "Ragione" in Italian Music Theory of the Late Sixteenth Century. In *The Second Sense: Studies in Hearing and Musical Judgement from Antiquity to the Seventeenth Century,* ed. Penelope Gouk, Charles Burnett, and Michael Fend, 199–221. London: Warburg Institute.

Ferrara, Lawrence. 1991. *Philosophy and the Analysis of Music: Bridges to Musical Sound, Form, and Reference.* Westport, Conn.: Greenwood.

Fétis, François F. [1836] 1972. *Biographie universelle des musiciens.* Ed. Arthur Pougin. Brussels: Culture et Civilisation.

Feyerabend, Paul. 1993. *Against Method.* London: Verso.

Fichte, Johann Gottlieb. [1792–99] 1988. *Early Philosophical Writings.* Trans. and ed. Daniel Breazeale. Ithaca, N.Y.: Cornell University Press.

Fischer, Wilhelm. 1915. Zur Entwicklungsgeschichte des Wiener klassischen Stils. *Studien zur Musikwissenschaft* 3, 24–84.

Foucault, Michel. [1966] 1971. *The Order of Things: An Archaeology of the Human Sciences—A Translation of Les Mots et les Choses*. New York: Pantheon.

———. [1969] 1972. *The Archaeology of Knowledge*. Trans. A. M. Sheridan Smith. New York: Pantheon.

———. 1984. What Is an Author? In *The Foucault Reader*, ed. Paul Rabinow, 101–20. New York: Pantheon.

Frank, Manfred. 1989a. *Einführung in die frühromantische Ästhetik: Vorlesungen*. Frankfurt am Main: Suhrkamp.

———. 1989b. *What Is Neostructuralism?* Trans. Sabine Wilke and Richard Gray, with a foreword by Martin Schwab. Minneapolis: University of Minnesota Press.

———. 1995. Philosophical Foundations of Early Romanticism. In *The Modern Subject: Conceptions of the Self in Classical German Philosophy*, ed. Karl Ameriks and Dieter Sturma, 65–85. Albany: State University of New York Press.

Frye, Northrop. 1957. *Anatomy of Criticism: Four Essays*. Princeton, N.J.: Princeton University Press.

Galilei, Vincenzo. [1589] 1934. *Discorso intorno all'opere di messer Gioseffo Zarlino da Chioggia*. Florence: Giorgio Marescotti. Facsimile, Milan: Bollettino Bibliografico Musicale.

———. [1581] 1967. *Dialogo della musica antica et della moderna*. Florence: Giorgio Marescotti. Facsimile, *Monuments of Music and Music Literature*, 2nd ser., vol. 20. New York: Broude Brothers.

———. 1989a. *A Special Discourse concerning the Diversity of the Ratios of the Diapason*. In *The Florentine Camerata: Documentary Studies and Translations*, ed. and trans. Claude V. Palisca, 180–97. New Haven, Conn.: Yale University Press.

———. 1989b. *A Special Discourse concerning the Unison*. In *The Florentine Camerata: Documentary Studies and Translations*, ed. and trans. Claude V. Palisca, 198–207. New Haven, Conn.: Yale University Press.

Gaukroger, Stephen. 1995. *Descartes: An Intellectual Biography*. Oxford: Clarendon Press.

———. 1997. Descartes's Early Doctrine of Clear and Distinct Ideas. In *The Genealogy of Knowledge: Analytic Essays in the History of Philosophy and Science*, 131–52. Aldershot: Ashgate.

Gebauer, Gunter, and Christoph Wulf. [1992] 1995. *Mimesis: Culture—Art—Society*. Trans. Don Reneau. Berkeley: University of California Press.

Genette, Gérard. [1972] 1980. *Narrative Discourse: An Essay on Method*. Trans. Jane E. Levin, with a foreword by Jonathan Culler. Ithaca, N.Y.: Cornell University Press.

Gjerdingen, Robert. 2002. The Psychology of Music. In *The Cambridge History of Western Music Theory*, ed. Thomas Christensen, 956–81. Cambridge: Cambridge University Press.

Godøy, Rolf Inge, and Harald Jørgensen, eds. 2001. *Musical Imagery*. Lisse, The Netherlands: Swets & Zeitlinger.

Greenblatt, Stephen. 1980. *Renaissance Self-fashioning: From More to Shakespeare*. Chicago: University of Chicago Press.

Gutting, Gary. 1989. *Michel Foucault's Archaeology of Scientific Reason*. Cambridge: Cambridge University Press.

Haar, James. 1971. Zarlino's Definition of Fugue and Imitation. *Journal of the American Musicological Society* 24 (2), 226–54.

Handwerk, Gary J. 1985. *Irony and Ethics in Narrative: From Schlegel to Lacan.* New Haven, Conn.: Yale University Press.

Harari, Josué. 1987. *Scenarios of the Imaginary: Theorizing the French Enlightenment.* Ithaca, N.Y.: Cornell University Press.

Hatten, Robert S. 1994. *Musical Meaning in Beethoven: Markedness, Correlation, and Interpretation.* Bloomington: Indiana University Press.

Heidegger, Martin. 1962. *Being and Time.* Trans. John Macquarrie and Edward Robinson. New York: Harper and Row.

———. 1971. *Poetry, Language, Thought.* Trans. and introduction by Albert Hofstadter. New York: HarperCollins.

Helfer, Martha B. 1996. *The Retreat of Representation: The Concept of* Darstellung *in German Critical Discourse.* Albany: State University of New York Press.

Herder, Johann Gottfried. [1770] 1965. *Über den Ursprung der Sprache.* Stuttgart: Verlag Freies Geistesleben.

Hobbes, Thomas. [1651] 1996. *Leviathan.* Ed. Richard Tuck. Cambridge: Cambridge University Press.

Howell, Peter, Robert West, and Ian Cross, eds. 1991. *Representing Musical Structure.* London: Academic.

Hume, David. 1826. *The Philosophical Works of David Hume.* Vol. I. Edinburgh: Adam Black and William Tait.

Huppert, George. 1974. "Divinatio et Eruditio": Thoughts on Foucault. *History and Theory* 13 (3), 191–207.

Husserl, Edmund. 1964. *The Phenomenology of Internal Time-Consciousness.* Ed. Martin Heidegger, trans. James S. Churchill, introduction by Calvin O. Schrag. Bloomington: Indiana University Press.

———. 1970. *The Crisis of the European Sciences and Transcendental Phenomenology.* Ed. and trans. David Carr. Evanston: Northwestern University Press.

Hyer, Brian. 1994. "Sighing Branches": Prosopopoeia in Rameau's "Pigmalion." *Music Analysis* 13 (1), 7–50.

———. 1995. Reimag(in)ing Riemann. *Journal of Music Theory* 39 (1), 101–38.

———. 1996a. Before Rameau and after. *Music Analysis* 15 (1), 75–100.

———. 1996b. Second Immediacies in the *Eroica.* In *Music Theory in the Age of Romanticism,* ed. Ian Bent, 77–104. Cambridge: Cambridge University Press.

Inwood, Michael. 1992. *A Hegel Dictionary.* Oxford: Blackwell.

Iser, Wolfgang. 1993. *The Fictive and the Imaginary: Charting Literary Anthropology.* Baltimore: Johns Hopkins University Press.

Jardine, Lisa. 1985. Experientia literata ou Novum Organum? Le dilemme de la méthode scientifique de Bacon. In *Francis Bacon: Science et méthode. Actes du Colloque de Nantes,* ed. Michel Malherbe and Jean-Marie Pousseur, 135–57. Paris: J. Vrin.

Jones, Matthew L. 2001. Descartes's Geometry as Spiritual Exercise. *Critical Inquiry* 28 (3), 40–71.

Judd, Cristle Collins. 2000. *Reading Renaissance Music Theory: Hearing with the Eyes.* Cambridge: Cambridge University Press.

Judovitz, Dalia. 1988. *Subjectivity and Representation in Descartes: The Origins of Modernity.* Cambridge: Cambridge University Press.

Kant, Immanuel. [1787] 1965. *Critique of Pure Reason.* Trans. Norman Kemp Smith. Boston: Bedford/St. Martin's Press.

Keiler, Allan R. 1981. Music as Metalanguage: Rameau's Fundamental Bass. In *Music*

Theory: Special Topics, ed. Richmond Browne, 83–100. New York: Academic Press.

Klumpenhouwer, Henry. 1992. The Cartesian Choir. *Music Theory Spectrum* 14 (1), 15–37.

Korsyn, Kevin. 1988. Schenker and Kantian Epistemology. *Theoria* 3, 1–58.

Kramer, Lawrence. 1995. *Classical Music and Postmodern Knowledge.* Berkeley: University of California Press.

———. 2001. The Mysteries of Animation: History, Analysis, and Musical Subjectivity. *Music Analysis* 20 (2), 153–78.

Kristeva, Julia. [1973] 1998. The Subject in Process. In *The "Tel Quel" Reader,* trans. Patrick Ffrench, ed. Patrick Ffrench and Roland-François Lack. London: Routledge.

Kuhn, Thomas. 1970. *The Structure of Scientific Revolutions.* Chicago: University of Chicago Press.

Kurtzman, Jeffrey. 1993. A Taxonomic and Affective Analysis of Monteverdi's "Hor che'l ciel e la terra." *Music Analysis* 12 (2), 169–95.

Lacoue-Labarthe, Philippe, and Jean-Luc Nancy. 1988. *The Literary Absolute: The Theory of Literature in German Romanticism.* Trans. Philip Barnard and Cheryl Lester. Albany: State University of New York Press.

La Motte-Haber, Helga de, and Peter Nitsche. 1982. Subjektivistische Begründung von Kompositionslehre. In *Neues Handbuch der Musikwissenschaft,* Band 10: *Systematische Musikwissenschaft,* ed. Carl Dahlhaus and Helga de la Motte-Haber, 54–56. Wiesbaden: Akademische Verlagsgesellschaft Athenaion.

Latour, Bruno. 1993. *We Have Never Been Moderns.* Trans. Catherine Porter. Cambridge, Mass.: Harvard University Press.

Leibniz, G. W. 1989. *Philosophical Writings.* Trans. Roger Ariew and Daniel Garber. Indianapolis: Hackett.

Lerdahl, Fred. 2001. *Tonal Pitch Space.* Oxford: Oxford University Press.

Lester, Joel. 1992. *Compositional Theory in the Eighteenth Century.* Cambridge, Mass.: Harvard University Press.

Lévi-Strauss, Claude. 1964. *Totemism.* Trans. Rodney Needham. Boston: Beacon Press.

———. 1966. *The Savage Mind.* Chicago: University of Chicago Press.

Lewin, David. 1986. Music Theory, Phenomenology, and Modes of Perception. *Music Perception* 3 (4), 327–92.

Lochhead, Judith. 1980. Some Musical Applications of Phenomenology. *Indiana Theory Review* 3, 18–27.

———. 1995. Hearing New Music: Pedagogy from a Phenomenological Perspective. *Philosophy of Music Education Review* 3, 34–42.

Lohmann, Johannes. 1979. Descartes' "Compendium musicae" und die Entstehung des neuzeitlichen Bewußtseins. *Archiv für Musikwissenschaft* 36, 81–104.

Longyear, Rey. 1970. Beethoven and Romantic Irony. In *The Creative World of Beethoven,* ed. Paul Henry Lang, 145–62. New York: W. W. Norton.

Manuel, Roland. 1957. Descartes et le problème de l'expression musicale. In *Descartes, Cahiers de Royaumont. Philosophie 2.* Paris: Éditions Minuit.

Marvin, Elizabeth West. 1987. "Tonpsychologie and Musikpsychologie": Historical Perspectives on the Study of Music Perception. *Theoria* 2, 59–84.

Matson, Wallace. 1966. Why Isn't the Mind-Body Problem Ancient? In *Mind, Matter and Method: Essays in Philosophy and Science in Honor of Herbert Feigl,* ed. Paul

Feyerabend and Grover Maxwell, 92–102. Minneapolis: University of Minnesota Press.

McKinnon, James W. 1978. Jubal vel Pythagoras, quis sit inventor musicae? *Musical Quarterly* 64 (1), 1–28.

Menninger, Karl. 1969. *Number Words and Number Symbols: A Cultural History of Numbers.* Trans. Paul Broneer. Cambridge, Mass.: MIT Press.

Merleau-Ponty, Maurice. 1964. *Signs.* Trans. and introduction by Richard C. McCleary. Evanston, Ill.: Northwestern University Press.

Mitchell, W. J. T. 1986. *Iconology: Image, Text, Ideology.* Chicago: University of Chicago Press.

———. 1990. Representation. In *Critical Terms for Literary Study,* ed. Frank Lentricchia and Thomas McLaughlin, 11–22. Chicago: University of Chicago Press.

Mitchell, William J. 1963. Chord and Context in 18th-Century Theory. *Journal of the American Musicological Society* 16, 221–39.

Montesquieu. [1721] 1964. *The Persian Letters.* Trans. and introduction by George R. Healy. Indianapolis: Bobbs-Merrill.

———. [1748] 1989. *The Spirit of the Laws.* Trans. and ed. Anne M. Cohler, Basia Carolyn Miller, and Harold Samuel Stone. Cambridge: Cambridge University Press.

Mooney, Kevin. 1996. "The Table of Relations" and Music Psychology in Hugo Riemann's Harmonic Theory. Ph.D. dissertation, Columbia University.

Moyer, Ann E. 1992. *Musica Scientia: Musical Scholarship in the Italian Renaissance.* Ithaca, N.Y.: Cornell University Press.

Nattiez, Jean Jacques. 1990. *Music as Discourse: Toward a Semiology of Music.* Trans. Carolyn Abbate. Princeton, N.J.: Princeton University Press.

Neuhoser, Frederick. 1990. *Fichte's Theory of Subjectivity.* Cambridge: Cambridge University Press.

Nichomachus of Gerasa. 1926. *Introduction to Arithmetic.* Trans. Martin Luther D'Ooge, with studies in Greek arithmetic by Frank Egleston Robbins and Louis Charles Karpinski. New York: Macmillan.

Novalis. 1957a. *Band 2 Werke/Briefe/ Dokumente: Fragmente I.* Ed. Ewald Wasmuth. Heidelberg: Verlag Lambert Schneider.

———. 1957b. *Band 3 Werke/Briefe/ Dokumente: Fragmente II.* Ed. Ewald Wasmuth. Heidelberg: Verlag Lambert Schneider.

Olivieri, Luigi, ed. 1983. *Aristotelismo veneto e scienza moderna. Atti del 25° anno accademico del Centro per la storia della tradizione aristotelica nel veneto.* 2 vols. Padua: Antenore.

Palisca, Claude V. 1985. *Humanism in Renaissance Musical Thought.* New Haven, Conn.: Yale University Press.

———. 1989. *The Florentine Camerata: Documentary Studies and Translations.* New Haven, Conn.: Yale University Press.

———. 1994. *Studies in the History of Italian Music and Music Theory.* Oxford: Clarendon Press.

Pirro, André. 1907. *Descartes et la musique.* Paris: Librairie Fischbacher.

Plato. 1961. *The Collected Dialogues of Plato.* Ed. Edith Hamilton and Huntington Cairns. New York: Bollingen Foundation.

———. 1992. *Complete Works.* Ed. with introduction and notes by John M. Cooper. Indianapolis: Hackett.

Polanyi, Michael. 1958. *Personal Knowledge: Towards a Post-critical Philosophy.* Chicago: University of Chicago Press.

Powell, C. Thomas. 1990. *Kant's Theory of Self-consciousness*. Oxford: Clarendon Press.

Racek, Jan. 1930. Contribution au problème de l'esthétique musicale de Descartes. *Revue Musicale* 11, 289–301.

Raffman, Diana. 1993. *Language, Music, and Mind*. Cambridge, Mass.: MIT Press.

Rameau, Jean-Philippe. [1722] 1967a. *Traité de l'harmonie reduite à ses principes naturels*. In *The Complete Theoretical Writings of Jean-Philippe Rameau*, vol. I, ed. Erwin Jacobi. Rome: American Institute of Musicology.

———. [1726] 1967b. Nouveau système de musique théorique. In *The Complete Theoretical Writings of Jean-Philippe Rameau*, vol. II, ed. Erwin Jacobi. Rome: American Institute of Musicology.

———. [1737] 1968. Génération harmonique. In *The Complete Theoretical Writings of Jean-Philippe Rameau*, vol. III, ed. Erwin Jacobi. Rome: American Institute of Musicology.

———. [1722] 1971. *Treatise on Harmony*. Trans. Philip Gossett. New York: Dover.

Rehding, Alexander. 1999. Nature and Nationhood in Hugo Riemann's Dualistic Theory of Harmony. Ph.D. dissertation, Cambridge University.

———. 2003. *Hugo Riemann and the Birth of Modern Musical Thought*. Cambridge: Cambridge University Press.

Reimer, Erich. 1978. Musicus und Cantor: Zur Socialgeschichte eines musikalischen Lehrstücks. *Archiv für Musikwissenschaft* 35, 1–32.

Reiss, Timothy J. 1976. Cartesian Discourse and Classical Ideology. *Diacritics* 6 (4), 19–27.

———. 1997. *Knowledge, Discovery and Imagination in Early Modern Europe: The Rise of Aesthetic Rationalism*. Cambridge: Cambridge University Press.

Revault d'Allonnes, Olivier. 1951. L'esthétique de Descartes. *Revue des Sciences Humaines* 61, 50–55.

Ricoeur, Paul. 1970. *Freud and Philosophy: An Essay on Interpretation*. Trans. Denis Savage. New Haven, Conn.: Yale University Press.

———. 1981. *Hermeneutics and the Human Sciences: Essays on Language, Action and Interpretation*. Ed. and trans. with introduction by John B. Thompson. Cambridge: Cambridge University Press.

Rorty, Richard. 1979. *Philosophy and the Mirror of Nature*. Princeton, N.J.: Princeton University Press.

Rosand, Ellen. 1977. Music in the Myth of Venice. *Renaissance Quarterly* 30 (4), 511–37.

Rose, Paul Lawrence. 1975. *The Italian Renaissance of Mathematics: Studies on Humanists and Mathematicians from Petrarch to Galileo*. Geneva: Droz.

Rosset, Clément. 1977. *Le réel: Traité de l'idiotie*. Paris: Les Éditions de Minuit.

———. 1989. Reality and the Untheorizable. In *The Limits of Theory*, ed. and introduction by Thomas M. Kavanagh, 76–118. Stanford, Calif.: Stanford University Press.

Rothfarb, Lee. 1988. *Ernst Kurth as Theorist and Analyst*. Philadelphia: University of Pennsylvania Press.

Rothstein, William. 1991. On Implied Tones. *Music Analysis* 10 (3), 289–328.

Rousseau, Jean-Jacques. [1762] 1961. *Émile*. Trans. Barbara Foxley, introduction by André Boutet de Monvel. New York: E. P. Dutton.

Sachs, Klaus-Jürgen. 1991. Boethius and the Judgement of the Ears: A Hidden Challenge in Medieval and Renaissance Music. In *The Second Sense: Studies in Hearing and Musical Judgement from Antiquity to the Seventeenth Century*, ed. Penelope Gouk, Charles Burnett, and Michael Fend, 169–98. London: Warburg Institute.

Salinas, Francisco de. 1577. *De musica, libri septem.* Available on the Thesaurus Musi-
carum Latinarum web site, http://www.music.indiana.edu/html.
Saslaw, Janna K. 1990. Gottfried Weber and Multiple Meaning. *Theoria* 5, 74–103.
———. 1991. Gottfried Weber's Cognitive Theory of Harmonic Progression. *Studies in
Music from the University of Western Ontario* 13, 121–44.
———. 1992. Gottfried Weber and the Concept of "Mehrdeutigkeit." Ph.D. dissertation,
Columbia University.
Saslaw, Janna K., and James P. Walsh. 1996. Musical Invariance as a Cognitive Structure:
"Multiple Meaning" in the Early Nineteenth Century. In *Music Theory in the Age
of Romanticism,* ed. Ian Bent, 221–32. Cambridge: Cambridge University Press.
Schlegel, Friedrich von. 1967. *Kritische Friedrich-Schlegel-Ausgabe.* Band 2. Ed. Hans
Eichner. Paderborn: Verlag Ferdinand Schöningh.
———. 1981. *Kritische Friedrich-Schlegel-Ausgabe.* Band 16. Ed. Ernst Behler, with the
collaboration of Jean-Jacques Anstett and Hans Eichner. Paderborn: Verlag
Ferdinand Schöningh.
Schmitt, Charles Bernard. 1976. L'introduction de la philosophie platonicienne dans
l'enseignement des universités à la Renaissance. In *Platon et Aristote à la Renaissance: XVIᵉ Colloque International de Tours,* 93–104. Paris: J. Vrin.
———. 1983. *Aristotle in the Renaissance.* Cambridge, Mass.: Harvard University Press.
———. 1984. *The Aristotelian Tradition and Renaissance Universities.* London: Variorum.
Schuster, John A. 1980. Descartes' "mathesis universalis": 1619–28. In *Descartes: Phi-
losophy, Mathematics and Physics,* ed. Stephen Gaukroger, 41–96. Totowa, N.J.:
Barnes and Noble Books.
Seidel, Wilhelm. 1970. Descartes' Bemerkungen zur musikalischen Zeit. *Archiv für Mu-
sikwissenschaft* 27, 287–303.
Sepper, Dennis L. 1996. *Descartes's Imagination: Proportion, Images, and the Activity of
Thinking.* Berkeley: University of California Press.
Seyhan, Azade. 1992. *Representation and Its Discontents: The Critical Legacy of German
Romanticism.* Berkeley: University of California Press.
Smith, Barbara Herrnstein. 1981. Narrative Versions, Narrative Theories. In *On Narra-
tive,* ed. W. J. T. Mitchell, 209–32. Chicago: University of Chicago Press.
Snarrenberg, Robert. 1997. *Schenker's Interpretive Practice.* Cambridge: Cambridge Uni-
versity Press.
Starobinski, Jean. 1986. *Montaigne in Motion.* Trans. Arthur Goldhammer. Chicago: Chi-
cago University Press.
Stone, Harriet. 1996. *The Classical Model: Literature and Knowledge in Seventeenth-
Century France.* Ithaca, N.Y.: Cornell University Press.
Strunk, Oliver. 1998. *Source Readings in Music History.* Rev. ed., general ed. Leo Treitler.
New York: W. W. Norton.
Taylor, Charles. 1989. *Sources of the Self: The Making of the Modern Identity.* Cambridge,
Mass.: Harvard University Press.
Telemann, Georg Philipp. 1965. Zwolf Pariser Quartette. In *Musikalische Werke,* Bd. 18–
19. Kassel: Bärenreiter.
Todorov, Tzvetan. 1982. *Theories of the Symbol.* Trans. Catherine Porter. Ithaca, N.Y.:
Cornell University Press.
Tomlinson, Gary. 1993. *Music in Renaissance Magic: Toward a Historiography of Others.*
Chicago: University of Chicago Press.
———. 1999. *Metaphysical Song: An Essay on Opera.* Princeton, N.J.: Princeton Univer-
sity Press.

Towey, Alan. 1991. Aristotle and Alexander on Hearing and Instantaneous Change: A Dilemma in Aristotle's Account of Hearing. In *The Second Sense: Studies in Hearing and Musical Judgement from Antiquity to the Seventeenth Century*, ed. Penelope Gouk, Charles Burnett, and Michael Fend, 7–18. London: Warburg Institute.

Van De Pitte, Frederick. 1988. Intuition and Judgment in Descartes's Theory of Truth. *Journal of the History of Philosophy* 31, 223–44.

Van Orden, Kate. 2002. Descartes on Musical Training and the Body. In *Music, Sensation, and Sensuality*, ed. Linda Austern, 17–38. New York: Routledge.

Van Wymeersch, Briggite. 1999. *Descartes et l'évolution de l'esthétique musicale*. Sprimont, Belgium: Mardaga.

Vertrees, Julie Anne. 1974. Mozart's String Quartet K. 465: The History of a Controversy. *Current Musicology* 17, 96–114.

Vickers, Brian. 1984. Analogy versus Identity: The Rejection of Occult Symbolism, 1580–1680. In *Occult and Scientific Mentalities in the Renaissance*, ed. Brian Vickers, 95–163. Cambridge: Cambridge University Press.

Walker, Daniel Pickering. 1958. *Spiritual and Demonic Magic from Ficino to Campanella*. London: Warburg Institute.

———. 1978. *Studies in Musical Science in the Late Renaissance*. London: Warburg Institute.

———. 1985. *Music, Spirit, and Language in the Renaissance*. Ed. Penelope Gouk. London: Variorum.

Weber, Gottfried. 1832. *Versuch einer geordneten Theorie der Tonsetzkunst zum Selbstunterricht*. 4 vols. 3rd ed. Mainz: Schott.

———. [1832] 1994. A Particularly Remarkable Passage in a String Quartet in C by Mozart. In *Music Analysis in the Nineteenth Century*, vol. I: *Fugue, Form and Style*, ed. and trans. with introduction by Ian Bent, 157–83. Cambridge: Cambridge University Press.

Weber, Jean-Paul. 1964. *La constitution du texte des "Regulae."* Paris: Société d'Édition d'Enseignment Supérieur.

White, Hayden. 1978. *Tropics of Discourse: Essays in Cultural Criticism*. Baltimore: Johns Hopkins University Press.

Whitehead, Alfred North. [1929] 1941. *Process and Reality: An Essay in Cosmology*. New York: Social Science Book Store.

Wienpahl, Robert W. 1959. Zarlino, the Senario, and Tonality. *Journal of the American Musicological Society* 12, 27–41.

Yates, Frances. 1966. *The Art of Memory*. Chicago: University of Chicago Press.

———. [1964] 1991. *Giordano Bruno and the Hermetic Tradition*. Chicago: University of Chicago Press.

Zarlino, Gioseffo. [1558] 1965. *Le istitutioni harmoniche*. Venice: Pietro Da Fino. Facsimile, New York: Broude Brothers.

———. [1588] 1966. *Sopplimenti musicali*. Venice: Francesco Sanese. Facsimile, Ridgewood, N.J.: Gregg.

———. [1558] 1983. *The Art of Counterpoint*. Part Three of *Le istitutioni harmoniche*. Trans. Guy A. Marco and Claude V. Palisca. New York: Da Capo.

Žižek, Slavoj. 1999. *The Ticklish Subject: The Absent Centre of Political Ontology*. London: Verso.

Index

Masson, Charles, 23
Mattheson, Johann, 22
Mediating Generalizations, 173n22
Mendelssohn, Moses, 128
Merleau-Ponty, Maurice, 163
Mersenne, Marin, 51, 55
Mitchell, W. J. T., 24, 126
Momigny, Jerome-Joseph, 19
Montesquieu, 17, 122, 123, 124; *Les lettres persanes*, 123, 124; *De l'esprit des lois*, 123
Musical imaginary, 16
Musical thought, 2, 11
Musico, 25, 26, 43

Nancy, Jean-Luc, 150, 218n68
Naturwissenschaften, 20
Neoplatonism, 13, 28, 50, 53, 55, 115, 131
Neuhoser, Frederick, 151
Newton, Isaac, 97, 115, 124
Novalis, 18, 130, 142, 143, 144, 145, 147, 148, 149, 158; and representation, 144, 145, 158; and self-consciousness, 143; and systemlessness, 147; and time, 143

Palisca, Claude, 48, 49
Panaetius, 47
Pareja, Bartolomé Ramos de, 38
Pirro, André, 57
Plato, 39, 40, 57, 68, 70, 71, 100–102, 104; *Philebus*, 101; *Republic*, 100; *Timaeus*, 101
Plutarch, 47
Polanyi, Michael, 10
Porphyry, 47
Port-Royal, 105, 205n61
Ptolemy, 30, 45, 47
Pythagoras, 1, 13, 28, 30, 36, 37, 38, 39, 46, 47, 48, 50, 90, 115, 131

Quadrivium, 36, 53, 76
Quintillian, 46, 57

Rameau, Jean-Philippe, 3, 4, 9, 14, 15, 16, 17, 18, 19, 21, 22, 84, 85–127, 128, 129, 131, 138, 140, 146, 147, 162, 164, 166; *Généra-tion harmonique*, 22, 97; *Nouveau système*, 22, 93, 97; *Nouvelle suites de pièces de clavecin* ("Les tricotets"), 85; *Traité de l'Harmonie*, 1, 15, 16, 85, 88, 89, 90, 91, 92, 93, 94, 95, 96, 106, 108, 116, 118, 119, 120, 121, 124, 125, 173n27; and cadence, 86, 90–92, 94, 117, 118, 198–199n14, 199–200n22; and the classical sign, 110–111; and cogni-tion, 116, 121, 138; and Corelli, Opus 5, 97, 126, 202n32; and counterinduction, 112,

116, 117, 119, 120, 121, 125, 208–209n94; and figured bass, 89, 92, 108–109; and fun-damental bass, 16, 22, 85, 86, 87, 89, 90, 91, 94, 97, 105, 106, 107, 108, 109, 110, 111, 116, 117, 118, 120, 125, 126, 146, 147; and imagination, 16, 87, 88, 89, 105, 112, 116, 118, 124, 125, 126; and implication, 87, 88, 94, 111, 117, 126; and implied dissonance, 15, 86, 87, 89, 94, 96, 98, 99, 104, 108, 109, 111, 112, 117, 119, 120, 124, 126; and im-plied tones, 87, 89, 126, 196–197n1; and in-teriority, 88; and intervallic progression, 90, 91, 198n14; and intuition, 106, 107, 108, 110, 111, 112, 115, 116, 117, 118, 119, 162; and *liaison en harmonie*, 92, 93, 94, 97, 124; and listener, 116, 119; and *mathesis univer-salis*, 89, 90; and metalanguage, 107; and modern era, 88; and musical imaginary, 16; and perception, 16, 106, 107, 116, 117, 118, 119, 120, 121; and the real, 100, 121, 124; and representation, 15, 88–89, 162; and se-quences, 87, 117, 118, 119; and *son fonda-mental*, 90, 91, 106, 107; and *sous-entendre* (implication), 15, 88, 94, 162, 164; and Tele-mann, *Zwölf Pariser Quartette*, 98
Reiss, Timothy, 59, 75, 76, 79
Representation, 6, 19, 172n8
Resemblance, 78, 79
Ricoeur, Paul, 129, 211n3
Riemann, Hugo, 1, 19, 20, 166
Rosset, Clément, 121
Rousseau, Jean-Jacques, 17, 122–123, 124; *Émile*, 122–123, 210n111

Sahlins, Marshall, 29
Saint-Lambert, Michel de, 23
Sarti, Giuseppe, 157
Schlegel, Friedrich von, 18, 130, 142, 145, 148, 153, 154, 156, 158; and allegory, 154; and consciousness, 153; and ironic conscious-ness, 153; and irony, 145, 154; and Roman-tic poetry, 156; and system, 158
Sepper, Dennis, 64
Signatura rerum, 13, 27
Smith, Barbara Herrnstein, 129, 154
Socrates, 118
Spataro, Giovanni, 38
Stamitz, Karl, 128
Stumpf, 166; *Musikpsychologie*, 20
Subject, 5, 7–8
Sulzer, Johann Georg, 128

Taylor, Charles, 141
Temporality, 19

Textuality, 21
Theophrastus, 47
Tomlinson, Gary, 29, 177n24
Trivium, 76

Vicentino, Nicola, 183n85
Vogler, Georg Joseph, 19, 146
Voltaire, 123, 124

Weber, Gottfried, 2, 3, 4, 7, 9, 17, 18, 19, 20, 21, 22, 128–159, 161, 163, 164, 166; *Versuch einer geordneten Theorie der Tonsetkunst zum Selbstunterricht*, 1, 22, 129, 133, 134, 135, 136, 139, 146; and allegory, 145, 154, 155, 156, 218–219n72; and chord structure, 140–141; and cognition, 18; and consciousness, 138, 143, 148, 154–156, 163; and *Darstellung*, 142, 214n27; and "das Gehör," 17, 18, 19, 131, 132, 134, 136, 140, 143, 148, 149, 154, 155, 157, 158, 161, 163, 212n11, 212n14; and intention, 132, 133; and interiority, 141; and irony, 17, 145–147, 148, 149, 153, 154, 155, 156, 157, 159; and language, 148–149, 155, 164; and listening subject, 141, 147, 163; and *mathesis*, 128, 141; and *Mehrdeutigkeit*, 17, 18, 131, 136, 137, 138, 139, 141, 142, 143, 147, 148, 156, 159, 164, 213n20; and Mozart's String Quartet in C Major, K. 465, 17, 19, 20, 128, 129, 132, 135, 136, 137, 141, 143, 144, 147, 148, 149, 153, 154, 155, 156, 157, 158, 163, 212–213n18; and perception, 18, 137, 159; and postfiguration, 155; and representation, 18, 19, 20, 144, 145, 146, 147, 148, 156, 157, 161; and Roman numerals, 17, 18, 19, 22,

147, 158, 164, 211n2, 216n46; and self-consciousness, 142, 143, 148–149, 154; and *Stufentheorie*, 137, 147; and subject-object relation, 137–138, 140, 141, 148, 164; and temporality, 143, 155, 156; and *Vorstellung*, 142, 144
White, Hayden, 14, 172n8, 210n118
Whitehead, Alfred North, 164, 165
Willaert, Adrian, 26, 27, 44, 45, 46, 50, 182n77

Yates, Frances, 49

Zarlino, Gioseffo, 2, 3, 7, 9, 12–13, 14, 15, 21, 22, 25–49, 50, 52, 60, 89, 131, 161, 165, 174–175n8; *Le istitutioni harmoniche*, 1, 13, 25, 26, 27, 28, 38, 42, 43, 44, 45, 46, 47, 50, 51, 55, 91; *Sopplimenti musicali*, 1, 13, 26, 27, 43, 46, 47, 48, 50, 51; and antipathies, 34; and and *convenientia*, 30, 31, 32, 33, 35, 41; *convenienza*, 28, 29, 43, 44; and counterpoint, 25, 26, 27, 38, 41; and form, matter, 37, 38, 40, 41, 45, 47; and hermeneutics, 30, 33; and historic knowledge, 26, 29, 30, 44, 46–47, 50; and methodic knowledge, 46–47; and minor sixth, 40, 41; and *musica mondana*, 28, 30, 34, 39, 180n61; and *musica prattica*, 25, 26, 38, 41, 44; and *musica scientia*, 13, 26, 27, 30, 37, 50; and *musica speculativa*, 25; and myth, 28, 44–45, 47; and *numero Senario*, 31, 38–41, 45, 46; and *numero sonoro*, 38; and perception, 12; and *scientia*, 37, 44; and semiology, 30, 33, 41, 48; and *soggetto*, 43; and *soggetto ben disposto*, 13, 45
Žižek, Slavoj, 166

JAIRO MORENO is Associate Professor of Music Theory at New York University. His research focuses on the critical history of music theory, cultural and musical analysis of Latin American music in the United States, and the poetics of jazz performance.